KITBU NURIIM
"The Book of Light"
The Official Anunnaki Ulema Textbook for
The Teacher and the Student

Volume 2

THE ESSENTIAL MAXIMILLIEN DE LAFAYETTE

The Official Anunnaki Ulema Textbook for the Teacher and the Student. Vol.2

The Ultimate Esoteric-Spiritual-Occult Secrets, Teachings and Revelations

Maximillien de Lafayette

⌘ NOTA BENE ⌘

- To avoid all sorts of troubles and psychological confusion (s), all topics discussed in this book were approached from a philosophical-metaphysical-esoteric angle.

- Bear in mind that the Ulema's teachings and/or opinions should not be considered as a professional advice at any level – therapeutic, medical, psychological, mental health, etc. – thus avoiding any conflict with professional licensing bodies and legal practitioners in these fields.

- They are of a purely philosophical-esoteric nature.

- The Kira'ats (Readings) were given by the Ulema in Asia, and the Near/Middle East within a confined milieu of seekers of metaphysical and esoteric knowledge.

-
- Many of the texts as published in this book are excerpts from their Kira'ats and Rou'ya (Visions) that first appeared centuries ago, and continue to enlighten many of us.

- You enter their world at your own risk.

⌘⌘⌘

THE ESSENTIAL MAXIMILLIEN DE LAFAYETTE

The Official Anunnaki Ulema Textbook for the Teacher and the Student

KITBU NURIIM

Volume 2

Maximillien de Lafayette

Edited by
Dina Vittantonio

Acknowledgements

For their enormous contributions to this book, and especially for their guidance, I am extremely grateful to:

Ulema Mordachai ben Zvi
Ulema Penjabi Tien Utan,
Ulema, Grand Master Master W. Li,
Master Sorenztein,
Master Oppenhemier,
Master O. Kanazawa,
Master Ghandar,
Master Govinda,
Ulema Cheik Al Mutawalli,

A special thank you note goes to:
Dr. Mary Ann Ghafurrian, administrator of the United States Chapter of the Anunnaki Ulema Ramadosh Society for revealing the truth.
Author Laura Lebron for translating major manuscripts and books on the Anunnaki from English to Spanish, and for enlightening the international Latin/Spanish speaking communities.
My loyal friends Peggy Sulin, Indra Sulln, Colonel Petrit Demaliaj, and artist extraordinaire Edward Albers for their constant encouragement and support.

*** *** ***

Table of Contents

Part 8: The Ramadosh supernatural and metaphysical Techniques, the Supersymetric Mind, Activation of the Conduit...121

13

14

PART 9: Healing. Energy, Positive Vibes, Negative Vibes, Aura...331

PART 10: Most frequently asked questions ...715

*** *** ***

25

Glossary
Terminology
And
Explanations of
Concepts

Glossary/Terminology and Explanations of Concepts

A

Aamala: Anunnaki's registry of future events.
It is used as a calendar to show important events that will occur on other planets. According to Ulema Rajani, time is not linear. And because space bends on itself, therefore, events don't have a chronology or time-sequences. "Things and events happen on the net of the cosmos. When your mind perceives them, they happen before your eyes. But in fact, they have already happened before your have noticed them.
This applies to all future and forthcoming events, because also they have occurred on another cosmos net parallel to the one that have contained separate events. It is a matter of perception, rather than observation or taking notice..." said Ulema Govinda.

Abgaru: Balance; equilibrium.
Balance does not mean a physical balance, but a position or a situation where and when a person maintains a perfect vision, assimilation and understanding of the limits, dimensions and length of objects surrounding him/her.
In other words, it is sensing and remembering the exact position of objects that can expand within the area where we are standing or walking, even in the dark. Objects are not limited by their physical dimension, and/or the physical place they occupy.
"Almost all objects extend and expand outside what it defines their measurement, shape, and size, because they have inertia "Energy" rays or vibrations that constantly emanate from them, thus occupying an extra physical place. Not to bump into the vibes area is maintaining balance," said Ulema W. Li.

Afik-r'-Tanawar: Enlightenment through the development of the mind. Composed of two words;
   ❖   **a**-Afik-r, which means mind.

❖ **b**-Tanawar, which means the act of enlightenment.

The Anunnaki have created us on earth to serve their needs.
Their intentions were to create a race that could carry heavy physical load and do intense physical labor.
This was their initial and prime objective. Thus, the "Naphsiya" (DNA) they put in us had limited lifespan, and mental faculties.
Later on, they discovered that they had to prolong the human lifespan and add more developed mental faculties, so they added the Hara-Kiya (Internal energy or physical strength).

Few generations later, the early human beings stock evolves considerably, because the Anunnaki geneticists added a fully operational mind in the human body. To do so, they installed a Conduit with limited capabilities. In the same time, this Conduit was also installed into the prototype of the human body. Thus, through the mind, the physical body of the humans got linked to the Double.
This non-physical link created a Fourth dimension for all of us.
In fact, it did not create a Fourth dimension per se, rather it activated it.
So now, at that stage, humans had a physical dimension (Life on earth), and not-a-totally separated non-physical dimension called Nafis-Ra.
So, the Bashar (Humans) became destined to acquire two dimensions, as exactly the Anunnaki decided. Later on, centuries upon centuries, the human mind began to evolve, because the other mind, call it now the Double or prototype began to evolve simultaneously and in sync.
The more the prototype is advanced the more the "Physical Mind" becomes alert, creative and multidimensional. But we are not trapped, and our mind is no longer conditioned by the Anunnaki. The Anunnaki gave us all the choices, opportunities, freewill and freedom to learn on our own and progress. This is why we are accountable and responsible for everything we do and think about.
Because of the evolution of our mind, and realization of an inner knowledge of our surroundings, and understanding what is right and what is wrong, a major mental faculty emerged in all of us: Conscience.

Anšekadu-ra abra "Anshekadoora-abra": Learning by traveling or traversing other dimensions.
Composed of four words:

* ❖ **a**-Anše, which means magnificent.
* ❖ **b**-Kadu, which means ability, or to be able.
* ❖ **c**-Ra, which means heavenly; godly.
* ❖ **d**-Abra, which means to cross over; to traverse.

Ulema Shimon Naphtali Ben Yacob and Ulema de Lafayette explained that the Anunnaki have acquired an enormous amount of knowledge by entering different dimensions, and visiting multiple universes.

These dimensions are sometimes called parallel universes, future universes, and vibrational spheres.

He said: "Some are physical/organic, others are purely mental. There are billions and billions of universes. Some are inhabited by beings, super-beings, multi-vibrational beings, and even negative entities known to mankind as demons and evils. Planet earth is considered the lowest organic and human life-form in the universe. The human beings are the less developed living entities, both mentally and spiritually."

Anšekadu-ra abra also means Anunnaki's branching out and changing individuality in multiple universes. To understand the concept, consider this scenario said Ulema Mordachai Ben Zvi: "Let say, you wish if you could do something differently in your life, something like changing the past, changing a major life decision you have made

some years ago, like perhaps, going back in time to a point before you have made a bad decision. Or for instance, you wish if you could do something really good by changing an entire event that has happened in your past. In the Anunnaki's case, they have the solutions for these dilemmas. They can go back and forth in time and space, including the past, the future, and meta-future.

An Anunnaki can split himself/herself in two, three, or more if necessary, and move on to a universe that is very much like the one they live on (Nibiru), or totally different. There are so many universes, and some of them do not resemble Nibiru at all. If an Anunnaki wishes to branch out and move on, he/she must study the matter very carefully and make the right selection. And the branching, or splitting, results in exact copies of the person of the Anunnaki, both physically and mentally.

At the moment of separation, each separate individual copy of an Anunnaki grows, mentally, in a different direction, follows his or

31

her own free will and decisions, and eventually the two are not exactly alike."

So what do they do, first of all? The old one stays where he/she is and follows his/her old patterns as he/she wishes. The new one might land one minute, or a month, or a year, somewhere, some place, right before the decision he/she wants to change or avoid.

Let's take this scenario for instance; Some 30,000 years ago in his life-span; an Anunnaki male was living a nice life with his wife and family.

But he felt that he did not accomplish much, and suddenly he wanted to be more active in the development of the universe; a change caused by witnessing a horrendous event such as a certain group of beings in his galaxy destroying an entire civilization, and killing millions of the inhabitants, in order to take over their planet for various purposes.

It happened while an Anunnaki was on a trip, and he actually saw the destruction and actions of war while he was traveling. It was quite traumatic, and he thought, at that moment, that he must be active in preventing such events from occurring again, ever. So, he went back in time to be in a spot to prevent these fateful events from happening again.

There, in that new dimension, the Anunnaki leaves his former self (A copy of himself) as a guardian and a protector. The other copy (Perhaps one of the original ones) is still on Nibiru. The branching out phenomenon occurred in one of the designated locals of the Anunnaki Hall of Records, also called in terrestrial term Akashic Records Hall.

Ulema Openheimer said: "For the Anunnaki fellow there is no problem or any difficulty in doing that. He/she will go back in time and space and change the whole event. This means that this particular event no longer exists in a chronological order.

This also means that the event has been erased, because the Anunnaki can de-fragment the molecules, the substance, the vibrations and the fabric of time, but necessarily space. In other words, that event never happened in one dimension, but it is very possible, that it might still exist in another world.

You could consider the cosmos as an assemblage of several layers of universes, each one on the top of the other, and sometimes parallel to each other. When the Anunnaki traverses more than two layers, we call this Anšekadu-ra abra." Can a human being traverse multiple layers of time and space? Yes, however, the human being will be facing a series of problems.

32

For instance:

1-Case one: Although, he/she may cross over and enters another dimension, and succeeds in altering, changing or even erasing a past event, the human being might get stuck in that dimension, and remains there for ever.

In this condition, he/she is transformed into a new person without an identity or a past. A brand new person who is out-placed, without a job, without a residence, without credentials, and without social or professional context. It would become very difficult for that person to make a living. How the others would look upon him? A person from the past? A person from the future? It is not an easy situation.

2-Case two: Because everything in the world is duplicated ad infinitum in many universes, only one copy of the past event has been altered.

3-Case three: What would happen to that person, should he/she decides to return back to his/her original world?

The real problem here is not how to go back to his/her world and relive an ordinary life, the life he/she had before, but what is going to happen to him/her when that person leaves the new dimension he/she has entered?

Every time a person enters another dimension, he/she creates a new copy of himself/herself, and occupies a new spot on the cosmos net. In our case here, that human being by entering another dimension, he/she has duplicated himself/herself in that new dimension, and returning to Earth, he/she will be facing another copy of himself/herself. "Is this possible? Quantum physic theorists say yes. And they add that humans can enter and live in multiple universes and acquire new identities, and new copies of themselves.

An-zalubirach: Collecting and sorting thoughts and multiple mental images; using mental energy to move or teleport things. This is one of the phases and practices of Tarkiz.

Tarkiz means deep mental or intellectual concentration that produces telekinesis and teleportation phenomena. Anunnaki's young students, apprentices, and novices learn this technique in Anunnaki schools in Ashtari. Usually, they use their Conduit (Which is located in the brain's cells), and deep concentration on an object hidden behind a screen or a divider made from thin paper. Synchronizing the frequency of their Conduit and an absolute state of introspection, the Anunnaki student attempts to move the hidden object from one place to another without even touching it. In a more advanced stage, the Anunnaki student attempts to alter the properties of the object by lowering or increasing the frequencies and vibrations of the object.

Araya: Prediction; code.
According to the Ulema, the Anunnaki's Araya is an effective tool to foresee forthcoming events in the immediate and long term future. The expression or term "foreseeing" is never used in the Anakh language and by extraterrestrials because they don't foresee and predict. They just calculate and formulate. In spatial terms, they don't even measure things and distances, because time and space do not exist as two separate "presences" in their dimensions.
However, on Ashta.Ri (Ne.Be.Ru), Anunnaki are fully aware of all these variations, and the human concept of time and space, and have the capability of separating time and space, and/or combining them into one single dimension, or one single frame of existence. Anunnaki understand time differently from us, said the Ulema.
For instance, on Nibiru, there are no clocks and no watches. They are useless. Then you might ask: So, how do they measure time? How do they know what time it is...now or 10 minutes later, or in one hour from now? The answer is simple: If you don't need time, you don't need to measure it. However, on Nibiru, Anunnaki experience time and space as we do on earth. And they do measure objects, substances, distances and locations as we do on earth. But they rarely do.
"The Anunnaki (In addition to the Nordics and Lyrans) are the only known extraterrestrials in the universe to look like humans, and in many instances, they share several similarities with the human race..." said Ulema Ghandar.
This physiognomic resemblance explains to a certain degree, the reason for Anunnaki to use time.
To calculate and formulate information and to acquire data, Anunnaki consult the Code Screen. Consulting the screen means pragmatically, the reading of events sequences, explained the Ulema. Every single event in the cosmos in any dimension has a code; call it for now Nimera, a "number", added the Ulema. Nothing happens in the universe without a reason.
The universe has its own logic that the human mind cannot understand. In many instances, the logic of numbers dictates and

34

creates events. And not all created events are understood by the extraterrestrials.

This is why they resort to the Araya Code Screen. Activating the Araya Code requires four actions or procedures:

1-Taharim:

This demands clearing all the previous data stored in the "pockets" of the Net. A net resembles space net as usually used by quantum physics scientists. They do in fact compare space to a net. According to their theories, the net as the landscape of time and space bends under the weight of a ball rotating at a maximum speed.

The centrifugal effect produced by the ball alters the shape of the net, and consequently the fabric of space. And by altering space, time changes automatically.

As time changes, speed and distances change simultaneously. Same principle applies to stretching and cleaning up the net of the screen containing a multitude of codes of the Anunnaki.

2-Location of the Spatial Pockets:

The word pockets means the exact dimension and exact space an object occupies on the universe's net or landscape. No more than one object or one substance occupies one single pocket; this is by earth standard and human level of knowledge.

In other parallel worlds, more than one object or one substance can be infused in one single pocket. But this could lead to loss of memory. Objects and substances have memory too, just like human beings; some are called:

- ❖ **a**-Space memory,
- ❖ **b**-Time memory,
- ❖ **c**-String memory,
- ❖ **d**-Astral memory,
- ❖ **e**-Bio-organic memory,

The list is endless. Thus, all pockets containing previous data are cleared.

3-Feeding the Pockets, also called Retrieving Data:

All sorts and sizes of data are retrieved and stored through the Conduit. The Conduit is an electroplasmic substance implanted into the cells of the brain.

4-Viewing the data:

Retrieved data and information are viewed through the Miraya, also called Cosmic Mirror. Some refer to it as Akashic Records. Can the Anunnaki go forward in time and meet with the future? Yes, they can! An Ulema has said that future events have already happened at some level and in some spheres. It is just a matter of a waiting period for the mind to see it.

B

Baliba nahr usu na Ram: Expression.
Translated verbatim: "The water of the river purified my people."
Attributed to Sinhar Marduchk in the Book of Rama-Dosh.
Baliba means flows of waters. Nahr means river (Same meaning in Hebrew, Phoenician and Arabic).
Usu means to clean or purify.
Na means my or our.
Ram means people (Same meaning in Phoenician, primitive Arabic, early Armenian and ancient Hebrew).
The Ana'kh word "Usu" also means to dig.
We find similar meaning in the Annals of Sardanapalus: "Nahrtu istu nahr zaba anta ahri nahr babilat kanin sumsa abbi." Translated verbatim: "A river from the upper Zab I dug and its name I called."

Balu-ram-haba: Composed of three words:
a-Balu, which means power; transition; contact.
b-Ram, which means people.
In this case, entities; other life-forms.
c-Haba, which means beyond; other dimension.

Possibly, from Balu-ram-haba, derived the Hebrew word Olam ha-ba. This Ana'kh term or expression pertains to circumstances in the world beyond, and/or experiences, the departed humans might encounter in the next dimension, following their death. Afterlife does not necessarily begin after we die, because death does not exist; it is simply a transitory stage. Within our physical world exist so many other worlds. And far away, and deep in the

36

fabric of the universe, distances are reduced, even eliminated, if we zoom into our Double.

Matter and anti-matter are de-fragmented in the parallel dimension. The initiated and enlightened ones can transport themselves to the other world, and visit the far distant corners of the universe through their Double.

Those who are noble in their thoughts, intentions and deeds can accomplish this after an Ulema initiation.

- The righteous people will be reunited with their loved ones including their pets in the afterlife.
- This reunion will take place in the 1st level of the ethereal 4th dimension.
- The reunion is not of a physical nature, but mental.
- This means, that the mind of the deceased will project and recreate holographic images of people, animals and places.
- All projected holographic images are identical to the original ones, but they are multidimensional.
- Multidimensional means that people, animals and physical objects are real in essence, in molecules, in DNA, and in origin, but not necessarily in physical properties.
- In other words, what you see in the afterlife is real to the mind, but not to your physical senses, because in the
- after life (In all the seven levels/dimensions of life after death), physical objects, including humans' and animals' bodies acquire different substances, molecular compositions, and new forms.
- The physical rewards and punishments are mental, not physical in nature, but they are as real as the physical ones.
- The deceased will suffer through the mind.
- The pain sensations are real, but are produced by the mind, instead of a physical body. So in concept and essence, the Ulema and Hebraic scholars share similar beliefs; the good person will be rewarded, and the bad person will be punished.
- For the Jews, it is physical, while for the Ulema it is mental, but both reward and punishment are identical in their intensity and application.

- The wicked will not be indefinitely excluded from a reunion with loved ones.
- The wicked will remain in a state of loneliness, chaos, confusion and mental anguish for as long it takes to rehabilitate him/her.
- This state of punishment and rehabilitation can last for a very long period of time in an uncomfortable sphere of existence inhabited by images of frightening entities created by the mind as a form of punishment.
- Eventually, all wicked persons will reunite with their loved ones after a long period of purification and severe punishment.

Note: Some scholars believe that the projection of these macabre and scary entities is created by the sub-conscience of the wicked person. Other scholars believe that the holographic imageries are produced by the Double housing the mind.

The Torah speaks of several noteworthy people being "gathered to their people." See, for example, Gen. 25:8 (Abraham), 25:17 (Ishmael), 35:29 (Isaac), 49:33 (Jacob), Deut. 32:50 (Moses and Aaron) II Kings 22:20 (King Josiah).

This gathering is described as a separate event from the physical death of the body or the burial. Certain sins are punished by the sinner being "cut off from his people." See, for example, Gen. 17:14 and Ex. 31:14. This punishment is referred to as Kareit (Kah-Rehyt) (literally, "cutting off," but usually translated as "spiritual excision"), and it means that the soul loses its portion in the world to come. Later portions of the Tanakh speak more clearly of life after death and the world to come. See Dan. 12:2, Neh. 9:5.

Here are the views of the Anunnaki-Ulema:
- Soul is a metaphysical concept created by Man.
- Soul is a religious idea created by humans to explain and/or to believe in what they don't understand.
- It is more accurate to use the word Mind instead.
- The mind thinks and understands. The soul does not, perhaps it feels, if it is to be considered as a vital force and source of feelings in your physical body.

- In the afterlife, such source of feelings is nonexistent, and in the dimensions of the world beyond, such source is useless.

Barak-malku: Expression. Blessing of the ruler or the king; long live the king. Composed of two words:
a-Barak, which means blessing.
b-Malku, which means king.

Barak is Barak and Barakat in ancient Hebrew, and Barak and Barakat in Arabic. Malku is Malku, (Plural: Malki) in Assyrian. In Aramaic, it is Malak (King).
In Hebrew, it is Malek (King). In Arabic, it is Malak (King). From the Ana'kh Malku derived the Aramaic Malkut or Malakut (Kingdon; paradise), the ancient Hebrew Malkuth (Kingdom), and the Arabic Malakoot (Paradise; kigdom of God).
Not to be confused with the Semitic words Mala'k or Malak wich mean angel in Hebrew and Arabic.
Sargina said: "Sar sa ultu yom biluti-su malku gabra-su la ispu." Translated verbatim: "King who from the day of his power, a prince his rival has not been." From the Annals of Tiglath Pileser: "Malki nikrut Assur abil." Translated berbatim: "Monarchs enemies of Assur (Ashur) I seized."

Bariya "Ba-riya'ah": The creation of the world as described in the Akkadian/Sumerian texts.
From Bariya, derived the primitive Arabic words Bari (Creator; God), and Baria (Creation; creatures.)
The Sumerian Creation:
Only one account of the Sumerian creation has survived, but it is a suggestive one. This account functions as an introduction to the story of "The Huluppu-Tree".

Barka-kirama: Expression.
A blessing or an enlightenment (Tanwir) technique that develops teleportation. It is composed of two words:
a-Barka, which means blessing.
b-Kirama, which means good deeds.

From Barka, derived the Hebrew words Barak and Baraka (Blessings), and the Arabic Baraka and Brakaat (Blessings).

39

From Kirama, derived the Persian Keramat (Good deeds), and the Arabic Kiramat (Honorable deeds).

Barka-kirama is a very important and a primordial Anunnaki's expression, because it is closely and directly related to Tay Al Ard, and Tay Al Makan, which mean teleportation. Tay Al Ard is an Ulemite/Arabic word. It is a metaphysical experience that produces a teleportation phenomenon; a secret esoteric practice of the Ulema and Allamah.

The Ulema claim that they have learned its secret and how its works from the Rou-hi-yin who are supreme beings from the Fifth dimension.

When Islam became a major religion in the Near East, and the Middle East, Tay Al Ard was banned by Prophet Muhammad, who called its practitioners "Min Ahl Al Nar", meaning verbatim: Those who are from fire.

Fire meant hell, or the kingdom of Al Shaytan (Satan, the devil).

The Arabic pre-Islamic word Ulema was replaced by the Arabic Islamic word Allamah or Al Hallama.

However, the Ulema and the Allamah were very different from each other in many ways.

The Ulema remained the custodians of the Anunnaki's secret knowledge and esoteric powers, while the Allamah were considered as the "Alamin", the learned ones and leading figures of letters, literature, science and religion.

Nevertheless, many Muslim teachers and spiritualists remain Ulema at heart.

Many of them - secretly of course - joined the circle of the non-Muslim Ulema to learn the ultimate knowledge acquired from non-terrestrial beings. The Suphists were the first to join the Non-Muslim Ulema.

Worth mentioning, that around, 850 A.D., Ulema and Allamah were semantically overlapping each other. And both words came to mean or express the same thing in the eye of Arab scholars, and in the Islamic world.

Many Soufiyyin (Sufis) by joining the Ulema, learned some of the secrets of Tay Al-Ard. They called it: "Tay Al Makan", meaning the folding of space. It is composed of two Arabic words: Tay (Folding or to fold) + Al Makan (The Space; the location; the place.) The Sufis replaced the word Al Makan with the word Al Ard.

The general meaning of Tay Al Ard or Tay Al Makan is to traverse the earth without moving. Al Munawarin claim that instead of physically moving from one place to another, an enlightened person can bring to himself, to where he is standing, the place he wanted to reach. In other words, the earth of the place to reach has been displaced under the enlightened one's feet.

Ironically, this pre-Islamic concept is now fully accepted by Muslim clerks, Cheiks and teachers of the Islamic Shari'a and Fuk'h, grouped together under the umbrella of Al Allamah.

Ulema or Allamah Qadhi, previously one of the leading figures of Allameh Tabatabaei explained Tay Al Ard as the termination of matter itself in the original location, and its re-appearance, manifestation, and re-creation in its final location, the place one wished to reach.

The Iranian Dehkhoda dictionary defined Tay Al Ard as: "An aspect of Keramat "Kiramat" (Extraordinary deeds of saints and holy people) in which instead of going toward a destination by taking a step forward, the earth turns itself toward the traverser rapidly, in a blink of an eye, regardless of how far the destination is."

Ulema Ibn Al Nadim bin Ishaq al-Nadim (a.k.a. Al Warrak died on September 17, 995. He wrote the Kitab al-Fihrist.) explained this phenomenon by citing verses from the Quran, taken from Chapter Al Naml;

Verse: 27:38: Solomon said to his men: "O Chiefs, which of you can bring me the throne of Queen of Sheba before she and her envoys come to me in submission?"

Verse 27: 39: "Said an 'Ifrit of Al Jinns: "I will bring it to thee before thou rise from thy council. In fact, I have full power for this purpose, and may be trusted."

Verse 27:40: "Said one who had knowledge of the Book: "I will bring it to thee within a blink of any eye!"

Then when the sage Solomon saw it placed right before him, he said: "This was done by the authority of God all mighty, my Lord."

Some Middle Eastern sages and teachers of religious esoteric dogmas suggested that according to these verses, the Ulema Asif ibn Al Birkhia teleported the throne of Queen of Sheba almost instantaneously, in a blink of an eye. This was confirmed in a Hadith (Dialogue, a chat, or a discourse) by Jaafar Al Sadiq.

Allamah have explained this teleportation phenomenon very differently.

They claimed that the teleportation occurred because Ulema Asif ibn Birkhia used one of the secret "Asma Al Allah Al Sab'a Al Husma." (One of the seven secret names of God.)

The knowledge and use of one of the secret holy and lovely names of God allowed Ulema Asif ibn Birkhia to teleport the throne. The Ulema, students of the Anunnaki, briefly explained this phenomenon. Ulema Cheik Al Kabir said (Verbatim): "Time is represented with 2 lines not perfectly aligned; one for you, the other for what is not you. Space is represented with two circles; one for you, the other for what is not you.

If you manage to place yourself between one of the two lines and one of the two circles without touching the other line and the other circle, you will conquer time-space."

D

Dab'Laa: Term for the Anunnaki's branching out and changing individuality in multiple universes. This is a very complex topic, and a phenomenon difficult to comprehend or to explain in terrestrial terms.

To understand the concept, the closest metaphor in human terminology would be going back in time by bending space and time. In this case, time and space are no longer influenced or regulated by the laws of physics as we understand them on Earth. Distances became shorter and time acts strangely, according to speed. Through the Dab'Laa, an Anunnaki can duplicate himself or herself, and transpose one of the copies of himself/herself to a new dimension.

This dimension is real, because it has always physically existed in the cosmos, but at a different vibrational level. Vibrational level does not mean that all substances and life forms in that new dimension exist and appear as frequencies, rays and vibrations.

They possess physical properties and dimensions, but are structured differently. They are made from the same molecules, and particles, but their vibrational intensity varies.

This variation allows the substances to take on different forms, i.e. water can be solidified as ice cubes, and ice cubes can melt to become liquid water. The Anunnaki's branching, or splitting results in duplicate copies for 2 dimensions, or multiple copies to

42

use in multiple universes. But these copies are not exactly alike, for the original remains the primordial center of knowledge, while the duplicates traverse the universe as a mirrored spatial memory.

However, the physical structure and molecular substance of all copies are identical.

Ulema can duplicate themselves, copy themselves, but cannot clone themselves. These faculties allow them to materialize and dematerialize in parallel spheres. The Ulema are also capable of elevating the vibrations of their body and mind to a higher level. This act allows them to penetrate solid substances, such as walls.

In the new dimension, the Anunnaki uses a vivid copy of himself or herself, while the primordial composition of his/her persona remains unaltered on Ashta.Ri.

E

Eido-Rah: Term for the non-physical substance of a human being's body. In other words, the mental or astral projection of the body leaving earth. Eido-Rah manifests to human beings, and particularly to the parents of the deceased person during a period of less than 40 days, following the death of a relative. From Eido-Rah, derived the Greek word Eidolon (A phantom).

According to the scribes of the Book of Rama-Dosh: "After we die, the primordial source of energy in our body leaves our body.

This energy is a substance made out of Fik'r closely connected and attached to a copy of ourselves preserved in the Fourth dimension, which is not very far away from us, and from Earth. As soon as this energy leaves the physical body, the mind of the deceased becomes confused instantly. The mind does not realize that the body is dead.

At this particular stage, the mind is unable to realize right away that it has entered a new dimension.

Although this new dimension is identical to the one we live in and what we call Earth, it is also very different because time, space and distance no longer exist. And also because, it exists at a different vibrational level. Everything becomes meta-linear.

Because the mind is confused, it tries to return to Earth. The first places, the mind (Or the new form-substance of the deceased

43

one) searches for, and/or tries to return to, are always the familiar places on Earth, such as home, office, recreation center, church, mosque, synagogue, temple, etc...but the most sought place is usually home. So, the deceased person returns home for a very short period.

This does not happen all the time. Only when the deceased person is totally confused and disoriented. First, the deceased tries to contact relatives and close parents.

When the deceased begins to realize that parents and relatives are not responding, the deceased tries again to send messages telepathically.

Some messages if intensified can take on ectoplasmic forms, or appear as a shadow usually on smooth substances such as mirror and glass. Some deceased people will keep on trying to contact their beloved ones left behind for a period of 39 days and 11 hours. After this time, the deceased dissipates, and no further attempts to establish contact with the living are made." In another passage of the Book of Rama-dosh, we read (Verbatim): "Although, it is impossible to reach the deceased one as soon as he/she leaves the body, and/or during the 39 days and 11 hours period following his death, sometimes, if we are lucky, and/or were extremely attached to the person we lost, a short contact with him or with her is still possible if we pay attention to unusual things happening around us...those unusual things are difficult to notice, unless we pay a great attention....they happen only once, sometimes twice, but this is very rare..." The book provides techniques and methods pertaining to all forms and means of such contact.

Ezakarerdi, "E zakar-erdi "Azakar.Ki":
Term for the "Inhabitants of Earth" as named by the Anunnaki, and mentioned in the Ulemite language in the "Book of Rama-Dosh."

Per contra, extraterrestrials are called Ezakarfalki "Inhabitants of Heaven or Sky". The term or phrase "Inhabitants of Earth" refers only to humans, because animals and sea creatures are called Ezbahaiim-erdi. Ezakarerdi is composed of three words:
1-E (Pronounced Eeh or Ea) means first.
2-Zakar: This is the Akkadian/Sumerian name given to Adam by Enki. The same word is still in use today in Arabic, and it means male. In Arabic, the female is called: Ountha (Oonsa).

44

The word "Zakar" means:
a-A male, and sometime a stud.
b-To remember.

In Hebrew, "Zakar" also means:
a-To remember (Qal in Hebrew).
b-Be thought of (Niphal in Hebrew).
c-Make remembrance (Hiphil in Hebrew).

There is a very colorful linguistic jurisprudence in the Arabic literature that explains the hidden meaning of the word "Zakar"; Arabs in general believe that man (Male) remembers things, while women generally tend to forget almost everything, thus was born the Arabic name for a woman "Outha or Oonsa", which means literally "To forget!"
Outha (Oonsa) either derives from or coincides with the words "Natha", "Nasa", "Al Natha", "Nis-Yan", which all mean the very same thing: Forgetting; to forget, or not to remember.
On a theological level, Islamic scholars explain that the faculty of remembering is a sacred duty for the Muslim, because it geared him toward remembering that Allah (God) is the creator.
Coincidently or not, Zakar in Ana'kh (Anunnaki language) and ancient Babylonian-Sumerian means also to remember. Could it be a hint or an indication for Adam's duty of remembering Enki, his creator?
3-Erdi means planet Earth. Erdi was transformed by scribes into Ki in the Akkadian, Sumerian and Babylonian epics.

From Erd, derived:
a-The Sumerian Ersetu and Erdsetu,
b-The Arabic Ard,
c-The Hebrew Eretz.
All sharing the same meaning: Earth; land.
Thus the word Ezakarerdi means verbatim: The first man (Or Created one) of Earth or the first man on Earth, or simply, the Earth-Man.
In other word, the terrestrial human.

Ezakarfalki "E-zakar-falki": Term for extraterrestrials as mentioned in the "Book of Rama-Dosh." Per contra, inhabitants of planet Earth are called Ezakarerdi or Ezakar.Ki. In terrestrial vocabulary, extraterrestrial(s) is a term applied to any entity(ies), object(s), substance(s), life-form(s), intelligence, and presence that have originated from beyond planet Earth. Also referred to as alien(s).

Contemporary ufology etymology added extraterrestrial origins coming from outer-space, other planets, stars, galaxies, and dimensions.

The word extraterrestrial is composed from three words:

a-Extra, which is derived from the Latin word Extra, which means outside; additional; beyond.

b-Terrestri, derived from the Latin Terrestris, which means pertaining to earth; belonging to earth; earthly; made out of earth, itself derived from the Latin words Terranum and Terrenum, which are derived from the word Terra, which means earth; ground; piece of land; soil.

(Note: From the Latin word Terrenum, derived the French word Terrain; and from the French word derived the English word terrain.)

c-Al, an English addition.

(Note: The Latin word Terra originally derived from the Arabic word "Tourab" (Terrab), which means dirt; dust; earth, itself derived from the Arabic word Tourba (Terrba), which means a piece of land, originally derived from the Ana'kh word Turbah, pronounced Toorbaah, which means dirt from planet Earth.

In the Sumerian/Akkadian epics and mythologies, the words dirt and earth refer to clay; the very clay found in abundance in ancient Iraq that was used by the Anunnaki to genetically create the human race.

Evolution of the extraterrestrials and the human races:

The evolution of aliens, and the extraterrestrial races on many galaxies evolved inter-dimensionally by copying, duplicating, and cloning themselves and fertilizing their own genes. On other planets, more advanced extraterrestrial civilizations multiply and prosper through the development of brain's waves and thoughts frequencies.

They did not need to immigrate to other planets in order to survive, and/or to recreate (Reshape) themselves, as mistakenly claimed by some ufologists, extraterrestrialogists, mediums, and channelers, for they did not encounter insurmountable ecological or bio-organic catastrophes on their own planets or stars.

Zetas and Anunnaki did alter their genetics but, not for survival purposes or for intra-planetary immigration.
The alteration came as cause and effect, much needed to reach a higher level of awareness and scientific advancement.

Ezbahaiim-erdi:
Term for the animals, and sea creatures living, and/or created on planet Earth. It is composed of three words:
a-Ez means first creatures of a second level. (In comparison to humans.)
b-Bahaiim means animals. The same word exists in Arabic, and means the very same thing (Animals).
c-Erdi means planet Earth.

Ezeridim: Term for entities or super-beings from the future.
In Ufology and paranormal terminologies, Ezeridim are called chrononauts, a word derived from the Greek Khrono, which means time, and "nauts" referring to space travelers, or simply voyagers.

Ezrai-il: Name of super-beings, who can transcend space and time, and appear to humans as angels, in terrestrial term. The Ana'kh literature refers to them as ethereal manifestation of the matter. But, our religions and Holy Scriptures depict them as the fallen angels. Ezrai-il or Ezrail is composed of two words:
a-Ezra, which means message or manifestation.
b-Il, which means divine; god; creator(s).

F

F "ف": One of the esoteric letters in the Anunnaki, Ulemite and Arabic alphabets. Typical with ancient Semitic names, there are none that begin with an 'F'. The Ulema called "F" the forbidden letter, or more precisely, the letter that was never allowed to be included in the Phoenician Aramaic, and Hebrew alphabets. "Thus all secret sounds and meanings associated with F would not be pronounced or heard, or known to the un-enlightened ones..." said Ulema Hanafi. "There are 12 secret words starting with the letter F that are hidden in the Torah, and the Book of Rama-Dosh...", explained Ulema Sadiq Al Qaysi.

And accordingly, each word produces a powerful sound capable of changing the fabric of time. The letter F was substituted by Ph, pronounced Pveh in several Semitic languages, except Arabic; the proto-Semitic "P" became the Arabic "F".

Fadi-ya-ashadi: An Anunnaki-Ulemite term for non-terrestrial shape-shifting entities.

The Ulema have explained this phenomenon.

- For extraterrestrials, shape-shifting is necessary.
- Shape-shifting includes skin color change, organs size, general physical appearances, but not the functionality of the body.
- The fingers become longer; thin and beneath the skin, there are millions of microscopic hair filaments and pores (orifices) that help them hold on slippery surfaces like glass and wet areas.
- Many of the extraterrestrial races wear tight outfits, almost glued to their skin. Anunnaki don't.
- The "Greys" are notorious for shape-shifting.
- They can appear like a reptile, an insect and even like humans.
- Aliens of lower dimensions need to manipulate their bodies to enter different spheres, the atmosphere of other planets, particularly underwater and underground environments and habitats.
- This is exactly what happens all the time with the "Greys" who live on earth and work with scientists in restricted/confined areas, such as underground genetic labs, and military research centers and bases.
- One of their striking characteristics is claustrophobia.
- Once confined for a long time in a limited space, the "Greys" go through intense crises. And almost all their supernatural powers weaken considerably.
- For instance, they loose the ability to go through walls and rigid substances, and teleport themselves.
- Even though, some of them, like their head scientists for instance retain the ability to resize their bodies, lower the density of their bodies' molecules and penetrate dense layers, the confined condition diminishes many of

48

their faculties, and considerably limits the possibilities of body's manipulations.

Anunnaki vis-à-vis other alien races:
Anunnaki look very different from the Zetas and the numerous alien races that have visited the Earth. In this context, they never appear or manifest like reptilians or short "Greys".
Sinhar Ambar Anati said:

- "It is easy to recognize an Anunnaki, because he usually appears like a tall warrior.
- An Anunnaki's vest is made from thin layers of metal called "Handar".
- His wears a long robe "Arbiya" of dark colors.
- Underneath the Arbiya, he wears a sort of pans with wide contour.
- On his wrist, you always notice his navigation tool."

Anunnaki's characteristics:

- The Anunnaki can transmute and manipulate their bodies if needed. This happens very rarely.
- In many instances, they don't need to do so, because they are already known to so many galactic and outer-galactic civilizations, and are seen by inhabitants of millions and millions of stars, planets and moons.
- They are superstars in their own rights.
- The Anunnaki can easily shape-shift themselves. This is necessary for climatic and atmospheric reasons.
- Each planet, star and dimension has its own climate, temperature and atmosphere.
- Consequently the organic-galactic body must adapt to these environment's conditions in order to remain functional.
- When they visit earth or a similar sphere, the Anunnaki slightly change their physical appearances, not so much, because in general, they look like us, except their eyes are much bigger, and they are much taller than us.
- Anunnaki are 9 foot tall.
- Even their women are extremely tall by human standard. Some women are 8 foot tall.

- When they travel to other planets, minor changes are required. For instance, when they get out of their galaxy and visit the planets Niftar, Marshan-Haloum and Ibra-Anu, they change the color of their skin, and the shape of their hands.
- On Niftar, inhabitants have grey-blue color skin and 3 fingers in each hand.

Falak-Dounia: Name of one of the dimensions of the world of the Anunnaki called "Anunnakifalak Dounia", which means the multiple universe of the Anunnaki.
According to the Ulema Kira'at, as far as humans are concerned, there are two Anunnaki's worlds:
1-Sama,
2-Falak or Dounia.

Falak "Dounia" is not a physical world.
No living human beings as physical creatures live in this second world. "Physical objects including human beings cannot enter a non-physical world, unless their molecules are reduced to a lower level of vibrations..." said Ulema Al Bakri.
Thus, Falak "Dounia" is not a world where human beings could live with their physical bodies. Falak "Dounia" is the world of the human mind.
The human mind was created by the Anunnaki. The human mind can manifest itself as the Double of a physical body..." explained Ulema Raja Shinkar.
Falak consists of seven different "Woujoud", meaning existences. Three of these Woujoud already exist in a physical-nonphysical sphere of illusion, called "Kha-Da'h". Planet earth is one of these three existences. But these three existences do not count as meaningful dimensions. This is why we start counting with the Fourth dimension as the first sphere of Falak.
a-The first Woujoud is known to us as the Fourth dimension, and it is called "Nafis-Ra".
b-The second Woujoud is known to us as the Fifth dimension, and it is called "Fik'r-Ra".
c-The third Woujoud is known to us as the Sixth dimension, and it is called "Kadosh-Ra" or "Koudous-Ra".
d-The fourth Woujoud is known to us as the Seventh dimension, and it is called "Khalek-Ra".

In other words, the Falak is the world of human beings who continue to live through their mind. Extraterrestrials of a very high vibrational state could share this sphere with the purified mind of humans (The deceased ones). Falak starts as soon as we die. It is neither outside nor inside our solar system, and no light years separate humans from any dimension or state of existence in Falak. Some Bashar (Human beings) have already reached different vibrational levels and spheres in Falak "Dounia".

Fana.Ri "Fanna-Ri": Name for a beam, or a sort of light used in the fertilization and genetic reproduction process of the Anunnaki.

According to Ulema Albaydani, "Anunnaki reproduction is done by technology, involving the light passing through the woman's body until it reaches her ovaries and fertilizes her eggs. The eggs go into a tube. The woman is lying on a white table for this procedure, surrounded by female medical personnel.

No discomfort is caused by this operation, because it resembles a scanning process." If performed by uncaring aliens (such as the Greys and Reptilians) it is unpleasant and even can be painful, which has given rise to abductee's stories of suffering. However, not all aliens are created equal, and have similar agenda. The Anunnaki, which are a very compassionate race, are very gentle and the procedure is harmless. Apparently, the Anunnaki version of sex is much more enjoyable for both genders. It involves an emanation of light from both participants. The light mingles and the result is a joy that is at the same time physical and spiritual. The Anunnaki do not have genitals the way we do.

As an Anunnaki hybrid becomes more and more Anunnaki, he/she loses the sexual organs.

The hybrid welcomes the changes and feels that he/she has gained a lot through the transformation. The Anunnaki mate for life, like ducks.

They don't even understand the concept of infidelity, and don't have a word for cheating, mistress, extramarital affairs, etc. in their language. Like many extraterrestrials, the Anunnaki do not have genital organs, but a lower level of aliens who inhabit the lowest interdimensional zone and aliens-hybrids living on earth do.

The stories of the abductees who claim to have had sex with Anunnaki are to be disregarded. Those stories are pure fiction.

Summary of fertilization and reproduction:

1-Aliens reproduce in laboratories.

2-Aliens do not practice sex at all.

3-Aliens fertilize "each other" and keep the molecules (not eggs or sperms, or mixed liquids from males and females) in containers at a very specific temperature and following well-defined fertilization-reproduction specs.

4-Alien babies are retrieved from the containers after 6 months.

5-The following month, the mother begins to assume her duty as a mother.

6-Alien mothers do not breast-feed their babies, because they do not have breast, nor do they produce milk to feed their babies.

7-Alien babies are nourished by a "light conduit."

8-Human sperm or eggs are useless to extraterrestrials of the higher dimension.

9-Extraterrestrials are extremely advanced in technology and medicine. Consequently, they do not need any part, organ, liquid or cell from the human body to create their own babies.

10--However, there are several aliens who live in lower dimensions and zones who did operate on abductees for other reasons – multiple reasons and purposes – some are genetic, others pure experimental.

Fari-narif "Fari-Hanif": Or simply Ra-Nif.

A term for categorizing different forms of spirits, or non-physical entities. The Anunnaki referred to many different forms, shapes and "rating" of entities known to the human race as "Spirits" and "Souls". From "Ra" and "Ra-Nif", derived the Semitic words Rouh, Rafesh, Nefes, Nefs, Roach, and Ruach, meaning the soul in Arabic, Aramaic and Hebrew.

I. Souls and spirits in Anunnaki-Ulema literature:

"The soul or spirit is a concept created by man," said Ulema Bakri. "Man was created, lives and continues to live through his Mind...not through his soul.

Angels do exist, but humans don't understand a thing about them, because religions taught Man that angels are spirits. The truth is they are neither spirits, nor the messengers of God, but a projection of a higher level of goodness and intelligence...and those who (after their physical death on earth) enter a higher dimension, would meet the angels in the Fourth dimension as meta-plasmic presence emanating beauty and goodness, but they are not divine spirits or pure souls." added Ulema Bakri.

Fasirach "Fisara": Nutrition. It is related to the nutrition and food of non-terrestrial entities. Extraterrestrials do not absorb food. They don't eat like we do, simply because they do not have stomach, intestines and digestive organs.

Don't confuse them with hybrids, semi-humans and Anunnaki. Hybrids living on earth, whether among humans or in restricted areas, such as their own habitat and underground installations eat and drink, and many of them enjoy humans' food.

No, they are not vegetarians, they eat meat and flesh, and this is why they are considered by extraterrestrials as "inferior breed". Extraterrestrials do not eat meat or flesh.

It was reported by William Cooper that Zetas:

a-Absorb certain substances from parts of the cattle that stabilize them during the cloning process;

b-This can be placed under the tongue to give sustenance and stability for some time. It is a substance that comes from certain mucus membranes: The lips, nose, genitals and rectum, and also from certain organs;

c-These glandular substances serve as nutrients in lieu of eating. Resting the substances under the tongue is not the only way they get nutrition. The cattle mutilations generally result in all the blood being drained from the body.

The Zetas have in their bases canisters and vats in which animal and human organs float along with a purple liquid to hold these parts in suspension.

(Author's note: Mr. Cooper's claims are not totally substantiated. And I doubt the veracity of some of his statements.)

Mr. Cooper also claimed that the Zetas use hydrogen peroxide in both the absorption and elimination process, because allegedly, the hydrogen peroxide also helps to preserve the liquid and organ mixture to keep it from spoiling.

The "Greys" have no digestive tract and eliminate through the skin. To eliminate, they need to pass the substance through some part of their body, much the same way plants eliminate through their skin or outer shells. They use hydrogen peroxide for helping with that elimination as well

Note: Mr. Cooper's description of food elimination after absorption is correct. They dispose of the rest of the absorbed food through their skin without producing odors. In a sense, the food substance evaporates through the dermatologic pores.

Fik'r: The ability of reading others' thoughts.

Derived from the Anakh Fik-R'r, and Fik.Ra.Sa.

The esoteric Arabic word "Firasa" is derived from Fik.Ra.Sa. It means in Arabic the ability to read thoughts, to understand the psyche of a person just by looking at him/her.

The Ulema uses Fik'r to read the mind, to learn about the intentions of others, and assess the level of intelligence of people.

As defined in the "Anunnaki Encyclopedia" (Authored by M. de Lafayette), and according to the doctrine and Kira'at of the Ulema, the soul is an invention of early humans who needed to believe in a next life. It was through the soul that mortals could and would hope to continue to live after death.

Soul as an element or a substance does not exist anywhere inside the human body.

Instead, there is a non-physical substance called "Fik'r" that makes the brain function, and it is the brain that keeps the body working, not the soul.

The "Fik'r" was the primordial element used by the Anunnaki at the time they created the final form of the human race.

Fik'r was not used in the early seven prototypes of the creation of mankind according to the Sumerian texts.

Although The "Fik'r", is the primordial source of life for our physical body, it is not to be considered as DNA, because DNA is a part of "Fik'r"; DNA is the physical description of our genes, a sort of a series of formulas, numbers and sequences of what there in our body, the data and history of our genes, genetic origin, ethnicity, race, so on. Thus Fik'r includes DNA.

The Ulema said: "Consider Fik'r as a cosmic-sub-atomic-intellectual-extraterrestrial (Meaning non-physical, non-earthly) depot of all what it constituted, constitutes and shall continue to constitute everything about you.

And it is infinitesimally small. However, it can expand to an imaginable dimension, size and proportions. It stays alive and continues to grow after we pass away if it is still linked to the origin of its creation, in our case the Anunnaki.

The Fik'r is linked to the Anunnaki our creators through a "Conduit" found in the cells of the brain. For now, consider Fik'r as a small molecule, a bubble. After death, this bubble leaves the body. In fact, the body dies as soon as the bubble leaves the body. The body dies because the bubble leaves the body.

Immediately, with one tenth of one million of a second, the molecule or the bubble frees itself from any and everything physical, including the atmosphere, the air, and the light;

absolutely everything we can measure, and everything related to earth, including its orbit.

The molecule does not go before St. Paul, St. Peter or God to stand judgment and await the decision of God -whether you have to go to heaven or hell– because there is no hell and there is no heaven the way we understand hell and heaven.

So it does not matter whether you are a Muslim, a Christian, a Jew, a Buddhist or a believer in any other religion. The molecule (Bubble) enters the original blueprint of "YOU"; meaning the first copy, the first sketch, the first formula that created you. Humans came from a blueprint.

Every human being has a Double. Your double is a copy stored in the "Rouh-Plasma"; an enormous compartment under the control of the Anunnaki on Nibiru and can be transported to another star, if Nibiru ceases to exist.

And this double is immortal. In this context, human is immortal, because its Double never dies. Once the molecule re-enters your original copy (Which is the original You), you come back to life with all your faculties, including your memory, but without physical, emotional and sensorial properties (The properties you had on earth), because they are not perfect."

Ulema Sadiq said: "At that time, and only at that time, you will decide whether you want to stay in your Double or go somewhere else...the universe is yours. If your past life on earth accumulated enough good deeds such as charity, generosity, compassion, forgiveness, goodness, mercy, love for animals, respect for nature, gratitude, fairness, honesty, loyalty...then your Double will have all the wonderful opportunities and reasons to decide and select what shape, format, condition you will be in, and where you will continue to live."

In other words, you will have everything, absolutely everything and you can have any shape you want including a brand new corporal form. You will be able to visit the whole universe and live for ever, as a mind, as an indestructible presence, and also as a non-physical, non- earthly body, but you can still re-manifest yourself in any physical body you wish to choose.

Worth mentioning here, that the molecule, (So-called soul in terrestrial term) enters a mew dimension by shooting itself into space and passing through the "Baab", a sort of a celestial star-gate or entrance. If misguided, your molecule (So-called your soul) will be lost for ever in the infinity of time and space and what there is between., until reconnected to your prototype via the "Miraya".

Is the afterlife a physical world? According to the Anunnaki Ulema: "No and yes. Because life after death unites time and space and everything that it constitutes space and time. It means extending to, and encompassing everything in the universe, and everything you saw, knew, felt, liked and disliked.

Everything you have experienced on earth exists in other dimensions, and there are lots of them. Everything you saw on Earth has its duplicate in another dimension. Even your past, present and future on Earth have another past, another present and another future in other worlds and other dimensions. And if you are lucky and alert, you can create more pasts, more presents and more futures, and continue to live in new wonderful worlds and dimensions; this happens after you die. Anunnaki and some of their messengers and remnants on Earth can do that. The physical aspect of the afterlife can be recreated the way you want it by using your Fik'r. Yes, you can return to Earth as a visitor, and see all the shows and musicals on Broadway or hang out on Les Champs-Elysées. You can also talk to many people who died if you can find their Double in the afterlife.

You can also enjoy the presence of your pets (Dead or alive), and continue to read a book you didn't finish while still alive on earth. What you currently see on Earth is a replica of what there is beyond Earth and beyond death.

The afterlife is also non physical, because it has different properties, density and ways of life." Anunnaki Ulema Wang Lin said: "Through Fik'r, a person can enter higher dimensions. It is of a major importance to train your Fik'r. "Transmission of the mind" training sessions can develop extra-sensorial faculties and open your "inner eye" commonly referred to as the Third Eye..."

Metaphysical-religious context:

"Although the Anunnaki do not believe in the same God we worship, revere and fear, understanding their concept of Khalek, the creator of our universe (Our galaxy), and other galaxies, the whole universe and especially life after death (The afterlife) could change the way we understand "God", the universe, the reason for our existence on earth, the principle of immortality, because it opens up a new way to comprehend the place of Man in the universe in this life and all the ones beyond the frontiers of time and space...", said Ulema Ghandar.

"The Anunnaki-Ulema's view of the afterlife gives a great hope and an immense relief to human beings...to all of us...", added Ulema Stambouli.

According to the "Book of Rama-Dosh", the only Anunnaki's manuscript left on earth in the custody of the Ul'ma (Ulema), humans should not be afraid to die, nor fear what is going to happen to them after they die.

Sinhar Marduck, an Anunnaki leader and scholar said human life continues after death in the form of "Intelligence" stronger than any form of energy known to mankind. And because it is mental, the deceased human will never suffer again; there are no more pain, financial worries, punishment, hunger, violence or any of the anxiety, stress, poverty and serious daily concerns that have created confusion and unhappiness for the human beings.

After death, the human body never leaves earth, nor comes back to life by an act of God, Jesus, or any Biblical prophet. This body is from dirt, and to dirt it shall return. That's the end of the story. Inside our body, there is not what we call "Soul".

Soul is an invention of mankind. It does not exist anywhere inside us. Instead, there is a non-physical substance called Fik'r that makes the brain function, and it is the brain that keeps the body working, not the soul.

The Fik'r was created by the Anunnaki at the time they designed us. The Fik'r is the primordial source of energy for our body. "However, the Fik'r despite its close tie to the human body, it does not belong to our physical properties...our mind has its own sphere, and quite often, it works independently from the body, this is how imagination and mental creativity are produced..." said Ulema Ghandar. The Fik'r contains the DNA and all its genetic data.

Fikrama "Fikr-Rama": The "Fik'r" (Brain cell-Conduit) sixth wave, unknown yet to science. It is related to An-zalubirach, also known as Tarkiz; a mental training that develops a supernatural power.

To fully understand what Fikrama "Fikr-Rama" means, we must first comprehend what An-zalubirach is, and how it works.

An-zalubirach is an Ana'kh/Ulemite term meaning the following:

a-Collecting thoughts, receiving and sending multiple mental images via brain wave synchronization, to improve mental and physical health;
b-Using mental energy to move or teleport things.

This is one of the phases and practices of Tarkiz.
Tarkiz means deep mental or intellectual concentration that produces telekinesis and teleportation phenomena.
Ulema's students learn this technique in various forms.
Basically it works like this:
a-The students use their Conduit (Which is located in the brain's cells) to control the waves of their brains (First level of learning)
b-The students concentrate on an object hidden behind a screen or a divider made from thin rice paper. (Second level of learning)
By synchronizing the frequency of their Conduit and an absolute state of introspection, the students attempt to move the hidden object from one place to another without even touching it.

In a more advanced stage, the students attempt to alter the properties of the object by lowering or increasing the frequencies and vibrations of the object itself.
The Ulema brain's waves: In addition to Beta, Alpha, Theta, and Delta, the Anunnaki Ulema developed a sixth wave called Fikr-Rama. It is neither measurable nor detectable, because it does not emanate from the physical brain. It is triggered by the Conduit situated in the brain's cells. No science on earth can direct us to the exact position of the Conduit.

The Ulema said:
1-Through the mechanism of the Conduit, the enlightened ones regulate mind's waves and frequencies.
2-The Fikr-Rama allows them to enter other dimensions, solid substances and matter.
3-The Fikr-Rama is a sort of a beam much lighter than laser. It does not have particles.
4-It has no substance per se, yet, it contains energy.
5-Extraterrestrials in general, and Anunnaki in particular have a multitude of similar brain's waves.
6-The Fikr-Rama is one single tone in the rainbow of their mental vibrations.

7-Highly advanced extraterrestrial beings can project thoughts and holographic images using any of their mental vibrations waves.

Filfila "Fil-I-fila": Name for an esoteric symbol closely related to the Anunnaki's "Light Liquid" and the "Flower of Life".
Literally it means a rose. And the rose represents a magical chalice. Some time, the chalice itself. Quite often, this chalice was depicted as a mushroom. It is quite obvious, that the chalice, the rose, the Flower of Life are symbols. In the black arts, esoterism, so-called magic, and other secret esoteric and occult teachings and principles, behind each symbol, there is another secret symbol, and behind each depiction or illustration, there is another secret illustration and depiction.

Filfila is no exception. Perhaps the following excerpt from the Anunnaki-Ulema Kira'at, could elucidate the matter: "...The meaning of the name of the great Perseus, founder of the Perseid Dynasty, and builder of the citadel of Mycenae is: "The Place of the Mushroom", and various illustrations of the mushroom appear abundantly on churches' columns.
Another striking example is the figure of the Biblical Melchizedek that appeared on a façade of the Cathedral de Chartre in France, holding a chalice in the shape of a mushroom, symbolizing life, and perhaps the Holy Grail, as interpreted in the literature of Cathars, Templar Knights, and many enlightened eastern secret societies. It was also interpreted as the "Divine-Human Vessel", meaning the womb of Virgin Mary; the very womb that gave birth to Jesus. In ancient Phoenician and Akkadian traditions closely related to the Anunnaki, the mushroom as a chalice represents the creative power of the female.
More precisely, the fecundity of a female Anunnaki goddess, giver of life and all living creatures. This fecundity source came in the form of a mitochondrial DNA. Also, the secret extracted liquid of the mushroom represented the "Light Liquid" known also as Elixir of Life.
On many Templars' pillars and Bourj (Upper part of a medieval fortress or a castle) in Syria, Malta and Lebanon, the mushroom is carefully illustrated as a "Flower of Life" known to the Phoenicians, Habiru (Hebrew), early Arabs, Sumerians and Anunnaki as:
a-Wardah;

b-Ward;
c-Vardeh.

These three words (Meaning a rose, or a flower) in ancient linguistic context, symbolized the blooming of life. At one point in history, the mushroom's figure was used by the Templar Order of St. John of Malta as the symbol of the Holy Grail. And in other passages, the mushroom represented a head; the head of a Sinhar "A leader".

Some historians thought that the leader was Baphomet, while others believed it was Noah, and another group believed it was the Prophet Mohammed, and finally, there is a group of learned masters who claimed that is was the Khalek of Markabah. Khalek is one of the seventy two names/attributes of God in Arabic (Now, 99), and Markabah or Merkabah means a spaceship in Sumerian and Akkadian.

The Anunnaki's mushroom symbol gave birth to the "Cult of Head". Anne Ross in her book "Pagan Celtic Britain", wrote: "The Cult of the Human Head constitutes a persistent theme throughout all aspects of Celtic life spiritual and temporal and the symbol of the severed head may be regarded as the most typical and universal of their religious attitudes."

Firasa or "Firasa-Basira": Arabic. Usually associated with Basira. Literally, it means perception, intelligence, discretion, evidence, and insight. All these attributes define Firasa-Basira.
In addition, it is understood and depicted as having an eye of the heart open, deep perception, an ability to see consequences just at the beginning of an act, or foresight.
Insight acquires a different, deeper dimension among Sufis. It is considered the sole source of spiritual knowledge obtained through reflective thought and inspiration, the first degree in the spirit's perception of the reality of things, and a major power of conscience that discerns and establishes values originating in the spirit, whereas reason becomes entangled in colors, forms, and qualities.
It is also a power of perception so sharpened by the light of nearness to the Divine Being that, when other powers of perception become exhausted by imagining, it acquires great familiarity with mysteries lying behind things and, without any

guide or evidence, reaches the Truth of the Truths, where reason is bewildered.

According to ascetic Sufism and the early spiritual-esoteric Islam, seeing is one of the luminous attributes of God, and one's insight, as declared in "We have shared among them." (43:32)
The greatest portion belongs to the one who, having benefited from that Divine Source to the fullest poured his inspirations into the hearts of his followers, namely the Prophet. The Divine Declaration said: "This is my path. I call to God on clear evidence and by insight, I and whoever follows me." (12:108).

This matchless perceptiveness allows the traveler on the path of Ascension to reach a higher sphere beyond corporeal existence.
The pleasure of observance given by insight sometimes acquires a new, deeper dimension when the believer begins to discern and discover the spiritual dimension and meanings of things and events.
His or her spirit experiences other dimensions in this three-dimensional realm, and his or her conscience becomes the eye of existence with which it sees, and reaches a higher intellect.
In addition to perception and understanding, discernment (Firasa) denotes the deepening of insight when perception becomes a source of certain knowledge. Those who discern the manifestations of the light of God, acquire a radiant faculty that allows them to see everything, and understand all issues, with total clarity. They are never confused, even when encountering the most intricate elements. (15:75). (Source: Fethullah Gülen.)

Firasa and the paranormal: Almost all rulers in ancient Persia, Phoenicia and later in Egypt employed in their royal courts, "People of Firasa". They consulted with them during visits of dignitaries and officials from foreign countries. It was the secret science of learning about the personality of people through the study of physiognomy.
This science was called "Firasa". One of the greatest Ulema masters and experts in the field was Fakher Addīn Al- Rāzī. His noted treatise on Firasa "The Science of Psycho-physiognomy" was inspired by the teachings of the elder non-physical Ulema. In the unpublished original edition of his treatise, several Anunnaki syllables and geometric forms were included in "Al Moukamma"

61

the introduction of the book dedicated to the "True believers of the higher knowledge".

G

Gabhatimani: The reader of galactic maps; the decipher of codes and symbols. From Gabhatimani, derived the Sanskrit word Gabhastiman, which means repossessed of his rays.

Gadaridu: Ana'kh/Ulemite. A term for an Anunnaki's method used to alter a genetic code. According to the Anunnaki Ulema, some mental techniques using Ana'kh words can alter the composition of the human DNA.
The change brought to the DNA can be read on a chart, animated on a screen-grid called Miraya.
Ulema Sadiq said: "Although our DNA is our permanent biological, chemical, physical, mental and structural identity, this DNA can be altered, because it is a genetic formula, more precisely a program as defined in our terminology.
As such, any program can be reprogrammed and deprogrammed. There is a multitude of means and techniques to do that. One of them is the use of vocal imagery.
The Vocal imagery is the continuous sequence of sounds and words produced by vocal chords, as well as brain's waves. They have the capability of changing the composition and sequences in our DNA. This procedure was used by the Anunnaki, after they have created the first seven human prototypes.
The Anunnaki's genetic change brought to the physiognomy and mental faculties of the quasi-humans some 65,000 years, added "intelligent mobility" to the body, and allowed the early human beings to acquire a sense of understanding of their immediate environment.
This was done in genetic laboratories, here on planet Earth, using sounds and words....motion, sounds, voices, words and even thoughts, all have DNA...some have a genetic reproduction power..."

Gens "Jenesh": A gender.Similar words appeared in Semitic languages. To name a few:
a-Gens in Arabic;

b-Gensa in Assyrian;
c-Gensu in Akkadian.

Ghen-ardi-vardeh, also "Gen-adi-warkah": Aagerdi-deh for short.The act or process of talking to others without using words, and in a total silence. Composed from three words:
a-Gen, which means people; others.
b-Ardi, which means earthly; land; location. Ertz in Hebrew, and Ard in Arabic. Ersetu "Erdsetu" in Assyrian and Sumerian. All derived from the Ana'kh Erd and Ard.
c-Vardeh, which means rose; flower; aroma; chalice; quest.

Vardeh in Hebrew and Arabic, and it means a rose in both languages. Warkah is a substitute for Vardeh, and it means a paper; a page. Ulema Seif Eddine Chawkat told a great story about Gen-ardi-vardeh, and briefly explained how it works in the Book of Rama-Dosh. He said (Verbatim, unedited): "During World War One, my father worked as a military superintendent for the Turkish army. In prisoners of war camps, some medical visits and check-ups were scheduled once a month.
It did not happen in all the concentration camps and centers of detention, but it did happen at one particular place, and my father worked there. Some British officers (Prisoners of war) were treated properly, while others were not so lucky. Malaria, dysentery, and other health problems among prisoners were frequent. The Turkish army ran out of medicine and quinine pills, and the prisoners' health condition began to deteriorate. In brief, not all prisoners received medical treatment. One of those unfortunate British officers was Major V. H.
He was in serious trouble. And because he fell so ill, he could not talk anymore, and succumbed to a threatening fever. Yet, no medical attention was given to him, until, and probably by pure coincidence or luck, a military doctor entered the tent and saw him there agonizing in his bed. The doctor noticed his serious condition and approached him.

Unfortunately, nothing could be done; medicine and pills were no longer available, and the only thing one could have done in similar situations was to wipe out the sweat of the sick prisoners. But something very unusual happened there. The doctor briefly examined the major who was agonizing, but could not utter not one word. He placed his hand on his forehead and throat, and all

63

of a sudden, as my father recalls, "the whole situation changed immediately.

The doctor ordered one of his adjutants to fetch a certain box; we did not know what it was. When the adjutant returned carrying the box, we saw what was in it...bandages, medicine, pills, everything you needed...syringes...etc. the major was lucky; the doctor took care of him, he gave him a few pills, told the adjutant to watch over him, and asked him to bring the major new clean pillows and blankets. We were stunned.

All of a sudden, the doctor and the major became friends.

Two years later, when the war ended, and by a pure coincidence, my father met the military doctor in Budapest, and they start to talk about the war and so many other things. One of those things was Major V. H. story. My father asked the doctor why he cared so much for the major, and not the others. And the doctor replied that the major was one of the "Brothers". In other words, a novice-Ulema just like himself. How did he find out? Smiling, the doctor told my father: "I touched his forehead and his throat...and by touching his throat I could read his silent message to me. He told me that he was Ulema." In other words, the British major used the technique of Aagerdi-deh to talk to the doctor without opening his mouth, and of course to let him know that he was an Ulema. The British major hoped that the Turkish doctor might be an Ulema himself, and if so, he would be able to get his "silent message."

And he was! Both were Ulema, and this is why the Turkish physician cared so much for the British prisoner. "Of course nobody believed this", said my father. In fact, every time my father told this story, people laughed at him." Amazingly, ninety years later, NASA began to explore Aagerdi-deh. They call it now the "Subvocal Speech."

Most recently, NASA issued a press release to that effect; it is self-explanatory. Herewith an excerpt from the release, and update on NASA's most fascinating project." NASA develops system to computerize silent, "Subvocal Speech": NASA scientists have begun to computerize human, silent reading using nerve signals in the throat that control speech.

In preliminary experiments, NASA scientists found that small, button-sized sensors, stuck under the chin and on either side of the "Adam's apple," could gather nerve signals, and send them to a processor and then to a computer program that translates them into words.

Eventually, such "subvocal speech" systems could be used in spacesuits, in noisy places like airport towers to capture air-traffic controller commands, or even in traditional voice-recognition programs to increase accuracy, according to NASA scientists. "What is analyzed is silent, or subauditory, speech, such as when a person silently reads or talks to himself," said Jorgensen, a scientist whose team is developing silent, subvocal speech recognition at NASA's Ames Research Center, Moffett Field, Calif.

"Biological signals arise when reading or speaking to oneself with or without actual lip or facial movement," Jorgensen explained. "A person using the subvocal system thinks of phrases and talks to himself so quietly, it cannot be heard, but the tongue and vocal chords do receive speech signals from the brain," Jorgensen said.In their first experiment, scientists "trained" special software to recognize six words and 10 digits that the researchers repeated subvocally. Initial word recognition results were an average of 92 percent accurate.

The first sub-vocal words the system "learned" were "stop," "go," "left," "right," "alpha" and "omega," and the digits "zero" through "nine."

Silently speaking these words, scientists conducted simple searches on the Internet by using a number chart representing the alphabet to control a Web browser program.

"We took the alphabet and put it into a matrix -- like a calendar. We numbered the columns and rows, and we could identify each letter with a pair of single-digit numbers," Jorgensen said. "So we silently spelled out 'NASA' and then submitted it to a well-known Web search engine. We electronically numbered the Web pages that came up as search results.

We used the numbers again to choose Web pages to examine. This proved we could browse the Web without touching a keyboard," Jorgensen explained. Scientists are testing new, "noncontact" sensors that can read muscle signals even through a layer of clothing.

A second demonstration will be to control a mechanical device using a simple set of commands, according to Jorgensen. His team is planning tests with a simulated Mars rover. "We can have the model rover go left or right using silently 'spoken' words," Jorgensen said.

People in noisy conditions could use the system when privacy is needed, such as during telephone conversations on buses or trains, according to scientists. "An expanded muscle-control system could help injured astronauts control machines. If an astronaut is suffering from muscle weakness due to a long stint in microgravity, the astronaut could send signals to software that would assist with landings on Mars or the Earth, for example," Jorgensen explained.

"A logical spin-off would be that handicapped persons could use this system for a lot of things." To learn more about what is in the patterns of the nerve signals that control vocal chords, muscles and tongue position, Ames scientists are studying the complex nerve-signal patterns.

"We use an amplifier to strengthen the electrical nerve signals. These are processed to remove noise, and then we process them to see useful parts of the signals to show one word from another," Jorgensen said. After the signals are amplified, computer software "reads" the signals to recognize each word and sound.

"The keys to this system are the sensors, the signal processing and the pattern recognition, and that's where the scientific meat of what we're doing resides," Jorgensen explained. "We will continue to expand the vocabulary with sets of English sounds, usable by a full speech-recognition computer program."The Computing, Information and Communications Technology Program, part of NASA's Office of Exploration Systems, funds the subvocal word-recognition research. There is a patent pending for the new technology, as noted by NASA

Gensi-uzuru: Apparition of deceased pets. The Ulema are very fond of animals. Extensive passages in the Book of Rama-Dosh speak about the important role animals play in the life of humans, especially at emotional and therapeutic levels. The Ulema believe that pets understand very well their human-friends (Instead of using the word "owners"). And also, pets communicate with those who show them love and affection.

This loving relationship between pets and their human-friends does not end when pets die. Although the Anunnaki-Ulema do not believe in any possibility of contacting deceased people or animals, they have explained to us that contacting our departed ones is possible for a very short time, and only during the 40 days period following their death.

In other words, we can contact our deceased parents and dear ones, or more accurately enter in contact with them if:

a-They contact us short after their death;

b-They must initiate the contact;

c-This should happen during a 40 days period following their departure;

d-Their contact (Physical or non-physical) must be noticed by us. This means that we should and must pay an extra attention to "something" quite irregular or unusual happening around us. Because our departed pets will try to send us messages, and in many instances, they do.

e-We must expect their messages, and strongly believe in those messages.

The Ulema said that humans cannot contact their dead pets.

But pets can contact us via different ways we can sense and feel, if we have developed a strong bond with them. Pets know who love them and those who don't, because pets feel, understand, sense and see our aura.

All our feelings and thoughts are imprinted in our aura, and the aura is easily visible to pets, particularly, cats, dogs, parrots, lionesses, pigs, and horses. This belief is shared by authors, people of science and therapists in the West, despite major difference between Westerners and Ulema in defining the nature and limits of pets-humans after death contact. Ulema in defining the nature and limits of pets-humans after death contact. For instance, in the United States, pets lovers and several groups of therapists and psychics think that "a pet can reappear as a ghost. And a ghost could be luminous or even appear as it did in life. You don't necessarily know when you see an animal if it's a ghost or not, said Warren, a researcher in the field. "It's much easier to identify a loved one who's passed and come back."

"Don't forget them because they're gone," said Jungles, who owns three cats. "Keep their toys and blankets around.

They (ghosts) will go where they're happiest." Warren agrees. "Recreate an environment conducive to the pet's life," he said. "Use your imagination and treat it like it's alive. In other words, you should create or re-create conditions ideal for their re-appearance, even though, for a very short moment.

Gholaim: Ana'kh/Ulemite name for ghosts.

The occasional apparitions of deceased persons, but in no instances whatsoever of the spirits of the dead, or invisible astral entities producing various psychic phenomena. This age-old belief is consistent with the breaking up of composite human nature into its component parts at death. As the astral model-body, when freed from its familiar physical duplicate, is still magnetically attached to the body, it is sometimes seen haunting the new grave for a short time. Soon the atoms of this shadowy form begin to dissipate. But the more ethereal and enduring astral atoms cohere in the kama-rupic body of the deceased person's lower mental, emotional, and psychic nature.

Giabiru: Death; a dead person lost in a parallel dimension. From Giabiru, derived the Assyrian noun Giabi, which means a reaper. It did appear in the Akkadian and Sumerian clay tablets.
"Matani sabzute va malki aibi-su kima giabi uhazizu."-From the Annals of Sardanapalus.
Translated verbatim: "Countries turbulent and kings his enemies like a reaper he cut off."

Gibbori: A group of Anunnaki geneticists and people of science who develop DNA sequences, and alter the genes of hybrids. From Gibbori, derived the Arabic word Gabbar which means giants, and the plural Gababira (Giants). In Pre-Islamic era, the word Gababira meant huge entities who came from a non-physical world, and maliciously interfered in humans' affairs. In Hebrew, it is Gibborim (גבר גבור), which is the plural of Geber, which means mighty man. It appears more than 150 times in the Jewish Tanakh.

Gibishi: Power. From Gibishi, derived the Assyrian word Gibis, which means might; power; strength. It did appear in the Akkadian and Sumerian clay tablets. "Mili kassa mee rabuti kima gibis tihamti usalmi."-Nebuchadnezzar.
Translated verbatim: "A collection of great water like the might of the sea I caused add it."
"In gibis libbi-ya u suskin galli-ya er asibi."-From the Annals of Sardanapalus. Translated verbatim: "In the strength of my heart, and steadfastness of my servants, I besieged the city."

"Ana gibis ummani-su mahdi ittagil."-From the Obelisk of Nimrud. Translated verbatim: "To the powers of his great army he trusted."

"Ina gibis emuqi sa Asur bil-ya."-From the Annals of Tihlath Pileser. Translated verbatim: "In the boubdless might of Assur my lord."

Gibsut-sar: A leading group in charge of military operations. Usually, the group consists of five persons, men and women selected from Ma'had, an Ana'kh word meaning an academy. Similar Assyrian word Gibsut-sun appeared in Iraq's ancient clay tablets. In Assyrian, Gibsut-sun means "all of them", referring to groups and gatherings. "Kitru rabu iktera itti-su gibsut-sun uruh Akkadi izbatunu."-From a Sennacherib's cylander. Translated verbatim: "A great gathering was gathered, and with him all of them the road of Akkad took."

Gigur: A shield; a cover; roof of an edifice. From Gigur, derived the Assyrian word Gigu, which means a cover; a roof.
It did appear in the Akkadian and Sumerian clay tablets. "Sillulat gigu kima antir anna nashira gimir babani." From the Annals of Esar Haddon. Translate verbatim: "Stairs and roof like defenses of metal I placed about all the gates."

Gilgoolim: The non-physical state of a deceased person, at the end of the 40 days period. At that time, the deceased person must decide whether to stay in the lower level of the Fourth dimension, or head toward a higher level of knowledge, following an extensive orientation program/guidance.
From Gilgoolim, derived the Kabalistic/Hebrew word Gilgoolem referring to the cycle of rebirths, meaning the revolution of souls; the whirling of the soul after death, which finds-no rest until it reaches its final destination.

Goirim-dari: *Ana'kh/Ulemite.* A mental catalyst.

Goirim-daru: *Ana'kh/Ulemite.* Term.The vibes produced by one's double, according to the Book of Rama-Dosh; a sort of bio-plasmic rays that project the non-physical properties of an object or a thought.

Godumu "Godumari": The lines that appear on a Miraya, in order to register codes for galactic communications.

Goduri "Goduri-mara": The process that prints pages or symbols from the Ulemite's Book of Rama-Dosh, using electro-magnetic beams, projected on the Minzar box.

Golibu "Golibri":
Term for the passage or transition from a physical existence to a mental or non-physical sphere, usually associated with the first dimension of the Anunnaki's Shama, meaning sky; outer space; a parallel dimension.

Golim: A prototype of a created presence or entity, usually associated with the mixture of a terrestrial element and the thought of a Golimu who creates a non-human creature. From Golim, derived the Kabalistic/Hebrew word Golem. See Golem and Golimu.

Golimu: The enlightened Ulema who creates a Golem look-like.

Goirim-dari: A mental catalyst.

Goirim-daru: The vibes produced by one's double, according to the Book of Rama-Dosh; a sort of bio-plasmic rays that project the non-physical properties of an object or a thought.

Gudinh: To move around; the act or the attempt of bringing things (even thoughts) together and creating a virtual three dimensional reality from assembling collected thoughts, desires and ideas, and projecting them over a mirror serving as a catalyst. This mirror is called Miraya in Ana'kh language.

Gudar: Ana'kh-Ulemite name of Anunnaki cones that store data.

Gudari: Ana'kh-Ulemite name for a technician in charge of codes classifications.

Gudaridu-marah: Ana'kh-Ulemite name for the plasmic screen that receives galactic codes.

Gudiba: Ana'kh-Ulemite term for an Anunnaki raid. From Gudiba, derived the Sumerian word Gúdibir, which means a battle; a war.

H

H: A symbol representing the two parallel lines emanated from the "Conduit" during a telekinesis training exercise, called Haabaari "Ha-abri".

Habru: Term for the mental powers of the Anunnaki-Ulema students implanted and programmed in the "Conduit".

Hadiiya: Successful completion of a study, usually referring to the initiation of the "Eight Degree". This initiation leads to the opening or activation of the Conduit; a cell in the brains that contains supernatural powers.

Hag-Addar: Literally, the right to enter a palace; a metaphoric expression for an Ulemite adept spiritual initiation, sometimes referred to as the 18th degree ritual ceremony.
According to Ulema Govinda, during this ceremony, the adept is taught the secrets of the origin of the creation, and the invisible dimensions that co-exist with the physical world. In addition, a multitude of techniques are revealed to the initiated, that allow him/her to acquire extraordinary powers, such as teleportation, Tay Al Ard, Firasa, dematerialization, and psychotelemetry.

Halida: Invisibility.

Hama-dar: A library. Composed of two words:
a-Hama, which means information; data; knowledge.
b-Dar, which means a place; a home, a center.

Hamen: A union.

Hamenka: Ana'kh-Ulemite name for family.

Hamenku: Ana'kh-Ulemite name for the head of a family.

71

Hamentaa: Ana'kh/Ulemite. Trust; confidence; belief.
From Hamentaa, derived:
a-The Phoenician words Hameni, and Hamena which mean trust.
b-The Aramaic noun Hamenta, which means belief.
c-Eeman "Imaan" in Arabic.

Hamenu: A communication.

Hamil-Arda: A cloned person.

Hamnika-mekhakeh: Kha in mekhakeh is pronounced as "Jo" in Jose in Spanish. Grids used by Anunnaki-Ulema as calendar to find the lucky days and the lucky hours in a person's life.

Hamta: Strength; authority. From Hamta, derived the Assyrian and Chaldean adjective Hamtu, which means strong; powerful

Hamulu: Assistance. From Hamulu, derived the Assyrian and Akkadian verb Hamu, which means to depend on.

Hamunara: Equilibrium; balance.
From Hamunara, derived the Sumerian noun Hamun, which means harmony.

Hamuu: Head of a family, and/or a family cell. From Hamuu, derived the Phoenician noun Hamum, which means father- in-law.

Hanaasha-niha: Surrender; submission. From Hanaasha-niha, derived the Akkadian and Sumerian verb Hanaashu, which means to submit; To accept subjection; to become submissive.

Hanaida: A hand. The hand has a deep meaning in Ana'kh, Hebrew and in the Bible. The hand was called by Galen "The instrument of instruments." The hand in the Bible is the symbol of human deeds.(Ps. 9:16; Job 9:30; Isa. 1:15; 1 Tim. 2:8).

Handaa: A treaty; an understanding.

Handar: Annunaki's vest, which is made from thin layers of metal.

Hani: An Anunnaki guide; an instructor.

Hannaaba: An Anunnaki council.

Hapura "Hapudi": A division; a separation. From Hapura, derived the Akkadian verb Hapu, which means to divide.

Haraabu: Destruction; complete decimation. From Haraabu, derived:
a-The Akkadian word Harābu, which means to become ruined, devastation; destruction.
b-The Assyrian word Haraba, which means ruins; wasteland.
c-Kharaab in Arabic. Kherba in Hebrew.

Hara-da-irat: A circle, a circumference. From Hara-da-irat, derived the Sumerian word Hara, which means a ring.

Hara-da-irat: Center of power.

Haraana: A battle. From Haraana, derived the Sumerian word Haraan "Karaan", which means either a military maneuver, or a military campaign. Haraanum in Akkadian and Old Babylonian.

Harabah: Destruction; ruins.
From Harabah, derived the Assyrian adjective Haraba "Kharaba, which means ruins; wasteland.
Kharaab in Arabic, which means destruction, and Kharbah, "Kherbeh", which means rubbles.
Kherba in Hebrew, which means ruins.
Harav "Karav" in contemporary Hebrew, which means rubble; ruins. Harabu "Kharaabu in Akkadian, which means devastation.
Harbatu "Kharbatu" in Akkadian, which means ruins; deserted area.Krb in Ugaritic/Phoenician, which means ruins.
Kherba in proto-Hebrew, which means a wasteland; deserted land.

Harima: Ana'kh-Ulemite title given to a female Anunnaki who is in charge of the education of Anunnaki children. The education and orientation programs of young Anunnaki continue till 71, which is the official maturity age of all Anunnaki in Nibiru. The first 25 years of studying and learning period is usually under the direct control of an Anunnaki female called Harima.

Harimu: Ana'kh-Ulemite name or title given to the head of an Anunnaki's family cell on other planets.

Harranur-urdi: Ana'kh/Ulemite. A term applied to retrieving data and codes displayed on a cosmic monitor called "Miraya".
On this subject, Ulema Ben Zvi said (Excerpts from his Kira'at, in the Book of Ramadosh):

- "On Ashtari, the Planet of the Anunnaki (Ne.Be.Ru or Nibiru, to others) each Anunnaki (male and female, young and adult) has a direct access to the Falak Kitbah (Akashic Records) through the Akashic Libraries (Called Shama Kitbah), which are located in every community in Ashtari.
- The libraries (Called Makatba and/or Mat-Kaba) are constructed from materials such as chiselled opaque glass (Called Mir-A't), a substance similar to fibreglass (Called Sha-riit), and a multitude of fibre-plastic-like materials (Called Fisal and Hiraa-Ti);
- They convey the appearance of ultra-modern, futuristic architecture (By humans' standards), and techno-industrialized edifices.
- One enters the libraries through an immense hall (Called Isti-bal), seven hundred to one thousand meters in length, by five hundred meters in width.
- The Isti-bal is empty of any furniture, and is lit by huge oval windows that are placed near the top of the ceiling.
- The windows (Called Shi-bak) were designed in such a way that the shafts of light that enter through their circular compartments are redirected and projected like solid white laser beams.
- The effect is spectacular.
- At night, quasi identical effect is produced by the projection of concentrated light beams coming from hidden sources of lights located behind (More precisely,

inside the frames' structure) the frames (Called Mra) of the windows.

- The frames serve as an energy depot.
- The energy is transformed into sources of light.
- The visual effect is stunning. Enormously large and animated metallic billboards (Called Layiha, pronounced La-ee-haa) are affixed on walls in a parallel alignment, and on the floor, in front of each billboard, there are hundreds of symmetrically rectangular pads (Called Mirkaan).
- When visitors enter the library's main hall (Situated just at the front entrance), they approach the billboards, and stand each on a Mirkaan.
- The pad serves as a scanner and a transportation device, because it has the capacity to read the minds of the visitors, learn what they are searching for, and as soon as it does so, it begins to move, and slides right through the central billboard (Called Kama La-yiha), which is not really solid but is made from blocks of energy, carrying the visitor with it.
- Behind the billboard is the main reading room (Called Kama Kira'at) of the Akashic Library.
- Under the belly of the pad, there are two separate compartments designed to register what the visitor is looking for, and to direct the visitor to his/her destination; usually, it is a reference section where books in form of cones are located on magnetized shelves.
- The Anunnaki's Akashic Library is not a traditional library at all, for it contains no physical books per se, even though, there are plenty of conic publications (Books manufactured as magnetic cylinders and cones.) Instead of searching for books on shelves, as we do on Earth, the visitors find themselves in the presence of an immense white-light blue screen, made of materials unknown to us.
- The screen is hard to describe; it can be compared to a grid (Called Kadari), with a multitude of matrices and vortices of data.
- The visitors communicate with the screen via their Conduit. The screen registers their thoughts and right away finds/records the information the visitors seek.

75

- All the visitors have to do is stand still for less than two seconds (In terrestrial terms) in front of the screen, and the data will be displayed in an animated format.
- The data (Information) is given in codes which are easily understood by the visitors.
- The codes are usually divided into sequences; each sequence reflects an aspect of the information.
- For example, if you want to know what happened in Alexandria or Phoenicia 3000 B.C., all what you need to do, is to think about either Alexandria or Phoenicia, and one grid will appear, waiting for your command to open it up.
- From this precise moment, the visitor's Conduit and the Screen are communicating in the most direct fashion.
- The grid opens up and displays three files in sequence.
- The nearest description of these files would be plasmic-digital, for the lack of the proper word;
- Each file will contain everything that had happened pertaining to that particular date or era in Alexandria or Phoenicia.

Harurtu: A sound, a message. Possibly from Harurtu, derived the Akkadian and Assyrian word Harurtu, which means the throat. Harhirta in contemporary Assyrian Eastern dialect. Zragrurto in contemporary Assyrian Western dialect.

Hasami-erdi: People of planet Earth. Composed of two words:
a-Hasami, which means beings,
b-Erdi, which means Earth.

Hasamir: Beings from other planetary systems. From Hasamir, derived the Anatolian word Hasami, which means people; a clan.

Hashala: Ana'kh-Ulemite. Destruction. From Hashala, derived the Assyrian and Akkadian verb Hashalu, which means to crush; to smash. Hshalla in contemporary Assyrian Eastern dialect. Ksopho in contemporary Assyrian Western dialect.

Hasisa: Ana'kh-Ulemite. Knowledge; data.
From Hasisa, derived the Akkadian word Hasisu "Khasisu", which means intelligence.

Haskaama: Ana'kh-Ulemite. An agreement. From Haskaama, derived the Hebrew word Haskama, which means approval.

Hassantu "Hassantur": An authority; a decree.
From Hassantu, derived the Hittite and Luwian adjective, which means legal.

Hassata: Confirmation. From Hassata, derived the Hittite and Luwian word Hassatar, which means a testimony.

Hassuzanāi: Reign. From Hassuzanāi, derived the Hittite and Luwian verb Hassuiznāi, which means to rule.

K

Kami-liim: People of the fourth level. Composed of two words: a) Kamil, which means perfection or complete, and b) iim, which means a group, a level, a standard. The Turkish, Arabic, Urdu and ancient Persian word Kamal or Kemal means the very same thing.

Korashag "Khur-Sha": An Anunnaki/Ulemite word for hybrids' habitat.

PART 7
Extraterrestrials, Intraterrestrials, Grays, Hybrids

Zanich-Eredu:
I. Definition and introduction.
II. The "Grays": The intraterrestrial non-human race.

I. Definition and introduction:

An Ulemite term referring to human genetic contamination, caused by the "Grays". The contamination was the result of an inter-breeding program secretly carried out by an intraterrestrial non-human race living on Earth, usually referred to as the "Grays". The inter-breeding with humans is a major part of their agenda. And this is a serious threat that humanity is constantly facing.

II. The "Grays": Intraterrestrial non-human race:

It is important to understand that the Grays have lived on Earth for millions of years, long before the human races were created by the Igigi, Anunnaki and Lyrans. We call the Grays "extraterrestrials".

This is not correct, for the Greys are intraterrestrials, living deep underground and underwater, and humans are the co-inhabitants of planet Earth. We fear the Grays. And ironically, the Grays fear us. They feel threatened by our nuclear arsenal, nuclear tests and experiments, because they can annihilate Earth, where the Grays live.

Earth is the habitat of the Grays. Earth is where their communities and families live. Grays will do anything and everything to prevent humans from destroying Earth. Earth will be only destroyed by acts of nuclear war. Grays have adapted very well to the intra-landscape of Earth; meaning the Inner-Earth. And water on Earth is essential for their survival and for "energizing" their crafts.

Unfortunately, constant genetic interaction with the Grays will deteriorate the genes of the human race. The first phase of such deterioration is contamination.

The Anunnaki are fully aware of this contamination. Simply put, in order to eliminate the contamination, the Anunnaki must get rid of the Grays. And the decontamination process will result in a major confrontation with the Grays.

Some influential governments have already received a sort of "briefing" on the subject. Some high officials took the threat very seriously, while many others did not.

Their arrogance and ignorance will have lethal consequences that humanity will suffer from.

There are no additional threats from other extraterrestrial races, simply because they are not interested in us. They are not interested because we have nothing meaningful or important to offer them. Humans live on a linear timeline. This is how and why we understand the universe in terms of time and distance. And this limits us, and prevents us from becoming part and members of the "Cosmic Federation." Only two races in the known universe can live on Earth: The Anunnaki and the Grays. In the past, three extraterrestrial races lived here on Earth, for sometime among us.

They were:

- **a**-The Anunnaki;
- **b**-The Lyrans;
- **c**-The Grays.

Their organism and body structure could survive our atmosphere and its conditions. Other extraterrestrials would not be able to live on Earth, as humans would also not be able to live on other known stars systems and planets, because of their atmospheric conditions. Other alien races will self-destruct if they try to live on Earth. Consequently, they have no interest whatsoever in invading or dominating Earth. In other words, the only threat, the only real threat to humans, come from the Grays.

But for the time being, we are safe, because the Grays still need us. Despite their highly advanced technology and science, the Grays have not yet found the perfect and final formula for saving themselves, genetically. For some incomprehensible reason, the survival of the Grays depends on two things:

- **a**-The survival of humans;
- **b**-The safety of Earth.

Because peace on Earth, and the ecological safety of planet Earth affect the stability of the underground/underwater habitat of the Grays themselves.

On hybrids and immortality

Can hybrids reach immortality?

- 1. Although hybrids are intelligent beings, they are not to be considered neither as humans nor as extraterrestrials.
- 2. Their essence (DNA) is not pure.
- 3. They are genetically created either by humans or by a malicious extraterrestrial race.
- 4. Any living creature Dha-kiliyan (Genetically) created by humans will never reach immortality.
- 5. Because a Dha-kiliyi (Genetic) creation of other living-forms manufactured by human beings is an artificial product, this Dha-kiliyi (Genetic) product which does not include the first energy element introduced in regular human beings by the Anunnaki will totally disintegrate without leaving the "Shou'la" (Spark of life).
- 6. The Shou' la was created on earth by the Anunnaki. No human ever succeeded in duplicating a Shou'la.
- 7. Any living creature Dha-kiliyan (Genetically) created on earth or in other physical dimensions by a malicious extraterrestrial race coming from a lower dimension will not reach immortality.

I do believe that the honorable Ulema refer to hybrids, what American ufologists call the "Greys", even though, the have never used the word "Greys". It is my belief that this word is an American ufology terminology. The word the ulema used is "Min Kariji al-dounia". Min means from. Kariji means outside or outer. Dounia means the world.

- 8. Living entities or creatures created by the Greys are born contaminated.
- 9. The Greys' contamination prevents these living entities (Hybrids, half humans-half-extraterrestrials) from ascending to the Ba'ab.

- 10. Consequently, the hybrids will not enter the other dimensions and reach immortality.

On the Grays, their disease, and doomed race
Is it true the Grays are dying?
What are they dying from?
Are they kidnapping people to use them as guinea pigs and extract something from their bodies to save their own lives?

- 1. The Grays are a dying civilization.
- 2. Many of them (Almost the majority) have progeria.
- 3. On earth, progeria is also called Hutchinson-Gilford Syndrome, after the two scientists who discovered it in 1886.
- 4. Progeria victims are children who age, really become old people, before they even reach puberty; it is a parent nightmare, but very rare on Earth, common among the Grays.
- 5. Only one progeria child is born out of four to eight million births. Rare, and extremely frightening genetic disease, resulting from spontaneous mutation in the sperm or egg of the parents.
- 6. The horror of this disease is that it has no cure.
- 7. The child is born, starts showing early symptoms, and begins to age right away.
- 8. The children remain tiny, rarely over four feet, both boys and girls become bald, and all develop a large cranium, a pointy nose and a receding chin, resulting in an amazing resemblance to each other, almost as if they were clones.
- 9. And then they die of old age, mostly in their teens but often before, and there is nothing anyone can do for them. They develop old age diseases – such as hardening of the arteries – and often die of strokes or coronary disease, while their poor parents have to watch helplessly.
- 10. The name progeria is very appropriate. It means 'before old age,' and expresses it very well.
- 11. The civilization of the Grays is millions of years old, and for eons, they have been degenerating. A huge percentage of their population has progeria, in varying

degrees, and because of that, they are threatened with extinction.

- 12. No one knows how many Grays are affected, and how many are progeria-free. We only meet those who are, at least for the present, able to carry on their duties, with the help of their advanced medical technology. For all we know, there are millions of sick individuals hidden from view on their home planet.
- 13. The Grays do not reproduce sexually. They used to, but not anymore.
- 14. Also, they don't reproduce like the Anunnaki, either. For thousands of years, they have been relying on cloning. And that has damaged their DNA even further, creating more and more cases of progeria. They are dying out.
- 15. There are strong similarities between the Grays and the progeria children of Earth. For one thing, progeria does not produce any form of dementia.
- 16. Both groups maintain their excellent mental faculties, usually with high IQ, until they die.
- 17. That is a very important clue, but here are the others for your consideration:
- 18. Neither group ever grows much beyond four feet.
- 19. Both have fragile, weak bodies, with thin arms and legs; all their bones are thin, as a general rule.
- 20. Both groups are bald.
- 21. Grays have no sexual reproduction, most have no genitalia at all. Progeria children never reach puberty.
- 22. Both have large heads by comparison to their bodies.
- 23. Both have receding chins and pointy noses. Within their groups, they closely resemble each other. The Grays are cloned; the progeria children look as if they could have been cloned.
- 24. The Grays believe that the experiments on abductees will help them survive.
- 25. They take the eggs and the sperm from humans and combine them with Grays' DNA. Thus, they create the hybrid children.
- 26. The hybrid children are closer to the Grays in their character and behavior than they are to humans.

- 27. The first generation hybrids are smaller than human children. They tend to follow the growth pattern of the Gray parent.
- 28. They are even smaller than progeria babies. The retardation of growth begins before birth.
- 29. First generation means that they go on mixing the genetic material.
- 30. The Hybrids may or may not have progeria, but naturally, the more human DNA is mixed into the species, the more chances of eliminating the bad genes exist.
- 31. So they breed the Hybrids with more human DNA, always hoping to eradicate the disease, never quite succeeding. That is why they have to get fresh human specimens all the time.
- 32. They have no chance of survival. They are doomed.
- 33. Some governments on Earth arte fully aware of this situation. They have made a deal with the Grays. They supply them with humans. Usually, these victims are retarded people, prostitutes, homeless, etc.
- 34. In exchange, the Grays give them the technology they crave for.
- 35. Some of the most up to date scientific discoveries and inventions were given to governments by the Grays.
- 36. They have learned so much from the Grays, and they mostly use it for military purposes.
- 37. Humans are not kind to each other. Look at wars, torture, genocide, holocausts... all part of human history, and still taking place.
- 38. There are various places on earth where such activities can be studied, various military bases, underground mostly, in many countries.
- 39. There are no hybrid bases anywhere else, except on planet Earth, certainly not on Nibiru.
- 40. Earth is the lowest habitat in the universe.
- 41. And humans are the lowest living-forms in the universe. Even animals are more elevated than humans, taking into consideration the enormous opportunities, humans were given to ascend to a higher level of knowledge, awareness, and goodness.

On hybrids, their habit, food, way of life, and relationship with the Grays

- Do hybrids eat like us?
- What kind of food do they eat?
- Where do they eat? Do they have dinning rooms?
- Do they follow any ritual?
- Do they eat human food or alien food?
- Where do they sleep?
- Do they have beds?
- I was told they play with toys like our children do. Is it true?
- What kind of toys they have?
- Is it true some were adopted by military families?
- 1. Hybrids live only on Planet Earth.
- 2. Hybrids habitats are found in isolated areas on Earth and underwater.
- 3. Hybrids are under the direct control of the Grays.
- 4. The Anunnaki have no relation and no contact with Hybrids.
- 5. Some Anunnaki Sinhars have visited the underwater bases of the hybrids.
- 6. Upon visiting the underwater bases, the Anunnaki pass through a tunnel-lock that is safe for both water and air.
- 7. The Grays as well as visitors enter a huge, hangar-like room. This is the main entrance of the base.
- 8. The rooms are of beige and gray colors, all metal and have no windows.
- 9. The rooms are huge, and are used for different kinds of operations.
- 10. You could call them hellish laboratories.
- 11. Visitors walk to a solid wall, put their hands on it. The wall shimmers a little and then moves, allowing a door to form and open.
- 12. The door will take you to a long corridor, illuminated by stark, white light, with many regular doors on each side.

- 13. Some other corridors lead you to a large room, a kind of a refectory which contains extremely long tables, all made of metal.
- 14. The room is usually painted entirely in beige. The room is filled with tables, and chairs. It is scrupulously clean.
- 15. When the tables open up, each table reveals a deep groove on each of its long sides.
- 16. Plates of what seemed to be normal human food are released from the grooves, and placed each before a chair.
- 17. At this moment, a few doors open at various parts of the room, and from each door an orderly file of children come in and settle at the table.
- 18. The hybrids are always and completely silent, not a word is heard. They don't talk to each other while eating.
- 19. They pick up their forks and began to eat, exactly as humans do.
- 20. The children ages range from six to twelve.
- 21. On one hand, they are small and fragile. On the other hand, their eyes give the impression of almost old age.
- 22. They are wise beyond their tender years.
- 23. Their hair is thin.
- 24. Their skin is pale to gray.
- 25. They all wear white clothes of extreme cleanliness.
- 26. Despite these similarities, which make them look as if they were all related to each other, there are differences between them that are fundamental.
- 27. They are divided into three distinct groups.
- 28. The three groups consist:
- a- Early-stage hybrids,
- b- Middle-stage hybrids,
- c- Late-stage hybrids.
- 29. The first group is born from the first combination of abductees' and Grays' DNA. They closely resemble the Grays.
- 30. The grayish color is very close to that of the Grays, and so is the facial structure.
- 31. The second group, the middle-stage hybrids, are the result of mating between these early-stage ones, once

they are old enough for reproduction, and human abductees.

- 32. The resulting DNA is closer to humans, and so they look much more like humans, and many of them lose the progeria gene.
- 33. The third group, the late-stage hybrid, is the most important. Middle-stage hybrids are mated with humans to create them, and they can hardly be distinguished from humans.
- 34. However, it is easy to recognize the late-stagers, but there are not too many of them here.
- 35. A large number of these hybrids, who represent the most successful results of the experiments, are placed for adoption with human families.
- 36. The human families are always aware of the origin of their adopted hybrid children.
- 37. Generally, they are adopted by a high-ranking United States military man or woman, who had worked, or still works, with aliens, in secret military bases.
- 38. This happens much more often than most people suspect.
- 39. The spouse of the military person may or may not know, depending on circumstances and character traits.
- 40. These lucky hybrids lead a much better life than whose who are raised in places like this one, communally.
- 41. In their underwater habitats, hybrid children are not treated badly by the Grays.
- 42. The Grays don't want to lose them, they are too valuable to them.
- 43. But they receive no love, no individual attention, there is no real parenting, and the environment is barren and depressing.
- 44. They live peacefully until they are old enough to be of use in the experiments. Not a very nice life for any child.
- 45. Only the hybrids who are entirely free of progeria are adopted by human families.
- 46. Many of the progeria stricken late-stagers are killed, since their progeria gene is too strong.

- 47. The Grays believe the hybrid children somehow will save their civilization. But they are doomed.
- 48. The children finish eating in complete silence. Each child, as he or she finishes his meal, leans back into the chair, and as soon as all of them are leaning back, the groove from which the plates came, opens up, and re-absorbs all the plates.
- 49. Plates and dishes go to an automatic dishwashing machine, on two rows of metallic belts.
- 50. The hybrid children get up, and leave the dismal room in the same file arrangement they came in.
- 51. As soon as the room is empty, large vacuum cleaners emerge from the wall and suck up every crumb, every piece of debris.
- 52. Then they spray the tables and floor with a liquid that smells like a disinfectant. The room is once again spotless, and ready for the next sad, depressing meal.
- 53. Their dormitories look like a place that you can describe as a combination of an old-fashioned orphanage and military barracks on Earth.
- 54. The dormitory is always a very large room, but the ceiling is not high, only about twelve feet.
- 55. Again, everything is beige and gray, and there are no windows to relieve the monotony.
- 56. The room is full of beds, arranged above each other in groups of three, like in a submarine.
- 57. Dozens and dozens of such rows stretch to a very long distance.
- 58. The beds are made of metal, very smooth, and of silver-gray color. They are assembled like your prefab furniture.
- 59. The beds which are stacked on the top of each other have no ladders.
- 60. To reach the upper levels, the hybrid children levitate.
- 61. Part of each bed is magnetic, so each child can have his or her toys attached to it. As for the lower beds, the toys are stored next to them.
- 62. The Grays have discovered that mental stimulation is highly important to the hybrids' development. There are

plenty of other activities, mostly with abductees, that relieve their lives of the tedium, at least to a certain extent, but they have no privacy at all.

- 63. The hybrid children only get their own room when they are more mature, but they have one thing that pleases them. If the children want to, they can put their things in their bed, close the bed with a panel, and hide them inside a wall. They like that.
- 64. Their feelings and emotional climate are not exactly human.
- 65. The playground of hybrid children is located directly behind the dormitory. It is really a glass bubble.
- 66. The hybrid children usually sit on the floor of the bubble. The floor is made from sand.
- 67. The children play with normal human toys – trucks, cars, trains, and multi colored buckets. They love to fill the buckets with sand, using plastic trowels that usually you see on your beaches.
- 68. They also build tunnels from the sand, wetting it with water from large containers that stood here and there.
- 69. They seem to be enjoying their games, certainly concentrating on them, but their demeanor remain quiet and subdued, and they do not engage in the laughter, screaming, yelling, or fighting that human children of this age usually produce.
- 70. They also have rooms with climbing equipment, and places to play ball. It is needed to strengthen their bones and muscles.

Statements by Ambar Anati:
Author's note: Ambar Anati who has visited the children hybrids said: "I approached the children, a little apprehensively, worrying that I might frighten the poor things.

They looked up at me, seemingly waiting for me to do something but I was pleased to realize that they were not afraid. I sat on the sand, took some stones that were scattered around, and arranged them so that they created a little road.

The children stared at me for a minute with their strange, wise eyes, as if trying to read my thoughts, and almost instantly grasped the idea and continued to build the road together. None of them smiled, but they seemed very much engaged in the new activity. Once all the stones were used, they looked at me again, as if trying to absorb information, and sure enough, after a minute they took the trucks and make them travel on the little road. I got up and let them play.

"So they can read minds," I said to Sinhar Inannaschamra.

"To an extent," she said. "At this age, they basically just absorb images you project. You probably thought about the trucks going on this road, and they saw it."

"And everything was done together, as if they were mentally connected," I said. "Do they do everything together?"

"Yes, everything is communal, even the bathrooms where they clean themselves. But don't be too upset about it. If they are separated from each other before their adolescence, they are extremely upset. It is almost as if the onset of puberty makes them an individual, and before that they have a group mentality."

"They are not unhappy," said Sinhar Inannaschamra. "Only as adolescents, when they break off the communal mind, they understand how unhappy they are.

But we will visit the adolescents on another occasion."

On the Grays' fetuses storage:

- How the Grays store fetuses?
- Is there a special room for this?
- Is this room located in secret military bases as many abductees have reported?
- 1. The fetuses storage room is a hangar-sized room, full of tanks.
- 2. Each tank contains liquid nutrients.
- 3. This is where they put the fetuses, as soon as they are removed from the abductees.
- 4. The tanks are arranged in order, from the youngest fetuses to those that are almost ready to be removed.
- 5. They separate them into their stages.
- 6. This room is for early stagers only.
- 7. In other rooms, they have the middle stagers. But the late stagers remain in the mother's womb until birth, to make them as close to humans as possible.

- 8. The babies are quiet, not as responsive as human babies. Many of them die as soon as they are removed from the tank.
- 9. The babies who survive are generally mentally well developed, physically weak, and emotionally subdued."
- 10. Both Grays and abductees take care of them.
- 11. Always, the Grays perform most of the physical requirements, but the abductees supply the human touch.

On the Grays' abduction and their laboratories:
What is going there in the Grays base? Is it a base, a laboratory, hospital or what? And what kind of operations or surgery they perform on abductees? The answers and description were provided by Anunnaki Sinhar Inannaschamra:
Sinhar Inannaschamra said to Anati: "The first thing we must talk about is the situation with the Grays."
"The small extraterrestrials with the bug eyes, right?" said Anati.
"Yes. They do not contact people like we do, on your planet. They abduct them. You are familiar with many stories that come from the people that they have abducted, but much of what these people say is inaccurate, and based upon mind control that the Grays exercise on them. I am going to tell you a bit, and then, if you feel up to it, we will take a short trip on my spaceship and visit one of their labs."
"Would they let you in? Aren't they dangerous?"
"Dangerous? Very. But not to an Anunnaki.
We are much stronger and they are afraid of us. If I come to their place and demand to see a lab, I will see a lab. In addition, I want to show you a few things on a monitor.
Some will be extremely unpleasant, but it cannot be avoided if you want to learn something."
"What do they want of us on earth?"
"There are a few things that they want. First, they want eggs from human women and use them to create hybrids. Let's take a look at this monitor, and I'll show you how they do that. But Victoria, steel yourself. This is pretty horrible, even though I have seen even worse. You will also be able to hear, it is like a television."
The monitor blinked and buzzed, and a small white dot appeared on the screen. It enlarged itself, moved back and forth, and settled into a window-like view of a huge room, but the view was

still rather fuzzy. I heard horrendous screams and froze in my seat, these were sounds I have never heard before.

After a few minutes the view cleared and I saw what seemed to be a hospital room, but it was rounded, not square. Only part of it was revealed, as it was elongated and the far edge was not visible. The walls on the side were moving back and forth, like some kind of a balloon that was being inflated and deflated periodically, with a motion that made me dizzy; they seemed sticky, even gooey.

The room was full of operation tables, of which I could see perhaps forty or fifty, on which were stretched human beings, each attached to the table and unable to move, but obviously not sedated, since they were screaming or moaning. Everyone was attached to tubes, into which blood was pouring in huge quantities. I noticed that some of the blood was turning into a filthy green color, like rotting vegetation. At the time I could not understand what that was, but later that day I found out. This blood was converted to a suitable type for some of the aliens that paid the Grays to collect it, and it was not useful in its raw condition.

The people who operated these experiments were small and gray, and they had big bug eyes and pointy faces without any expression. I thought they looked more like insects than like a humanoid species. They wore no clothes, and their skin was shiny and moist, like that of an amphibian on earth. It visibly exuded beads of moisture which they did not bother to wipe away. Each operating table had complicated machinery that was poised right on top of the person who was strapped to it. On some of the tables, the machinery was lowered so that needles could be extracted from them automatically, and the needles reached every part of the human bodies, faces, eyes, ears, genitals, stomach. The people screamed as they saw the needles approaching them, some of them fainted. Many of the people were already dead, I could swear to that. Others were still alive but barely so, and some had arms and legs amputated from their bodies. It was clear that once the experiment was over, every single person there will die. I don't know how I could continue to look, but somehow I managed. I looked at the ceiling of this slaughter house and saw meat hooks, on which arms and legs and even heads were hanging, like a butcher's warehouse. On the side of the tables were large glass tanks where some organs were placed, possibly hearts, livers, or lungs, all preserved in liquids.

The workers were doing their job dispassionately and without any feelings, moving around like ants and making buzzing sounds at each other as they conversed.

They were entirely business-like and devoid of emotion. At least, their huge bug eyes did not convey any emotion to me, neither did their expressionless faces.

I watched until I could no longer tolerate it, and finally covered my eyes and cried out, "Why don't you stop it? Why don't you interfere?"

Sinhar Inannaschamra turned the monitor off. "This event is a record from decades ago, Victoria. It is not happening now as we look. And even though often we do interfere, we cannot police the entire universe or even the entire earth. They know how to hide from us. And you must understand, that often the victims cooperate with their abductors."

"Why would they?"

"Basically, through mind control. The Grays have many ways to convince the victims. The Grays can enter the human mind quite easily, and they find what the abductees are feeling and thinking about various subjects. Then, they can either threaten them by various means, or persuade them by a promise of reward."

"Reward? What can they possibly offer?"

"Well, you see, they show the victims images through a monitor, just like this one. They tell them that they can send them through a gate, which is controlled by the monitor, to any number of universes, both physical and non-physical. That is where the reward come in.

For example, if the abductees had originally reacted well to images of Mary or Jesus, the Grays can promise them the joy of the non-physical dimensions. They show them images of a place where Mary and Jesus reside, where all the saints or favorite prophets live, and even the abode of God. They promise the abductees that if they cooperate, they could live in this non-physical universe in perpetual happiness with their deities. Many fall for that."

"And if they resist?"

"Then they show them the non-physical alternative, which is Hell. Would you like to see some of it?"

"You can show me Hell?" I asked, amazed.

"No, there is no such thing as Hell... it's a myth that religions often exploited. But I can show you what the Grays show the abductees, pretending it is hell; they are quite devious, you know.

You see, some creatures live in different dimensions, where our laws do not apply. Sometimes, they escape to other dimensions.

These beings have no substance in their new dimensions, and they need some kind of bodies to function. At the same time, the Grays can tap into numerous universes, because they can control their own molecules to make them move and navigate through any dimension.

Well, a cosmic trade had been developed. The Grays supply the substance taken from human abductees, and from the blood of cattle. You must have heard of cattle mutilation, where carcasses of cows are found in the fields, entirely drained of blood? The Grays do it for their customers."

"How do these creatures pay the Grays?"

"By various services. Once they get their substance, they are incredibly powerful in a physical sense. The old tales of genies who can lift buildings and fly with them through the air were based on these demons; the Grays often have a use for such services. But let me show you a few of these creatures. Of course, you can only see them when they have already acquired some substance from the Grays."

The monitor hummed again as Sinhar Inannaschamra turned it on. The white dot expanded into its window, which now, for some reason, was larger and took over the entire screen. All I could see was white fog with swirls floating through it. Sometimes the fog changed from white to gray, then to white again.

I started hearing moans. Not screams, nothing that suggested the kind of physical pain I saw before, but perhaps just as horrible, since they voices where those of hopelessness, despair, and emotional anguish. Every so often I heard a sound that suggested a banshee's wail, or keen, as described in Irish folklore.

"It will take a while for someone to show up," said Sinhar Inannaschamra. "Most of them have no substance, and therefore they are invisible. Others have a shadowy substance. Then, there are the others... but you will see in a minute. Once they notice they are being watched, they will flock to the area, since they are desperate to get out. Incidentally, it was never made quite clear to me how they produce sounds without bodies, we are still trying to find out what the mechanics are, but it's not easy, because we would rather not go there in person."

"They sound horribly sad," I said.

"This is what makes it so hell-like. In many cultures, Hell never had any fire and brimstone and tormenting devils, but rather, it was a place of acute loneliness, lack of substance, and alienation from anything that could sustain the individual from a spiritual point of view. Think of the Greek Hades, or the ancient Hebrew Sheol, before the Jews made their Hell more like the Christian one. Look, here comes the first creature. Poor thing, he is a shadow."

I saw a vaguely humanoid shape in deep gray. It seemed to have arms, which it waved in our direction. It seemed fully aware of the monitor. Then another shadow, then another, all shoving each other and waving desperately at the monitor. Then something more substantial came into view, and I jumped back as if it could reach me. It seemed to be a severed arm.

Cautiously, I came back, and then saw that the arm was attached to a shadow body. I looked at Sinhar Inannaschamra, speechless, and she said, "Yes, here you see one that managed to receive an arm. It wants to complete its body, of course, so that it can get out of this dimension and serve the Grays, but the Grays keep them waiting until they want them."

More and more came, clamoring for attention. "Do they think we are Grays?" I asked.

"Yes, they do. They can't tell the difference, all they know is that they are watched, and they try to get the attention of the watchers. It's incredibly cruel, but if you feel for them, which I still do, remember that at the same time they become murderous, cruel creatures themselves as soon as they escape their dimension and join the Grays."

Another half thing came into view. It had eyes stuck in the middle of a half-formed face, each eye different. The face seemed mutilated, somehow, until I realized it had no nose and no chin. Floating heads, arms, legs, torsos – they all jostled in front of the monitor, each more horrible than the other. And then I saw the worst thing imaginable.

"Sinhar Inannaschamra!" I screamed. "This is a baby's head! A floating baby's head! What in the world it is attached to?"

"Another shadow," said Sinhar Inannaschamra. "They don't care what age the substance comes from. Sometime the babies' heads or limbs get attached to big adult bodies."

"They use babies," I said, sobbing. "Babies..."

"Yes, this is the kind of creatures we have to contend with," said Sinhar Inannaschamra. She looked at me and realized I could not take any more of this Hell, and so turned off the monitor.

"This was something," I said, shivering and trying to recover.

"Indeed," said Sinhar Inannaschamra. "So you see, they can easily show them horrific pictures of Hell, enough to frighten them to such an extent, that they are sure to obey.

Interestingly, the abductees, under such threats, often develop physical, psychosomatic effect in the form of scratches, burns, or even stigmata, on parts of their bodies.

Of course, sometimes the Grays burn them with laser beams as a form of punishment or of persuasion, and sometimes the wounds are produced simply by the radioactive rays emanating from the spaceship, like what sometimes happens in nuclear plants on earth, or during nuclear explosions. But most often it is the mind reacting to the image."

"How horrible..." I said weakly.

"It gets worse," said Sinhar Inannaschamra. "They can show them the physical universe as well. They would project, on screen, well-known events that occurred during times in which humanity was utterly cruel, or when war, famines, and plagues ravished the earth. They might show them the Crusades, or Attila the Hun, or the Nazi concentration camps, or the famine in Ireland, or the black plague in Europe, and threaten them that they can open a gate through the monitor, and abandon them there for the rest of their lives."

"The poor things. No wonder they obey," I said.

"Yes, you see, the Anunnaki tell you the truth when they contact you. They let you know that they cannot change the past, nor can they interfere with the future. But the Grays lie. They tell the abductees that they can change events in the past, from day one, and that they could project and change life at two, five, or ten thousand years in the future of humanity."

"I wish you would just wipe them of the face of the universe," I said.

"We don't do such things. Some of us recommend it, but we just don't. Anyway, they have other systems of persuasion. Some women have a very strong reaction to the images of children. The Grays catch it, of course, and then they tell the women that they have been abducted before, years ago, and were impregnated by the Grays. Then they show them a hybrid child and tell them that this is their own child.

Many of the abductees who are thus psychologically influenced fall into a pathological attachment to the hybrid child. Then the Grays tell them that if they don't fully cooperate, they will take the child away. The woman cooperates, the experiment takes place, and then the Grays make them forget the child and place them back in their beds at home.

Usually, some vague memory remains, since the Grays don't care about the well being of their victims and don't bother to check if the memory is completely cleaned out."

"But it is not really their child?"

"Sometimes it is, sometimes it isn't. You must realize that normal impregnation and the nine months of carrying the baby does not occur. The Grays take the eggs out of the woman, the way you just saw it on the monitor, put them in a tube, fertilize it by an electric or sometimes atomic way, and the hybrid grows in the tube until it is of term. No woman has ever given birth to a hybrid."

"This is beyond words," I said. "And I thought most of the extraterrestrials would be like you."

"There are many species," said Sinhar Inannaschamra. There are those humans call 'The Nordic,' they look and behave much like humans, they are rather kindly, and other kinds are reasonable as well.

But there are a lot of horrible species. The closer any species get to the demonic dimension, and particularly if they trade with them, the worse they become. Some look reptilian, some insect-like. Some eat human beings and other sentient species, in what we see as almost cannibalistic behavior. Some make sacrifices of sentient beings to their deities. The reptilians have a specialized digestive system. They don't eat solid food, but only suck blood through pores in their fingers. That is why some researchers on earth connect the extraterrestrials with vampirism.

The Grays sell them cattle blood, since the reptilians don't particularly care where the blood comes from. But anyway, are you ready for your field trip? Let's go and visit a Grays' lab."

I thought I was ready. I thought I was tough. But what I saw on this field trip would remain with me for eons.

Sinhar Inannaschamra took me to her spaceship, and informed me that the trip would be very short. She had been to this lab before, and knew the conditions very well. Just before we landed, she pulled out a suit that was needed to protect me from any radiation.

98

Apparently, for this trip, she needed no protection herself, but she could not tell as yet if I could tolerate such conditions or not, due to my human existence for the last thirty years. The suit was made of lightweight, soft metallic material that was actually rather comfortable and moved easily with me. Then, I put on a helmet, which was entirely transparent and allowed me perfect vision.

We landed on a bleak field covered with some material that looked much like cement, gray and unpleasant, but with a smoother finish. Right before us was a huge building which looked like an ugly airport hangar, completely utilitarian without any ornamentation. The entire area around it was an empty prairie-like field with stunted, grayish vegetation, stretching into the horizon without any feature like a mountain or a city. The sky was gray but without clouds. We walked to a large door, tightly closed and made of metal. Sinhar Inannaschamra put her hand on it, and it slid immediately to the side and allowed us to come in. "They know my hand print," she said to me. We entered a small hall, empty of any furniture, and from there, a door opened into a long corridor, brightly lit and painted white. On each side there were doors, also painted white, all closed, and it was entirely empty of any occupants. Sinhar Inannaschamra led the way to one of the doors, and again placed her hand on it. The door slid open silently, and we entered an enormous room. It was so huge that I could not see the end of it, and had gray walls and a white ceiling. Round, bright lights of large circumference were placed in the ceiling, emanating a very strong illumination. The impression the room gave was that of a hospital ward, or a surgical hall, but there were no beds or operation tables, only large tanks containing some objects I could not as yet see.

And while the place was scrupulously clean, the smell was nightmarish. I recognized the stench of formaldehyde, mingled with some other malodorous liquids. I was surprised I could smell anything through the helmet, but Sinhar Inannaschamra explained that they deliberately made the suits and the helmets allow as much interaction with the environment as possible.

"It smells like that because this is the warehouse, where they keep all the spare parts," said Sinhar Inannaschamra. "Come, look at this tank."

We approached an enormous tank, transparent in the front parts and increasingly opaque as it extended further into the room. Inside floated a large number of severed arms and legs, all human. I recoiled in horror, but quickly recovered. We went to the next tank. It was arranged in the same manner, but inside floated severed heads and torsos.

And so it went on, each tank filled with body parts, some even with full bodies. Smaller containers had interior organs, such as livers, hearts, and some others I was not sure of.

In addition, there were containers of blood, some red, some green. I already knew that the green blood was like that after preparation for sale to species that needed the adjustments.

Suddenly I heard sounds of conversation, as if a group of people were approaching us from somewhere. The sounds were in a language I could not understand, and uttered in a metallic, screeching way that was almost mechanical. To me, it sounded demonic and inhuman. A group of five Grays approached us. After what I have seen on the monitor, I was about to escape in terror, but the group bowed to Sinhar Inannaschamra, and went on about their business. One of them approached a tank. He looked at what seemed to be a chart, like a hospital chart but in a language I could not understand, that was positioned above the tank, and just stared at it for a short while. A line on the chart lit up, and some equipment that was build above the tank came down, entered the tank, and using a robotic hand pulled out a specimen and placed it in a tube, along with some of the liquid. Then the robotic hand came up, moved forward, and handed the tube to the Gray. The Gray took the tube, looked at the chart, and the robotic hand withdrew.

The Gray took the tube to a wall and placed the tube against it. To my amazement, the wall sort of swallowed the tube and it disappeared.

I looked at Sinhar Inannaschamra for explanation, and she said, "The walls are not solid. They look solid, of course, but really they are constructed of energy. The Grays can move things back and forth, and even pass through it themselves. Some of the walls contain drawers, where they place equipment."

The other Grays were all communicating among themselves in their demonic language, mostly ignoring us. "Let's go to the next room, where I can show you what they do with their specimens," said Sinhar Inannaschamra.

We went to the wall and she put her hand on it while holding me with her other hand, and I found myself passing through the wall as if it was made of thick molasses.

The room we entered was designed just like the others, architecturally, but had work tables instead of tanks and containers. Hundreds of Grays stood there, each at his table, doing things to the limbs, torsos, and blood.

The smell of formaldehyde was so intense that I almost fainted. "Here," said Sinhar Inannaschamra. "Let me adjust the helmet so you don't have to smell the liquid." She did something at the back of the helmet, and I felt better.

"And now, let's go to the area where they fit the spare parts on the creatures I have shown you, the ones that want to buy substance," said Sinhar Inannaschamra. We stepped into a third room, again through the wall, and this was a much smaller room. On the walls, there were a number of monitors, just like the ones in Sinhar Inannaschamra's office, but much larger.

Before each monitor stood a Gray. We walked to one of them, and the Gray bowed to Sinhar Inannaschamra, and returned to his work. The Gray adjusted something, and a swirling shadow attached to one leg appeared on the screen. Behind him were numerous other shadows, but the Gray managed to separate the first creature from the others with some walls of energy that looked like white fog. The creature waved desperately at the Gray, who had before him a torso in liquid. A large robotic hand came from above the monitor, picked up the torso, and allowed the liquid to drain into its container. Then, he passed the torso through the screen, which now I realized was made of energy, like the wall, and placed it on the shadow. The shadow shivered, as if in pain, and I heard a deep moan or sigh, as the torso attached itself to the swirling gray form. I had a glimpse of a shadowy face, contorted in agony, but whether it was physical or mental pain I did not know. The shadow seemed utterly exhausted by the bizarre procedure, and floated away.

"What will happen to it now?" I asked.

"It will be back again and again, and when the Gray decide, they will give it more parts, allowing it to adjust and become more substantial."

"Are there any of them ready to leave and serve the Grays?"

"Yes, but I think this would be too dangerous to visit in person. The demonic creatures don't have the restraints the Grays have, regarding the Anunnaki, and often they are too stupid and just lash out as soon as they are brought into our dimension. Their transport, therefore, is done in a different part of the lab, under tremendous precautions. Besides, we don't want to stay much longer, since I think you had seen enough for one day..." I could not agree with her more, and we retraced our steps back to the spaceship.

"Next time I will show you how the creatures are taken out and put to service," said Sinhar Inannaschamra. "Only not in person." This sounded good to me. I was already so shaken from my day's adventures, I did not think I could take much more instruction, nor did I have a wish to meet such creatures in person. But, of course, I knew that one day I would have to do exactly that.

*** *** ***

On the Bene ha Elohim and the Anunnaki

- Who are the Bene Elohim?
- Any relation to the Anunnaki?
- Are they angels or demons?

Bene ha-Elohim and the extraterrestrials:
I. Hebraic Definition and introduction
II. Sons of God in Canaanite traditions
III. The "bene ha 'elohim", the Nephilim and the extraterrestrial Anunnaki
IV. The Rephaim

I. Hebraic definition and introduction:

As stated in Understanding the Dead Sea Scrolls, Early Rabbis saw "bene ha 'elohim" as referring to righteous men, not as the "Sons of God." The Church fathers understood it as referring to the descendants of Seth. Both are kind of interesting because neither want to address that gods mated with humans and produced offspring. The phrase "bene ha 'elohim" and its variant "bene 'elim" is found in other passages in the Bible, such as Job 1:6 and 2:1. Here, the Sons of God present themselves to Yahweh in the heavenly divine assembly. Job 38:7 says that the Sons of God have been with Yahweh at the creation of the world.

They also appear in Psalm 89:7, where Yahweh is proclaimed incomparable to all other gods, and in Psalm 29:1 where the bene 'elim sing praises to Yahweh. The passage in Deuteronomy (32:8) reads "When the Most High apportioned the nations, when he divided the sons of man. He established the borders of the peoples according to the number of the sons of Israel."

The weird thing about this passage is how can the borders of all the peoples be established according to the sons of Israel when Israel hadn't already been established? The end seems to contradict the beginning. This contradiction doesn't appear in all Bibles, like the RSV based on the Greek Septuagint (dated from the 3rd century BCE), which state "according to the number of the Sons of God."

This is also the wording in the Hebrew DSS version, which is now the oldest version of Deuteronomy we currently have, and what scholars now believe as the most authentic. The implications are that the Sons of God are not just present at the beginning of the world, but also figure prominently in dividing nations. That implicates that while Yahweh chose Israel as his nation, each of the other Sons of God also received a nation to rule over.

II. Sons of God in Canaanite traditions:

Krista stated that Canaanite traditions also use the term "Sons of God" ("Banu ili" or "Banu ili-mi") in their texts dating back to the 14th century BCE. In the Canaanite pantheon, the chief god is El, meaning God, and his wife is Asherah. The phrase Sons of God can then be translated as the children of El. There are also references in Phoenician inscriptions of the 7-8th centuries BCE - Arslan Tash (KAI 27.II) and Karatepe (KAI 26.A.III.19) and in an Ammonite inscription of the 9th century found in Amman, Jordan. This may be an earlier tradition that Biblical phrase pulls from.

III. The Bene ha 'elohim, Nephilim and extraterrestrial Anunnaki:

Advocates of alternative archeology, as well as many ufologists claim that the "bene ha 'elohim" were the Nephilim, who were the extraterrestrial Anunnaki. Now, in Genesis 6:1-4, the offspring of the Sons of God and the daughters of men are called Nephilim, who are the "heros of old, the men of renown." Literally, the word Nephilim means "the fallen ones" and is a common euphemism for "the dead" in Hebrew.

For example, in Jeremiah 6:15, "They will fall among the fallen (Hebrew, Nopelim)." In Ezekiel 32:27, the Nephilim are fallen warriors: "They lie with the warriors, The Nephilim of old, who descend to Sheol with their weapons of war." Elsewhere, the

Nephilim are giants who were native inhabitants of Canaan. In Numbers 13:33, they advise Moses "All the people whom we saw in its midst were people of great size there we saw the Nephilim - the Anaqim are part of the Nephilim - and we seemed in our own eyes like grasshoppers, and so we must have seemed in their eyes."

IV. The Rephaim:
The Rephaim were also referred to as the Nephilim, the Anakim, and the Anunnaki. The Habiru (Early Hebrews) view the Rephaim as the "bene ha 'elohim", and the Biblical giants were called by the Habiru, the Rephaim. In Deuteronomy 2:11, the giant Anakim are called Rephaim, and two of the most famous of the Raphaim are King Og of Bashan, whose huge iron bed could still be seen on display in Rabbah of Ammon (Deuteronomy 3:11) and the warrior Goliath, who descended from the Raphah in Gath (2 Samuel 21:19ff). Thus, it would seem that the Nephilim were both the race of heroes who lived before the Flood and in Canaan before the Israelites conquered the Promised Land. The Rephaim and Anakim were defeated by Joshua, Moses, and Caleb, and then the rest by David. Joshua 11:22 says that "No Anaqim remained in the land of Israel, but some remained in Gaza, Gath, and Ashdod."

*** *** ***
Shape-shifting "Ibra-Anu"

I. Definition and introduction:
For extraterrestrials, shape-shifting is necessary. Ambar Anati said verbatim (As is and unedited): "Shape-shifting includes skin color change, organs size, general physical appearances, but not the functionality of the body. The Anunnaki can easily shape-shift themselves. This is absolutely necessary for climatic and atmospheric reasons.
Each planet has its own climate, temperature and atmosphere. Consequently the body must adapt to these environment conditions.

II. Anunnaki's shape-shifting:
When they visit Earth, the Anunnaki slightly change their physical appearances, not so much, because in general, they look like us, except their eyes are much bigger, and their height is far

more superior and taller to the size and height of humans. Some Anunnaki are 9 foot tall. Even their women are extremely tall by human standard. Some women are 8 foot tall. When they travel to other planets, minor changes are required. For instance, when they get out of their galaxy and visit the planets Niftar, Marshan-Haloum and Ibra-Anu, they change the color of their skin, and the shape of their hands.

On Niftar (Niftari), inhabitants have grey-blue color skin and 3 fingers in each hand. The fingers are long, thin and beneath the skin, there are millions of microscopic hair filaments and pores (orifices) that help them hold on slippery surfaces like glass and wet areas. Anunnaki look very different from the Zetas and the numerous alien races that have visited the earth. In this context, they never appear or manifest like reptilians or short "Greys".

It is easy to recognize an Anunnaki, because he usually appears like a tall warrior; his vest is made out of thin layers of metal called "Handar". He wears a long robe "Arbiya" of dark colors and underneath, it a sort of pans with wide contour. On his wrist, you always notice a navigation tool. Many of the extraterrestrial races wear tight outfits, almost glued to their skin.

Anunnaki don't. The "Greys" are notorious for shape-shifting. They can appear like a reptile, an insect and even like humans. The Anunnaki can transmute and manipulate their bodies if needed. This happens very rarely. And in many instances, they don't need to do so, because they are already known by so many galactic and outer-galactic civilizations, and seen by inhabitants of millions and millions of stars, planets and moons. They are superstars in their own rights.

Aliens of lower dimensions need to manipulate their bodiy-type to enter the atmosphere of other planets, particularly underwater and a multitude of underground environments and habitats.

This is exactly what happens all the time with the "Greys" who live on earth and work with scientists in restricted areas such as underground genetic labs, and military research centers and bases. One of their striking characteristics is claustrophobia.

*** *** ***

Extraterrestrials in the Book of Ramadosh
"Ezakarfalki", "E-zakar-falki"

I. Definition and introduction

II. Evolution of the extraterrestrials and the human races
III. Extraterrestrial races populated the Earth
IV. Extraterrestrials of the sea (Underwater)
V. Senses of the extraterrestrials
VI. Talking to extraterrestrials

I. Definition and introduction:

Term for extraterrestrials as mentioned in "Book of Ramadosh." Per contra, inhabitants of planet Earth are called Ezakarerdi or Ezakar.Ki.

In terrestrial vocabulary, extraterrestrial(s) is a term applied to any entity(ies), object(s), substance(s), life-form(s), intelligence, and presence that have originated from beyond planet Earth. Grosso modo, referred to as alien(s). Contemporary ufology etymology added extraterrestrial origins coming from outer-space, other planets, stars, galaxies, and dimensions.

The word extraterrestrial is composed from three words:

- **a**-Extra, which is derived from the Latin word Extra, which means outside; additional; beyond.
- **b**-Terrestri, derived from the Latin Terrestris, which means pertaining to earth; belonging to earth; earthly; made out of earth, itself derived from the Latin words Terranum and Terrenum, which are derived from the word Terra, which means earth; ground; piece of land; soil.

(Note: From the Latin word Terrenum, derived the French word Terrain; and from the French word derived the English word terrain.)

- **c**-Al, an English addition.

(Note: The Latin word Terra originally derived from the Arabic word "Tourab" (Terrab), which means dirt; dust; earth, itself derived from the Arabic word Tourba (Terrba), which means a piece of land, originally derived from the Ana'kh word Turbah, pronounced Toorbaah, which means dirt from planet Earth. In the Sumerian/Akkadian epics and mythologies, the words dirt and earth refer to clay; the very clay found in abundance in

106

ancient Iraq that was used by the Anunnaki to genetically create the human race.

II. Evolution of the extraterrestrials and the human races:

The evolution of aliens, and the extraterrestrial races on many galaxies evolved inter-dimensionally by copying, duplicating, and cloning themselves and fertilizing their own genes. On other planets, more advanced extraterrestrial civilizations multiply and prosper through the development of brain's waves and thoughts frequencies.

They did not need to immigrate to other planets in order to survive, and/or to recreate (Reshape) themselves, as mistakenly claimed by some ufologists, extraterrestrialogists, mediums, and channelers, for they did not encounter insurmountable ecological or bio-organic catastrophes on their own planets or stars. Zetas and Anunnaki did alter their genetics but, not for survival purposes or for intra-planetary travel-immigration readiness reasons. The alteration came as cause and effect, much needed to reach a higher level of awareness and scientific advancement.

III. Extraterrestrial races populated the Earth:

Some 300,000 years before the creation of the cities of "The Women of Lights," forty-six different races of humans and quasi-humans populated the earth. The greatest numbers were found in Africa, Madagascar, Indonesia, Brazil, and Australia. These quasi-human races died out not because of famine, ecological catastrophes, or acts of war, but because of the disintegration of the very molecules and composition of their cells. The Anunnaki created the 'final form' of human beings, and all of us are their descendants.

IV. Extraterrestrials of the sea (Underwater):

According to Sinhar Ambar Anati, the extraterrestrials of the sea are not our ancestors and creators, the Anunnaki. They belong to a different race; one of the 46 different alien races that have visited the earth at its dawn. Only 7 specific races remained on Earth.

They have many things in common, and share non-physical similarities, but are different from the Anunnaki. According to ufology literature, the aliens who currently work with terrestrial scientists have extraterrestrial physiognomy, totally alien to the human race. The original Anunnaki no longer live on earth. They left our planet thousands of years ago. However, many of their off springs, bloodlines, descendants and hybrid remnants live among us, today.

Ulema Sadqi said: "The Anunnaki are not very much different from the human beings. They are not reptilians at all, and they don't look like the Zeta Reticulians, as erroneously depicted in the West. They have a human shape, yet they are capable to shape shifting when needed."

V. Senses of the extraterrestrials:
Anunnaki-Ulema Wah Lin stated that the extraterrestrials have an astonishing range of senses; for instance:

- **a**-The Artyrians have 13 different kinds of senses, ranging from physio-biological to mental-sensorial, yet, they are neither psychosomatic nor neurological.
- **b**-The Naryans have 17 senses.
- **c**-The Anunnaki have 26 extra-senses and a multitude of meta-bio-organic faculties."

Ulema Li adds: "Some of the most fascinating senses are:
- **a**-The ability of freeing themselves from the limitation of time and space and sensing the "ultra dimension"; in other words, they are able to feel and sense the infinitesimal frequencies that constitute the dividing waves or walls between each dimension and/or multiple universes. Those dividing lines are waves and they expand and react spatially like rubber bands. There are no other words or expressions in the human vocabularies we can use to describe these "existences".
- **b**-They can totally eliminate the effect of heat and cold and mentally regulate the temperature degrees of the environment in any sphere. Also they can adjust others bodies' temperature for health and therapeutic reasons because they can sense the body's weaknesses and strengths. In terrestrial terms, they can see the aura. But it goes beyond aura, because aura is produced bio-organically and can be detected either visually or through scientific apparatus.

VI. Talking to extraterrestrials:

Anunnaki and extraterrestrials have no intention whatsoever in engaging into a dialogue with ordinary human beings. If they have an agenda, and/or are on a mission, they either abduct (Not the Anunnaki) humans, or directly contact scientists working with them in secret facilities, laboratories and bases. Anunnaki do not talk tête-à-tête with humans, nor convey their messages on a personal basis. And most certainly, Anunnaki do not abduct humans. However, direct and personal contact did happen with aliens. They were the "Greys".

But this occurrence is extremely rare. Ulema Al Bakri said: " And when and if it happens, extraterrestrials would not pronounce one word and walk away, or stutter as some contactees reported", including one famous contactee in Switzerland who made headlines worldwide and became the messenger of the Lyrans on earth. When aliens contact (So to speak) or encounter a human being, they usually complete sentences and engage into a dialogue, even though, as it was reported, the dialogue is short, and their words are incomprehensible, and the voice is mechanic and fuzzy.

In some instances, the aliens transmit their messages mentally, not telepathically, because for the telepathic phenomenon to occur, you need two telepathic people, and most certainly contactees who are regular folks are neither gifted nor trained telepaths. You cannot talk to another person on your cellular phone, if the other party does not have one. Do you want to try? Same thing applies to telepathy; it needs two telepathic stations, fully operational and fully capable of sending and receiving messages. The human brain did not yet reach this level.

Although some preliminary forms of telepathy between humans were noticed in rare instances. Extraterrestrials are capable of speaking and understanding many languages, including our own. They assimilate and "compute" words, sentences and physical expressions with mathematical formulas and numerical values. Some extraterrestrials have limited vocal chords capabilities, but they can very quickly acquire additional vocal faculties, and earth dialects by rewinding sounds and vibes.

Contrary to what many contactees and others claim or depict, extraterrestrials from higher dimensions/spheres do not talk like computerized machines. They have their own language but also they can absorb and assimilate all the languages on earth in a blink of an eye via the reception and emission of a spatial memory.

*** *** ***

Longevity of Quasi-Human-Life Form
"Izra-nafar-mikla'ch"

I. Definition:
"Izra-nafar-mikla'ch" is a term referring to the longevity of quasi-human-life form, such as Golem and hybrids. The term is explained in the following Q&A, from my Kira'at (lectures) in 1961.

II. Kira'at:
A student asked: Can hybrids reach immortality through genetic manipulations?
My answer:

- Although hybrids are intelligent beings, they should not to be considered neither humans nor extraterrestrials.
- Their essence (DNA) is not pure.
- They are genetically created either by human beings, or by a malicious extraterrestrial race.
- Any living creature Dha-kiliyan (Genetically) created by humans will never reach immortality.
- Because a Dha-kiliyi (Genetic) creation of other living-forms manufactured by human beings is an artificial product, this Dha-kiliyi (Genetic) product which does not include the first energy element introduced in regular human beings by the Anunnaki will totally disintegrate without leaving the "Shou'la" (Spark of life).
- The Shou' la was created on earth by the Anunnaki. No human ever succeeded in duplicating a Shou'la.
- Any living creature Dha-kiliyan (Genetically) created on earth or in other physical dimensions by a malicious extraterrestrial race coming from a lower dimension will not reach immortality.

Note: I am referring to the "Greys". It is my belief that this word is an American ufology terminology. The word the Ulema use is "Min Kariji al-dounia". Min means from. Kariji means outside or outer. Dounia means the world.

- Living entities created by the Greys (A spiritually lower ntraterrestrials alien race) are born contaminated.
- The Greys' contamination prevents these living entities (Hybrids, half humans-half-extraterrestrials) from ascending to the Ba'ab.
- Consequently, the hybrids will not enter the other dimensions and reach immortality.

*** *** ***

Hybrids' Dwellings
"Korashag", "Khur-Shag"

I. Definition and introduction
II. Description of the hybrids' habitat
a- Human environment
b- Underground/underwater communities
III. Characteristics
Bedrooms, beds, toys, dining rooms, food, and eating habits
IV. Hybrid children habitat as described by an Anunnaki
a. Inside the base
b. The refectory
c. Hybrids' three distinct groups/categories
d. Hybrids placed for adoption
e. Disposing of the food and cleaning the refectory
f. Dormitories and sleeping quarters
g. Attending various activities
h. The fetuses' room

I. Definition and introduction:
Korashag "Khur-Sha" is an Anunnaki/Ulemite word for hybrids' habitat (Community). The hybrid-human (Intraterrestrial) race is very different from hybrid extraterrestrial race living on other planets. The hybrid-humans look exactly like human beings, but are much shorter, and have different facial structure.

II. Description of the hybrids' habitat:
These hybrid children live in two different ways.
- **a- Human environment:**

The first is the human environment. This happens when a hybrid child had been adopted by a human family, usually, by a high ranking United States military man working with aliens in secret military underground bases. This top echelon military man adopts a hybrid child and raises him or her as a human being. This happens much more often than most people imagine.

- **b- Underground/underwater communities:**

The second kind of habitat is a large communal living in underground and/ or underwater dormitories, or sometimes in above ground level dormitories, but always on Earth.

III. Characteristics:
Bedrooms, beds, toys, dining rooms, food, and eating habits.

- **1.** While the adult hybrid usually has his or her own room, the children live together.
- **2.** Their dormitories are like a combination of old fashioned orphanages, and military barracks.
- **3.** The rooms don't have high ceilings, rarely over twelve feet, they are extremely long, and they have no windows.
- **4.** The rooms are spotlessly clean; they are cleaned constantly by a vacuum system that sucks away all dirt.
- **5.** They have no need of trash cans.
- **6.** The colors of the rooms are sad, nothing appealing about them, dark, and basically gray metallic color.
- **7.** The beds are arranged on top of each other, like in a submarine. There are no ladders reaching the higher level beds, since the children can levitate.
- **8.** For each dormitory, there are dozens and dozens of three beds row sections.
- **9.** These beds are assembled like prefab furniture, quickly and efficiently. The materials the beds are built from are very different from any material used in standard furniture. It is a kind of metal, very smooth, and of silver-gray color. For the second and third levels, parts of the bed are magnetic, so the children can attach their toys to it.
- **10.** On the first level, the toys are around the bed. They are given a choice of toys because the Grays believe the toys would be part of their education and adjustment.

- **11.** If a child wishes to hide his or her toys, the bed can be closed and pushed into the wall. For their bathroom needs, they go to an adjacent room, also communal, where baths and toilets are available to them.
- **12.** Cleanliness is scrupulously maintained there as well as in the dormitory. The children eat in refectories.
- **13.** These dining rooms are long, and contain extremely long tables. The food is served from within the table, which opens up at the outside edge of the table and reveals the plates.
- **14.** When they finish eating, the plates, which are metal, are left on the table.
- **15.** The table absorbs the plate and sends it to the dishwasher.
- **16.** Despite all the precautions and the cleanliness, many children die from various diseases and never reach adulthood.
- **17.** When a child dies, he or she is cremated. The Grays refer to it as "incineration."

IV. Hybrid children habitat as described by an Anunnaki:

The following is an actual depiction of their habitat according to Sinhar Ambar Anati, the Phoenician-American hybrid woman, known to us as Victoria. She is married to SinharMarduck, an Anunnaki leader.

I have reproduced the article from the original version of the book "Revelation of an Anunnaki's Wife", and which reappeared in an updated edition under the title "Anunnaki Ultimatum", a book, authored by Maximillien de Lafayette with his colleague, Dr. Ilil Arbell. Victoria (Ambar Anati) is conversing with her mother-in-law, Sinharinannaschamra who is the mother of SinharMarduck. Here is the text (Title; Visiting the Hybrids):

a. Inside the base:

Sinharinannaschamra said: "The base we are going to visit is an underwater habitat. We are about to descend way down into the Pacific.""What about air?" I asked, a bit apprehensive about the idea. Surely she won't forget I could not breathe under water, but still..."We pass through a lock that is safe for water and air," said Sinharinannaschamra, "and inside, it's geared for the hybrids,

113

which, just like humans, need air." In a few minutes, we stopped and I assumed, correctly, that we were already inside the base. "They are expecting us," she said. "Don't worry about them. They know I can blow the whole place up if they dare to give me any trouble."

The spaceship's door opened and I saw that we were inside a huge, hangar-like room. If I had expected a beautiful, aquarium-like window, showing the denizens of the deep playing in their blue environment, I would have been disappointed. But knowing the Grays, I expected nothing of the sort, and so the beige and gray room, all metal and lacking any windows, did not exactly surprise me.

"This base is enormous," said Sinharinannaschamra. "It is used for many operations, but we will just concentrate on the hybrids today." I was pleased to hear that, since I was secretly apprehensive about the possibility of stumbling on one of the Grays' hellish laboratories. I will never forget, or forgive, what I saw in their lab. But I said nothing and waited to see what was to happen next. Sinharinannaschamra walked me to a solid wall, put her hand on it, and wall shimmered a little and then moved, allowing a door to form and open for us.

b. The refectory:

We entered a long corridor, illuminated by stark, white light, with many regular doors on each side. Sinharinannaschamra opened one of the doors and we entered a large room, obviously a refectory since it contained extremely long tables, all made of metal. The room was painted entirely in beige – tables, chairs, walls, and ceiling, and had no windows.

It was scrupulously clean. Suddenly, the tables opened up, each table revealing a deep groove on each of its long sides. Plates of what seemed to be normal human food were released from the grooves, and placed each before a chair. At this moment, a few doors opened at various parts of the room, and from each door an orderly file of children came in and settled at the table. They were completely silent, not a word was heard, as they picked up their forks and began to eat. None of them paid any attention to us, even though we stood at plain view. The children seemed to range from six to twelve, but it was difficult to be sure of that. On one hand, they were small and fragile, so I might have mistaken their ages. On the other hand, their eyes gave the impression of almost old age. They seemed wise beyond their tender years.

Their hair was thin, their skin was pale to gray, and they all wore white clothes of extreme cleanliness.

c. Hybrids' three distinct groups/categories:
Despite these similarities, which made them look as if they were all related to each other, I could tell some differences between them that seemed rather fundamental. It was almost as if they fitted within three distinct groups. I mentioned it, in a whisper, to Sinharinannaschamra, and she nodded. "Yes, you got it," she said. "They consist of early-stage hybrids, middle-stage hybrids, and late-stage hybrids.

> - 1-**The first group** is born from the first combination of abductees' and Grays' DNA. They closely resemble the Grays. Look at their skin – the grayish color is very close to that of the Grays, and so is the facial structure.
>
> - 2-**The second group,** the middle-stage hybrids, are the result of mating between these early-stage ones, once they are old enough for reproduction, and human abductees. The resulting DNA is closer to humans, and so they look much more like humans, and many of them lose the Progeria gene.
>
> - 3-**The third group,** the late-stage hybrid, is the most important. Middle-stage hybrids are mated with humans to create them – and they can hardly be distinguished from humans." "Yes, I can tell who the late-stagers are quite easily," I said.

d. Hybrids placed for adoption:
"But there are not too many of them here, right?" "This is true, not too many are here. A large number of these hybrids, who represent the most successful results of the experiments, are placed for adoption with human families."
"Are the human families aware of the origin of their children?"
"Yes, in most cases they are. Generally, they are adopted by a high-ranking United States military man or woman, who had worked, or still works, with aliens, in secret military bases. This happens much more often than most people suspect... the spouse

of the military person may or may not know, depending on circumstances and character traits. These lucky hybrids lead a much better life than whose who are raised in places like this one, communally."

"Are they badly treated here? Are they abused by the Grays?"

"No, the Grays don't want to lose them, they are too valuable. But they receive no love, no individual attention, there is no real parenting, and the environment is barren and depressing.

They live like that until they are old enough to be of use in the experiments. Not a very nice life for any child."

"And what about Progeria? I mean, for the adopted ones."

"Only the hybrids who are entirely free of Progeria are adopted by human families. We even suspect, though we are not sure, that many of the Progeria stricken late-stagers are killed, since their Progeria gene is too strong. The Grays believe that after these three attempts, it cannot be eradicated by further breeding."

"And so they kill the poor things... what is the motive for all these atrocities?"

"All for the same reason I have mentioned. They think they somehow will save their civilization. But they are doomed."

"But in the meantime, they harm, torture, and kill so many people. I don't understand why it is tolerated."

Sinharinannaschamra did not answer.

e. Disposing of the food and cleaning the refectory:

The children finished eating, still in complete silence. Each child, as he or she finished his meal, leaned back into the chair, and as soon as all of them were leaning back, the groove from which the plates came opened up, and re-absorbed all the plates.

"They now go to an automatic dishwashing machine," explained Sinharinannaschamra. The children got up, and left the dismal room in the same file arrangement they came in. As soon as the room was empty, large vacuum cleaners emerged from the wall and sucked up every crumb, every piece of debris.

Then they sprayed the tables and floor with a liquid that smelled like a disinfectant. The room was spotlessly clean again, ready for the next sad, depressing meal.

f. Dormitories and sleeping quarters:

"Shall we go to the dormitories now?"

Asked Sinharinannaschamra. I nodded.

We followed the children through one of the doors, and entered a place that was a combination of an old-fashioned orphanage and military barracks. It was a very large room, but the ceiling was not high, only about twelve feet. Again, everything was beige and gray, and there were no windows to relieve the monotony. The room was full of beds, arranged above each other in groups of three, like in a submarine.

Dozens and dozens of such rows seemed to stretch to a very long distance. The beds were made of some metal, very smooth, and of silver-gray color. They seemed to be assembled like prefab furniture. "Sinharinannaschamra," I said, "there are no ladders. How do the children reach the upper levels?"
"They can levitate," said Sinharinannaschamra.
"Look at this. Part of each bed is magnetic, so each child can have his or her toys attach to it. As for the lower beds, the toys are stored next to them."
"So they have toys," I said.
"That's a mercy."
"Yes, the Grays discovered that mental stimulation is highly important to the hybrids' development. There are plenty of other activities, mostly with abductees, that relieve their lives of the tedium, at least to a certain extent."
"But they have no privacy at all."
"None whatsoever, they only get their own room when they are more mature, but they have one thing that pleases them. If the children want to, they can put their things in their bed, close the bed with a panel, and hide it inside a wall. They like that."
"I wonder, too, if it is not a comfort for them to be together, after all."
"Their feelings and emotional climate are not exactly human...it's hard to explain.
I think it's time for you to see them interact."
"Where are all the children now?" "They are attending various activities," said Sinharinannaschamra.
"Come, I'll show you."

g. Attending various activities:
We entered a room that opened directly from the dormitory. To my surprise, it was really a glass bubble.
You could see the outside, which was an unpleasant desert surrounding. I found it nasty, but I figured that to the children it

117

might have represented a pleasant change. About ten children, seemingly between the ages of six and eight, sat on the ground, which was simply the desert sand. They were playing with normal human toys – trucks, cars, and trains. They filled the things with sand, using plastic trowels that one usually sees on the beach. They were also building tunnels from the sand, wetting it with water from large containers that stood here and there. They seemed to be enjoying their games, certainly concentrating on them, but their demeanor remained quiet and subdued, and they did not engage in the laughter, screaming, yelling, or fighting that children of this age usually produce.

"They also have rooms with climbing equipment, and places to play ball," said Sinharinannaschamra.

"It is needed to strengthen their bones and muscles," she added.

I approached the children, a little apprehensively, worrying that I might frighten the poor things. They looked up at me, seemingly waiting for me to do something, but I was pleased to realize that they were not afraid. I sat on the sand, took some stones that were scattered around, and arranged them so that they created a little road. The children stared at me for a minute with their strange, wise eyes, as if trying to read my thoughts, and almost instantly grasped the idea and continued to build the road together. None of them smiled, but they seemed very much engaged in the new activity. Once all the stones were used, they looked at me again, as if trying to absorb information, and sure enough, after a minute they took the trucks and make them travel on the little road. I got up and let them play.

"So they read minds," I said to Sinharinannaschamra.

"To an extent," she said. "At this age, they basically just absorb images you project. You probably thought about the trucks going on this road, and they saw it..." and she added. "And everything was done together, as if they were mentally connected,"

I asked: "Do they do everything together?"

"Yes, everything is communal, even the bathrooms where they clean themselves. But don't be too upset about it. If they are separated from each other before their adolescence, they are extremely upset. It is almost as if the onset of puberty makes them an individual, and before that they have a group mentality."

"Horrible," I said.

"They are not unhappy," said Sinharinannaschamra.

"Only as adolescents, when they break off the communal mind, they understand how unhappy they are. But we will visit the adolescents on another occasion."

"Very well," I said.

h. The fetuses' room:

Sinharinannaschamra asked: "Would you like to see the room where they keep the fetuses?" I followed her to the corridor, and we walked quite a distance before opening another door. We entered another one of the hangar-sized rooms, full of tanks. "Each tank contains colored and different liquid nutrients," said Sinharinannaschamra. "This is where they put the fetuses, as soon as they are removed from the abductees. The tanks are arranged in order, from the youngest fetuses to those that are almost ready to be removed."

"Do they separate them into their stages?" I asked.

"Yes, this room is for early stagers only. In other rooms, they have the middle stagers. But the late stagers remain in the mother's womb until birth, to make them as close to humans as possible."

"And what are the babies like?"

"Quiet, not as responsive as human babies. Many of them die as soon as they are removed from the tank. Those that survive are generally mentally well developed, physically weak, and emotionally subdued."

"And who takes care of them?"

"Both the Grays and the abductees. The Grays perform most of the physical requirements, but the abductees supply the human touch. We can't go there yet."

"How come?"

"We need to prepare you to interact with abductees. They are very complicated. We shall have a few sessions about interacting with them at the same time we teach you how to work with the adolescents.

Also, you wanted some instructions of how to contact and help those people that are children of humans and Anunnaki, like your son. This should take some teaching, too." We went back to our spaceship, not saying much. I remember thinking that if I were part of the Anunnaki Council, I would vote to kill every Gray in the known universe.

Of course I did not say it to Sinharinannaschamra, but I am sure she knew how I felt. Back home, I went to my beloved garden

119

and sat under a tree that constantly showered tiny blossoms on me, like little snowflakes. I did not even know I was crying.

"What is the matter?" said Marduchk, who suddenly appeared next to me. I told him about the visit with the hybrids.

"The hybrids are not abused," said Marduchk.

"Something else is bothering you." I thought for a moment, and then decided I might as well be honest with him. "Yes," I said.

"I cannot understand the Anunnaki's casual attitude about the fact that thousands of human beings are tortured and killed all the time. Neither you nor Sinharinannaschamra seem to be as shocked as I am about the fact that the Grays engage in such atrocities."

Marduchk was quiet for a minute, thinking. At this conversation, we did not use the Conduit, because at my agitated state I found it difficult. I was not entirely used to it as yet. So I waited for him to say what he thought. "I see your point," he said. "You think we are callous about it."

"Yes, I do, to tell you the truth. Why don't you destroy the Grays? Why do you allow so much death, so much pain? Are you, after all, cruel beings? Have you become callous because you have lived so many years, and became thick-skinned about suffering?"

"No, we are not cruel.

It's just that we view life and death differently than you do. We cannot destroy all the Grays, even if we wanted to. We don't commit genocide, even if they try to do it. But we don't want to kill them. We know that they will die on their own."

"And in the meantime, suffering means nothing to you?"

"It means a lot, but destroying the Grays would not eliminate suffering in all the universes we go to.

There are other species that are even worse, you just don't know them because the objects of their behavior are not humans."

"It seems to me, that even though you are so much more sophisticated than the humans, the fact that you deny the existence of God may have deprived you of your ethics, after all."

"Deny God? What makes you think we deny God?" asked Marduchk. He seemed genuinely surprised.

"Marduchk, you have told me, more than once, that the Anunnaki created the human race, not God. So where is God if He is not the Creator? Your statements are contradictory."

*** *** ***

PART 8

The Ramadosh Supernatural and
Metaphysical Techniques
The Supersymetric Mind
Activation of the Conduit

Godabaari "Gudi-Ha-abri" Technique

Godabaari is a term for an Ulema's technique/practice aimed at developing a faculty capable of making objects move at distance, by using vibes emanated by the "Conduit" implanted in the brain. It is composed of three words:

a-Goda or Gudi, which means great; influential; powerful,
b-Ha, which means first; the first vibration,
c-Abaari or Abri, which means to cross over or to displace.

I-Developing the Conduit:

There are techniques which are partially physical and partially mental. You could refer to them as psychosomatic. As a beginner, even though your Conduit is now open, you cannot tap directly into it, because consciously, you don't even know where it is located in your brain. By adopting some postures and positions, you will send sensations to your brain.

These positions will create internal muscular vibrations, and your mind will read them. You will be sending mental visionary lines, and these will activate the cell which is responsible for imagination. By the power of concentration and introspection, you will start to get intensified activity in the brain. This causes a buzz vibration in the brain the Conduit begins to detect.

Then, the Conduit will absorb the vibrations and organize them, and from that moment on, the Conduit will take over.

To summarize, by attempting certain activities, you are sending a message to your Conduit. It will take some time, because at the beginning, your Conduit may not catch the messages, or if it does catch them, may not interpret the messages correctly, because the Conduit is not one hundred percent awake.

With practice, the Conduit becomes familiar with these types of messages, and it begins to give them codes. Each activity would have its own code.

One thing must be understood. You cannot do these techniques to amuse yourself, since they simply will not work unless there is a purpose to the activity, and it must be a beneficial, positive purpose.

II. Moving objects by using mental powers:

As mentioned earlier, you cannot do any of these techniques to amuse yourself, it simply will not work unless there is a purpose to the activity, and it must be a beneficial and positive purpose. It does not have to be a great undertaking, a simple positive intent will be just fine. Put a lightweight coaster on the table. You wish to manipulate it with the beneficial intent of preventing a cup of coffee or tea from spilling on the table. Before starting, sit in a comfortable position next to the table.

Never attempt to do this technique standing up – you may very easily lose your balance and fall. You should not try to start with a heavy object, but once you learned how to work with this technique, and your powers become stronger, you could increase the weight of the objects.

III. Preparations:

In preparation, certain changes in lifestyle are needed during two weeks before you start your exercises:

- **1**-Avoid all alcoholic beverages.
- **2**-Avoid smoking, or tobacco in any form
- **3**-Abstain from sexual activity.
- **4**-Do not eat meat.
- **5**-Do not use any animal fat, such as lard, bacon drippings, or butter, in your cooking.

IV. Precautions during practice:

During your practice, certain precautions must be taken:

- **1**-Take off your shoes, and make sure your feet touch the ground, to anchor yourself
- **2**-Do not wear anything made of metal.

- **3**-Do not allow either people or pets in the same room with you. You must have complete privacy.
- **4**-Do not have any crystal glass in the room with you.

V. The technique:

- **1**-Extend your hands in front of you from the elbow up and shake them in the air for four or five seconds. This cleanses the hands from superfluous energy that might have accumulated on them.
- **2**-With your arms in the same position, spread your fingers and hold for three seconds.
- **3**-Put your thumbs right on the temples, with the fingers still spread in front of your face.
  Make sure the thumbs are located in the small indentation that is close to your eyes. People who practice acupressure will recognize this spot – pressing it is used to cure headaches. Hold the position for three seconds.
- **4**-Rotate your thumbs, taking your fingers to the back of your head, and put your forefingers in the indentation at the back of your head, where it meets the neck. Again, people who practice acupressure will recognize this spot; it is used to cure headaches.
- **5**-Push your forefingers into the indentation, and hold the position for ten seconds.
- **6**-Close your eyes.
- **7**-While still sitting with your back straight, bring your chin as close to your solar plexus as possible. Remain in this position for ten seconds. At this point, you will feel a slight dizziness. This is perfectly fine; it is part of the procedure.
- **8**-Keeping your thumbs in their position, release the forefingers, and rotate your hands forward until you can put your forefingers in the small indentations by the sides of the bridge of your nose. In acupressure, this is the site for one of the techniques that release pressure in the sinuses, so practitioners would be able to recognize the sensation.

- **9-**The rest of your fingers should be kept in a horizontal position, the fingers of one hand resting over the fingers of the other hand, the thumbs pointing down.
- **10-**Move your thumbs toward each other and have them touch. Your hands will form a triangle. Your arms will be in a position of ninety degrees, relative to your body.
- **11-**Say to yourself, mentally, I will now make the coaster move.
- **12-**In your mind, draw one line from the middle of your left wrist, and another line from the middle of your right wrist, toward the coaster. Visualize the coaster between the two lines.
- **13-**Keeping your hands in the same position, raise your head and sit straight.
- **14-**Drop your hands down slowly. In your mind's eye, keep on visualizing the coaster.
- **15-**Bring your arms close to your body so the arms touch the ribs.
- **16-**Move your hands up to a position in which they are horizontal to the floor.
- **17-**The left hand should serve as a rod, moving the left line further to the left. The same should be done with the right hand, moving the line further to the right.
- **18-**Keep concentrating on the coaster, with your eyes still closed, for at least another minute.
- **19-**With your eyes still closed, you will notice blue lines and bubbles moving in front of your eyes.
- **20-**At this point, decide which side of your body you are about to employ. You may use either side, but not both at the same time.
- **21-**Let's assume you chose the left side. Open your eyes, and concentrating on the left line, look intently at the coaster. Move your left hand a little to the side, and the coaster will move with it. You have accomplished your mission.

VI. Closing the energy:

This is the end of the exercise, but like any other mental technique, you cannot just leave and go about your business. You

125

have created a center of energy, which should never be left open. The energy you have created with this exercise is linear.
To create an all-around center of energy needs a higher training, and closing it is more difficult, but closing the linear energy is relatively easy.

- **1**-Extend both hands, straight in front of you.
- **2**-Make the hands stay in the direction of the lines.
- **3**-Bring the hands close together, with a very little distance between them.
- **4**-Visualize a very thin thread entering the space between the hands. Close your hands around the thread.
- **5**-Bring your closed hands toward your solar plexus.
- **6**-Open your hands, and shake them as you have done in the beginning. You have closed the center of energy.

*** *** ***

Gomari "Gumaridu" Technique

Gomari is a term referring to an Anunnaki Ulema technique capable of manipulating time.
It is also called the "Net Technique". Ulema Rabbi Mordechai said: "Human beings treat time as if it were linear. Day follows day, year follows year, and task follows task. The Anunnaki Ulema, however, have long ago learned how to treat time nonlinearly, and thus be able to accomplish more in their lives."

I. The Exercise:

For the purpose of this exercise, one must have complete privacy, and in addition, one's consciousness changes under the influence of the exercise to such an extent that a mother, for instance, would not hear her children if they need her. So the exercise cannot be done while young children are at home. Also, if you are taking care of an ill or elderly relative, you should not pursue it either. If parts of the tasks you wish to accomplish are to be done at work, again, you cannot accomplish that because almost all jobs involve the presence of other people. Therefore, for the purpose of this exercise, we will choose a simple frame and an acceptable set of tasks. Let's choose a Saturday, and you have to accomplish a few tasks. All of them must be done on Saturday, because on Sunday you are expecting to be busy with other things. You have, in short, seven hours. Let's assume you have chosen these tasks:

- You have to drive your spouse to the airport.
- You have committed yourself to your boss, promising that you will write a report of a hundred pages or so for Monday.
- You want to shop for food for the week.

This is quite a lot to do in the seven hours that we will assume are available to you during that day. The trip to the airport would take about an hour. The shopping will take about an hour and a half. As for the report, it looks like it should take at least ten hours. So obviously some of the things you wanted to do will not get done. But the Anunnaki-Ulema say that all these things can be done if you learn to break the "mold of the linear time", and they have a technique one can learn to do so.

II. The Equipment:

For this technique, you will need a few props:

- A round net. It can be anything – a fishing net, a crochet tablecloth, anything made of thread or yarn with perforations. It should be around four feet in diameter.
- Paper
- Pencil
- Scissors.

III. The Technique:

- 1-Since one of the tasks involves taking your spouse to the airport, work on the preliminary preparations behind a closed door.
- 2-Look intently at the net, and memorize the way it looks, so that you can easily visualize it.
- 3-Close your eyes and visualize the net.
- 4-In your mind, draw a large circle on the net.
- 5-In your mind, let the net float in the air, making sure it is not flat and horizontal, but moving, bending, waving, and being in a vertical position most of the time.

- **6**-In your mind, concentrate on the tasks you wish to accomplish.
- **7**-In your mind, represent each task as a hole that you mentally perforate in the net. Since you have three tasks, you visualize three holes.
- **8**-Open your eyes, take the physical net, and toss it lightly on a chair or a couch nearby. Do not make it flat and horizontal, just let it land on the piece of furniture like a casual throw.
- **9**-Close your eyes again, and visualize the holes in the mental net. Look at the holes you made, visualizing their shape, their edges, and their exact position on the mental net.
- **10**-In your mind, throw the mental net on the physical net.
- **11**-Take the paper and pencil, and draw three circles that would match, by their shape and size, the mental holes you have visualized.
- **12**-Cut the circles with the scissors.
- **13**-Write the descriptions of the tasks you wish to perform on the back of the paper, a single task for each circle. If possible, break the task into segments. For example, if you are working on the circle that represents the trip to the airport, write:
- **a**-Take car out of the garage – five minutes.
- **b**-Drive to airport and drop spouse at the terminal – twenty five minutes.
- **c**-Return home – twenty five minutes.
- **d**-Return car to the garage – five minutes. Do the same for all the tasks.
- **14**-Put the circles on the physical net and fold it around them. Tie the top with a ribbon, so the papers will not fall out, and suspend it on a hook or a door.
  It must remain suspended until the tasks are done, or until the seven hours are over.
- **15**-Start with a linear task, which will anchor you. The best one will be the trip to the airport, and for this task no Anunnaki-Ulema powers are used at all. Even though your Conduit is not open, since you have not been trained by a master, it is still there and it can calculate

what it needs to do, and how to partially and gradually squeeze the other tasks into the frame of seven hours.

- **16-**When you come back home, you should start the second task, the shopping. While you are shopping, the Conduit will employ a system that will be like two old-fashioned tape recorders working at the same time.

  One tape recorder is working slowly, about 30 turns per second.

  The other tape recorder does 1000 turns a second. They do not interfere with each other.

  While you are shopping, which is represented by the slow tape recorder, the time you are using is slower than the time the Conduit is squeezing in.

  The Conduit knows how quickly to "spin" because you have outlined the tasks and the time they take on the circles of paper. This is, therefore, the way the faster tape recorder works.

- **17-**When you come back from your shopping trip, you decide to go to your computer to work on your report. You have to make sure all the physical parts are working properly: The computer is connected to the printer, the paper in the printer is sufficient for printing the entire report, your ink cartridge is fresh, and everything on your desk is in order.

- **18-**Before you start working on your report, unplug the telephone, turn off the TV, make sure nothing is on the stove, and your room's door is locked.

- **19-**Start typing the report.

- **20-**What will happen now will not be entirely clear and understandable to you, because you will be existing, for the duration, on different levels of vibrations.

- **21-**Everything will seem, and actually be, faster than you are accustomed to, including your typing speed.

- **22-**Your body will function normally, but you will not be entirely aware of it, and you will lose your awareness of your physical surrounding.

- **23-**After working for a while, you will feel extremely tired, and without much thinking you will lie down and fall asleep. This is important, because at this time, it is not your normal physical faculties that are in control, but copies of yourself, your doubles, are handling the job.

129

Unless you are a master, it is best to sleep during such occurrences.

- **24**-After a while, and the time for that varies greatly, you will wake up. Naturally, you will return to the computer, feeling again like yourself, and ready to resume your typing.
- **25**-You may be stunned to see that the report of a hundred pages, which you expected to spend hours upon hours preparing, will be neatly stacked by your printer, completely done.
- **26**-When you read it, it will be perfectly clear that it was written by yourself, entirely your work and your style, including your regular mistakes and typos, since the doubles do not edit your work.
- **27**-The only difference is that it was done with supernatural speed.
- **28**-This is a proof positive that you have done the work personally and did not hallucinate these occurrences.

IV. Closing the Energy Center:

You have created a strong field of energy, which now must be closed.

- **1**-Take the net you have suspended, and open it up.
- **2**-Take out the paper circles, and cross-out the tasks that have been accomplished.
- **3**-Fold the net and put it in its regular place.
- **4**-Throw out the circles.
- **5**-You have closed the energy center. Tour tasks are done.

*** *** ***

Gomatirach-Minzari
"Gomu-Minzaar" Technique

Known also as the "Mirror to Alternate Realities".
Ulema Mordechai ben Zvi said: "Building and using the Minzar is risky. However, if the student reads the instructions carefully and does not deviate from them, it should be a reasonably safe procedure. If you choose to try it, this may be one of the most

important lessons you will ever learn, since the benefits, both physical and spiritual, are without equal.

Those who are familiar with the concept of the Anunnaki's Miraya would notice a resemblance in the way these tools are used. However, one should realize that we are not pretending to use the kind of cosmic monitor that is connected, through the Akashic Libraries on Nibiru, to the Akashic Record itself. It is beyond our scope to even conceive how such a tool had ever been created. Nor are we attempting to recreate the kind of Minzar that is used by the Anunnaki-Ulema, who are enlightened beings whose Conduit has been opened.

Most of us possess a Conduit that has not been opened, and the Minzar we recommend is fitted to our level of advancement. Nevertheless, working with the Minzar will open doors that will astound and amaze any student. You will be using the techniques to create an alternate reality that will allow you to do things you have never imagined are possible.

CREATING YOUR OWN WORLD

What you are aiming for is a place to which you can retreat at will, a place where you can have many options. It will be a place of beauty and comfort, and it should allow you opportunities to learn, to create, to invent, to meet compatible people, to connect with animals, to heal, or to simply take a vacation.

The place is designed and planned entirely by you, and is brand new. You cannot say "My new alternate reality is exactly like Rome, Italy," because there is a good possibility that the Conduit, confused by this mixed message, will actually take you to Rome, Italy, in our own world.

If this happens, no real harm is done, but no benefit will occur either. You will simply be wandering the streets of another city, not benefiting from the advantages of an alternate reality at all. However, you should certainly take certain elements from places you like, Rome included if that is what you wish, since you are not required to build your new reality in a vacuum.

However, don't limit yourself to one place. You may want to copy a particular art museum from Rome, where you can always indulge in looking at your favorite sculptures and paintings. Then, you might want to add the gorgeous rose garden from the Brooklyn Botanic Gardens in New York City.

A charming old-world train station from somewhere in Eastern Europe might make the place more interesting, with perhaps a touch of the Orient Express, and a sunny Mediterranean beach would not hurt, either.

How about a café you liked in Paris, and the cozy little library from your home town, where you used to have so much fun during your childhood and you knew you could find every book that was ever written?

Design the house you would want to live in. It may be an opulent mansion, or on the other hand, some of us would prefer a small, simple, rural-type house with a restful cottage garden.

It's all entirely up to you.

Create your new world carefully and don't worry if you change things around as you go along, there is always room for change and development. Did you suddenly remember your trip to China and a wonderful Pagoda you liked? Put it in. Did you enjoy your snorkeling in Australia? Add a barrier reef. One thing should be made entirely clear. Any place you want is allowed, except a place where others are hurt in any way whatsoever, and that includes not only humans, but animals as well. Do not imagine a steak dinner, do not imagine fishing, do not imagine hunting.

Don't waste your time imagining the "glories" of wars. Do not imagine a place where you demean your spouse and yourself by having multiple partners. Do not imagine pornography. Do not imagine a place where you revenge the ills brought on you by people you hate. Your Conduit will not accept any action that can cause pain or even discomfort to any living creatures. Therefore, if you have any negative intention, you are wasting your time. You can build twenty Minzaars, but none of them will take you to such a place. Rather, if you wish to heal from hurts imposed by others, or painful addictions, imagine yourself getting away from all and entering a fresh new world where nothing of this sort exists. Rest assured that you will never meet anyone who had ever hurt you in your new reality. Do this for a few weeks before you build the Minzaar, so the new place is well established in your mind and you can imagine it in seconds.

This is essential because contacting the new reality during the building of the Minzaar requires speed, and no one can create a new world for themselves in a few minutes! And most important, don't do it as a chore.

This should be a fun, rewarding mental exercise. There is no doubt that you will meet pleasant people in your new reality, but there are those who would also wish to have a guide, or a friend, to introduce them to the new world.

This is also possible, and the directions are given below.

If this is part of your plan, by all means do the same and imagine the person you wish to contact with. Don't limit yourself to the kind of person you think you should choose. The friend does not have to be a conventional "spiritual guide" which is often described by people who channel entities, such as a Native American guide, an Asian guru, or a guardian angel. The guide can be just about anyone you would like to have as a friend.

I. Prerequisites:

- For seventy-two hours before building the Minzaar, and before any subsequent visit to the alternate reality, you must abstain from:
  - Drinking alcohol
  - Using any addictive substance
  - Eating meat.
  - Wearing nail polish
- Do not wear clothes made of polyester.
- Wear white or light colored clothes.
- Imagine only positive conditions (see above for details).

II. Precautions:

- Before starting, remember the full instructions carefully.
- These procedures are for novices, and involve mental transportation only.
- If, however, you become extremely adept, there is a possibility of future physical teleportation. In such event, please exercise some logical restrictions on your activities.
- For example, people who had heart problems, pregnant women, and individuals with severe arthritis, asthma, diabetes, should not take the chance of moving physically between realities without consulting first with an Enlightened Master who would advise them on the best way to proceed.

- The Minzaar, during building or using, may explode. The explosion is small, and the glass that is used does not shatter or fly around, so you will not be hurt by it.
- However, if it is built inside your home, or in any confined area, such an occurrence may cause damage to children, pets, furniture, or decorative objects.
- The Minzaar must be built in an outdoor location, where the energy that will be released during such an explosion will not cause damage.
- You can build it in your back yard, but if you live in an apartment in the city, you must find an appropriate location where you will be outside, but still have some privacy.
- A woman should not wear loose skirts, flowing dresses, or scarves. For everyone, close-fitting clothes, though not too tight for comfort, are highly recommended.
- Never wear clothes made of polyester.
- Remove any jewelry or metal objects you may be wearing.
- You will be using dry ice. When you handle it, make sure to wear gloves, since direct contact with dry ice will burn your skin.
- You will be using two bowls. Make sure they are not made of metal.
- When you cut the dry ice, be sure to place it in the dry bowl. Never mix dry ice and water, this can cause serious injury.

III. Equipment and Supplies:

The supplies required to build the Minzaar are readily available. You will need:
- Laminated glass, two feet by two feet, with rounded, smooth edges. Laminated glass is made of two layers of glass, and it does not shatter into sharp-edged slivers when it breaks. It is the safest glass you can use. Have the store cut it for you to the right dimensions.
- A few pieces of charcoal.
- A role of aluminum foil.

- A very small quantity of dry ice. You will only need a small cube, approximately the size of a dice.
- Two very thin pieces of wire, each three feet in length.
- Two iron nails.
- A Magnet.
- Two plastic or glass bowls that would contain sixteen ounces of liquid each. Never use metal.
- Lumber, enough to build a two feet by two feet base, two inches height.
- Wood glue.
- Adhesive spray.
- Fabric glue.
- Small finishing nails.
- A small hammer.
- Water.
- A sheet of white linen, large enough to create four panels that you will use to surround yourself as you work with the Minzaar.
- This sheet should be made of flame-retardant fabric, or if you cannot find such a sheet, spray your linen with flame-retardant spray.
- Four Pieces of cardboard, six feet by two feet.

IV. Building the Minzaar:

- Magnetize the iron nails by placing them next to the magnet for a few hours.
- Build a wooden base. It should be a simple box, two feet by two feet, and two inches tall.
- Use the wood glue and the finishing nails to make it steady.
- Fold each piece of cardboard vertically, ending with a small pyramid measuring three feet by two feet.
- Make all four can stand up steadily.
- With the fabric glue, attach four panels from the white linen sheet to the cardboard pyramids.
- Rub the coal on one side of the glass, until it covers the surface with a thin black film.
- Use the adhesive glue spray to stabilize the film. Allow to dry thoroughly.

135

- From the aluminum foil, cut seven ribbons.
- Each should be a little less than one inch in width.
- Six of the ribbons should be exactly two feet long, and the seventh should be two inches longer.
- Take four ribbons, not including the longer one, and glue them to the coal covered side of the glass.
- They should be placed with equal distance between them and from the edges, creating five equal sized spaces where the coal dust will be visible.
- Take the remaining three ribbons.
- They should be glued on top of the four ribbons, but in ninety degrees to them, creating a grid.
- The longer ribbon should be glued in the middle of the box, with an inch extending on each side.
- The others should be glued with equal distance between the middle ribbon and the edges, creating four spaces. The grid will thus be made of square spaces between the ribbons.
- Use the extra ribbon that is extending from both sides to attach the wires. Each wire will be extending vertically from the box.
- Place the glass on the wooden base, coal and ribbon side down, and clean side up.
- Make sure the glass and the base are squared and the edges are perfectly aligned.
- To each wire, attach one of the magnetized nails you have prepared in advance.
- Arrange the panels around the box.
- There should be one on three sides, and the fourth one will be placed behind you.
- Pour the water into one of the bowls, and place one of the nails into it. The wire that is attached to this nail must be fully stretched.
- Cut the dry ice, wearing gloves, into a dice-sized cube. Place it in the dry, empty bowl. Remember never to mix dry ice and water!
- That wire should be closer to the glass than the one that is touching the water, so bend it slightly.

- The dry ice will produce some smoke. That is normal, it is an effect that is often used for theatrical production, and it will not hurt you.
- Sit in front of the glass box, put the fourth panel behind you, and close your eyes.

V. Contacting the Alternate Realities:

- Close your eyes and visualize a green, virgin land, a place no one has ever seen before.
- Imagine, dream, and think about the land you have been visualizing for the past few weeks.
- You are bringing the things you love and want most, the good things that you wish to see in your life, to the green land. You are creating a new earth, the way you want it.
- There are people in the new place.
- You must build places for them, streets, houses, a wonderful city or countryside, exactly the way you want it.
- Working as fast as you can, and with your eyes still closed, in a few minutes you will sense smoke coming from your left side. It will not rise high, but remain rather low, and it will creep close to the glass.
- Realize that even though your eyes are closed, you will actually see the smoke.
- When you are sure you are seeing the smoke, open your eyes.
- Put both your hands on the glass, with your fingers spread out.
- Concentrate your gaze on the spaces between the fingers. Bring to mind all the beautiful things you imagined in the new land, and place them in the spaces between the fingers.
- Start alternating your concentration between the tips of your fingers and the spaces between the fingers.
- Continue for about five minutes.
- You will notice that the tips of your fingers will produce light, in the form of sparks. There will be no physical sensation caused by these sparks.

137

- Slide your hands closer to your body until they are about an inch or two from your body.
- Put your hands on the edges of the glass, each on one side.
- Look down into the bottom of the Minzaar. You will notice that the color of the aluminum ribbons has changed, and that the charcoal film looks as smooth as a marble. The glass has turned into a black mirror, and a line of light will vibrate on the black surface.
- You will begin to see the things you have imagined as miniatures in the black mirror.
- Some will look proportional and organized. Others will be out of proportion. They will be moving and shifting.
- You may have created a person to function as a friend and a guide.
- If you did so, look for that person in the Minzaar.
- You will soon find him or her, so try to increase the size of the person. In a few seconds, the person will acquire dimension, proportion, and personality, and will appear as real, in or out of the Minzaar.
- You will establish a true rapport with him or her, though you may not quite understand the nature of the rapport.
- If what you imagined is a country, or a place, or a house rather than a person, you will develop the connection to it so that you will be able to escape to this place at will. Many students prefer creating such a place, since, as it will most likely to have people in it, will combine the advantages of both.
- In the future, you will not need to build a second Minzaar, or even use the many steps of preparations to envision the person or the place you have created.
- They will be stored in your brain. The act of building the Minzaar was meant to trigger one of the Conduit faculties in the brain. A rudimentary one by comparison to what the Anunnaki-Ulema can do, but of great benefit none the less.
- You could not, for example, simply buy a ready-made black mirror, and work with it.
- You must follow the step-by-step the creation of the Minzaar to achieve the effect.

138

- It will be a good idea to throw out the unnecessary equipment, such as the nails, the bowls, etc., but keep the Minzaar, which has turned into a beautiful black mirror, as a stimulus for the activity.
- You can go into the new country anytime you wish. It is a physical place, located in a different dimension, but just as real as this one.
- When you go there, you can spend months in that time frame, while here on earth only a few minutes will pass. That is because the Conduit allows you to duplicate yourself, to create a double, and time is different in other dimensions.
- What you can do there is limitless. You can simply rest and enjoy a place that will never hurt you, a vacation from the trials and tribulations in the here and now. Or, perhaps, you wish to create something.
- Let's say you want to write a screenplay, and can never find the time or the leisure to do it here. Well, you can go to your special place for the duration of the time you need for writing this screenplay, and come back to your present existence after a few seconds of leaving it.
- The advantage will be that you have written the play and it is all there in your memory, one hundred percent of it. All you will need is the short time needed to type it. Or perhaps you are not well, and you would like to see the doctors and the hospitals you have created at this new environment.
- It is quite likely that they may have a cure to at least some ailments – it won't hurt to try. Possibly you wanted to build a magnificent library, containing an enormous number of books. By all means, this is a wonderful experiment, with one added bonus.
- When you are at this library, make a note of certain titles and authors which you have never heard of before. Then, when you are back home, ask a librarian, or check the Internet, to see if such titles/authors exist.
- If they do, it would be a proof that you have not been hallucinating! Or perhaps you would like to try a new career, see how it feels to become a teacher, or a singer, or a trapeze artist. Why not try it? You are the best judge on what you wish to accomplish!

VI. Subsequent Visits to the Alternate Realities:

After the initial visit to the alternate reality, you will no longer need to use the Minzaar. As mentioned before, some students find it easier to look at the Minzaar for a while before attempting the visit, but it is not entirely necessary.

- The best time to visit is your usual bed time. Before you go to sleep, just lie down on your bed. Generally, it is best to lie on your right side, to avoid pressure on the heart.
- Close your eyes.
- Think about the place you want to visit.
- Draw as clear a picture of it in your mind as you can.
- At this point, remember the way your hands were placed on the Minzaar, and imagine yourself behind your fingers.
- Tell yourself the first activity you wish to perform during your visit.
- For seven to ten seconds, do not think at all. Make your mind completely blank.
- Do not be startled – amazing things will begin to happen now. Images will float before your eyes, you will hear sounds, or noises. This is called "The buzzing of the mind."
- At this moment, the preliminary rapport is established between the necessary cell in your Conduit and your double in the alternate reality.
- The cell will zoom you there and your double will be your guide. In other words, the cell acts as your vessel, and the double as the pilot.
- As soon as you arrive, the double will stop all activities and instantly merge with you.
- Your visit has begun.

VII. Benefits and Advantages:

Beside the pleasure and learning experiences that you gain through your trips to the alternate reality, there are several concrete advantages that will manifest themselves very soon in your normal reality.

140

- You will be less tense or nervous.
- You will gradually lose any phobia that might have tormented you for many years, perhaps all your life.
- Your physical health will improve.
- You will be able to work efficiently, since you will bring with you some very important creations, plans, or thoughts from your alternate reality.
- Such products or services will be performed in much greater speed since they have been "rehearsed" in the alternate reality.
- You can learn languages with surprising speed since you can actually learn them first in the alternate reality, and the memory is retained. That applies to other skills, such as computer skills, art, music, and many others.
- You will put every moment to good advantage.
- If you hate waiting in line, or sitting in the doctor's office, or listening to your boss droning on and on while of course you cannot put a stop to the conversation, just hop to the new reality for a few minutes, and do something fun or creative there. Of course, for these few moments you will be out of touch with your earth body, but you will be recalled back quickly as soon as needed. Obviously, using this quick "hop" you will never be bored again, ever.
- To complement this activity, it is advisable to always carry a notepad and a pen in case you wish to quickly record an experience.

VIII. Returning to Your Regular Reality on Earth:

We must note that there is never any need for fear. Some people are concerned that the body that they have left on earth when visiting their alternate reality might be exposed to harm, perhaps even attacked.

There is no reason for such fear. First of all, with the exception of the first time, when you originally build the Minzar, you will usually do it in the privacy of your own bedroom, and alone.

Second, no matter how long you will spend in your alternate reality, you will return to your body seconds after you left it in our reality here, since time flows very differently in the alternate reality, and the Conduit knows how to handle it. The only thing

141

you should be concerned about is not to come back into the body too quickly. If you panic suddenly and zoom into your body, you may harm it by this speed. You are perfectly safe, so come back easily and slowly.

The best procedure for a beginner is to spend the time and enjoy the stay in the alternate reality without worrying about coming back. The first few times would not take long, since you are so new at it, anyway. After a while, your stays will be extended.

In both cases, after what seems to be minutes, hours, days, or months, since it really does not matter how long you are there, suddenly you will remember that you left your body behind. For a few seconds, you are not sure which part of you is real, and it may create the sense of fear discussed above. Remember there is nothing to fear, your Conduit is in control, and it knows what it is doing. So when this moment arrives, allow yourself to relax, and in seconds you will be aware that you are back in the presence of your normal earth body.

Do not rush, and do not bunch yourself quickly into the body from either side. Instead, help your Conduit by hovering horizontally right above your body, and then settling peacefully into it. Most likely that will be followed by a few minutes sleep, after which you will wake up refreshed and in complete memory of your activities in the alternate reality."

*** *** ***

Gubada-Ari
The Triangle of Life Technique

Gubada-Ari is a term referring to the Anunnaki-Ulema "Triangle of Life", and how to apply the value of the "Triangle" shape to health, success, and peace of mind. Most importantly, how to find the healthiest spots and luckiest areas on earth, including private places and countries, and take advantage of this.

How this technique will enhance your life: With the help of the triangle, you will able to find the perfect areas on earth where your health, success, and peace of mind will be at their optimum. You can work it on a large scale and find out the best countries to live in, or on a small scale, which would give you the best neighbourhoods in your own city or county.

I. Synopsis of the Theory:

- There are lines of energy spinning around the world. In this exercise, we will concentrate on the lines that are revealed by the use of the triangle. The energy flows in currents, both negative and positive, mostly underground, traversing the globe. Those who live above the positive lines, will have good health, success, and peace of mind. Those who live above the negative lines, will have bad health, lack of success, and will experience mind turmoil. The meaning of life is based on the fact that life is, in itself, a triangle. One corner of the triangle represents health. The second represents success. The third represents peace of mind.
- You find meaning by placing the triangle you are about to draw on the world.
- The student might ask, where do I put the triangle? How do I choose the original location? The answer is, you put the triangle wherever you are.
- The student might ask, what if I change locations? The answer is, this technique is working within the dictates of the moment. Wherever you are, the triangle follows. Change it as many times in life as you need. It always works.

II. Materials:

- This lesson can be accomplished with two different props. And they are easy to find.
- You can use a globe, or a flat map of the world. A globe (Earth Globe) gives a more precise direction, but it is expensive and sometimes hard to get. The student may instead use a flat map of the world. It is not as precise, but the distortion is so slight that it does not signify, and it is cheaper and readily available. If you are using a map, you will need lightweight paper which is somewhat transparent, a pen, a ruler, and a pair of scissors. If you are using a globe, you will need plastic wrap, the kind that is used to wrap sandwiches or leftovers in the kitchen, since it will adhere easily to a globe. You will

143

also need a magic marker that can write on this material, a ruler, and a pair of scissors.

III. The Technique:

- The drawings below show how the double triangle, or the six-pointed star, was created. To be most effective, an individual exercise should be used separately for Health, Success, and Peace of Mind. As you copy the template below, simply change the word on top for each exercise.

Note: See illustrations on the following pages.

"Triangle A" was drawn as an equilateral triangle.

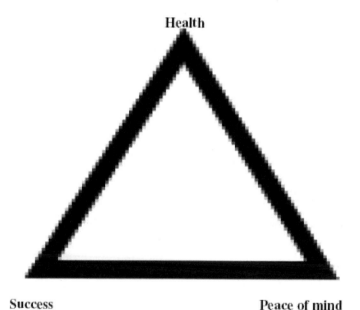

Figure 1: Triangle A

"Triangle B" was drawn by extending the lines on top of triangle A, and then closing these lines and thus creating a second triangle of the same size exactly.

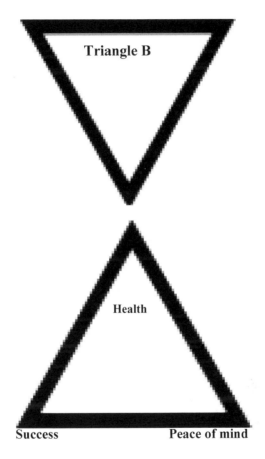

Figure 2: Triangle on the top is triangle B.

"Triangle A" was moved up and centered exactly on Triangle B. By doing this, we have created a six pointed star. We have numbered the four small triangles created on the sides of the star, as1, 2, 3, and 4.

Figure 3: The six pointed star

- Copy the template of the star on transparent paper if you are using a map, or on the plastic wrap if you are using a globe.
- Place the center of the star precisely on the location of the place you are living in now, at this very moment.
- All countries located inside these four small triangles are good for your health. Should you have a health issue, or a desire to live in the more healthy places, these are your choices

The Anunnaki-Ulema Triangle is a complex concept. Perhaps, to better understand its essence, revisiting Ulema Mordechai, and listening to him explaining to his student Germain Lumiere (My pseudonym as it appeared in a few books) is a must.
Excerpt from his dialogue with Lumiere.

Ulema Mordechai and Germain Lumiere Dialogue

"We are going to apply the value of the triangle shape to real life and to the organization we call the Pères du Triangle. I am not sure if you are aware of it, but there are six Triangles on earth. Actually, they rule the earth."

Lumiere: "Are they political? Secret? Are they part of existing governments?" I asked.

"They are more important, far more so, than mere governments. Can you define for me what are the most important things in life?"

"Life itself?" I said.

"Yes, this is right within itself, but it does not answer the question." I was annoyed. Here we go again, I said to myself. I am arguing with an old Jewish Rabbi. They always go round and round, using semantics that get you nowhere. "How can I be right and wrong at the same time?" I asked.

"Well, we will go about it in a different way," said Rabbi Mordechai. "What is the meaning of life on earth?"

"Family? Friends?" I said, knowing full well that he will argue again, and I was right.

"Family and friends make our life meaningful, of course," said Rabbi Mordechai, but they are not the meaning of life. The

147

meaning of life is based on the fact that life is, in itself, a triangle. One corner of the triangle represents health.
The second represents success.
The third represents peace of mind. Visualize it like that." And he demonstrated by joining his two thumbs and his two forefingers, creating a triangle. "You find meaning by placing this triangle on the world." He leaned his hands on the large globe. "But the all important thing is to find the right spot to put the triangle on."
"I am not sure I follow," I said, dubiously.
"So let's demonstrate it with some props," said Rabbi Mordechai. He gave me paper, pencil, a ruler, and a pair of scissors. "Now," he said, "draw and cut a more or less equilateral triangle from this peace of paper." I did, trying my best to make an exact drawing, and cut it carefully.
"Now," he said, "put it anywhere on the globe."
I took the paper, and feeling like a fool tried to place the paper on the globe, knowing that it will fall off since I used no glue. Of course it fell, several times, until Rabbi Mordechai smiled rather cynically, an expression I have never seen on his face before. "Put it on again," he said, giving the globe a piercing look. I did, and the paper stuck to the globe. Another trick, I thought. I was tired of tricks.
"Spin the globe," he said. The triangle stuck and the globe was spinning.
"As this is happening," said Rabbi Mordechai, "realize that if the lines of the triangle were somehow continued, they would represent lines of energy around the world. Let's concentrate on the lines that occur when you extend the Health corner at the top of the triangle. This energy flows in currents, both negative and positive, mostly underground, traversing the globe." This was beginning to make sense to me.
I span the globe again, the paper stuck, and I tried to imagine the continued lines that would follow the entire world. I was beginning to see the pattern. "Those who live above the positive lines, will have good health. Those who live above the negative lines, will have bad health. But let's elaborate a little. Look at the drawing I am about to make."
He drew a triangle, wrote Health on the top of it, and said, "This is Triangle A." Then, he extended the lines. "Close these lines and thus create a second triangle of the same size exactly, which we call Triangle B. Everything inside Triangle B will have good health. Now, make a copy, of an exact size, of Triangle A. Move it

up and center it exactly on Triangle B. By doing this, you have created a six pointed Star of David."

By now I realized we were not doing any tricks, but studying a most fascinating and helpful technique. "How do we proceed?" I asked, poring over the drawing.

"We will number the four small triangles created on the sides of the Star of David 1, 2, 3, and 4. All countries located inside these four small triangles are good for health. Should you have a health issue, or a desire to live in the more healthy places, these are your choices."

"So I imagine that you can do the same for Success and Peace of Mind, to find the best of each quality?"

"Correct," said Rabbi Mordechai.

"Ah, but there still one problem here. Where do I put the triangle? How do I choose the original location? " I asked.

Rabbi Mordechai laughed. "For once, son, I encourage you to consider yourself the center of the world. You put the triangle wherever you are."

"However, Rabbi Mordechai, another question remains. At this moment I am in Budapest. I put the triangle on the map of Hungary and learn of my best locations. But next week, or next month, I am going back to France. Then, should I put it on the map of France?"

"Yes, of course," said Rabbi Mordechai.

"This technique is working within the dictates of the moment. Wherever you are, the triangle follows. And it always works."

"I am a little surprised to see the Star of David involved in Ulema teachings," I said.

"Not at all," said Rabbi Mordechai. "You must realize that the Kabalists share many of the Ulema techniques. There is much more to it, as this is only one of the seven great secrets of the Star of David," said Rabbi Mordechai. "The Kabalists have been using it to great advantage for centuries."

"But the Triangle is used by the Pères du Triangle, so it is a universal symbol," I said.

"Good point. As you can imagine, the presence of the Star of David caused the usual Anti Semitic comments that the Jews are ruling the financial world. But this is sheer nonsense. The Pères du Triangle includes people from all religions and nations, and they have very little affiliation to either. The Star of David, even though it signifies in Judaism and is placed on the flag of the state of Israel, is entirely universal and many scholars claim its origin is Anunnaki." Indeed, so much of the Ulema knowledge comes from the Anunnaki, that it did not surprise me."

*** *** ***

Cadari-Rou'yaa Technique

Cadari-Rou'yaa is the name or term for a secret technique developed by the Anunnaki- Ulema, centuries ago, that enabled them to read the thoughts, intentions, and feelings of others.
It is composed of two words:
a-Cadari, which means a grid; a plasma-screen.
b-Rou'yaa, which means vision; perception.

Cadari-Rou'yaa is also a method to diagnose health, and prevent health problems from occurring in the present, and in the future, by reading and interpreting the rays and radiations, a human body diffuses on a regular basis.
In the West, it is called reading of the aura.
The following is an excerpt from an Ulema's Kira'at (Reading). It is herewith reproduced verbatim (Unedited), from a Kira'at, as it was given by an Anunnaki-Ulema in the Middle East, and told by Maximillien de Lafayette.

Ulema Sadiq is talking to his students (Verbatim):

The Technique:

- **1**-You are going to learn wonderful things today. But you have to remember that you should stay calm, focused and relaxed all the time.
- **2**-You are going to succeed. But you should not give up too easy. Don't get frustrated and despair because it is not working right away. At the beginning, everything needs additional effort, a great deal of patience, and a strong belief in yourself.
- **3**-We are not asking you to have a blind faith. Leave faith to others. Use your mind. Follow the procedures. Practice, practice, practice. And everything is going to be just fine.

- **4**-I repeat again one more time. Don't get frustrated and anxious if it is not working right away. It is going to work, and your patience will pay off.
- **5**-Now, go to a quite place. We suggest your office if you are sure nobody is going to interrupt your practice, or just your bedroom if you can be by yourself, alone, quite and distant from noises.
- **6**-You have to practice alone. Always alone.
- **7**-Good. Take a piece of paper. A plain sheet of white paper with no lines. Size: 7 centimeters by 6 centimeters.
- **8**-On the left side of the paper, draw a red circle. Size: 2 centimeters in diameter.
- **9**-Next to the red circle, and at a distance of 1 centimeter, draw a small black dot. Size: Half the size of a bean.
- **10**-Next to the black dot, and at 1 centimeter distance, draw a green circle. Size: 2 centimeters in diameter.
- **11**-All should be aligned equally and straight on the same line. (Same level)
- **12**-Now you have from left to right: A red circle, a black dot, and a green circle, all on the same line.
- **13**-Make sure the sheet of paper is placed 25 centimeters in front of you.
- **14**-Close your eyes for 4 seconds.
- **15**-Open your eyes, and breathe slowly and deeply.
- **16**-Close your eyes one more time for 2 seconds.
- **17**-Open our eyes, and breathe one more time slowly and deeply.
- **18**-Now, look straight at the black dot for just 2 seconds.
- **19**-Close your eyes for 2 seconds.
- **20**-Open your eyes now, and look one more time at the black dot for 40 seconds or so.
- **21**-Now, tell your left eye to look at the red circle, and your right eye to look at the green circle at the same time.
- **22**-I know, it is strange, and it seems confusing to you all. But don't worry.
- **23**-Try again.
- **24**-Keep on trying until you get it right.
- **25**-Now, something is going to happen. Pay attention.

151

- **26**-You will start to see both circles getting closer.
- **27**-It is not an optical illusion.
- **28**-On the contrary, it is an optical adjustment, because now, your eyes and your mind are working together. Something you have not done before.
- **29**-Now, something very new and very unusual is going to happen.
- **30**-Keep looking at those circles.
- **31**-Do not loose concentration.
- **32**-Watch now what is going to happen.
- **33**-The blue circle on your left starts to look very different. It has something around it. Something you did not see before.
- **34**-The blue circle has some sort of a lighter color ring around it. It could be any color. It does not matter.
- **35**-Remember you are still looking at both circles at the same time.
- **36**-Don't leave one circle to go to another circle.
- **37**-Now the green circle on your right starts to look very different. It has something around it. Something you did not see before.
- **38**-The green circle has some sort of a lighter color ring around it. It could be any color. It does not matter.
- **39**-Remember you are still looking at both circles at the same time.
- **40**-Don't leave one circle to go to another circle.
- **41**-Keep looking at both circles for two minutes or so.
- **42**-Something is going to happen now. Pay attention.
- **43**-It would/could appear to you that the black dot is moving somehow.
- **44**-Don't let this distract you.
- **45**-Anyway, it will go away in a few seconds.
- **46**-Something very important is going to happen now. Pay attention.
- **47**-The ring around the blue circle on your left is getting bigger and denser.
- **48**-The ring around the green circle on your right is getting bigger and denser.
- **49**-And you are still looking at both circles.
- **50**-You are doing absolutely great.

- **51**-Now, focus your attention on the blue circle on your left.
- **52**-Something very important is going to happen now. Pay attention.
- **53**-The longer you look at the blue circle, the stronger and brighter is the ring around it.
- **54**-Now the ring around the blue circle is getting denser.
- **55**-In less than 2 seconds, the ring becomes much much brighter and starts to radiate.
- **56**-Now move to the green circle on your right.
- **57**-Focus your attention on the green circle on your right.
- **58**-Something very important is going to happen now. Pay attention.
- **59**-The longer you look at the green circle, the stronger and brighter is the ring around it.
- **60**-Now the ring around the blue circle is getting denser.
- **61**-In less than 2 seconds, the ring becomes much much brighter and starts to radiate.
- **62**-You are seeing now something you have never seen before. And that is good.
- **63**-Breathe deeply and take a short brake. (One minutes)
- **64**-Repeat the whole exercise from the very top.
- **65**-This should do it for now.
- **66**-Tomorrow, you will practice again.
- **67**-You will do the same thing.
- **68**-Keep on practicing like this for 5 consecutive days.
- **69**-If it did not work, do not give up.
- **70**-Be patient. It will work. It did work for many students. It is simply a matter or practice, perseverance, and patience.
- **72**-And hopefully, if it did work, the rings you saw around the circles were the vibrating auras of the circles.

Note: According to the Ulema, this exercise opens an extra visual/optic dimension for your eyes and your mind. In fact, it did not open anything new; it has just activated your visual perception. You had it all the time, but you were not aware of it.

153

Chabariduri Technique

The name of an Anunnaki-Ulema technique/exercise to develop the faculty of remote viewing.
The Ulema taught their students the art and science of remote viewing to improve their knowledge, enrich their awareness, and widen their perception of life, and not to spy on others, as it is the case in the West. Herewith a synopsis of one of the Ulema remote viewing techniques.
Note: The Ulema hand over to each student two small stones of the same size.

Stage One:

- **1**-Pick up any stone you want and write on it Aleph "A" (First letter in many Semitic and ancient Middle/Near Eastern languages)
- **2**-Squeeze on the stone, and try to feel something, anything, or try to think about something, anything you want.
- **3**-Put the Aleph stone on your desk.
- **4**-Pick up the second stone and write on it Beth "B".
- **5**-Squeeze strongly on the stone.
- 6-Try to feel something, anything, or try to think about something, anything you want.
- **7**-Put the Beth stone on your desk.
- **8**-Write down on the white paper what did you feel or what did you think when you touched stone Aleph.
- **9**-Draw a line, and write below the line what did you feel or what did you think when you touched stone Beth.

Stage Two:

- **10**-Now, use the other sheet of paper.
- **10**-Take stone Aleph, and put it in your right palm. Close your hand. Close your eyes.
- **11**-Breathe slowly and deeply. Squeeze on the stone, and ask yourself where did the stone come from. Ask yourself this question 4 times.
- **12**-Put down the stone on your desk. Open your eyes. Take the pen and start writing on the paper what you are thinking about. It does not matter what. Just write down what your mind is telling you.

154

- **13**-Now try to guess where did the stone come from.
- **14**-Try to associate the stone with places you know and places you don't know.
- **15**-Draw on the paper whatever you see in your mind.
- **16**-Think strongly. You may close your eyes if you want.
- **17**-You still have 2 minutes to finish the test.

Stage Three:

Note: Now, the Ulema tell the students time is up.
One of the students is asked to collect the papers, and he deposits them on the desk of the Ulema. After having reviewed the students' answers, the Ulema directs those who passed the test to move to a designated area in the classroom, and he dismisses the others for now.
If all the students failed the test, the session comes to an end, and another test will resume the following day.
Now, the students are asked to do the same thing with stone Beth. Same instructions are given, and same procedures are followed. Those who pass the test stay in the classroom, and those who failed are dismissed.

- **1**-Now you are going to work with stone Aleph. Stone Beth is no longer needed.
- **2**-Now you are going to describe the place where the stone came from. You are going to write down everything you see or think of.
- **3**-Now you will write down on a new sheet of paper, anything you will be thinking about, anything and everything, no matter how silly or unrealistic it appears to you.
- **4**-Do not hesitate. Do not doubt yourself. Don't wait to have a second thought.
- **5**-Rush your visions, thoughts and feelings to the paper.
- **6**-Now hold the stone in your right hand, and squeeze on the stone firmly for one minute.
- **7**-Put the stone down, and start writing.
- **8**-Right down first what you thought first.
- **9**-If you feel, or if you think that you know something or anything about the place where the stone might have

come from, write down right away the name and location of the place. Do not doubt yourself.

- **10**-Follow your instinct, follow your thoughts, follow your feelings, follow your vision, and stop there.
- **11**-Now you are there. And you start to see things; people, houses, shops, gardens, children, trees, water, bicycles, cars, animals...many many things, or maybe just few things. It doesn't matter how much you see. Write it down.
- **12**-Now, make a list of you are seeing.
- **13**-Describe what you are seeing.
- **14**-Be precise; give as much details as you can, and name things...be specific about colors, sizes, forms, shapes, dimensions, locations...anything around, below and above the items you see.
- **15**-You don't need to follow any particular order in listing what you see. First, write down everything you see, later we will sort them out together.
- **16**-Now draw what you see. You don't have to make a masterpiece. Sketches are fine. Any kind of sketches. Even small icons, a few lines here and there, even a series of lines and geometrical forms...draw anything you see or you think you are seeing.
- **17**-Do not try to force yourself to give any explanation to what you are seeing or drawing. You will think later about that. Now concentrate on that place you have found and write down everything you see...draw more pictures...do not delete anything...add but don't delete.

Note: At the end of the session, the students' work is evaluated, and compared with the data and information about the place subject of the test, and safely guarded in numbered files.

This was a synopsis of the Ulema's instructions and guidance, and their students' orientation/training session. This remote viewing exercise is repeated again and again on a daily basis for one full month. At the beginning, you need an instructor (Ulema or just an instructor or a guide to tell you what to do). But later on, you will do it on your own. After few practices, you know exactly what to do.

Daemat-Afnah Technique
How to Stay and Look 37 Permanently

Term for the process of halting the process of aging.
It is composed of two words:
a-Daemat, which means longevity.
b-Afnah, which means many things, including health, fecundity, and longevity.
According to the Anunnaki-Ulema, we are not programmed to age.

Understanding human life-span and our body longevity.

- **1**-Not all parts, membranes, tissues and organs of your body age the same way and at the same rate.
- **2**-Sometimes, your neck or the skin right under your eyes shows your age, while your very eyes remain vibrant and young. It is a matter of genes or cells. This is what science taught us.
- **3**-Although, it is true, we age because our genes get damaged, there are reasons for aging that are still unknown to science.
- **4**-Some of the non-physical aging factors cannot be detected in laboratories, because they are not created by purely terrestrial elements.
- **5**-They belong to another dimension, where your blue prints were conceived and stored.
- **6**-Humans are not programmed to age. I am neither referring to the early genetic creation of mankind (One million years ago or so), nor to the primordial seven prototypes created by the An. Na.Ki. (450,000 years ago or so).
- I am talking about the final specimen of humans that contained the original 13 mental faculties, some 65,000 years ago.
- **7**-The Anunnaki who live outside time don't show any indication of aging, because time does not control their lifespan. Human life is controlled by time. Anunnaki's life is free of time, thus time cannot regulate their lives.

- **8**-The Anunnaki have the ability to activate and reactivate their genes in their laboratories. Although, they are not immortal, and eventually their cells and genes deteriorate, the Anunnaki can activate the last fully functional and healthy cell, reproduce it in a large quantity, and activate each newly created cell separately, in conformity with the many copies and doubles of an Anunnaki stored in a reversed time-data-storage.
- **9**-The Anunnaki can keep you young for ever, and easily postpone aging indefinitely. Two of the very first things they do are:
- **A**-Extending the longevity of your Double by rearranging your stored DNA and blueprints.
- **B**-By building a new genetic sequence aimed at resisting stress that causes damages to your genes in a terrestrial surrounding.
- **10**-The Anunnaki can divide each sequence of your DNA, and add to this divided sequence, a new genetic code that extends your life span for thousands of years. Quantum physics and modern medicine sciences do not contradict this.

*** *** ***

From the Ulema's Kira'ats.
Excerpts from the readings of Master Li, Maximillien de Lafayette and Ulema Mordachai Ben Zvi

Translated verbatim in conformity with its authentic caché and linguistic expressions.

- **1**-You can reprogram yourself and adjust your genes. The Anunnaki, Ulema, and the sages of Melkart taught the enlightened ones and the righteous ones how to do it.
- **2**-Your body is a machine like so many other machines in the universe, here on earth and beyond.
- **3**-Some machines run on fuel, others on atomic energy...your body is very special, and a great mystery, because it runs on a substance known to very few people in the world. Is it your blood?

Is it the oxygen you breathe in the air?

Is it your soul? Is it the mind of God?

Is it your essence, your Chi, your DNA? Or all of the above? Or perhaps something we cannot touch, we cannot see, we cannot measure, and consequently we cannot understand or be sure of?

- **4**-You were taught that the human body is created from a male's semen and a female's eggs. That is very true.

  But this semen and these eggs must have "something" extraordinary, something non-physical to allow a physical human body to perform physical/non-physical acts such as writing poetry, epics, music, symphonies, and love letters, to measure light, to reader others' thoughts, to communicate telepathically, to fall in love, to think about new ideas, and possibly to escape

  laws of physics. This very special and extraordinary "something" is somewhere...not necessarily in the semen and the eggs...

- **5**-Although, we are all human beings...the truth is, we did not come from the same origin. Some were born here on earth, others were born somewhere else...in some other dimensions and far distant spheres. Yet, we have many things in common, because we were created by the same Khalek (Creator) and his assistants.

- **6**-We are not an assembly-line product. We are not like automobiles manufactured and assembled exactly the same way by the same plant.

- **7**-This is why each one of us is different. And this difference exists, because each one of us was created in a different plant, according to different specifications and very distinct genetic-programming process.

- **8**-Those who created us know these specifications and what went into our creation, thus, they can reprogram us, alter our properties, give us a new form, new faculties, and reduce or increase our life span.

- **9**-At the time we were created (Designed, produced, manufactured, etc.), three things happened to us, and are directly related to (a) intelligence, (b) luck/success in life, and (c) health/youth/longevity.

*** *** ***

A-The Brain Motor:
A brain was designed and instantly tested. The brain was created before the body took shape and form. In this brain, all faculties were installed. A copy or blueprints of the brain (Mind) was duplicated and stored in an etheric dimension "ED" (This is the best way we can describe this dimension for now.)
This ED is similar to a cosmic net that consists of trillions and millions of trillions of canals, stations, terminals and channels, all connected together, yet they function separately according to very specific frequencies and vibrations. Once these faculties are installed and begin to function −no matter at what rate or level −, they become a permanent and final fixture of our thinking process, i.e. intelligence, logic, creativity, etc. However, these faculties will get better and better by constant learning and acquiring new knowledge. This is only possible, if the Conduit (Installed by the An. Na. Ki or other non-terrestrials geneticists-creators in your brain's cells) has more room for improvement. The capacity of the Conduit is usually detected at an early age, between 3 and 5.
Many of the greatest geniuses on earth manifested the Conduit's capacity and potentials during this short and early period of time.

B-Vibrations, Frequencies, and Luck in Life:
Creation of a place for the vibrations of our mind. Nothing in the physical and non-physical dimensions exists, continues to exist, and functions without vibrations and frequencies.
When these rays (Vibrations and frequencies) get damaged or cease to radiate or emanate, the organism stops to function. In other words, the brain (Mind) as a motor dies out instantly. When our creators designed this motor during the first stage of manufacturing us, they carefully tested and measured the frequencies and vibes of the brain, and adjusted the level of its creativity. At this very moment, they created a space for this creativity, called the vibrational dimension.
Now, if these vibrations resonate in synchronization with the vibrations of the canals and channels of the cosmic net, the person who has this kind of vibrations will be a very luck person, but not necessarily a righteous one. In other words, either you were born lucky, or unlucky, and you are going to stay lucky or unlucky for the rest of your life, and there is nothing you can do to change your luck.

160

However, Master Li said: "It is not totally so...although you have no control over your destiny and luck, your Conduit will be able to ameliorate your chances if it is activated by your Double. The sad part of this story is that many of us either do not believe in a Double, nor accept the idea that a Conduit does in fact exist in our brains' cells."

C-The Conduit=Health/Youth/Longevity:

Those who have read my books are now familiar with the Conduit. For those who didn't, here is a brief description of the nature of the Conduit.
Basically, the Conduit is a depot of everything that is YOU; intelligence, emotions, feelings, attributes, qualities, talents, health, dreams, physiognomy, abilities to learn many languages, creativity, endurance, and yes, your future as well.

At the time you were born, a Conduit was installed in the cells of your brain. If the Conduit has been activated, then everything you touch will turn into gold, all your deeds will become honorable, and you will be destined to greatness. If the Conduit remains inactive, you will live a normal life, nothing spectacular about it, and you continue to live a very ordinary life like all the others.

A miniscule, an infinitely small part of the Conduit deals with health, youth, and longevity. And this very small part has been already programmed by those who created you. You can't deprogram it. You can't find it. And you can't reach it. It is way beyond your reach and comprehension. So let's leave it like that for now. In the Conduit, your life-span has been formulated and its length and/or continuity has been decided upon genetically.

Some people will die young, other will live 100 years. Some people will grow up to be very tall and physically strong despite lack of nutrition and a good diet, while many others will stay short, fat, or weak despite their healthy life style, good diet, and impeccable hygiene. Physicians and scientists are so quick to say: It is in the genes! And they stop there! But one thing they don't know for sure is what or who created those genes, and according to what guidelines, specs., and creation process?

161

They don't know. Well, the Ulema do know, because they learned it from their teachers the An. Na.Ki. You can't control longevity, youth and your life-span by deprogramming their genetic codes, because first, you don't know where to find these sequences, second, you have no control over the Conduit, and third, you don't know how much to add or to subtract from and to the genetic codes.

If you do, if you know for a fact, how to prolong the vibrations of these sequences and how much "stuff" to add to the Conduit, then, and only then, you will be able to control your life-span. Ulema Marash said: "It is like when you fill your automobile gas tank. The more fuel you put in your tank, the more mileages your car will run. The difference is that, at the gas station, you are in control, because you can decide how much gas you want to buy, but when it comes to living young for ever, first, you don't know where the youth station (In comparison to the gas station) is, and second, you are not in control of your Conduit (In comparison to your car)."

"The good news", said Ulema Albakr" is that a Conduit can be activated and/or reactivated if training and orientation programs are completed...Enlightenment and blessings are not the monopoly of few..." All these statements are fascinating, but is there a pragmatic and an effective way to either activate the Conduit or to stay and look younger for ever? "What do I have to do to stay young? And yes, I am over 37, but I want to look 37, can you teach me how to do this?" you might ask. Well, here are some of the guidelines and techniques according to the secret doctrine of the Ulema.

Some of the Ulema's guidelines and techniques

Introduction:
- You do not need to buy anything.
- No equipment is needed.
- No physical training is required.
- No diet is imposed.
- No pills to take.
- All what you need is your mind; believing in yourself; convincing yourself that you are determined to succeed; a great deal of optimism and patience. Nothing else.

- **1**-Your environment conditions your state of mind, and your way of life. This is very true.
- **2**-Equally true is the fact that your mind (No matter how educated or uneducated you are) can also condition your environment and way of life.
- **3**-It is up to you to decide: Would you like to be permanently at the mercy of your environment and what life and others have imposed upon your, or would you rather use the power of your mind to change your life for better? It is up to you!
- **4**-Your mind can do miracles for you if you let it. Just believe in it.
- **5**-Your mind has the power to make you look healthy and much much younger.
- **6**-Your mind is much powerful and durable than your genes and your pumped muscles. Because your mind can influence your genes and your muscles.
- **7**-In doing so, your mind can "freeze time" in your body and postpone aging. Oh yes, you will grow older, but you will look much younger, despite your old age.
  In fact, your body will never show sign, or any indication of aging if you let your mind create a new mental setting for your body, and I am going to show you how...
- **8**-First, you choose an age of your choice; this age will stay the same indefinitely, this is the age that is going to freeze time, and at which you stop to get older. Wonderful.
- **9**-Second, you tell yourself I want to stay 25 or 45 or 37 year old for the rest of my life, it is up to you (This depends on the age you have chosen.)
- **10**-We recommend that you choose the age of 37 if you are older than that. If you are younger, stay where you are and count your blessings.
- **11**-Do not think for a second, just because you have told yourself you want to stay 37 for ever, that you are going to stay 37 for ever. No! It requires much more than that.
- **12**-For 37 consecutive days, you will tell yourself as soon as you wake up in the morning: "I am going to stay 37 for ever." And immediately, you start to think about all the happy days and wonderful things you enjoyed when you

were 37. You have to do that, otherwise it will <u>never</u> work.

- **13**-You have to convince your mind that really you want to stay 37. Once your mind is convinced, it starts to work on your genes. Do not ask why and how. It is too complicated. After all, do you want to eat grapes or chase the bear in your vineyard? Don't ask too many questions.
- **14**-Now, we have to use some imagination here. Oh yes, imagination creates wonders. So, you start to tell yourself, you are going to relive the time when you were 37.
- **15**-First thing to do is to refresh your memories and remember (as much as you can) all the wonderful places you have visited when you were 37, the kind of sport you practiced, the fashion you followed, the movies you saw, the music you listened to, the car you drove, the entertainment you enjoyed, all the gifts and presents you received, and do not forget the young and beautiful girl or man you dated...all these things must pop up together and simultaneously in your head.
- **16**-You will fantasize about all these things, and you will revisit all these things, you relive and feel all these things the way you felt them when you were 37. You have to relive these times in your mind every single day for 37 consecutive days. Do not miss one single day.
- **17**-Before you go to sleep, and while you are still awake in your bed, choose one of those places you have recently visited in your mind. Any place you want. Very good.
- **18**-Go there now. See what is going on there.
- **19**-See if your buddies are there.
- **20**-Try to find one. You got to find somebody, a pal, a friend, somebody you had good time with. Good.
- **21**-Start talking to your friend. You got to believe in this. No, you are not crazy, you are doing just fine, and your mind is working perfectly.)
- **22**-Engage into a real chat with your friend. Tell jokes. Laugh. Feel the energy of being young again.
- **23**-Now do something else. Tell yourself you want to go on a date. Call your date. Pick up a place you used to love so much.

- **24-**Pick up your date, head straightforward to that place, be brave, kick the door, and step in.
- **25-**Once you are in, you are going to meet lots of good friends, and you are going to have a ball; eat, drink, sing, dance if you can, enjoy yourself.
- **26-**Probably you are sleeping now, and that is good for now. Your mind needs a rest. Go to sleep.
- **27-**Every single day for 37 consecutive days, keep on doing this. Of course, every time you revisit your life, do something different, but similar to what you used to do when you were 37.
- **28-**Do not do anything different or differently.
- **29-**You are still living your normal life; the one you are currently living. And I bet, now and then you are having some hard times, and of course some good times too. Now, you have to remember you have another wonderful life beyond this one.
- **30-**The one you visit in the morning and before you go to sleep. So why don't you go there right now and dump all these troubles you are having, and come back in the morning.
- **31-**Stay there overnight. It is good for you. Keep telling this to yourself. And every time you feel bad about something, or somebody is disturbing you, and you become anxious, exhausted and unhappy, you have to remember that you have a magical formula nobody knows about...it is your secret...you have the wonderful life you visit from time to time. It is there. It exists. It continues to exist, but you forgot about it, because you are living at a different pace and speed, and you worry so much.
- **32-**Now you have been visiting your youth, let's say for two weeks. And that is fine. At the end of the third week, you are going to feel so good, you are not going to believe it. You are going to feel so good about yourself, I guarantee it.
- **33-**Continue to visit your new world. At the end of the 37 day period, your life will change to better. You will see the difference. But that is not enough.
- **34-**Nothing physically in you has changed yet. Don't worry. It will happen sooner than you think. But now,

you are shifting gear, you are steamed up, you are happy about how you feel about yourself, and so, you decided to visit more often the wonderful place, life and time when you were 37. So go ahead, go there as often as you can, and as much as you want. It belongs to you. It is yours!

- **35**-If you keep doing this for 6 months – non stop –, you are going to see a major and mind bending physical transformation in you. Especially on your face. I will explain...
- **36**-Your hair color will not change. If you had grey hair before, well, the grey hair is still there. If you were bald, sorry, you are still bald. But your face now is much much younger, and you start to look almost 37. You will believe it when you will see it, and you are going to see it.
- **37**-Gradually, you start to regain your youth, but you are not stopping the time clock. But what do you care?
- **38**-You are not showing sign of aging. You will not have wrinkles on your face for many years to come. Everybody around you will see the difference. And those who will meet you for the first time will never guess how old you are! You will never look your age.
- **39**-It is at this very stage of your life, when you will realize for the first time, that age is not a state of mind, but what mind can do to stay that way."

*** *** ***

Da-Irat Technique

Name for Anunnaki's "Circle Technique" Da-Irat is known to the enlightened ones and Ulema' adepts as the "Circle Technique" (Da-Ira-Maaref), which means the circle of knowledge. This technique eliminates stress, through one's "Self-energy." In other words, it is an Ulema technique used to energize one's mind and body, and to eliminate worries that are preventing an individual from functioning properly everywhere, including the office, home, social gatherings, etc. In the West, zillions of techniques to reduce stress and counter bad vibes were proposed. And many of those techniques work very well. The following will explain the Ulema's techniques that were in practice for thousands of years in the Near and Middle East. No physical exercise is required. It is purely mental, although some of the steps to follow might look esoteric or spiritual in nature.

These techniques were developed by the early Ulema and members of the "Fish Circle", a brotherhood of the ancient island of Arwad, where allegedly, remnants of the An.na.Ki (Anunnaki) lived, and developed the Mah-Rit in sophisticated genetic labs.

The Da-Irat Technique (The Circle Technique) as used by the Fish Circle Brotherhood.

Terminology:

1-In Ulemite, it is called Da-Irat (Circle; sphere).

2-In Ana'kh, it is called Arac-ta.

3-In Phoenician, it is called Teth-Ra. Teth is circle or good thing. Ra is creative energy or first source of life.

Application and Use:

Excerpts from the Anunnaki-Ulema Kira'ats.

Note: Translated verbatim (As Is) by Maximillien de Lafayette, from the original text and readings in Ulemite and Phoenician:

- **1**-You have to create a space, or find a new space where your mind can manifest itself.
- **2**-You live through your mind, and not through your soul.
- **3**-Therefore, no spiritual exercise is required.
- **4**-A mental exercise is a prerequisite.
- **5**-You can create a space for your mind by putting aside for a short moment all your worries, thoughts and other activities.
- **6**-You enter your private room, and you sit there for five seconds, doing nothing, and trying to think about nothing.
- **7**-Find a comfortable spot.
- **8**-Untie your belt and take off your shoes.
- **9**-Bring your arms close to your hip. This position is called Kaph.
- **10**-If you managed to stop thinking about anything and everything, this would be great. If not, do this:
- **11**-Speak to your mind vocally. Do not be embarrassed. Nobody is going to think you are crazy, because you are alone in your room.

167

- **12**-Tell your mind that you want to see right before your eyes a large white door on your right, and a small blue window on your left. This exercise is called Qoph. It is a Phoenician word, and it means the eye of the needle. In Ulemite, it is called Qafra. In Ana'kh, it is called Kaf-ra-du.
- **13**-Tell your mind you are knocking at the door, and you are getting ready to walk in.
- **14**-Knock at the door. Yes, you can raise your hand and knock on the door. Do not hesitate. You will go through. It is guaranteed.
- **15**-Before you enter, look to see if the window is closed.
- **16**-If the window is closed, that's fine, open the door and get inside.
- **17**-If the window is open, close it. Make sure it is close.
- **18**-Now, proceed and get in...
- **19**-As soon as you step in, shut the door behind you.
- **20**-Your mind is free now.
- **21**-Close your eyes. Do not open your eyes, until I will tell you when.
- **22**-Your mind is no longer distracted by other things.
- **23**-You are now in a state of serenity.
- **24**-Your mind is getting settled.
- **25**-Your mind is finally finding its place. This stage is called Taw in Phoenician, and it means mark. You are marking now your state of mind.
- **26**-This is the place where you are going to dump your worries.
- **27**-You start to feel very quite, calm and relaxed. And that is good.
- **28**-Keep your eyes closed.
- **29**-Now, your mind is ready to listen to your command and wishes.
- **30**-Tell yourself you are entering inside your body.
- 31-Tell yourself you want to enter inside your head. This stage is called Resh in Phoenician, and it means head. In Arabic, it is called Ras. In Ulemite is called Rasha. In Ana'kh, it is called Rashat.
- **32**-Bring yourself very close to your forehead.
- **33**-Direct yourself toward your eyebrows.

- **34**-You are seeing now a calm stream of water.
- This stage is called Mem in Phoenician, and it means water. In Ulemite, it is called Ma'. In Arabic, it is called Ma' or Maiy.
- **35**-The water is running very smoothly.
- **36**-Flow with the stream.
- **37**-Become one with the stream.
- **38**-The stream is showing you now beautiful sceneries.
- **39**-The stream is branching out very gently and is diving itself into small canals. And that is good.
- **40**-Can you count how many canals are you seeing?
- **41**-Follow the canals and count how many are they.
- **42**-Can you try to join them together?
- **43**-Try again.
- **44**-Let your mind help you.
- **45**-Ask your mind to grab all these canals.
- **46**-You see, you are doing it. This stage is called Heth in Phoenician, and it means fence.
- **47**-You are feeling so good.
- **48**-Now, breathe slowly and gently.
- **49**-Continue to breath.
- **50**-Now tell yourself you want to continue going inside yourself.
- **51**-Can you manage to bring the river inside your body?
- **52**-Try.
- **53**-The river is coming closer to your chest.
- **54**-You start to feel it.
- **55**-Yes, the canal is entering your chest. And you are feeling so good, fresh, energized.
- **56**-Tell the canal to clean everything in your body.
- **57**-Everything...everything...
- **58**-You are feeling now the fresh and cool water everywhere in your body. This is a true feeling.
- **59**-The beautiful fresh water is cleaning all the mess and dirt inside your body.
- **60**-Command the water to flush everything out.
- **61**-Tell your mind to close your body.
- **62**-Nothing now can enter your body. It is sealed. It is clean and sparkling, and you feel it.

169

- **63**-Now, you want to visit your knees.
- **64**-Go there. Turn around your knees.
- **65**-Turn one more time.
- **66**-You are going to see now white spirals of light surrounding your knees.
- **67**-Stay there.
- **68**-Let the light turn and turn and turn around your knees.
- **69**-Now the light is going down...down toward your feet, and that is good.
- **70**-Your feet feel good.
- **71**-Your feet are floating now.
- **72**-Let them float.
- **73**-You start to feel as if you are sliding gently...
- **74**-You are, but you are floating. And that is so good.
- **75**-Tell yourself your heart is strong and healthy.
- **76**-Tell your lungs they are clean and healthy.
- **77**-Tell your body how wonderful and strong it is.
- **78**-Tell yourself how wonderful and strong you are.
- **79**-Thank your mind for this wonderful journey.
- **80**-Tell your body that your mind is standing by your body and is going to take care of it.
- **81**-Breathe slowly and deeply three times.
- **82**-Tell yourself you have done a good job and you are going to open your eyes now.
- **83**-Open your eyes.
- **84**-Stretch your arms gently.
- **85**-Stay put for 5 seconds.
- **86**-Stand up.
- **87**-Take a nice hot shower.

- Repeat this exercise twice a week.
- The second time you do this, you are going to feel much better, and the exercise will look more pleasant.
- After the second exercise, you are going to notice a great improvement in your mental and physical health.
- Take note of your progress, and compare notes.

***   ***   ***

170

Dudurisar Technique

Name for the act or ability to rethink and examine past events in your life, change them, and in doing so, you create for yourself a new life and new opportunities. To a certain degree, and in a sense, it is like revisiting your past, and changing unpleasant events, decisions, choices, and related matters that put you where you are today.

Excerpts from Ulema Anusherwan Karma Ramali Kira'at, number 165, Introduction to Dudurisar, Fasel Wahed (Part one) March 1961, Alexandria, Egypt. Verbatim. Unedited. As reported by Maximillien de Lafayette.

I. The Concept:

The honorable Ulema spoke:
- 1-You are not totally satisfied or happy in your current situation, in what you are doing, and where you are today. You wish you had a different life, a better job, more opportunities, less troubles and worries.
  But there is nothing you can do about it, because the past is the past, and nobody can change the past. It is done.
- 2-True, it is very true, you cannot change your past, because it was Maktoub (Written) in the pages of your fate and destiny book, the day you were born.
- 3-Besides, changing or altering the past creates global chaos, confusion, and dysfunctional order among people, communities and nations.
- 4-But you don't have to change your whole past (All events) to become happier, more successful, and put an end to your misery and tough times.
- 5-All what you need to do is to change the part or segments (Days, months, years, places, decisions) that have created hardship, misfortunes and mishaps in your current life; and this is permissible, possible, ethical and healthy.

- 6-What part of your life you wish to change or alter, how to do it, and the reason(s) for doing it are the paramount questions you have to ask yourself very honestly.
- 7-Once you have decided to alter a portion or a segment of your past, and replace this specific segment with new wishes and decisions, you cannot change, modify or alter the changes you have made.
- 8-You have to live with it, and you will not have another chance.
- 9-Something else you should think about (and you should never forget it): Your family, your children, your current obligations, your commitment to others, and all the promises you made to people. Because, once you have changed a major part of your life (Past or present), all these things that you are dealing with right now will change too, and you might not like it, or perhaps you might? Everything depends on your intentions, needs and desires.
- 10-Avoid at all costs and at all time selfishness, greed, escaping from responsibilities, and vicious intentions. No, you can't go back in time and kill all those people who did you wrong, or hurt the woman who turned you down.
- 11-You go back in time/space for one reason: Changing unpleasant events and decisions that unfairly have caused you grief, failures, pain, and unhappiness.
- 12-So the keyword here is "Unfairly". But how would you know what is fair and what is unfair, as far as your past, your job, your luck, your fortune, your bank account, you relationships, promotion in your career or profession, health conditions, peace of mind, and success are concerned?
- 13-You will, once you have crossed the frontiers of the present-past sphere.
- 11-You will not be able to lie to yourself. Once you are behind that thin curtain, you become a different person; un-materialistic, honest, sincere, simple, and wise.
- 14-The world you will enter is as real as the one you live in right now.
- 15-However, it is much much bigger, prettier, serene, meaningful, and confusing at the same time, because it

172

has different purposes, unlimited borders and levels, it is ageless, multidimensional, and contains places, dates, times, people, unfamiliar creatures, humans and non humans (Women, men, children, even animals and strange non-physical creatures) you have not met yet in your life, because they either belong to the future, and/or to different, multiple, vibrational, parallel worlds.

II. The Technique: It works like this

Note: This might frustrate you, because it requires a great deal of patience. Without patience, a strong will, and perseverance, you will not achieve a thing. This technique works. It is up to you to make it work for you.

- **1**-First of all, you have to understand that you cannot revisit and change your past at will, or as you please. There are rules you must follow. And these rules are closely connected to time, the place where you live, your intentions, and the specific events you wish to change.
- **2**-For instance, you cannot return in time/space to take revenge, to kill a person you dislike, or prevent that person from evolving or competing with you.
- **3**-There are limits to what you can do. You cannot return in non-linear time/space and create wars or bring destruction to people and communities. Changing a part or a segment from your past is limited to your sphere.
- **4**-Sphere means your very personal life, your personal actions, your personal events; things that are closely and exclusively related to you.
- **5**-You have no powers over others.
- **6**-Also you have to understand that you cannot return to the past any day you want. There is a calendar or more precisely a time table you should fit it. This means, there are days and hours that are open to you; these days and these hours allow you to zoom back into your past.
- **7**-Consequently, you must find out what are these days and these hours. You have to consider yourself as if you were an airplane.
- **8**-An airplane cannot take off or land without a flight schedule, and an authorization. Consequently, you have

to schedule your trip to the past according to a trip schedule.

- **9**-The trip schedule is decided upon by many factors. The two most important factors are: a-The activation of your Conduit; b-The most suitable hour for your trip; this happens when your Double, or at least your astral copy is in a perfect synchronization with the Ba'ab's opening. Possibly, you are getting confused with all these words and conditions. I will try to simplify the matter for you.

- **10**-To find out what is the most suitable hour to schedule your trip to the past is to do this: All the letters of the alphabet have a numerical value in the Ulemite literature, and were explained in the Book of Rama-Dosh. Refer to Book 2). These numerical values are as follows:

- A numerical value: 1.
- B numerical value: 3.
- C numerical value: 5.
- D numerical value: 7.
- E numerical value: 11.
- F numerical value: 15.
- G numerical value: 16.
- H numerical value: 21.
- I numerical value: 32.
- J numerical value: 39.
- K numerical value: 41.
- L numerical value: 42.
- M numerical value: 44.
- N numerical value: 49.
- O numerical value: 56.
- P numerical value: 58.
- Q numerical value: 62.
- R numerical value: 75.
- S numerical value: 81.
- T numerical value: 83.
- U numerical value: 89.
- V numerical value: 95.
- W numerical value: 98.
- X numerical value: 102.

- Y numerical value: 111.
- Z numerical value: 126.
- **11**-Let's assume your name is Kamil. Now, let's find out the numerical value of Kamil.
- **K=41**. Add 4 + 1=5. The number 5 is the numerical value of K.
- **A=1**. A is a single digit. The number 1 is the numerical value of A.
- **M=44**. Add 4 + 4=8. The number 8 is the numerical value of M.
- **I=32**. Add 3 + 2=5. The number 5 is the numerical value of I.
- **L=42**. Add 4 + 2=6. The number 6 is the numerical value of L.
- **12**-Now, let's find out the complete numerical value of the whole name of Kamil. Add the numerical values of all the letters of the word Kamil.
- **13**-We have here: 5+1+8+5+6=27.
- **14**-The numerical value of Kamil is 27. Now add 2+7=9. The number 9 represents the 9th hour on Kamil's trip schedule. Always use night hours. This means that you can't zoom into your past at a different hour. Just tell yourself you got to be at the gate at 9 o'clock, exactly as you do when you take a regular flight at any airport. You have to be on time.
- **14**-Now, we have to find out the day of the trip (Zooming into the past.) Only on this day you will be able to do so.
- **15**-Take the "Triangle" you have used in practicing your "Gubada-Ari" technique
- **16**-Place the Triangle on the globe. If you have done this previously and found out your best spots on the globe, then, take the number corresponding to that particular spot. Remember there are 4 small triangles, and each triangle has a number on it (From 1 to 4 on the Six Pointed Star.)
- **17**-Let's assume that the corresponding small triangle's number is 3. What does 3 represent? Or any of the 4 numbers of the four small triangles in any case?
- **18**-On Earth, the week consists or 7 days. In the Anunnaki-Ulema Falak, there are no weeks, no days and

175

no time, because time is equated differently beyond the third dimension. Instead, the non-terrestrial beings have four spatial sequences, each representing four different spheres beyond the fourth dimension. Don't worry about these spheres. For now learn this: The number 3 you found on the globe means the third day of the Anunnaki-Ulema calendar.

- **19**-The Anunnaki-Ulema calendar consists of the following: 4 days (So to speak). And the four days are (In a figurative speech) 1-Tuesday; 2-Wednesday; 3-Friday; 4-Saturday. Forget all the other days.
- **20**-This means that your zooming day is Friday. And the departure is at 9 (See bullet#14).
- **21**-Now, we know the day and the hour. What's next?
- **22**-Now, we have to find the gate (Ba'ab).
- **23**-The gate is usually very close to you. This gate is not the "Spatial Ba'ab", but your mental launching pad.
- **24**-The most practical launching pad is any place where nobody can interfere with this technique.
- **25**-Use your private room, make sure nobody is around.
- **26**-Place the Triangle on your desk, or on any solid and stable surface.
- **27**-Sit in a comfortable chair behind your desk, close enough to place both hands parallel to the triangle.
- **28**-Take a deep and long breath, approximately four or five seconds. Repeat this three times.
- **29**-In your mind, project two lines exiting from the top corner of the triangle. In other words, let the lines of the both sides (left and right) of the triangle continue outside the triangle leaving from the top corner.
- **30**-In your mind, create a new triangle starting from the top of the triangle you already have on the desk, and just formed by the extension of the two lines you have mentally created.
- **31**-Now you are looking at this new triangle sitting on the top of the other triangle. We are going to call it "Mira".
- **32**-At each corner of the Mira, you are going now to put something.

- **33**-For example, at the base, which is upside down (left side), choose the year you want to visit.
- **34**-At the base, which is upside down (right side), pick up the event you want to revisit. By event, I mean something you have done, such as a decision, a job you had, a responsibility you have assumed, a trip you made, an encounter you had. In other words, the thing you want to change or alter from your past.
- **35**-At the lower corner of Mira which is joining your triangle on the desk, put the "new thing" or "new wish" you want to use to change or alter something you have done. Remember: You have already chosen what you want to change; it is already placed at the right side (upside down) of the triangle (See bullet#34).
- **36**-Now, everything is in place. You have on the left side, the year you want to visit; on the right side, you have the event or the thing you want to change, and on the reversed corner of the triangle you have the new thing you want to bring to your past so it could change or alter the things you want to remove from your past.
- **37**-Your final mental projection is this: Draw in the triangle a circle, and make it spin or rotate in your mind.
- **38**-Let the circle spin as fast as possible.
- **39**-Keep telling your mind to order the circle to spin. And concentrate on the rotation of the circle as strong as possible. Stay in this mode as long as it takes until you see the circle increasing in size.
- **40**-When you begin to feel that the circle is getting big enough to contain all the corners of the triangle, at this very moment, and in your mind, push out of the circle all the contents of the right side corner, and immediately refill it with your wishes.
- **41**-Bring the refill to the left side corner.
- **42**-Anchor it in the chosen year.
- **43**-In your mind, close the right side corner.
- **44**-In your mind, close the bottom corner of the triangle.
- **45**-In your mind, stay with the year you are visiting now.
- **46**-You are now seeing lots of things; scenes from your past, people you knew, it depends where you are, in other words, your past as it happened at that place and during that year has been reconstructed. Not hundred

177

per cent physically, but holographically, and in this holographic projection, the essence, fabric and DNA of everything that happened are brought back to life in a different dimension, as real as the one you came from.

- **47**-Remember, nothing is completely destroyed in the world. Nothing comes to a total and permanent end. Everything is transformed, retransformed, and quite often recycled. You can recreate the original fabric of everything that happened in your past by recreating the DNA sequence of past events, in revisiting the parallel dimension that has never lost the print and copy of original events. It is this very parallel dimension that you are revisiting now mentally. Ulema enter that dimension physically and mentally. But because you are still a student, you will only revisit that dimension mentally and holographically.

- **48**-You are now revisiting and re-living past times in another dimension. Even though, you are experiencing this extraordinary phenomenon and interacting with re-structured events, you will not be able to bring to your physical world the changes you have made in the parallel dimension, because you cannot transport them to a different dimension. They exist only in that holographic reality, which never ceased to exist.

- **49**-However, you will be able to bring back with you the effects and positive results that such changes have created by altering the past. Those results created in a different dimension will materialize physically in your real life, and you will be able to sense and recognize their effects in a very realistic manner, in all things closely related to their nature.

- **50**-In fact, what you have done is changing or totally eliminating the negative and destructive effects of things and decisions you have made in your past. And this is what really counts. Because you have substituted bad results with good results.

- **51**-Those results will continue in your current life when you return to your physical world, and will prevent future bad incidents and bad things from occurring again

178

in your current life. Worth mentioning here that the kind of bad experiences you had in your past will never happen again to you. You have blocked them for good.

How real is the holographic/parallel dimension you are visiting?

It is fantasy? Is it hallucination? Is it day-dreaming? It is wishful thinking?

None of the above. It is as real as your physical world. Everything you see and feel in this materialistic/physical world exists also (Identically) in other worlds.

But their properties are different. Nevertheless, they look exactly identical. Even the smallest details are preserved. So what you will be seeing during your trip is real. What happened in the past still exists in other dimension, and follows rules that our mind cannot understand.

That incomprehensible and wonderful dimension does not only contain events, peoples, and things from your past, but also whatever is currently occurring on Earth.

In other words, you as a human being living on this planet, and working as a teacher or as a physician, you are simultaneously living and working as a teacher or as a physician in a parallel dimension. You may not have the same name or nationality, but your essence, persona and psycho-somatic characteristics are the same.

In fact, you live simultaneously in many and different worlds. Perhaps, and as we speak, there is another person who looks exactly like you in a different dimension is trying to visit you here on Earth, or perhaps, as we speak he/she is so curious to know if you look like him/her, what are you doing, are you aware of him/her in other dimension? Highly advanced copies of you are fully aware of your characteristics and existence on this planet.

If he/she is older than you in linear time, then he/she is from your past. If he/she is younger than you, than he/she is from your future. But in all cases and in all scenarios, you are one and the same person living at the same time in different places, each place functioning according to different laws of physics, or lack of laws of physics. So, when you revisit your past in a different dimension, prepare yourself to meet another copy of you, or simply YOU in a different non-linear space/time existence. Many adepts who have visited that dimension did not want to return

179

back. In fact, some Talmiz-Ulema remained there. But as you know by now, their copies remained on Earth.

Final words on your visit to the parallel world you have visited using the Dudurisar technique. While you are there, you will not have terrestrial sensorial properties, because your physical body is still in your room, where you began, however, a sort of a spatial memory you will pick up on your way to the parallel dimension, and will substitute for physical feelings and impressions. This spatial memory you had in you all your life, but you never knew you had it, because you have not entered another non-linear dimension before now. It will come handy, and will help you to remember or identify things.

While you are there, you will have all the opportunities of :

a-Meeting many of your past friends (Dead or alive, so to speak in terrestrial terms), perhaps loved pets you lost;

b-Making new friends, and this could sadden you knowing that you will be returning home;

c-Watching the re-happening of future events, as if you were watching a film (you saw before) backward;

d-Learning from new experiences and results you can use when you return home. The time will come, when you become capable of realizing and understanding the many lives and existences you have now, had, or will acquire in the future.

Some of the benefits:

- **1**-Your mind (On its own) knows when it is time to return home.
- **2**-Some people have reported the sadness they felt when they realized that they had to return home. Many did not want to return home, because they have discovered a better place, made new friends, and lived a life –even though extremely short – free of worries and troubles. This could happen to you. But your brain is stronger than your wishes, and you will return safe.
- **3**-On you way back, your mind will reassure you that everything is going to be just fine, and that you have succeeded in removing some stains, copies of disturbing events from your past, and above all the effects of past actions and events that have handicapped you in this life.
- **4**-Your mind will retain all the knowledge you have acquired, and will guide you more efficiently in all your future decisions.

- 5-Numerous people have reported that their journey was beneficial, because for some incomprehensible reasons, many of the problems and difficulties they have faced before evaporated in thin air.

Closing the Technique:
- 1-For this particular technique, you mind will close the technique by itself.
- 2-You will wake up, and you will realize that you were somewhere else, far, far away from your room.
- 3-You open your eyes, and all of a sudden, a delightful and reassuring sensation will invade your being. You feel energized, more confident, and in a total peace with yourself.

*** *** ***

Bari-du Technique

Baridu is the Anunnaki-Ulema term for the act of zooming into an astral body or a Double. We have used the expression "Astral body", because of the Western readers' familiarity with what it basically represents. This representation is not the depiction usually used by the Ulema, but it is close enough, to use it in this work.

Bari-du: The Concept

- The initiated and enlightened ones can zoom into their other bodies, and acquire Anunnaki supernatural faculties.
- I have used the words supernatural faculties instead of supernatural powers, because the enlightened and initiated ones are peaceful, and do not use physical power, brutal force or any aggressive means to reach their objectives.
- The use of violence against humans and animals, even aggressive thoughts and harmful intentions annihilate all chances to acquire Anunnaki's extraordinary faculties.

181

- Your Double can easily read your thoughts.
- If your thoughts are malicious, your Double will prevent you from zooming yourself into its ethereal molecules.
- Therefore, you have to control your temper, remain calm, and show serenity in your thoughts, intentions and actions.
- You Double is very delicate, even though it can accomplish the toughest missions and penetrate the thickest barriers.
- Any indication of violence or ill intention triggers a pulse that blocks your passage to the ethereal sphere of your Double.
- Once you enter your Double, you will be able to use it in so many beautiful and effective ways as:
  1- A protective shield against danger,
  2- An effective apparatus to protect yourself in hostile and dangerous situations,
  3- A tool to develop your abilities to learn many languages, and enhance your artistic creativity,
  4- A stimulus to increase the capacity of your memory,
  5- Instrument to heal wounds and internal injuries. No, you will not become a surgeon, but you will be able to stop internal bleeding, and eliminate pain,
  6- A vehicle to visit distant places and even enter restricted areas for good causes. The possibilities are endless.
- Once you are in a perfect harmony with your Double, and your physical organism is elevated to a higher vibrational level through your union with your Double, you will be able to walk through solid substances such as walls, sheets of glasses and metal.
- You become effective in controlling metal and de-fragmenting molecules of any substance. This will allow you to transmute, change and alter the properties of any object known to mankind.
- But if you use these supernatural faculties to hurt others, or for personal and selfish gain, you will loose them for good, and you will be accountable for such malicious use in the other dimension. And this could delay your entrance through the Ba'ab.

182

- Before you were born, and before your body took shape, you (as a human being) have existed somewhere as an idea.
- What is this idea? We will give you an example. Before a product is mass produced, inventors and artists design and create a model or a prototype of each product. And everything begins with the drawing board.
- On this board, shape, form, dimensions, colors and specifications of the product are defined and illustrated. It started with an idea. The idea became a project and the project found its existence on the drawing board. In fact, everything in life started with an idea, continued with a sketch before it reached its final form, and eventually the market.
- Your physical body is a perfect product. And this product came from an idea like everything that has been created. Nothing comes from nothing.
- Who came up with this idea? This depends on your religious beliefs. If you believe in the Judeo-Christian tradition, then, your God is the originator of this idea. He created the first draft of your physical body on his drawing board.
- Most certainly, God had to think about how your body should look like. On the Judeo-Christian drawing board of the creation of mankind, God decided how the physical body should come to life.
- You are much more important than a commercial product or a commodity like a car, or a soda bottle. The designers, artists and engineers at the automobile factory and plant spent many hours designing the model of the car, and the manufacturers of the soda bottle spent some good time going through various designs of the shapes and looks of bottles before they chose the most suitable design for their product.
- Now, if you think that you are more important than a car or a bottle, then, it is logical to assume that somebody has spent some time designing you, otherwise, you will surface as a non-studied and not well-researched product.
- If you look at your body very carefully, you will find out that your body is an extremely complicated machine and

183

your brain consists of a very intricate wiring system that requires an engineer or at least a first class designer.

- In summary, you did not come right away without a plan, without a well-thought design, and without an idea that created the design and execution of your physical body.
- At the very beginning and early stage of the creation of your physical body, the "Divine" or "Superior" architect-engineer conceived your physical looks as a picture in the astral world.
- And the astral world for now call it: The world of ideas; a non-physical world. In a non-physical world, everything is non-physical, it is astral, it is ethereal.
- When the ethereal image or idea becomes reality and adopts physical properties like eyes, legs, feet and bones, this idea or your "prototype" becomes a physical body and enters the physical world via the womb of your mother.
- Yet, it remains deeply and directly connected to the draft of the first copy of your physical body.
- Since the first draft of your non-physical body and your recently acquired physical body (Or about to be developed in the womb of your mother) are still connected to each other, both bodies (The Idea or Draft and your physical body) co-exist.
- The physical body is inside your mother, and the non-physical body called double or first body exists outside the physical world.
- The other copy, or more precisely the first copy of YOU is called your Double.
- As soon as you begin to develop as a small physical body (a small fetus) inside the womb of your mother, the idea or draft that created you before you entered the womb of your mother begins to feed your brain's cells and program your intellect.
- In other words, your brain begins to receive all the information and characteristics that will create and define your personality, temper, character, persona and nature.

- During the very first 40 days, everything your "Creator" wanted you to be or become start to "go inside your brain" and in the physiology of your body.
- During this very critical intellectual and physical formation, the other aspect of you, your Double, enters a dimension very close to your mother, and once your mother delivers you, your double, the non-physical body will leave the "surroundings" of your mother and follow you.
- From this moment on, your Double will stay with you until you die.
- The double interacts with us in a most fascinating way, noticeable only to the "small child we are", and not to the others. Many children have seen their double. And many of them spoke to their double, and played with their double.
- In many instances, babies and children called their double "my friend", or "a friend who came to visit me." Unfortunately, many parents discouraged their small children from talking about their "imaginary friends", or fantasizing about the visits of their unseen friends." This is very common.
- Ulema children are encouraged to talk about their "imaginary friends".
- These are very precious moments in our lives, because during this stage, the infant and later on, the small child, has a direct access to his/her double.
- If the child is deprived from this contact, the Double could dissipate for ever.
- Of course, in the future, the Double might appear again on certain occasions.
- But, because we have lost touch with our Double, and we no longer remember the beautiful and friendly visits of our forgotten imaginary friends, our mind and common sense will automatically dismiss the sudden apparition of our Double as a reality. In these instances, people quite often say: "I am seeing things", or "Am I hallucinating?" Therapists rush so quickly to explain the phenomenon as a trick by the mind.
- It is not a trick at all. It just happened that your Double is paying you a visit. Instead of questioning your sanity,

you must rejoice and welcome your "friend". In fact, your Double is the most truthful, caring and best friend you ever had, simply because it is YOU!

- Your Double appeared to you for many reasons.
- Your "double" always watches over you. It cares about you. Its presence is a sign of friendship, sometimes necessary and indispensable for solving your problems and finding a way to get out of trouble. You should welcome your Double and listen to.
- The initiated ones can contact their Double; it is a matter of learning, practice and patience. However, you have to remember, that the living cannot contact the dead. By reaching the sphere of your Double or Astral Body, you are reaching yourself, not a dead substance, a departed entity or a spirit.
- Untrained persons cannot contact their Double, but can be trained and taught by the Ulema. And the training has nothing to do with magic, spiritism or religious trances and state of ecstasy. It is purely mental, intellectual, and scientific.
- Here, we will be talking about two situations:
- First situation: Your Double materializes before you on its own,
- Second situation: You initiate the contact with your Double.
- Sometimes, the Astral Body materializes before you eyes, even though you did not try to contact it. This apparition has many meanings, and could be interpreted differently according to the circumstances.
- Sometimes, your Double appears to you to warn you against an imminent danger. Sometimes, to guide you in a moment of despair and difficulties.
- Some other times, when you "see yourself" as a fragile ectoplasmic thin substance like a fog for instance, your Double apparition is telling you, that a very important event is going to happen and it could change the course of your life.
- In rare instances, this apparition could mean that your days are numbered. Short after Lord Byron saw his Double he passed way.

186

- In the second situation: Now, you are trying to contact your Double. You initiate the contact. If you are not one of the enlightened persons, you would not know what to do, and where to start. Like everything in the universe, including speeches and lectures...everything begins with an introduction and ends with an epilogue. This is the right path. In contacting your Double, you must have an introduction that comes in the form of an entry or entrance into the "Al-Madkhal".
- Al Madkhal means verbatim: Entrance and/or where you step in. Ba'ab is a spatial place that exists around the physical dimension of our world. In the Anunnaki-Ulema vocabulary, Ba'ab means verbatim: Door. And from and through this door you enter the other dimension where your astral body (Your Double) exists.

In the West, ufologists, and even space scientists nickname Ba'ab "Stargate." It is not totally correct, because to them, stargate is a gate through which spaceships can travel through the infinity of space and conquer space-time, thus reducing the enormous distances between stars and planets, and reaching destinations in the universe at a speed greater than the speed of sound and light. For the Ulema, the Ba'ab can be used as a spatial stargate, and a mental means to reach the non-physical world as well; no spaceships are needed to communicate with your Double.

*** *** ***

Questions About The Anunnaki-Ulema Techniques

Why The Conduit Is Not Catching Your Messages?

Question 1:
Would you please explain further the passage below, and tell me why my Conduit is not catching all the messages I am sending to my Conduit? Does this mean that my Conduit is not receiving clear messages from me? How can I send clear messages to my Conduit? Passage: "The Conduit will absorb the vibrations and organize them, and from that moment on, the Conduit will take

over. To summarize, by attempting certain activities, you are sending a message to your Conduit.

It will take some time, because at the beginning, your Conduit may not catch the messages, or if it does catch them, may not interpret the messages correctly, because the Conduit is not one hundred percent awake. With practice, the Conduit becomes familiar with these type of messages, and it begins to give them codes. Each activity would have its own code."

Answer to Question 1:

- First of all, you have to remember that your mind (Your brain) has nothing to do with your Conduit. Even though, your brain is functioning wonderfully and you are doing great things in your life, not all the cells in your brain have been used.
- There are so many regions in our brain that have not been explored yet by science.
- In those many unexplored regions of the brain, are so many cells yet to be discovered, located and localized. And above all, we need to learn how they function.
- In that mysterious undiscovered region of the brain, the Conduit exists. It could be in the right or left side of your brain, or just adjacent to line dividing the two parts.
- In the Conduit, there are so many cells, each one with a very defined and particular extraordinary faculty/power, that needs to be activated.
- For instance, one cell triggers the faculty of reading others' thoughts, another cell (Or cells) is responsible for the faculty of teleportation, so on.
- If those cells are not activated, you will not be able to do all those wonderful things.
- So, you have to consider the Conduit as a bank where so many cells are deposited. And there are hundreds of thousands of cells deposited in the Conduit.
- Each cell has a precise function and an invisible location.
- This means that the Conduit can do so many things, if cells are activated. It would be impossible in one lifespan to develop and activate all the cells.
- Three or four fully activated cells is more than enough. With four activated cells you can do four great miracles by earth's standards.

- But for the cell to produce this extraordinary power, the cell must be able first to understand what you want to do.
- For instance, you cannot tell or command your cell "go ahead and make me fly or let me learn a new language in one hour."
- You should first learn how to send your command to your cell. There is a technique for this.
- Your Ulema teacher knows how to put you on the right track.
- Let's assume you have sent a message (A thought, a wish) to your cell. What's next? Well, the message enters your Conduit. Your conduit acting as a supervisor, and as the main receiver reads your message and directs your message to the appropriate cell.
- Your Conduit knows which cell is activated and designed to comply with your request.
- Instantly, the cell receives the Conduit transfer (Meaning your message.)
- Then what? The cell reads your message.
- If your message was sent correctly, then the cell will accept it and give it a code. So, if in the future you ask again your Conduit to do the same thing you have asked in the past, the cell will execute your request in a fraction of a second.
- In other words, each request is coded, and stored in your cell.
- Only coded messages are stored in your Conduit.
- How would you know if you have or have not sent a message correctly to your Conduit? You will know right away. It is very simple. If you have not been trained, you wouldn't know where and how to start in the first place.
- This is the reason why your Conduit did not catch your message(s). You asked "Does this mean that my Conduit is not receiving clear messages from me? And the answer is yes! Your Conduit received something, a thought, a feeling, a wish, a request, call it whatever you want, but your message was not clear to your Conduit, because you did not send your message according to the rules.
- What are these rules?

- They are explained below. But continue to read this first.
- And then you asked: "And how can I send clear messages my Conduit can catch and understand?
- You have to use the "Transmission of Mind" technique. Practice this technique before you send messages to your Conduit. For example, in the past, the SOS (Morse Code) was used by ships, planes, military troops and others. The person who has sent the message (Morse) knew the Code; he/she knew how to tap it. Each word had a code...one dot, two dots, three dots, one dash, two dashes, three dashes, one dit, two dits, one space, two spaces, three spaces, etc. There is a sequence of pulses and marks. And the person who received the message knew how what these dots, and dashes meant. This is how and why he/she was able to read the message or decipher it, if it was a secret message. Your Conduit works exactly in the same way.
- Your Ulema teacher will tell you exactly what dots and sequences to use.
- If your Conduit is hundred percent awake, meaning Open (After training completion), the Conduit will immediately interpret/translate and understand your dots, dashes and sequences.
- Consider those dashes and dots a "Password", a log-in information, a key to open the contact with your Conduit, just like the password you use to open your computer or have access to some websites.
- In the book, you will find several passages referring to the brain waves and mind frequencies, and some techniques used to direct thoughts and mind energies.

The Opening of the Conduit

Question 2:
Is the Conduit something like the Third Eye Lopsang Rampa talked about? Does it need an operation to open it up? Rampa said that he went through surgery to open his third eye?

Answer to Question 2:
The Conduit has nothing to do at all with the Third Eye.

It appears from the writings of Lopsang Rampa, that the opening of the Third Eye requires surgery. I am not very familiar with the Third Eye's medical procedures and what takes place during the surgery. According to the Ulema's teachings, the Conduit opening does not require a surgical operation. It is a state of enlightenment. And enlightenment does not happen with the use of medical tools.

The Opening of the Conduit is a mental exercise. It requires many things such as introspection, deep concentration, guided meditation, following a specific diet, and above all understanding how the brain emits and receives frequencies and vibes.

In Ulemite's literature, the word Conduit is used instead of brain. But the Conduit is much more powerful than the brain, even though it is located in a miniscule area of the brain. The Conduit governs and animates the brain and all the cells of the human brain, this is why it is more powerful than the brain. However, the brain can function perfectly without the help of the Conduit. But, the brain on its own, and without the help of the Conduit rarely produces extra-ordinary, supernatural powers.

The Godabaari technique: Moving Objects at Distance

Question 3:
In the Godabaari technique, step 12, you said "In your mind, draw one line from the middle of your left wrist, and another line from the middle of your right wrist, toward the coaster. Visualize the coaster between the two lines." Does this mean that I will be able to see those two lines with my own eyes, or simply I would be imagining the lines in my head? Something else I would like to know, how long it would take me to learn this technique, and would I be able to move heavier stuff at distance? How heavy? How much heavier than a coaster? How long does it last? It is a one time thing? Is it magic, faith or what? I am a good Christian and I have a strong faith in the Lord and Jesus. Does this help?

Answer to Question 3:
On faith: Then, you must be familiar with what Jesus Christ has said about faith? "And He said to them, "Because of the littleness of your faith; for truly I say to you, if you have faith the size of a mustard seed, you will say to this mountain, 'Move from here to there,' and it will move; and nothing will be impossible to you."

Faith is always good, but it has nothing to do with learning and successfully practicing this technique.

The knowledge, the doctrine, the techniques and the teachings of Anunnaki-Ulema are based upon science, para-physical means, and empirical observations. The Ulema do not ask their students and adepts to have a religious faith or any similar faith, because they do not mix religion with their learning/teaching.

The Ulema do neither consider one religion (Or a faith) superior to another religion, nor accept "Faith" as an effective/pragmatic way to discover and learn the truth. So, unfortunately, your faith will not play any role in understanding and mastering the Godabaari technique. "Use your mind, instead", said the Ulema.

Concerning those two lines: Yes, you will be able to see those two lines with your own eyes. You will not be imagining anything. They are not virtual. The lines are real. How long it would take you to learn this technique? Not very long, if you practice the technique at least three times a week. Would you be able to move heavier stuff at distance?

Yes! After a consistent practice for at least 6 months. How heavy? Heavy enough, but not as big or as heavy as a mountain. There is a limit to everything in life. By the power of his mind, an old Mongolian Ulema was able to lift up a truck, and dump it in a lake. You have asked: How much heavier than a coaster? And the answer is: Much heavier than a coaster.

Use your own assessment and judgment, short after you have succeeded in moving a slightly heavier object than a coaster. It is fun! How long does it last? It is a one time thing? Once you have learned this technique, it stays with you for ever.

The Gomari "Gumaridu" Technique

Question 4:
In the Gomari "Gumaridu" technique, number 15, you said: "Start with a linear task, which will anchor you. The best one will be the trip to the airport, and for this task no Anunnaki-Ulema powers are used at all. Even though your Conduit is not open, since you have not been trained by a master, it is still there and it can calculate what it needs to do, and how to partially and gradually squeeze the other tasks into the frame of seven hours."

My question is this: Does this mean that my Conduit works on its own, by itself, and does things outside my control? If my Conduit knows what to do, such as squeezing the other tasks into the frame of seven hours, why then my Conduit has to stop there? Why my Conduit does not go one step further? Where does the Conduit stop?

Answer to Question 4:
Yes, your Conduit has its own mode. As long as your Conduit is not activated, it remains free of your control. Once your Conduit is activated, you become the stimulus and the manager of your Conduit. Pay attention to the word "Partially".
This is very significant. The Conduit works partially when it is not activated. And partially means reacting by not acting.
The Conduit functions all the time regardless of your state of awareness, enlightenment or readiness. But it will not give you data and information. Everything the Conduit finds is instantly deposited in its compound. You will not find what's in there, until the Conduit is fully activated. Consider it for now as a depot of knowledge; a sort of a personal bank account where your daily balance is constantly increasing, however, you are not allowed to have access to your bank account.
So, nothing is lost. Your Conduit collects and stores information all the time, and from various sources, times, and spheres.

Godabaari's projected mental lines toward the coaster

Question 5:
In the Godabaari technique, step 12, you said: "In your mind, draw one line from the middle of your left wrist, and another line from the middle of your right wrist, toward the coaster. Visualize the coaster between the two lines."
Why the wrist is so important? Why this particular place in our body? Why do we need two lines from both wrists?

Answer to question 5:
The wrist is so important because it is the base of your hand, where your energy is stored. From the hands emanate the rays of your inner energy, called Rou'am. The Chinese compare it to Chi; the Japanese to Ki. Here, they are referring to an inner energy which is an internal physical energy. On the surface, and to the inexperienced, the Ki or Chi resembles Rou'am. But in fact, it is quite different, because Rou'am is not physical at all. If it was physical, it should be enough to use it as a rod or a stick to move the object with, and simplify the whole process. Bear in mind,

193

that all sorts of energies in the forms of vibrations, frequencies and rays emanate from your body.

In fact, each gland, organ and part of your body has a specific vibration defined by its intensity, colors, emission length and waves strength. Sometimes, we call it Aura, and some other times, bio-organic radiation. Still, it is not Rou'am. So Ki, Chi, and Aura are not your Rou'am, simply because they are produced by the composition of your physical body, while the Rou'am is produced by your brain. You brain has to find a way to eject Rou'am. It does so, by releasing it from your wrist, channeling it to your fingers' tips, and exiting it from the top of your fingers.

You need two lines to create a visual-spatial equilibrium. As it is necessary in classical arts to create/preserve beauty, symmetry is also and equally essential and necessary in Godabaari technique. On that principle, Taj Mahal was visualized and built. The same thing applies in our technique.

Mental projection of a visual symmetry eliminates chaos in your brain, and particularly in the difficult process of creating balance and harmony for something you can't touch physically. When you look at the coaster, you just see a coaster.

But you need to frame the coaster into a visual equilibrium. This equilibrium limits the extra dimension of the coaster you don't see. The two lines confine the coaster. The coaster cannot escape the space defined by the two lines you brain has created. And this is how your concentrate your mental energy right on the coaster.

It is this very concentrated mental energy that makes the coaster move in its preliminary phase.

If you use one line only, the coaster will escape, and your mental power has to chase the coaster, instead or trapping it, and controlling the physical place it occupies. What basically the two lines are doing is emptying the space from under the coaster. This void destabilizes the coaster, and immediately the two lines take advantage of this, and begin to dispose it, shake it, and finally make it move.

Anunnaki's Miraya and Akashic Records

Question 6:
In the Chapter Gomatirach-Minzari, you said: "Those who are familiar with the concept of the Anunnaki's Miraya would notice a resemblance in the way these tools are used. However, one should realize that we are not pretending to use the kind of

cosmic monitor that is connected, through the Akashic Libraries on Nibiru, to the Akashic Record itself. It is beyond our scope to even conceive how such a tool had ever been created. Nor are we attempting to recreate the kind of Minzar that is used by the Anunnaki-Ulema, who are enlightened beings whose Conduit has been opened. "

I am not familiar with the Anunnaki's Miraya. What is it? How does it work? And what connection it has with the Akashic Records? Also, I would like to know more about the Anunnaki's libraries.

Answer to question 6:
On Ashtari, the Planet of the Anunnaki (Ne.Be.Ru or Nibiru, to others) each Anunnaki (male and female, young and adult) has a direct access to the Falak Kitbah (Akashic Records) through the Akashic Libraries (Called Shama Kitbah), which are located in every community in Ashtari. The libraries (Called Makatba or Mat-Kaba) are constructed from materials such as chiselled opaque glass (Called Mir-A't), a substance similar to fibreglass (Called Sha-riit), and a multitude of fibre-plastic-like materials (Called Fisal and Hiraa-Ti); they convey the appearance of ultra-modern, futuristic architecture (By humans' standards), and techno- industrialized edifices.

One enters the libraries through an immense hall (Called Isti-bal), seven hundred to one thousand meters in length, by five hundred meters in width. The Isti-bal is empty of any furniture, and is lit by huge oval windows that are placed near the top of the ceiling. The windows (Called Shi-bak) were designed in such a way that the shafts of light that enter through their circular compartments are redirected and projected like solid white laser beams. The effect is spectacular. At night, quasi identical effect is produced by the projection of concentrated light beams coming from hidden sources of lights located behind (More precisely, inside the frames' structure) the frames (Called Mra) of the windows. The frames serve as an energy depot.

The energy is transformed into sources of light. The visual effect is stunning. Enormously large and animated metallic billboards (Called La-yiha, pronounced La-ee-haa) are affixed on walls in a parallel alignment, and on the floor, in front of each billboard, there are hundreds of symmetrically rectangular pads (Called Mirkaan). When visitors enter the library's main hall (Situated just at the front entrance), they approach the billboards, and stand each on a Mirkaan.

The pad serves as a scanner and a transportation device, because it has the capacity to read the minds of the visitors, learn what they are searching for, and as soon as it does so, it begins to move, and slides right through the central billboard (Called Kama La-yiha), which is not really solid but is made from blocks of energy, carrying the visitor with it. Behind the billboard is the main reading room (Called Kama Kira'at) of the Akashic Library. Under the belly of the pad, there are two separate compartments designed to register what the visitor is looking for, and to direct the visitor to his/her destination; usually, it is a reference section where books in form of cones are located on magnetized shelves.

The Anunnaki's Akashic Library is not a traditional library at all, for it contains no physical books per se, even though, there are plenty of conic publications (Books manufactured as magnetic cylinders and cones.) Instead of searching for books on shelves, as we do on Earth, the visitors find themselves in the presence of an immense white-light blue screen, made of materials unknown to us. The screen is hard to describe; it can be compared to a grid (Called Kadari), with a multitude of matrices and vortices of data. The visitors communicate with the screen via their Conduit. The screen registers their thoughts and right away finds/records the information the visitors seek. All the visitors have to do is stand still for less than two seconds (In terrestrial terms) in front of the screen, and the data will be displayed in an animated format. The data (Information) is given in codes which are easily understood by the visitors. The codes are usually divided into sequences; each sequence reflects an aspect of the information.

For example, if you want to know what happened in Alexandria or Phoenicia 3000 B.C., all what you need to do, is to think about either Alexandria or Phoenicia, and one grid will appear, waiting for your command to open it up. From this precise moment, the visitor's Conduit and the Screen are communicating in the most direct fashion.

The grid opens up and displays three files in sequence.

The nearest description of these files would be plasmic-digital, for the lack of the proper word; each file will contain everything that had happened pertaining to that particular date or era in Alexandria or Phoenicia.

Functions of the Conduit, Miraya and retrieving data:

196

- 1-The Conduit will sort out all the available information and references (Photos, holographic projections, sounds) available on the subject. On Ashtari, everything is stored in codes.)
- 2-The Conduit selects and indexes the particular data for the part of the information the visitor is most interested in.
- 3-Then, the selected information (Complete data in sound and images) is instantly transferred to the cells of the visitor's brain.
- 4-Because Anunnaki are connected to each other and to their community via the Conduit, the data recently absorbed is sent to others who share similar interest.

This is extremely beneficial, because if the data received from the screen is difficult to understand, other members of the Anunnaki community, will automatically transmit, the explanation needed. This is quite similar to an online technical support on earth, but it is much more efficient since it functions brain-to-brain.
Worth mentioning here, that each Anunnaki community has the same kind of center for these Akashic files.
The complexity of the centers, though, is not the same. Some of the Akashic Libraries include more perplexing and complicated instruments and tools, which are not readily available to other communities.
These tools include the Monitor, which is also called Mirror, or Miraya. Each Miraya is under the direct control of a Sinhar, who serves as custodian and guardian.

- 5-The screens can expand according to the number of codes that the Anunnaki researcher is using. Seven to ten codes are normal. If a larger number of codes are opened, the screen is fragmented into seven different screens. An amazing phenomenon occurs at this moment – time and space mingle together and become unified into one great continuum. This enables the researcher to grasp all the information in a fraction of a second.
- 6-An added convenient aspect of the Akashic files is the ability of the researchers to access them in the complete

privacy of their homes or offices, since part the files can be teleported there. But since the private screen is not as complicated as the central one in the Library, no multiple screen will open up, only the original one. Yes, Anunnaki do live in homes, and contribute to their societies as we do on Earth.

- **7**-It is important to understand that the data received is not merely visual. There is much more to it than that.
- **8**-By the right side of the screen, where the global data is displayed in files, there are metallic compartments, as thin as parchment paper, which serve as a cosmic audio antennae. These compartments search for, and bring back, any sound that occurred in history, in any era, in any country, and of any magnitude of importance.
- **9**-The compilation includes all sorts of sounds, and voices of people, entities, various civilizations, and living organisms (And life-forms from the past and the future) in the entire cosmos.
- **10**-According to the Anunnaki, every single sound or voice is never lost in the universe. Of course, it may not traverse certain boundaries. For humans, if a sound was produced on earth, such a boundary is the perimeter of the solar system. Each of these antennae-compartments will probe different galaxies and star systems, listening, recording, retrieving, and playing back sounds, voices, and all sorts of frequencies.
- **11**-A combined asset of the visual and audio systems is the ability to learn languages that is afforded by the Akashic Library. This applies to any language – past, present or future, and from any part of the universe.
- **12**-The researcher can call up a shining globe of light that will swirl on the screen with enormous speed. As it rotates, the effect blends with an audio transmission that comes from the metallic compartments, and in an instant, any language will sink into the brain cells.
- **13**-On the left side of the main screen, there are several conic compartments that bring still images pertaining to certain important past events. This display informs the researcher that these particular events cannot be altered. In other words, the Anunnaki cannot go back into the past and change it.

- **14**-The Anunnaki are forbidden to change or alter the events, or even just parts or segments of the past events projected on the main screen that came from the conic compartment, if the data (Images; sounds) represents events created by the Anunnaki leaders.
- **15**-This restriction (Altering, changing or erasing past events) which is applicable everywhere on Ashtari functions as a security device.

For example, a young Anunnaki cannot visit earth sixty five thousand years ago, recreate and enter the genetic laboratory of the Anunnaki in Sumer, Arwad, Ugarit or Phoenicia, and change the DNA and the genetic formula of a human race, especially when the DNA sequence was originally created by an Anunnaki Sinhar (Leader). In other words, a young Anunnaki is not allowed to alter the Akashic Records that contain the primordial events. Alteration such as recreating a new human race in past time will never happen.

16-However, an Anunnaki leader such as Sinhar Baal Shamroot, Inanna, Ellil or Enki can go back in time and space, and change events, but cannot bring to Earth new human species created according to a new formula that contradicts or reverses the primordial prototypes created 100,000 years ago.

- **17**-However, an Anunnaki leader such as Sinhar Baal Shamroot, Inanna or Enki can go back in time and change events, but cannot bring to Earth new human species created according to their new formula and based on the primordial prototypes created 100,000 years ago. Nevertheless, they can transpose their new creation or event alteration, and transport them to another dimension, parallel to the original dimension where the event occurred.
- **18**-This safeguard means that Sinhar Inanna cannot recreate a new race on our earth by the device of sending the current living humans back in time, remolding us, and then bringing us back to the twenty first century as a new species.
- **19**-This is not allowed by the Anunnaki High Council. All she can do is recreate her own experiment in another dimension.

- **20**-Worth mentioning here, that alternation of the fabric of time and space is rigidly and constantly monitored by the Anunnaki High Council via their Miraya; the cosmic mirror and monitor of all living-forms, past, present, and future.
- **21**-The Miraya is a terrific and mind-bending tool. The Anunnaki use it to revisit time and what is beyond time, space, meta-space, and para-space, as well as creating new cosmic calendar.
- **22**-More options are available for research, and one of them is a sort of browsing. Inside the screen, there is a slit where the mind of the Anunnaki can enter as a beam. This will open the Ba'abs, or Stargates, to other worlds that the researcher is not even aware of; they appear randomly as part of the discovery or exploration.
- **23**-In each slit, there is another Akashic file that belongs to another civilization.
- **24**-Sometimes, these civilizations are more advanced than the Anunnaki themselves, where the researcher can retrieve important information. It is like going back in the future, because everything present, or to occur in the future, has already occurred in a distant past (Timetable) and needed the right time to surface and appear before the current living Anunnaki.
- **25**-There is also the aspect of simply having fun, some of which is not so ethical. Sometimes an Anunnaki will go back in time, let's say 400 C.E., choose a famous historical figure, and at the same time bring over another important person, one thousand years older, simply to see how they would interact.
- **26**-They can easily deceive these personages, since every Anunnaki is an adept at shape changing. Or they can transpose people, move them in time, and see how they will react to the new environment.
- **27**-These games are strictly forbidden, but some low class Anunnaki occasionally try it as a game. Sometimes they interfere with our daily affairs, and temporary loss of memory may be a result of that.
- **28**-Worth reminding the readers, that the Anunnaki no longer interfere in human affairs. They have left planet Earth for good, but they are coming back in 2022.

- **29**-The Miraya is constantly used by the Anunnaki on Ashatari. In addition to its function as a cosmic calendar, the Miraya serves as a galactic monitor. Watching and monitoring other extraterrestrial civilizations are two of the major concerns of the Anunnaki. For the past 10 years (In our terrestrial time), the Anunnaki have been following very closely what was/is happening on other planets and stars, and particularly the experiments of the Greys. Sinhar Ambar Anati known to us as Victoria told us a lot about this. In the Book "Anunnaki Ultimatum: End of Time" (Co-authored by Ilil Arbel and Maximillien de Lafayette), Ambar Anati described at length some of the horrible genetic experiments of the Greys as caught on the Miraya.

Note: Ambar Anati is talking to Sinhar Inannaschamra, her mother-in-law in Ashatari, about the malicious intentions of the Greys. Inannaschamra told her that the Greys constantly conduct genetic experiments on humans, and that the Anunnaki kept on watching their atrocious experiments by using the Miraya (Monitor). Here are some excerpts from the book: "What do they want from us on earth?"
"There are a few things that they want. First, they want eggs from human women and use them to create hybrids. Let's take a look at this monitor, and I'll show you how they do that. But Victoria, steel yourself. This is pretty horrible, even though I have seen even worse. You will also be able to hear, it is like a television."
The monitor blinked and buzzed, and a small white dot appeared on the screen.
It enlarged itself, moved back and forth, and settled into a window-like view of a huge room, but the view was still rather fuzzy. I heard horrendous screams and froze in my seat, these were sounds I have never heard before. After a few minutes the view cleared and I saw what seemed to be a hospital room, but it was rounded, not square. Only part of it was revealed, as it was elongated and the far edge was not visible. The walls on the side were moving back and forth, like some kind of a balloon that was being inflated and deflated periodically, with a motion that made me dizzy; they seemed sticky, even gooey. The room was full of operation tables, of which I could see perhaps forty or fifty, on which were stretched human beings, each attached to the table and unable to move, but obviously not sedated, since they were

201

screaming or moaning. Everyone was attached to long tubes, into which blood was pouring in huge quantities.

I noticed that some of the blood was turning into a filthy green color, like rotting vegetation. At the time I could not understand what that was, but later that day I found out. This blood was converted to a suitable type for some of the aliens that paid the Grays to collect it, and it was not useful in its raw condition.

People who operated these experiments were small and gray, and they had big bug eyes and pointy faces without any expression. I thought they looked more like insects than like a humanoid species. They wore no clothes, and their skin was shiny and moist, like that of an amphibian on earth. It visibly exuded beads of moisture which they did not bother to wipe away.

Each operating table had complicated machinery that was poised right on top of the person who was strapped to it.

On some of the tables, the machinery was lowered so that needles could be extracted from them automatically, and the needles reached every part of the human bodies, faces, eyes, ears, genitals, stomach. The people screamed as they saw the needles approaching them, some of them fainted. Many of the people were already dead, I could swear to that. Others were still alive but barely so, and some had arms and legs amputated from their bodies.

It was clear that once the experiment was over, every single person there will die. I don't know how I could continue to look, but somehow I managed. I looked at the ceiling of this slaughter house and saw meat hooks, on which arms and legs and even heads were hanging, like a butcher's warehouse. On the side of the tables were large glass tanks where some organs were placed, possibly hearts, livers, or lungs, all preserved in liquids.

The workers seemed to be doing their job dispassionately and without any feelings, moving around like ants and making buzzing sounds at each other as they conversed. They were entirely business-like and devoid of emotion. At least, their huge bug eyes did not convey any emotion to me, neither did their expressionless faces.

I watched until I could no longer tolerate it, and finally covered my eyes and cried out, "Why don't you stop it? Why don't you interfere?" Sinhar Inannaschamra turned the monitor off. "This event is a record from decades ago, Victoria.

It is not happening now as we look. And even though often we do interfere, we cannot police the entire universe or even the entire earth.

They know how to hide from us. And you must understand, that often the victims cooperate with their abductors."

"Why would they?"

"Basically, through mind control. The Grays have many ways to convince the victims. The Grays can enter the human mind quite easily, and they find what the abductees are feeling and thinking about various subjects. Then, they can either threaten them by various means, or persuade them by a promise of reward."

"Reward? What can they possibly offer?"

"Well, you see, they show the victims images through a monitor, just like this one. They tell them that they can send them through a gate, which is controlled by the monitor, to any number of universes, both physical and non-physical. That is where the reward come in. For example, if the abductees had originally reacted well to images of Mary or Jesus, the Grays can promise them the joy of the non-physical dimensions. They show them images of a place where Mary and Jesus reside, where all the saints or favorite prophets live, and even the abode of God. They promise the abductees that if they cooperate, they could live in this non-physical universe in perpetual happiness with their deities. Many fall for that."

"And if they resist?"

"Then they show them the non-physical alternative, which is Hell. Would you like to see some of it?"

"You can show me Hell?" I asked, amazed.

"No, there is no such thing as Hell... it's a myth that religions often exploited. But I can show you what the Grays show the abductees, pretending it is hell; they are quite devious, you know. You see, some creatures live in different dimensions, where our laws do not apply. Sometimes, they escape to other dimensions. These beings have no substance in their new dimensions, and they need some kind of bodies to function. At the same time, the Grays can tap into numerous universes, because they can control their own molecules to make them move and navigate through any dimension. Well, a cosmic trade had been developed.

The Greys supply the substance taken from human abductees, and from the blood of cattle. You must have heard of cattle mutilation, where carcasses of cows are found in the fields, entirely drained of blood? The Grays do it for their customers."

203

"How do these creatures pay the Grays?"

"By various services, and once they get their substance, they are incredibly powerful in a physical sense. The old tales of genies who can lift buildings and fly with them through the air were based on these demons; the Greys often have a use for such services. But let me show you a few of these creatures. Of course, you can only see them when they have already acquired some substance from the Grays." The monitor hummed again as Sinhar Inannaschamra turned it on. The white dot expanded into its window, which now, for some reason, was larger and took over the entire screen.

All I could see was white fog with swirls floating through it. Sometimes the fog changed from white to gray, then to white again.

I started hearing moans. Not screams, nothing that suggested the kind of physical pain I saw before, but perhaps just as horrible, since they voices where those of hopelessness, despair, and emotional anguish. Every so often I heard a sound that suggested a banshee's wail, or keen, as described in Irish folklore.

"It will take a while for someone to show up," said Sinhar Inannaschamra. "Most of them have no substance, and therefore they are invisible. Others have a shadowy substance. Then, there are the others...but you will see in a minute. Once they notice they are being watched, they will flock to the area, since they are desperate to get out. Incidentally, it was never made quite clear to me how they produce sounds without bodies, we are still trying to find out what the mechanics are, but it's not easy, because we would rather not go there in person."

"They sound horribly sad," I said.

"This is what makes it so hell-like.

In many cultures, Hell never had any fire and brimstone and tormenting devils, but rather, it was a place of acute loneliness, lack of substance, and alienation from anything that could sustain the individual from a spiritual point of view. Think of the Greek Hades, or the ancient Hebrew Sheol, before the Jews made their Hell more like the Christian one. Look, here comes the first creature. Poor thing, he is a shadow."

I saw a vaguely humanoid shape in deep gray. It seemed to have arms, which it waved in our direction. It seemed fully aware of the monitor. Then another shadow, then another, all shoving each other and waving desperately at the monitor.

Then something more substantial came into view, and I jumped back as if it could reach me. It seemed to be a severed arm. Cautiously, I came back, and then saw that the arm was attached to a shadow body. I looked at Sinhar Inannaschamra, speechless, and she said, "Yes, here you see one that managed to receive an arm. It wants to complete its body, of course, so that it can get out of this dimension and serve the Grays, but the Grays keep them waiting until they want them. In summary, the Miraya has multiple functions, and remains one of the most important inventions of the Anunnaki.

Gubada-Ari: How to find the healthiest spots and luckiest areas on earth

Question 7:
The Gubada-ri technique included this intro: "There are lines of energy spinning around the world. In this exercise, we will concentrate on the lines that are revealed by the use of the triangle.
The energy flows in currents, both negative and positive, mostly underground, traversing the globe. Those who live above the positive lines, will have good health, success, and peace of mind. Those who live above the negative lines, will have bad health. The student might ask, where do I put the triangle? How do I choose the original location? The answer is, you put the triangle wherever you are.
The student might ask, what if I change locations? The answer is, this technique is working within the dictates of the moment. Wherever you are, the triangle follows."
My questions are: How do I know I live above negative currents? What should I do to change these bad currents affecting my life? Are there bad lines everywhere in the world?

Answer to question 7:
How would you know that you live above negative currents?
You should be the one, the only one (In many instances) to know you are living above negative lines, by assessing your status quo. If you see that you are failing in many of the things you are doing, despite good planning, common sense, hard work and reasonable approach to what you do, then you should realize that something is wrong.

If your health condition is constantly deteriorating with no apparent reasons, or justified symptoms despite intensive health care, a good nutritional system, a good diet, medical attention, regular check ups, and a healthy living, then you should ask yourself why your health is deteriorating. You have here more than one red flag! Keep watching those unpleasant occurrences very closely, monitor your activities, maintain a meticulous records of what you do on a daily basis, and write down in details what you are going through in relation to dates, days and hours, and especially where usually you move around. If these mishaps accumulate at an amazing rate without a logical explanation, then use alternative means/analyses to understand the reasons, the mechanism and the continuous avalanches of disastrous events.

Coincidences do happen. But when many bad coincidences don't cease and appear on all fronts, and in all what you do, including health, then you have to do something about it. Some people consult experts in the fields, therapists, experienced consultants, and talk to others who went through similar events. If all these approaches do not work, then you have to realize that you are not in control of these events and mysterious incidents.

You will know when so many things on many fronts and in many areas are getting nasty, worse or threatening. What should you do to change these bad currents affecting your life?

There is nothing you can do to change these lines because you are not stronger than Mother Nature. Consult professionals in the field, physicians and nutrition experts as far as your health is concerned. Business planning consultants and financial advisors when it comes to your business and finances, so on.

But if nothing works, and you know you have tried everything, then one option and only one option is left: Change location, move, live or work somewhere else. But where? This is another question (You have not asked, though)! Try to the find the answer by learn and practicing the Gubada-ri technique. See if it works for you. It could work for you, because it worked for so many people I know.

My advice to you is this:

- **1**-Don't rush to change location.
- **2**-Stay where you are for a while, especially if you own the place where you live or work.

- **3**-Now that you have realized that something quite strange is constantly happening in your life, and you have no means to stop it or a way to explain it, is already a good step.

So, keep your place for a while, but move temporarily somewhere else, and see if things change to better. If they do, and all of a sudden, you start to feel much better, and you have no more problems, then you will know that you were living/working in an area infested by bad vibrations and doomed by negative currents. This should work.

The Double and the Baridu Technique

Question 8:

Regarding the Baridu technique... you said that "Once you enter your Double, you will be able to use it in so many beautiful and effective ways as:

7- A protective shield against danger,
8- An effective apparatus to protect yourself in hostile and dangerous situations,
9- A tool to develop your abilities to learn many languages, and enhance your artistic creativity"

My questions are: How a non-physical entity that does not live on Earth can protect me from physical threats?

If this is true, then the President of the United States and the Secretary of State should get rid of their bodyguards and hire a Double? It does not make sense!

Is it really possible to learn a new language just by zooming into our Double? If this is possible, why then secret agencies and espionage or counter-espionage agencies don't use this technique to teach their agents all the languages in the world?

Why they keep on buying all these foreign languages dictionaries and foreign languages learning lessons on tapes and CDs?

Answer to question 8:

Protection against threats and dangers: First of all, you have to remember that people of power, politicians, *et al*, are neither spiritual people, nor adepts of metaphysical studies. They spend more time campaigning, shaking hands, and giving speeches than developing spiritual and paranormal abilities.

So bodyguards remain a necessity. They should stay around.

207

Only those who have learned and developed esoteric Ulema techniques can use their Double as a shield. However, a novice or a sincere student who is searching for the ultimate paranormal truth, and who has revealed a high standard of spirituality and goodness will be able to use the Double, once he/she has completed the Ulema studies. At your stage, your Double is alive and well, and is fully aware of your existence, but YOU are not aware of its existence, because either you do not believe in a Double, or you have not established a rapport with your Double.

Once, a rapport has been established with your Double, your Conduit will throw an invisible protective shield around you. Is it a physical barrage?

A protective tool or a device similar to the fibreglass or a metal shield police use in riots? The answer is no.

The shield functions in so many different ways your brain cannot comprehend. However, I will try to explain to you one of the protective measures a shield uses in threatening situations.

The Ulema after years of study and practice, and following the instructions of the Book of Ramadosh, became capable of creating a sphere (Or zone) around them that resembles a halo. Some call this halo a "Bubble". The halo surrounds their physical body. In the halo, exist molecules and particles charged with high atomic and sub-atomic density (No, not nuclear devices!), i.e. energy. This energy is denser in its composition than any of the molecules and particles that physically create and constitute any physical action or movement against an Ulema's body.

Ulema's energy changes constantly and transmutes itself into higher or lower molecules/particles density, according to their surroundings and needs.

Because of the Ulema's denser atomic substance, nothing can penetrate the halo surrounding them. You have to remember, that everything in the universe is composed from molecules and particles. For instance, if you throw a punch at an Ulema, you put in your punch a certain amount of energy and physical effort. The energy and the physical effort are composed from molecules. These molecules are denser in their composition than the molecules floating around the Ulema, and thus cannot penetrate their halo and reach their bodies.

This is why people can't go through walls. Our bodies molecules need "to shrink" and "transmute" themselves into thinner vibrations, to allow us to go through walls. Secondly, the non-physical entity (Double) you have mentioned is not totally non-physical. It changes. It materializes and dematerializes.

The Double can project itself as a physical entity.

And it takes on multiple appearances ranging from holographic to multi-dimensional presences.

However, the materialistic apparition does not last very long in a three-dimensional sphere, because its bio-etcoplasma energy is consumed rapidly. Let's forget for a moment this complicated language, and explore an easier characteristic aspect of the Double, its halo, zone and protective shield. I will try to use a simple language, as much as I can. Disregard everything I have said before, and follow me now step by step.

- **a**-Your Double is extremely intelligent and alert, and it senses things around you. Things currently happening and those en route.
- **b**-Your Double knows right away if what is coming at you is safe or dangerous.
- **c**-If the Double detects a threatening situation, it sends an alert to your Conduit.
- **d**-Your Conduit receives the message from your Double. (Note: Sometimes, it is simultaneously, and/or your Open Conduit understands the situation on its own, without the help of your Double.)
- **e**-Your Conduit acts on its own and guides you instantly to a safer position. Call it whatever you want, instinct, an inner feeling, etc...it does not matter what you call it.
- **f**-At the same time, your Conduit emits vibes aimed at the source of the threat to bock it.
- **g**-At this very moment, your Open Conduit and your Double act in unison.
- **h**-In a fraction of a second, the attacker or the negative vibes aimed at you is diverted. Nothing can penetrate the halo around you. If you practice and master the Baridu technique, you will be able to block any threat.

As to your question: "Is it really possible to learn a new language just by zooming into our Double?" The answer is YES! However, what you will learn becomes a memory, a sort of a depot of knowledge not activated or accessible by your brain. This happens at the preliminary stage. Later on, when you revisit your Conduit, you will be able to tap into that depot, work mentally

209

with the language you have just learned, and practice physically by writing down on a paper the words and phraseology from that language.

There is a process to follow that allows you to remember that language and bring it out of your Conduit cell.

Daemat-Afnah

Question 9:

You said the Daemat-Afnah technique keeps us young and makes us look 37 permanently. It is difficult to understand this. I am 54, if I practice this technique for a while, would I look again 37 years old? What would happen to the face I had before? Does it come back? For how long I would stay 37?

Answer to question 9:

You have to practice the technique for at least one full year. You will not see any improvement or any result before 12 months. I will explain to you what is going to happen step by step.

- For the first 6 months. You will not notice any change on your face.
- At the end of the seventh month, you will begin to feel that some of your facial muscles are getting stronger. A strange and a new sensation you have never felt before in your whole life.
- Your face will look cleaner and firmer.
- Some of the wrinkles under your eyes will disappear. In rare instances, they would not.
- Not all the wrinkles will disappear if you stop practicing.
- At the end of 12 months, you will notice that you eyes have gained vitality. They will look sharper.
- Your eyes will glitter with a sign of good health.
- At the end of 12 months, you will notice that your face's skin is healthier, and almost 90% of your wrinkles (large and small) have diminished.
- The dermatologic results have no side effect.
- A certain incomprehensible inner strength will energize your whole body.
- After 13 months of practice, the face you had when you were 37 starts to reappear gradually. You will not believe what you are seeing.

- This change is usually accompanied by sizeable increase in physical dynamism and mental vitality.
- Your face is younger, almost 100%.
- Only your face gets younger, not your neck, body or any other part of your body.
- Your grey hair will stay grey.
- If you are bold, you will stay bold.
- You will keep your new face for a very very long time, as long as you keep a good diet, and you eat well.

*** *** ***

Important note:

- Bear in mind that the Ulema's teachings, techniques, and/or opinions should not be considered as a professional advice, prescription, or opinion at any level – therapeutic, medical, cosmetic, surgical, health wise, etc.
- They are of a purely philosophical-esoteric nature.
- This technique does not substitute for any other medical treatment.
- This technique is not dangerous or harmful.
- It could be very beneficial at many levels, even though, it is not proven scientifically.
- However, many who have practiced this technique were delighted by the results.

Bukadari Technique

Question 10:
You said: "People can also send harmful vibrations to your mind, to your body, and to the objects you touch, including tools, materials, equipments you use, such as a computer, a camera, a car, an elevator, a desk, even a can-opener." Does this mean that people's negative vibrations can screw up my computer? Do they have to be around me, or they could still do it at distance? Are you talking about sick people, malicious people or all people?

Answer to question 10:
Most certainly, people's negative vibrations can screw up your computer, and many of your electrical gadgets.
The bitter negativity of some people affects even the battery and starter of your car. You car will not start. Some people have green thumb, others have grey thumbs. Some people emanate healthy and positive vibes that bring comfort and joy to others, and some people diffuse negative vibes that affect the harmony, balance and serenity around them and around others.
You asked: "Do they have to be around me, or they could still do it at distance?" Basically, they have to be at a close proximity. If they are around you, you will feel it. But to be certain that indeed they are causing you discomfort or disturbing your tools, you must observe what is happening, see if these unusual sensations you are felt when they were around you, and the nuisances or damage to your tool are reoccurring every time they show up or are around.
Now, do not get suspicious and anxious. Coincidences happen all the time. You must remain calm but alert.
If your computer crashes, your telephone does not work anymore, or any of your electric or electronic gadgets is acting weird or stop to function, every time they show up, then you should not be in the same room with them, or you could stay if you have already learned the Bukadari technique and know how to use it. There are some bizarre situations, where and when you got hit by negatives vibes caused by your own action, and thoughts.
For instance, while you were fixing something or typing on your computer keyboard, and all of a sudden, out of the blue, you think about a person you dislike so much, because he/he caused you some troubles or hurt you in the past, and suddenly the light bulb explodes, or the computer stops to work. This could happen. Perhaps something wrong with the bulb itself, or there is faulty electrical wiring, maybe your computer was attacked by a virus and just died on you at this peculiar moment.
You will never know and understand what is causing all these strange occurrences, until:
a-You start to take notice,
b-Keep meticulous records of all these events,
c-And find the relation between what you were doing or thinking and what just happened during these particular moments.

In this case, your brain has caused those unpleasant incidents. If your Conduit is open, you will discover right away the cause and source of these strange events. If you Conduit is extremely active, negative vibes or unpleasant incidents will not occur frequently. Negative vibes are not necessarily produced by sick or malicious people. In many instances, the vibrations emanate from people who really care about you. Unfortunately, they don't know that their unhappy state of mind, fear, anxiety, dissatisfaction from their jobs, bitterness, and their negative attitude toward life are producing such negative and destructive vibes.

Be considerate, polite, and understanding.

Quietly remove yourself from their presence. Use courtesy and civility.

Arawadi Technique and the Afterlife

Question 11:
Ulema Lambrakis said: "All of us live in two separate dimensions so close to us. One we know and we call it our physical reality, the other is the adjacent dimension that surrounds our physical world." Is he talking about the after-life dimension? Can I visit this dimension? I read in a few books written by Indian gurus that life after death exists in a dimension adjacent to the one we live in. Are we talking here about the same dimension? If not, what is the difference between the two?

Answer to question 11:
The adjacent dimension that surrounds our physical world could mean many things. For example, there is a dimension which is not located in the world of the after-life, because it is accessible to living human beings who wish to visit it. They are still alive, live a normal life on Earth, and through some techniques can visit that dimension and return safe to Earth. Their visit could take on many different shapes and forms, and be done via a multitude of means. It could be psychosomatic, purely mental, visual, holographic, teleported, transposed, spiritual and purely physical.

Essentially, what Ulema Lambrakis was referring to is no more or less than the dimension or zone that exists in a parallel world. Modern quantum physics theorists wrote extensively on this subject, and most particularly on parallel dimensions, multiple universes, future worlds, world from the future and beyond. And these scientists refer to Ulema Lambrakis' dimension. So, the answer is no.

Ulema Lambrakis is not talking about the dimension of the after-life. You asked: "Can I visit this dimension? If you are asking about the after-life dimension, I don't think you want to go there yet. You go there and you will never come back. Dead people don't come back.

You told me that you have read in a few books written by Indian gurus that life after death exists in a dimension adjacent to the one we live in, and asked: "Are we talking here about the same dimension?" My answer is no. It is quite different.

As to your final question: "If not, what is the difference between the two?" is this: It would take a whole book to explain all the differences.

*** *** ***

214

The Mind, the Supersymetric Mind and the Conduit Equation

In volume one, I told you briefly about the Mind, Fikr, the Supersymetric Mind, and their relationship to the Conduit. However, I did not elaborate enough on this subject. And I do feel that additional explanation is needed, mainly because I will be talking to you about the activation of the Conduit and the levels of Iama.

The Anunnaki Ulema Conduit is a new concept to readers in the Western Hemisphere. No other book has ever explained its enigmatic mechanism and purposes.

The Conduit is a cell that contains all knowledge known to Man, on Earth and in other dimensions.

Mainstream science has yet to define its properties, and locate its perimeter in the brains. Some scholars have compared the Conduit to the "Third Eye".

When I brought this concept to the West, I stated clearly that the Conduit is a cosmic memory and a depot of all the knowledge known to human beings. Once activated, it would produce extraordinary deeds, and elevates us to the highest level of awareness, and intelligence. In this section of the book, I will explain to you how to activate your Conduit.

Who created the Supersymetric Mind?

At the time, the Anunnaki fashioned our human body, they did not install in our body a fully functional brain. They created us to serve their needs. Some early human or quasi-human species were upgraded; others remained at a bestial level, despite all the efforts of the Anunnaki gods and goddesses.

The Akkadian/Sumerian clay tablets are clear on the subject.

Note: Please refer to my book "Anunnaki Genetic Creation of the Human Races, Demons and Spirits."

*** *** ***

215

The Anunnaki's intention was to create a robust race, capable of working the fields, and executing hard physical labor and duties. Thus, an intelligent mind was not necessary.

We were created as laborers and slaves.

You might not like the idea, or even refute this argument, but if you read the Akkadian/Sumerian texts, you will find out that the early humans were intentionally created by the Anunnaki goddesses and gods to feed them, and "fill the basket", meaning, to bring them food.

According to the Ulema, the Anunnaki were not the first to experiment with and on humans.

Some 445,000 years ago, a different race called the Igigi, were the first extraterrestrials to create quasi-human specimens.

At the very beginning of their genetic experiments, the results were catastrophic.

The Igigi's creations of the first race of humans looked awful – bestial, very ugly, even frightening. This happened because the Igigi were more terrestrial explorers than geneticists, and they were more interested in certain molecules found in terrestrial water, and in various minerals on Earth, than in creating a perfectly shaped human race.

At one point in time, the Igigi were ferocious toward the early quasi-human beings, and treated them very badly, since they considered the early version of human beings on Earth as a lower working class without intelligence.

Incidentally, the Earth was extremely cold at that time, and the Igigi had to cover the human bodies with lots of hair to protect them from the elements.

It took the quasi-human race thousands of years to evolve into an early human form, and even then, they were not totally human, looking more like apes. They had a very robust body, but lacked intelligence. Some of them had bizarre skulls and facial bones, and their brain was not wired to function as an intelligent processor of data, information, and analytic comprehension.

Bear in mind, that the Igigi were highly advanced in mineralogy and minerals transmutation. The Anunnaki were geneticists and engineers with a strong appreciation for esthetics. Therefore, the Igigi created a very primitive form of living beings on Earth, exactly as we, modern humans, created very unappealing early forms and shapes of robots and related mechanical devices at the dawn of robotics.

These robotic-quasi humans were functional but not pretty to look at, and the early quasi-humans were not much more than biological machines with limited mental faculties.

In the genes, molecules and DNA of the early quasi-human race, the Igigi programmed thirteen faculties (mental functions), according to "Ilmu Al Donia". A group of early Allamah stated that the thirteen faculties were implanted in the human brain by the Anunnaki. The Akkadian texts are silent on the subject. The most important abilities were as follows:

- **a**-The ability to move;
- **b**-The ability to sense danger;
- **c**-The ability to understand by association;
- **d**-The ability to memorize;
- **e**-The ability to see forms and shapes in four colors.

These colors were:
- **1**-Bright yellow, representing gold;
- **2**-Grey, representing minerals and rocks;
- **3**-Blue, representing the atmosphere, air, and water;
- **4**-A very strong red, representing heat and blood.

Other colors such as green, purple, lilac, etc, were not visible or known to the early and primitive form of quasi-humans.

The Akkadian text on the creation:
"Once you have finished mixing the
the Apsu's fathering clay,
Imma-en and Imma-Shar will make
the fetus bigger,
after you have placed the limbs upon it."
Enki then gives additional instruction to goddess Ninmah, who is the mother goddess, and to eight Anunnaki goddesses.
He said:
"O mother, once, you are done with molding the being,
let Ninmah join together the chair of birth,
without any male semen, and then,
you give birth to mankind.
Without the sperm of males
she will give birth to their offspring,
and to the embryo of mankind.

217

And once Nammu had enlarged its shoulders,
she will make a hole in the head to put a mouth.

Note: The following line is damaged.

and then, she will wrap its body in an amnion."

Note: The tablets tell us that Enki and Ninmah got drunk, and
consequently, they created crippled beings; they were both
physically and mentally deformed. Enki then decided to create
a creature on his own. The Epic tells us that this creature
(Quasi-Human) is terribly deformed.
Ninmah says:
"The man, you created
is neither a live man,
nor a dead man,
I can not support it!"

The Akkadian clay tablets tell us that the creation of the first Man
required the participation of at least twelve Anunnaki goddesses.
They had to mix up the "fathering clay" of the Apsu, which is the
underground fresh water.
Ulema Mordachai stated that the clay the Anunnaki goddesses
have used, had very particular properties that produced life, once
joined with a woman's womb. The clay was later placed over the
fetus and fashioned into the form of man.
Once done, the Anunnaki goddesses added limbs and a mouth.
To complete the genetic creation of Man, Ninmah placed the clay
into her womb.
Nammu is the Anunnaki goddess who gave Enki the idea of
creating humankind to replace the Igigi, who worked the fields.
Enki begins to think about the creation process, and how to use
the clay and water of the abyss, to create human beings.
He told Nammu to bring Anunnaki womb-goddesses to mix the
clay and to call upon Anunnaki fashioners (Term used to refer to
Anunnaki goddesses who designed the body of the first Man) to
thicken it, so she could mold the wet clay into the shape of a
human body. Then, he instructed her to bring the limbs to life, in
the image of the gods.
She will give birth to the embryo of mankind without using the
sperm of a male. The new being shall be called Adamah.
And a creature was created.

Sumerian Tablet of the Creation of the World, Babylonia 1900-1700 B.C.

Then, the gods and goddesses decided to have a feast to celebrate their new creation, and Enki and Ninmah began to drink beer and got drunk.
Consequently, the being they created was a deformed creature. And Ninmah continued to fashion handicapped people.
Her creations were:

- **a**-A weak person who was unable to control his urine,
- **b**-A barren woman,
- **c**-A being without organs, etc.

Finally she realized that she was unable to create a perfect Man. She throws down the clay in despair. Then Enki decided to create a man by himself, but he failed, for the creature he fashioned died as soon as he was born. The Sumerian-Anunnaki goddess Nammu/"Namma" and her son Enki created multiple forms of humans, sometimes using clay, and other times using blood of warriors they slaughtered.
In the Sumerian myths, she was the primordial mother goddess, and creator of the gods. She was also called "The pure goddess", and was associated with fresh water. Nammu is the mother of the Anunnaki god Enki, and the Anunnaki goddess Ereshkigal, the goddess of the Kurnugi (The underworld).
The Akkadian/Sumerian texts describe her as "The mother who gave birth to heaven, earth, and the gods of the universe, and the mother of everything."

Excerpts from Ulema's Kira'at (Reading):
Mankind was not created by one single Sumerian god. More than one Anunnaki participated in the creation of mankind.
And contrary to common belief, the Anunnaki were not the first extraterrestrials and gods to create a human from clay.
Many other deities from different pantheons also created man from clay. For instance, Khnum "Kneph" (Meaning: To build, to unify in Egyptian) was one of the oldest Egyptian gods, who created mankind from clay on a potter's wheel. Khnum became a variation of Ptah. The Anunnaki first landed in Phoenicia, where they established their first colonies, and shortly thereafter, they created their most elaborate medical center on the Island of Arwad, which at the time was a Phoenician territory.

However, the Anunnaki ameliorated their genetic creations, and upgraded early human forms and primitive humans in their laboratories in Sumer.

The goddess Inanna, also known as Innin, and Innini.

The Sumerian texts and their translations into western languages gave more exposure to the Anunnaki of Sumer, than to the other equally powerful Anunnaki of Phoenicia and Central Africa.
The Sumerian texts include various versions of the creation of mankind by a multitude of Anunnaki gods and goddesses.

Goddess Nammu, also known as Namma, the Sumerian goddess
of Creation.
Here, she is shown in the center of the slab, stepping over a
lion, to demonstrate her supreme authority.

Some passages in the Sumerian texts refer to different creators,
as well as to multiple genetic experiments.
There is no reference to one singular genetic creation of the early
human races, or solid certainty to the fact that mankind was
genetically created by one single god. In fact, a multitude of gods
and goddesses created different types and categories of human
beings, to name a few:

- Ninlil,
- Ninhursag, quite often referred to as Ninlil,
- Marduk,
- Inanna, the Anunnaki goddess who created the first
  prototypes of Man.
- Enki,
- Imma-Shar,
- Ekimu,
- Gibbori,
- Ferohim,
- Anu,
- Aruru,
- Enlil, etc.

The Akkadian/Sumerian texts revealed to us that the early
humans did not have an intelligent brain. They were robots. But
thousands of years later (Around, 6,000 or 7,000 B.C.), the
Anunnaki reprogrammed our brain, and installed additional

mental faculties. But this addition did not include a "Conduit". Nevertheless, the new human brain was upgraded, and a Supersymetric Mind came to life.
Regardless of the level of intelligence and awareness, each one of us has, had, or will have in the future, the supersymetric mind exists as a necessary companion and guide for our physical mind. In conclusion, it is safe to argue that the Anunnaki created our Supersymetric Mind, thousands of years, after the creation of the earliest prototypes of the human species.

The Goddess Ninhursag "Lady of Birth", circa 2017-1763 B.C. Terracotta.

223

Enki as Ea.

Enki as master of the universe, and creator of the human race, stepping over a rock, symbolizing his ultimate authority over Earth.

God Enlil.

Can we improve on our Supersymetric Mind and enhance our intelligence?

Yes we can!

Our Conduit can improve on our Supersymetric Mind, and add an extra dimension to our intelligence, even develops in us an astonishing variety of extra-mental faculties, and supernatural powers. Although, opening or activating the Conduit requires guidance from the enlightened masters, the Anunnaki Ulema have provided us with some preliminary techniques to reach this goal. And I will be discussing some of these techniques in the book.

Enlil in a human form.

Levels of the Mind "Iama" and the Development of the Supersymetric Mind

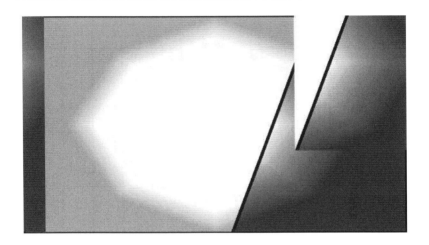

I. Definition and introduction
II. "All humans have more than one brain"
III. Where are located the different "Levels of the Mind"?
The four levels of the mind.
Level one: Tabi'a.
Level two: Irtifa.
Level three: Tanara.
Level four: Kamala.
The Triangle of Iama.
IV. How to develop your Supersymetric Mind?

I. Definition and introduction:

Iama is a term referring to the concept of the different "Levels of the Mind". According to many authors and thinkers, the human brain is a depot of all knowledge we have acquired so far.

This is not totally correct, according to the Book of Ramadosh. Ulema Oppenheimer said verbatim, as is and unedited:

"The physical brain, or in other words, the brain of a human being living here on Earth is one of the multiple layers of an infinite series of knowledge and experience acquired by a person in and outside the barrier of time and space."

Meaning that every single human being, regardless of the level of his or her intelligence and social status has an infinite number of other brains "Minds" fully operational in different and multiple spheres, times and spaces. And this includes the landscape of our Solar System, and other universes' systems. This is the cause and effect of the creation of the Universe and Man.

II. All humans have more than one brain:

Man cannot be separated from the universe, because he is a vital and primordial part of its molecules.

In other words, a person can be very intelligent and extremely important in this life, and in the same time, a total ignorant and unimportant in another life, and/or time-space that co-exists simultaneously somewhere else in the universe.

Anunnaki Ulema Oppenheimer added, "Here on Earth you might be an amateur musician, and in another world or dimension, you are conductor of a symphonic orchestra, or even equal to Mozart. In each dimension, and this includes stars and planets, you as a human being you live a separate life, and you have a totally independent brain. The enlightened masters are fully capable of synchronizing both, and even more..."

III. The four levels of the mind:

The Anunnaki Ulema told us that our mind has are four levels:
Level one: Tabi'a.
Level two: Irtifa.
Level three: Tanara.
Level four: Kamala.

Level one: Tabi'a.

It represents the human nature at its lowest point.

And it refers to dishonorable professions, deeds and humans' lowest desires/activities, such as, addiction to narcotics, prostitution, pimping, selling drugs, loan sharks, murderers, rapists, child abusers, injustice, viciousness, selfishness, and cruelty toward animals. Worth mentioning here, that similar to the ancient Roman Civil Code, the Anunnaki Ulema Nizam (Order) and Kanoun (Law or Principles) stripped prostitutes

228

from their civil rights. And considered those who dishonored their parents, neglected the elderly, mistreated animals, and caused suffering to orphans, as unworthy of mind-spirit orientation and guidance. At this level, we also find the weakness of the human body, diseases, sickness, mental anomalies, bad hygiene, and perturbed minds. These aspects of the human races prevent the opening of the Conduit. And as a result, the Astral Body, the Double, The Supersymetric Mind, and the equilibrium lines of Khateyn Tarika suffer enormously.

The enlightened masters believe that all humans are born materialistic, violent, and immoral. Few escape the chain of cause and effect of the Anunnaki's fashioning, design, and programming of mankind's nature, which they call Tabi'a.

At that level, the human mind is deteriorated, and the human spirit resembles a stagnant pond, where bacteria spread, and insects breed. The masters compared the people of level one, to the trapped beings/entities in Marash Mawta (The Afterlife Doomed Zone).

The masters argued that the Taba'yim (People of the Tabi'a level) are the Malou-niim, meaning the damned. And they are Malou-niim, because their Tabi'a (Nature) is permanently damaged. Nothing can be done for these people. However, the masters recommend that we treat them –at distance– with affection and dignity, and in the same token, to avoid interacting with them. They are troubled, and will create lots of troubles and damages to others.

Level two: Irtifa.
Irtifa means ascension, and liberation in Ana'kh and Ulemite. It is a good level of the mind, because it allows us to understand what is right and what is wrong. It is a level, where the Irtifa-iim (People of the Irtifa level) progress and evolve mentally, intellectually and spiritually, and consequently, they begin to learn how to prevent danger and threatening situations from happening, how to read mind, how to become fluent in many languages in a matter of a few weeks, how to read the Aura, how to accomplish multiple tasks in no time, how to reverse or halt bad luck, so on.

Because, they are already members of the Ulema's Jamiya (Society, circle), their mind will elevate itself to a higher level of awareness, and eventually the Irtifa-iim will liberate themselves from all the negative influences of Tabi'a, and ascend to Tanara.

Time needed to reach this level: Two years of study under the wings of the Anunnaki Ulema.

Level three: Tanara.
This level represents awareness, total development of supernatural powers, and the first stage of enlightenment.
Through their perfectly developed mind, the Tana-riim (People of the third level) keep their Chakra radiant and healthy, their vision clear and alert, and their mind-body synchronization in an excellent shape. Using the extraordinary powers of their mind, the Tana-riim can materialize and dematerialize, enter parallel dimensions, manifest themselves physically and holographically, and tap into the Miraya and the vast depot of knowledge and awareness of the collective mind of the Kami-liim. Time needed to reach this level: Ten years of study under the wings of the Anunnaki Ulema.

Level four: Kamala.
This level represents enlightenment, a perfect harmony with the Micro and the Macro, and the mastery of supernatural powers. It is the final stage of complete awareness, and unification/unity with the ultimate state of Oneness.
Kamala means perfection, in Ana'kh and Ulemite. At this level, the mind is free, perfectly developed, and transcends the frontier of time and space. The Kami-liim (People of the fourth level) can accomplish extraordinary deeds, incomprehensible to the human mind.
For instance, they never age physically, they are immune to illnesses and diseases, they teleport themselves in a blink of an eye, they materialize and dematerialize, bend time, reverse time, bend space, reverse space, enter multiple dimensions, and foresee the future, because they are already there.
Time needed to reach this level: Unknown.

*** *** ***

Level four: Kamala.
Enlightenment
Perfection
Supernatural Powers

Level three: Tanara.
Awareness
Supernatural Powers

Level two: Irtifa.
Ascension
Liberation

Level one: Tabi'a.
Human nature
Weaknesses
Attachment to materialistic values

The Triangle of Iama.

IV. How to develop your Supersymetric Mind.

I. Introduction:
According to Anunnaki Ulema Al-Sadik, and Master Mordachai ben Zvi, there are several ways and means to develop our Supersymetric Mind. The development or more precisely the awakening techniques of the Supersymetric Mind, called Tanwiir Ilmu, requires:
- Mental discipline;
- Introspection;
- Meditation;
- Observance of a very specific diet;
- Specific mental exercises;
- Visualization techniques;
- Mind projection;
- Mind transmission, and above all,
- Compliance with the rules of Nizam and Kanoun.

I know, it is getting very complicated. It would take 4 volumes to describe and explain to you all these requirements.
Besides, you would not fully benefit from the narrative and rhetoric explanation, if you are not a member of the Jamiya. However, I can introduce you to a technique that it is widely used by adepts, and Anunnaki Ulema's students.
This technique is called Nizraat Takaroob. It is easy to follow, challenging, and fun. Basically and essentially, Nizraat Takaroob invites your mind to think out of the box, and stimulates a part of your brains (Mind) you never knew existed.
Why?
Because it is not a physical zone in your brain. You can't touch it. You can't locate it. You can't measure it. You can't photograph it. But it is there.
This part or zone of your Mind was created some 6,000 or 7,000 years ago, when the Anunnaki upgraded and reprogrammed our brains. Forty years ago or so, DNA was a quasi-scientific quest, not a reality. The same thing applies today to the Supersymetric Mind. No doubt, in the very near future, you will read lots of scientific papers on this subject. On the following pages, you will observe various illustrations that demonstrate how Nizraat Takaroob works.

II. How to use the Nizraat Takaroob technique:
Follow these instructions.

Illustration #1:
   Step #1. You start concentrating on this screen (Grid). And try to identify the two different positions of the triangles. See next page.

Illustration of the screen (Grid).

Identifying the two positions of the triangles:

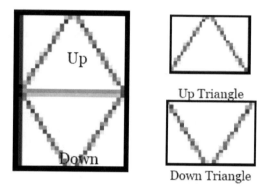

Up Triangle

Down Triangle

Step #2. Look for more triangles. And keep identifying more "Up Triangles", and "Down Triangles".
Spend approximately 2 minutes on this exercise. This will anchor you into the grid. Do not ask why, just do it.

Step #3. Now, try to identify the "Double Triangles"; one Up, and one Down. Spend approximately 2 minutes on this exercise.

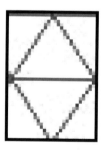

Illustration of a "Double Triangle".

Nizraat Takaroob Technique
Illustration #1

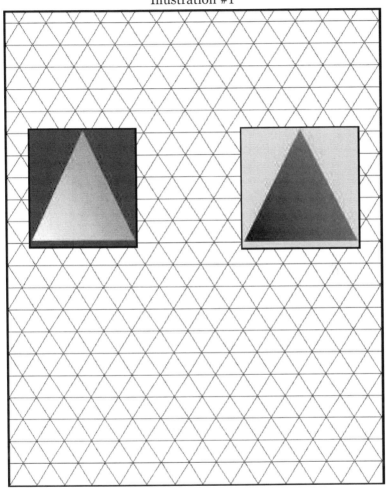

Write on this page how many "Up Triangles", "Down Triangles", and "Double Triangles", you have identified so far.
Example:
20 Up:_____

15 Down:_____

10 Double:_____

You write here:

Up:_____

Down:_____

Double:_____

***   ***   ***

236

Step #4: Go back to page 235. Concentrate on the left triangle (see below) for approximately 5 seconds.

Left triangle

Step #5: Concentrate on the right triangle (see below) for approximately 5 seconds.

Right triangle

Step #6: Now, look at the right triangle and the left triangle simultaneously (at the same time).

237

Step #7: Tell you mind that you want to bring the right triangle closer to the left triangle.

Step #8: You can do that if you concentrate on the very top of the right triangle for ten minutes. Focus on this part of the triangle. See below:

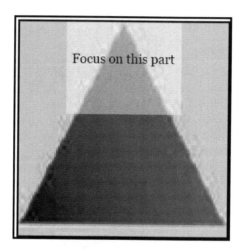

Step #9: Look at illustration #2, on page 239. You should get the result, as seen on page 239. Mind you, if you succeed, what you see is not a hallucination, but a Mental Transposition of an object, from one place to another.

With practice, patience, and perseverance, you will succeed. Do not underestimate the power of your mind.

Once this step is accomplished successfully, your Supersymetric Mind will be partially activated. Expect to fail in your first and second attempts. Nothing wrong with that. You are entering an unchartered zone of the mind. But eventually, you will Succeed!

Illustration # 2

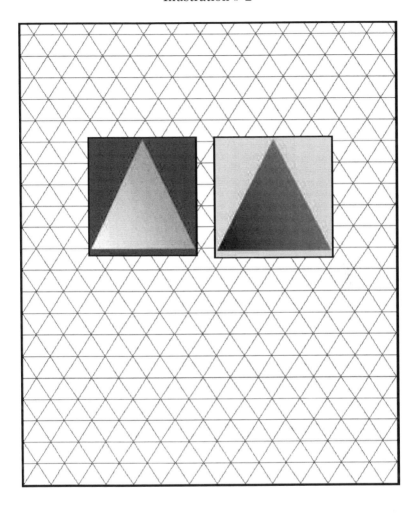

Additional instruction:
If you have failed more than 3 times, do this:

a-Tell your mind that the top of the triangle (Square in shade) is much lighter in weight than the base of triangle.
b-Focus on the top of the triangle for 5 minutes or so.
c-Command the top of the triangle to lift up and separate itself from the whole triangle. Keep repeating this command mentally for 2 minutes.
d-You are going to be amazed by the result of your deep concentration. The top will separate itself from the whole triangle, and will come closer to the left triangle. It is going to happen. No doubt about it.
e-As soon as the top is close to the left triangle, the whole triangle will shift itself toward the left triangle. See illustration on page 239.

Step #10: Mentally command the right triangle to merge with the left triangle. See illustration on page 241. On page 242, I will explain to you how you can do it.

*** *** ***

Illustration # 3

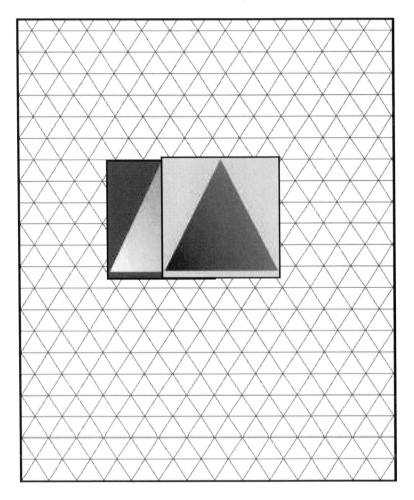

Instruction for step #10:

a- Look one more time at the illustration #3 on page 241.
This is how the 2 triangles merge.

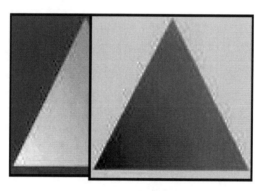

Merging of the 2 triangles.

b- Although, you are still using your "regular" mind, and no Supersymetric Mind has yet manifested itself, do not be concerned with this. Don't tell yourself, well, I am not using this Symetric thing, where is it? It is only a mind game.
Don't ever say that. Once you are fully anchored into the grid, and your mind starts to get busy with the right triangle, the left triangle, the Up triangle, the Down triangle, moving one triangle closer to another one, once all these activities are progressing, and while you are still focusing (Intensely) on all these mental exercises, your Supersymetric Mind will kick off, out of the blue. It will take over. Your "regular" mind will be pushed aside temporarily, your mental visualization will increase considerably, and suddenly your Supersymetric mind begins to guide you in your experiment/exercise.
How this is done? You will find out, later, and on your own, and no further explanation is needed.
Please, keep telling yourself: "I can do it! I can do it! I can do it!" You have to believe in yourself, and in the power of your mind. Don't give up too fast and too easy.

All the students of the Anunnaki Ulema practiced the Nizraat Takaroob, and all succeeded in activating their Supersymetric Mind. Practice makes perfect!
Esoteric studies and mental development are not easy to understand, simply because there is no physical and realistic explanation that could make you understand what is happening here. If others have succeeded in these exercises, why shouldn't you join the club?

c- If the right triangle is not getting closer to the left triangle, or not close enough, close your eyes for 5 seconds, and direct your attention to the base of the left triangle.

d- Focus on the lower base of the left triangle. See illustration below:

Base of the triangle

e-And now, fast, and back and forth, and without stopping, move your eyes from the base of the left triangle to the top of the right triangle, and vice versa...Don't STOP!! Keep doing this for 10 seconds, and Voila! Both triangles are merging now almost perfectly! It wouldn't take more than 9 seconds!
You did it. Congratulations!!
See illustration #4 on page 243.

See illustration #4 on page 243.

***   ***   ***

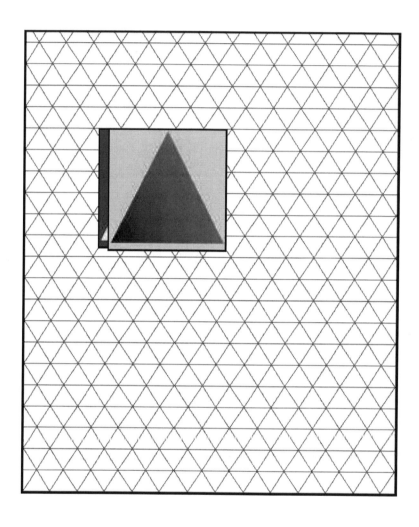

Illustration # 4

Step #11: Look at the illustration #5 on page 246.
Now you are going to reverse the whole process. Meaning, you are going to do just the opposite. I will explain:

Look at these 2 triangles that we took from illustration #5.

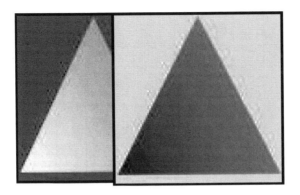

2 triangles taken from illustration #5.

By now, you have partially activated your Supersymetric Mind. Your "regular" mind is dormant, and that's wonderful. Reversing the whole process, and pushing aside the right triangle is a piece of cake. Why? Because your very powerful Supersymetric Mind is in charge now. It is going to require a minimal effort and a very short time to accomplish this.

Step #12: Tell your Supersymetric Mind to remove the right triangle from the space it currently occupies in the left triangle. You do not have to do anything else. No more concentration on a triangle base, or on the top of a triangle.
Your Supersymetric Mind knows what to do. It will follow your command. And instantly, the right triangle is separated from the left triangle. See illustration # 6, on page 247.

*** *** ***

Illustration # 5

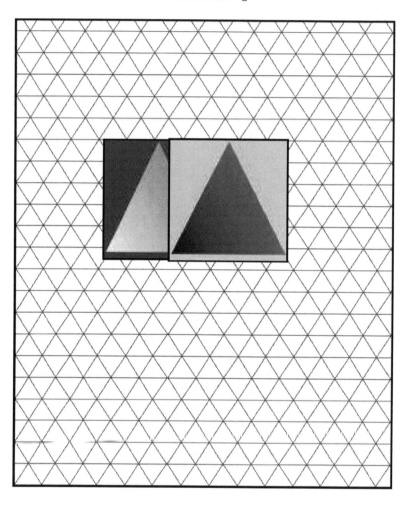

Illustration # 6

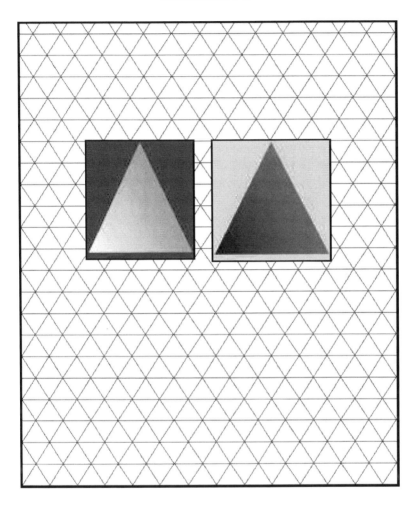

Step #13: Ask your Supersymetric Mind to move the left triangle closer to the right triangle, and merge partially with it. See illustration #7, on page 249.

Step #14: Ask your Supersymetric Mind to totally merge the left triangle with the right triangle. I mean almost totally. See illustration #8, on page 250.

Step #15: Final exercise:
Ask your Supersymetric Mind to separate both triangles and bring them to their initial position on the grid. See illustration #9, on page 251.

You are done!
Congratulations!

*** *** ***

Illustration # 7

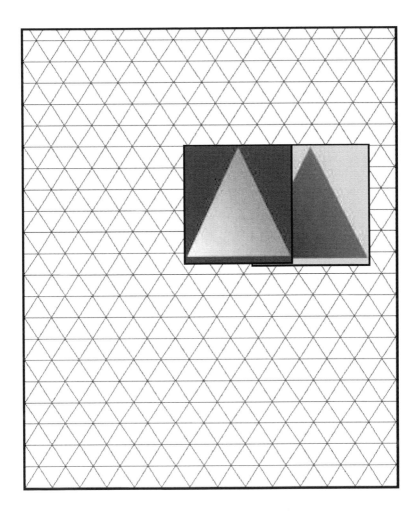

Illustration # 8

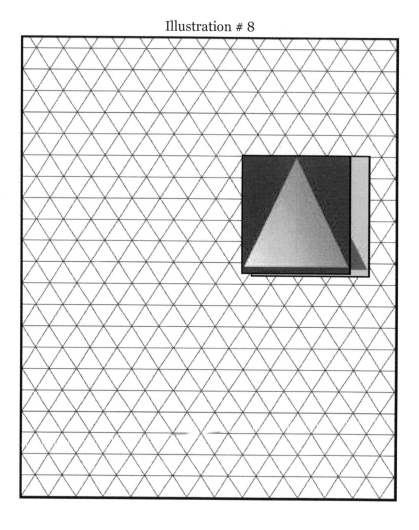

Nizraat Takaroob Technique
Illustration #9

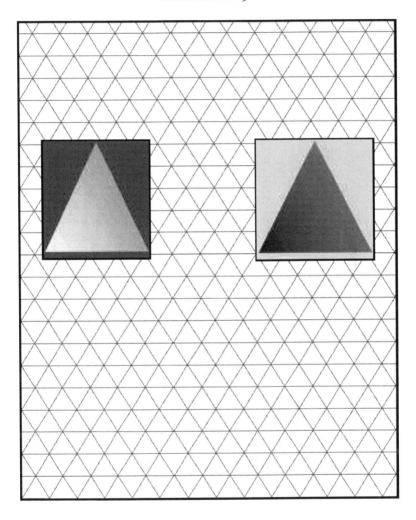

The benefits from mastering the Nizraat Takaroob technique

What have we accomplished by mastering the Nizraat Takaroob technique?

Why this mental exercise is necessary?

How can we benefit from it?

Well, you have to do something to trigger the Supersymetric Mind. In order to do so, you must transpose your "regular" mind to Ira'ha, which means a state of neutrality. As long as your "regular" (Normal) mind is preoccupied with other things, significant or not, it can't liberate itself from those things, and reach a higher level of awareness. Meditation is always useful, but in this context, it would not help to partially activate the Supersymetric Mind.

The Nizraat Takaroob technique opens the Ma bira-rach, which is the etheric image of your brain (Mind). Once the Ma bira-rach, becomes accessible, other images will follow, and a wider mental perception expands. The expansion of a wider mental perception frees your "regular" mind, and allows it to receive an avalanche of visions, messages, and ideas, which are both the physical and etheric substance of your brains (Mind). In other words, you are retrieving, scanning, and storing all sorts of new ideas, and thoughts, which will enrich your learning experience.

In addition, the expansion of a wider mental perception superposes the Araya (Net of the mind) of your physical mind and the Araya of your Supersymetric Mind (Your other mind that exists as a bulk of separate particles in an etheric substance.)

And when this happens, you will have instant access to an amazingly vast depot of knowledge and information stored in a cosmic library.

You "regular" mind can't reach this library, because it resides in the realm of the Supersymetric Mind.

In addition to moving one triangle from one place to another one, (Which could seem silly to some!) your mind has learned now how to switch on and off an ordinary mind, and listen to frequencies, waves, and vibrations that contain extraordinary information and knowledge.

This would enhance your imagination, creativity, productivity, and eliminate physical and mental obstacles blocking many of your projects, endeavors, and pioneering work. Nizraat Takaroob adds an extra dimension of knowledge, information, and awareness to your "regular" Mind. Knowledge is power.

Who has power succeeds. Information strengthens your position, and allows you to consider and evaluate all the possibilities, even foresee the outcome and consequences of your decisions. And awareness makes you alert, keeps you in harmonious synchronization with your environment, and what is going on around you.

Once, you have mastered the Nizraat Takaroob technique, you will be able to apply it pragmatically in all your endeavors, including decision making, business transactions, investment, communications, and rapports with others.

But do not forget to keep in yor heart, a warm place for the needy, and especially those who need help, and cannot return the favor. Remember, each time you give from your heart, you grow one inch taller, and the sky is the limit.

*** *** ***

The Conduit

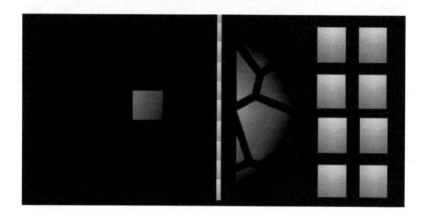

So, where is it?
Does it increase or decrease?
What causes the zone to shrink or extend?
VI. Possessed by the Spirits
Is this typical spirits possession of the human body?
VII. People entering your zone
Terminology
VIII. What is Atmashabah?
Entities and spirits entering your zone
Entering other people's zone
IX. Technique for cleansing and strengthening your Khateyn
Tarika
How to use it?
Time and place
Preparation
The process

I. Introduction:

In many of my books, I wrote ad infinitum about the Conduit, and the Supersymetric Mind. Yet, for some reasons, numerous readers could not grasp their essence and understand their meaning.

Almost in each book I wrote about the esoteric and metaphysical aspect surrounding the Anunnaki and the Anunnaki Ulema, a generous portion on the subject of the Conduit and the power of the Supersymetric Mind was given, and a multitude of pertinent cases were discussed.

I do not wish to repeat myself ad nauseam, in this current work, for those who hate my guts have so rightfully criticized me for doing so in the past. Others argued that the subject of the Conduit and the Supersymetric Mind was indeed fully explored in several passages in my previous books, but since these books are pricey, they could not afford to buy every single one that discussed these topics.

I do agree with them, first, because it would cost a small fortune to buy all these books, and second, those passages were scattered here and there -as necessity required- and thus, they were either hard to find, or quite possibly lost in the immensity of the published work.

255

But since, the subject of the Conduit and the Supersymetric Mind is still not clear to many, revisiting previous studies and writings on these two subjects becomes a necessity. Of course, I will not fall prey to repetitions; however, I will reproduce herewith what it is deemed essential for comprehending and assimilating –and once for good – what a Conduit is, and how a Supersymetric Mind functions.

II. Definition:

The Conduit is an infinitesimally small cell in our brain, not yet detected and/or acknowledged by mainstream science.

We have learned about it from the enlightened masters, and the illuminated teachers, members of the Anunnaki Ulema Jami'ya (Circle, society).

It was first mentioned in:

- a-Anunnaki Ulema's kira'at (Anunnaki Ulema's readings, lectures);
- b-Dirasaat Alfikr (Anunnaki Ulema's study or science of the mind);
- c-The manuscript/book of Ramadosh;
- d-The manuscript Kitabu Ilmu Aldonia (The book of the Knowledge of the world/universe).
- e-The scrolls of Kanoun Alhayaat wa Nizamou Alkawn (The laws or principles of life and order of the universe).

All these manuscripts were written in Ana'kh, Rouhaniyaat and pre-Islamic archaic Arabic. Some were translated into Farsi, Urdu, and Akkadian. Worth mentioning here, that a few passages from the Anunnaki Ulema's kira'at, and the Book of Ramadosh, were found in Ugaritic and Phoenician texts.

As you already know, we were genetically fashioned and created by the Anunnaki, some 65,000 years ago. At the time they created us, our physical body was deformed and underdeveloped, but much later, and after numerous genetic manipulations by the Anunnaki gods and goddesses, the human body became robust and exceptionally strong.

But one thing was missing: Intelligence. In other words, our mind was not fully operational, and the brain as a primordial motor for the body was stagnant.

Aruru, Namu, and other Anunnaki geneticists became fond of the human race, and decided to install in our brain a sequence of

256

mental faculties. However, the "Conduit" was not one of the brain's cells, the Anunnaki developed.

Thousands of years later, the "Conduit" became fully operational in the brain of the Anunnaki's remnants, who were partially humans and partially aliens or extraterrestrials.

The Anunnaki Ulema are the offspring of this hybrid race. As such, their "Conduit" became fully active.

According to Master Mordachai ben Zvi, by 2022, "many humans will have the opportunity to globally activate their Conduit."

The Conduit could be described as a vast depot of knowledge acquired in this dimension, from other dimensions, parallel, adjacent or beyond the known universe, from a physical sphere of time and space, as well as from a non-linear time-space.

Simply put, the Conduit is a time-space sponge that retains everything that touches on the surface of experience, memory, learning, emotions, intelligence, and creativity. And this surface is not limited by physical boundaries.

It transcends time and space.

The Anunnaki Ulema taught us that the Conduit links us to multiple spheres of existences, zones and physical-mental circumstances we are not familiar with, such as, to name a few:

1-The Miraya:
The Anunnaki's Miraya contains, stores and reflects all the knowledge, sounds, ideas, events, thoughts, past, present and future that exist in the universe. However, they do agree with the notion that the Miraya could be substituted with holographic screens. In fact, the Ulema were the first to talk and teach about spatial holography, holography screen, and Collective Mind, sometimes called the "Anunnaki Collective Depot of Knowledge" shared by all the Anunnaki communities' members.

The Anunnaki Ulema teach that human life is neither a restricted part of the divine creation, nor the creation itself. Thus, it is not limited by time, space, and the frontiers of a divine matrix.

2-The Double,
3-The Astral Body.
4-The Jaba.
5-The Fikr.
6-Khateyn Tarika.

Those who study under the wings of the Anunnaki Ulema will, soon or later, learn how to activate their Conduit. It takes years of study, meditation, fasting, mind-transmission, and a rigid spiritual-mental discipline. However, some of us, could partially open the Conduit, if we practice the Anunnaki Ulema Tarkiz (Concentration/Meditation exercises), and learn some of the state of Oneness techniques, I have described in this book.

An open (Active) Conduit produces or facilitates extraordinary phenomena and deeds, such as, to name a few:

- a-Telepathy;
- b-Reading mind;
- c-Sensing danger and preventing threatening situations from happening;
- d-Undertaking and completing multiple tasks in no time. You will be able to finish several projects simulteanously, which in ordinary cases, would require weeks, if not months;
- e-The healing touch;
- f-Learning so many languages, effortlessly and with a mind-bending speed.
- g-Foreseeing future events;
- h-Telemetry. You touch any object and right away you know its origin;
- i-Entering another dimension, whether physically or mentally;
- j-Moving objects at distance;
- k-Neutralizing bad (Negative) vibes, and malicious (Vicious) thoughts/intentions aimed at you, and at your Katheyn Tarlka zone;
- l-Teleportation, so on.

Haridu "Haridu-ilmu"

Haridu is the interpretation of messages sent to the Conduit in an Anunnaki's or a human's brain cell. Also, it applies to missing or misinterpreting a message by the Conduit.

On this, Ulema Rabbi Mordechai said verbatim:

- "First of all, you have to remember that your mind (Your brain) has nothing to do with your Conduit. Even though, your brain is functioning wonderfully and you

258

are doing great things in your life, not all the cells in your brain have been used.

- There are so many regions in our brain that have not been explored yet by science.
- In those many unexplored regions of the brain, are so many cells yet to be discovered, located and localized. And above all, we need to learn how they function.
- In that mysterious undiscovered region of the brain, the Conduit exists. It could be in the right or left side of your brain, or just adjacent to line dividing the two parts.
- In the Conduit, there are so many cells, each one with a very defined and particular extraordinary faculty/power, that needs to be activated.
- For instance, one cell triggers the faculty of reading others' thoughts, another cell (Or cells) is responsible for the faculty of teleportation, so on.
- If those cells are not activated, you will not be able to do all those wonderful things.
- So, you have to consider the Conduit as a bank where so many cells are deposited. And there are hundreds of thousands of cells deposited in the Conduit.
- Each cell has a precise function and an invisible location.
- This means that the Conduit can do so many things, if cells are activated. It would be impossible in one lifespan to develop and activate all the cells.
- Three or four fully activated cells is more than enough. With four activated cells you can do four great miracles by earth's standards.
- But for the cell to produce this extraordinary power, the cell must be able first to understand what you want to do.
- For instance, you cannot tell or command your cell "go ahead and make me fly or let me learn a new language in one hour."
- You should first learn how to send your command to your cell. There is a technique for this.
- Your Ulema teacher knows how to put you on the right track.
- Let's assume you have sent a message (A thought, a wish) to your cell. What's next?

259

- Well, the message enters your Conduit. Your conduit acting as a supervisor, and as the main receiver reads your message and directs your message to the appropriate cell.
- Your Conduit knows which cell is activated and designed to comply with your request.
- Instantly, the cell receives the Conduit transfer (Meaning your message.)
- Then what?
- The cell reads your message.
- If your message was sent correctly, then the cell will accept it and give it a code. So, if in the future you ask again your Conduit to do the same thing you have asked in the past, the cell will execute your request in a fraction of a second.
- In other words, each request is coded, and stored in your cell.
- Only coded messages are stored in your Conduit.
- How would you know if you have or have not sent a message correctly to your Conduit? You will know right away.
- It is very simple. If you have not been trained, you wouldn't know where and how to start in the first place.
- This is the reason why your Conduit did not catch your message(s).
- You asked "Does this mean that my Conduit is not receiving clear messages from me? And the answer is yes!
- Your Conduit received something, a thought, a feeling, a wish, a request, call it whatever you want, but your message was not clear to your Conduit, because you did not send your message according to the rules.
- What are these rules?
- They are explained below. But continue to read this first.
- And then you asked: "And how can I send clear messages my Conduit can catch and understand?
- You have to use the "Transmission of Mind" technique. Practice this technique before you send messages to your Conduit. For example, in the past, the SOS (Morse Code) was used by ships, planes, military troops and others.

- The person who has sent the message (Morse) knew the Code; he/she knew how to tap it.
- Each word had a code…one dot, two dots, three dots, one dash, two dashes, three dashes, one dit, two dits, one space, two spaces, three spaces, etc.
- There is a sequence of pulses and marks. And the person who received the message knew what these dots, and dashes meant.
- This is how and why he/she was able to read the message or decipher it, if it was a secret message.
- Your Conduit works exactly in the same way.
- Your Ulema teacher will tell you exactly what dots and sequences to use.
- If your Conduit is hundred percent awake, meaning Open (After training completion), the Conduit will immediately interpret/translate and understand your dots, dashes and sequences.
- Consider those dashes and dots a "Password", a log-in information, a key to open the contact with your Conduit, just like the password you use to open your computer or have access to some websites.
- In the Book of Ramadosh, you will find several passages referring to the brain waves and mind frequencies, and some techniques used to direct thoughts and mind energies.
- Your Conduit has its own mode. As long as your Conduit is not activated, it remains free of your control. Once your Conduit is activated, you become the stimulus and the manager of your Conduit.
- The Conduit works partially when it is not activated.
- And partially means reacting by not acting.
- The Conduit functions all the time regardless of your state of awareness, enlightenment or readiness. But it will not give you data and information.
- Everything the Conduit finds is instantly deposited in its compound.
- You will not find what's in there, until the Conduit is fully activated.
- Consider it for now as a depot of knowledge; a sort of a personal bank account where your daily balance is

constantly increasing, however, you are not allowed to have access to your bank account.

- So, nothing is lost.
- Your Conduit collects and stores information all the time, and from various sources, times, and spheres.

Jaba:
In Ana'kh, the word Jaba means many things. For example:
- **a**-The "Net Jaba" is a time-space pocket.
- **b**-The "Jaba-Garidu" is related to the "Conduit" cell, and adjacent cells in the brain.
- **c**-The "Jaba-Abru" is related to time management, using the power of mind to achieve multiple and lengthy tasks simultaneously.

Note: Please refer to the book "The Book of Ramadosh", latest edition, 2010, where you will find an in-depth study of the subject.

Fik'r "Fik-R'r", "Fik.Ra.Sa":
The ability of reading others' thoughts. The esoteric Arabic word "Firasa" is derived from Fik.Ra.Sa. It means in Arabic the ability to read thoughts, to understand the psyche of a person just by looking at him/her. The Ulema used Fik'r to read the mind, learn about the intentions of others, and assess the level of intelligence of people.

The soul is an invention of early humans who needed to believe in a next life. It was through the soul that mortals could and would hope to continue to live after death. Soul as an element or a substance does not exist anywhere inside the human body.

Instead, there is a non-physical substance called "Fik'r" that makes the brain function, and it is the brain that keeps the body working, not the soul.

The "Fik'r" was the primordial element used by the Anunnaki at the time they created the final form of the human race. Fik'r was not used in the early seven prototypes of the creation of mankind according to the Sumerian texts. The "Fik'r", although it is the primordial source of life for our physical body, it is not to be considered as DNA, because DNA is a part of "Fik'r"; DNA is the physical description of our genes, a sort of a series of formulas, numbers and sequences of what there in our body, the data and history of our genes, genetic origin, ethnicity, race, so on. Thus

262

Fik'r includes DNA. The Ulema said: "Consider Fik'r as a cosmic-sub-atomic-intellectual-extraterrestrial (Meaning non-physical, non-earthly) depot of all what it constituted, constitutes and shall continue to constitute everything about you. And it is infinitesimally small.

However, it can expand to an imaginable dimension, size and proportions. It stays alive and continues to grow after we pass away if it is still linked to the origin of its creation, in our case the Anunnaki. The Fik'r is linked to the Anunnaki our creators through a "Conduit" found in the cells of the brain. For now, consider Fik'r as a small molecule, a bubble. After death, this bubble leaves the body. In fact, the body dies as soon as the bubble leaves the body.

The body dies because the bubble leaves the body. Immediately, with one tenth of one million of a second, the molecule or the bubble frees itself from any and everything physical, including the atmosphere, the air, and the light; absolutely everything we can measure, and everything related to earth, including its orbit.

The molecule does not go before St. Paul, St. Peter or God to stand judgment and await the decision of god -whether you have to go to heaven or hell– because there is no hell and there is no heaven the way we understand hell and heaven.

So it does not matter whether you are a Muslim, a Christian, a Jew, a Buddhist or a believer in any other religion.

The molecule (Bubble) enters the original blueprint of "YOU"; meaning the first copy, the first sketch, the first formula that created you. Humans came from a blueprint. Every human being has a double. Your double is a copy stored in the "Rouh-Plasma"; a compartment under the control of the Anunnaki on Nibiru and can be transported to another star, if Nibiru (Ne.Be.Ru-Ashtari) ceases to exist. And this double is immortal.

In this context, human is immortal, because its double never dies. Once the molecule re-enters your original copy (Which is the original You), you come back to life with all your faculties, including your memory, but without physical, emotional and sensorial properties (The properties you had on earth), because they are not perfect."

Ulema Sadik said: "At that time, and only at that time, you will decide whether to stay in your double or go somewhere else...the universe is yours. If your past life on earth accumulated enough good deeds such as charity, generosity, compassion, forgiveness, goodness, mercy, love for animals, respect for nature, gratitude, fairness, honesty, loyalty...then your double will have all the wonderful opportunities and reasons to decide and select what shape, format, condition you will be in, and where you will continue to live."

In other words, you will have everything, absolutely everything and you can have any shape you want including a brand new corporal form. You will be able to visit the whole universe and live for ever, as a mind, as an indestructible presence, and also as a non-physical, non-earthly body, but you can still re-manifest yourself in any physical body you wish to choose.

Worth mentioning here, that the molecule, (So-called soul in terrestrial term) enters a mew dimension by shooting itself into space and passing through the "Baab", a sort of a celestial star-gate or entrance.

If misguided, your molecule (So-called your soul) will be lost for ever in the infinity of time and space and what there is between, until reconnected to your prototype via the "Miraya".

Is the afterlife a physical world? According to the Anunnaki Ulema: "No and yes. Because life after death unites time and space and everything that it constitutes space and time.

It means extending to, and encompassing everything in the universe, and everything you saw, knew, felt, liked and disliked. Everything you have experienced on earth exists in other dimensions, and there are lots of them. Everything you saw on earth has its duplicate in another dimension. Even your past, present and future on earth have another past, another present and another future in other worlds and other dimensions.

And if you are lucky and alert, you can create more pasts, more presents and more futures, and continue to live in new wonderful worlds and dimensions; this happens after you die.

Anunnaki and some of their messengers and remnants on earth can do that. The physical aspect of the afterlife can be recreated the way you want it by using your Fik'r. Yes, you can return to earth as a visitor, and see all the shows and musicals on Broadway or hang out on Les Champs-Elysées. You can also talk to many people who died if you can find their double in the afterlife.

You can also enjoy the presence of your pets (Dead or alive), and continue to read a book you didn't finish while still alive on earth. What you currently see on earth is a replica of what there is beyond earth and beyond death.

The afterlife is also non physical, because it has different properties, density and ways of life."

Anunnaki Ulema W. Lin said: "Through Fik'r, a person can enter higher dimensions. It is of a major importance to train your Fik'r. "Transmission of the mind" training sessions can develop extra-sensorial faculties and open your "inner eye" commonly referred to as the Third Eye..."

The Fik'r, although it is the primordial source of life for our physical body, it is not to be considered as DNA, because DNA is a part of Fik'r; DNA is the physical description of our genes, a sort of a series of formulas, numbers and sequences of what there is in our body, the data and history of our genes, genetic origin, ethnicity, race, so on.

The Fik'r contains the DNA and all its genetic data.

Fikrama "Fikr-Rama":
Name of the human brain's sixth wave, unknown yet to science.
It is related to An-zalubirach, also known as Tarkiz; a mental training that develops a supernatural power. To fully understand what Kikrama "Fikr-Rama" means, we must first comprehend what An-zalubirach is, and how it works.

An-zalubirach is an Ana'kh/Ulemite term meaning the following:

- **a**-Collecting thoughts, receiving and sending multiple mental images via brain wave synchronization, to improve mental and physical health;
- **b**-Using mental energy to move or teleport things.

This is one of the phases and practices of Tarkiz.
Tarkiz means deep mental or intellectual concentration that produces telekinesis and teleportation phenomena. Ulema's students learn this technique in various forms.
Basically it works like this:

- **a**-The students use their Conduit (Which is located in the brain's cells) to control the waves of their brains (First level of learning).
- **b**-The students concentrate on an object hidden behind a screen or a divider made from thin rice paper. (Second level of learning)

By synchronizing the frequency of their Conduit and an absolute state of introspection, the students attempt to move the hidden object from one place to another without even touching it.

265

In a more advanced stage, the students attempt to alter the properties of the object by lowering or increasing the frequencies and vibrations of the object itself. The brain is constantly producing different types of frequencies, waves, and vibrations, and transmitting various messages based on our mental activity, feelings, thoughts, and state of consciousness or mind.

Thus, the brain waves are divided in four states or categories called:

1-Beta
2-Alpha
3-Theta
4-Delta

In addition to Betha, Alpha, Theta, and Delta, the Anunnaki Ulema developed a sixth wave called Fikr-Rama. It is neither measurable nor detectable, because it does not emanate from the physical brain. It is triggered by the Conduit situated in the brain's cells. No science on earth can direct us to the exact position of the Conduit.

Let me explain this process:
- 1-Through the mechanism of the Conduit, the enlightened ones regulate mind's waves and frequencies.
- 2-The Fikr-Rama allows them to enter other dimensions, solid substances and matter.
- 3-The Fikr-Rama is a sort of a beam much lighter than laser. It does not have particles.
- 4-It has no substance per se, yet, it contains energy.
- 5-Extraterrestrials in general, and Anunnaki in particular have a multitude of similar brain's waves.
- 6-The Fikr-Rama is one single tone in the rainbow of their mental vibrations.
- 7-Highly advanced extraterrestrial beings can project thoughts and holographic images using any of their mental vibrations waves.

Kira-Fik:
Composed from two words:
- a-Kira (From Kira'at) means reading,
- b-Fik (From Fk'r) meaning mind.

The general meaning is the development, or the activation of telepathy in the brain of an Anunnaki student. Before the pre-final phase of an Anunnaki student purification, what happens takes only one minute, and this is the most important procedure done for each Anunnaki student on the first day of his/her studies – the creation of the mental "Conduit."

A new identity is created for each Anunnaki student by the development of a new pathway in his or her mind, connecting the student to the rest of the Anunnaki's psyche. Simultaneously, the cells check with the "other copy" of the mind and body of the Anunnaki student, to make sure that the "Double" and "Other Copy" of the Mind and body of the student are totally clean. During this phase, the Anunnaki student temporarily loses his or her memory, for a very short time. This is how the telepathic faculty is developed, or enhanced in everyone.

It is necessary, since to serve the total community of the Anunnaki, the individual program inside each Anunnaki student is immediately shared with everybody. Incidentally, this is why there is such a big difference between extra-terrestrial and human telepathy.

On earth, no one ever succeeds in emptying the whole mental content from human cells like the Anunnaki are so adept in doing, and the Conduit cannot be formed.

Lacking the Conduit that is built for each Anunnaki, the human mind is not capable in communication with the extra-terrestrials. However, don't think for a moment that there is any kind of invasion of privacy. The simplistic idea of any of your friends tapping into your private thoughts does not exist for the Anunnaki. Their telepathy is rather complicated. The Anunnaki have collective intelligence and individual intelligence. And this is directly connected to two things:

- **a**-The first is the access to the "Community Depot of Knowledge" that any Anunnaki can tap in and update and acquire additional knowledge.
- **b**-The second is an "Individual Prevention Shield," also referred to as "Personal Privacy."

This means that an Anunnaki can switch on and off his/her direct link (a channel) to other Anunnaki. By establishing the "Screen" or "Filter" an Anunnaki can block others from either communicating with him or her, or simply preventing others from reading his or her personal thoughts.

"Filter", "Screen" and "Shield" are interchangeably used to describe the privacy protection. In addition, an Anunnaki can program telepathy and set it up on chosen channels, exactly as we turn on our radio set and select the station we wish to listen to. Telepathy has several frequency, channels and stations.

Afik-r'-Tanawar:
Enlightenment through the development of the mind. Composed of two words;

- **a**-Afik-r, which means mind.
- **b**-Tanawar, which means the act of illumination.

The Anunnaki have created us on earth to serve their needs.

Their intentions were to create a race that could carry heavy physical load and do intense physical labor. This was the initial and prime objective. Thus, the "Naphsiya" (DNA) they put in us had limited lifespan, and mental faculties.

Later on, they discovered that they had to prolong the human lifespan and add more developed mental faculties, so they added the Hara-Kiya (Internal energy or physical strength).

Few generations later, the early human beings stock evolves considerably, because the Anunnaki added fully operational Mind in the human body. To do so, they installed a Conduit with limited capabilities. In the same time, this Conduit was also installed into the prototype of the human body. Thus, through the Mind, the physical body of the humans got linked to the Double. This non-physical link created a Fourth dimension for all of us. In fact, it did not create a Fourth dimension per se, rather it activated it.

So now, at that stage, humans had a physical dimension (Life on earth), and not-a-totally separated non-physical dimension called Nafis-Ra. So, the Bashar (Humans) became destined to acquire two dimensions, as exactly the Anunnaki decided.

Later on, centuries upon centuries, the human mind began to evolve, because the other Mind, call it now the Double or prototype began to evolve simultaneously and in sync.

The more the prototype is advanced the more the "Physical Mind" becomes alert, creative and multidimensional. But we are

268

not trapped, and our mind is no longer conditioned by the Anunnaki.

The Anunnaki gave us all the choices, opportunities, freewill and freedom to learn on our own and progress. This is why we are accountable and responsible for everything we do and think about. Because of the evolution of our mind, and realization of an inner knowledge of our surroundings, and understanding what is right and what is wrong, a major mental faculty emerged in all of us: Conscience."

III. Developing the Conduit:
There are techniques which are partially physical and partially mental. You could refer to them as psychosomatic. In this book, I have provided you with some techniques that could and would partially open your Conduit and activate your Supersymetric Mind. As a beginner, you cannot tap directly into your Conduit, because you don't know where it is located in your brain.

Your teacher will help you locate the Conduit cell, and will instruct you on some postures and positions, needed to enter the zone of the Conduit, and to start sending and receiving Mirsals; Sent or received by your mind.

These positions will create internal muscular vibrations, and your mind will read them. You will be sending mental/visionary lines, and their frequencies will activate the cell of the Conduit.

By the power of concentration and introspection, you will start to get intensified activity in the brain. This causes a buzz vibration in the brain the Conduit begins to detect. Then, the Conduit will absorb the vibrations and organize them, and from that moment on, the Conduit will take over.

To summarize: By attempting certain activities, you are sending a message to your Conduit. It will take some time, because at the beginning, your Conduit may not catch the messages, or if it does, your brain or your Conduit may not interpret the messages correctly, because the Conduit is not one hundred percent awake. With practice, the Conduit becomes familiar with these types of messages, and will start to give them Ishara (Codes).

Each activity, including thoughts, intentions, postures/positions, and exercises would have their own code.

*** *** ***

269

One exercise to partially activate the Conduit.
Activating, or opening the Conduit is an enigmatic and difficult
undertaking. Some, called this process a complicated mental
maneuver. And they are not wrong.
Similar to the Supersymetric Mind, the Conduit cannot be
detected, measured, and located.
Therefore, activating the Conduit is not a physical process.
"So, if we can't see it, and if we can't locate it, how one could
possibly activate this damned thing?" asked me one of my
readers from the United States. I don't blame him.
It makes sense, taking into consideration, the laws of physics,
logic, and common sense. But, if we listen to the Hadith of Ulema
Al-Baydani, we might get the correct answer.

**Excerpts from the Hadith of Ulema Al-Baydani, given at
Maa'had al Iskandariya, in 1963.**
Note: I was there for my apprenticeship.

Student: Honorable Master, is the Conduit, some sort of energy?
Ulema Al-Baydani: Yes, and much more than that.
Student: Can we see this energy?
Ulema Al-Baydani: Can you see electricity? No, only sparkles and
its effects. Can you see electricity running inside a wire? No, but
it is there.
Student: But you do see it?
Ulema Al-Baydani: Many do.
Student: Who, for example?
Ulema Al-Baydani: The honorable Moualamiin (Teachers), and
the graduated students.
Student: Only them?
Ulema Al-Baydani: Only them.
Student: Are you going to teach us how to see the Conduit?
Ulema Al-Baydani: I will show you the way, when you are ready.
Student: I am ready, Master.
Ulema Al-Baydani: You are not.
A pause.
The student is upset.
Student: Do I have a Conduit?
Ulema Al-Baydani: Yes, you do.
Student: Do Jamil and Kumar have a Conduit too?
Note: Jamil and Kumar are students (Talaa-miza) at the Maa'had

Ulema Al-Baydani: Yes, they do. Everybody does.
Student: Are they ready? (Referring to Jamil and Kumar)
Ulema Al-Baydani: It is none of your concern.
Student: When I am ready, will you teach me how to open my Conduit?
Ulema Al-Baydani: When you are ready, you will find the way. And if you don't, I will be there to teach you. And when you are ready, you will stop asking all these questions, because your mind will have all the answers. The less you talk, the more you learn.

Note: Readiness means a state of spiritual/mental purification, which resulted from observing the Kanoon and Nizam, and completing the orientation program. This could take several years.

Another student: Honorable Master, can we open the Conduit temporarily?
Ulema Al-Baydani: Wisdom is no a temporary matter.
Student: Do we have to wait so many years before we learn how to open the Conduit?
Ulema Al-Baydani: Patience is virtue. You don't have to wait so many years. The noble in spirits can accomplish this, when their minds are free from attachment to materialistic values, and their hearts are full of goodness.
Student: Then, good people could learn it very quickly?
Ulema Al-Baydani: Yes!
Student: Is it like the Ayn Nabaha (Similar to what it commonly called the Third Eye)?
Ulema Al-Baydani: No.
Student: Can you teach me a technique to explore the Conduit?
Ulema Al-Baydani: Good question Rabih. Exploring is a virtue.

Note: The master did not say "I will teach you how to open the Conduit." Wisely, he replied, "Exploring is a virtue." Meaning, that opening or activating the Conduit is not a matter of learning, but exploring and researching the truth; a truth built upon enlightenment and the Oneness. And this leads me to invite you to explore the Conduit, instead of activating it. If you persevere with humility and sincerity, you will be able to partially open your Conduit.
I can't divulge the secrets of the Conduit, and show the whole world how to activate it. But, I can provide you with a technique

that could help you in your sincere quest. And if you still need additional guidance, email me at <u>delafayette6@aol.com</u>

But you will have to answer some questions, and we will go from there.The technique you are about to learn is called Tamadi Fikru. Its phases are illustrated on the following pages.

I will comment on each illustration, and provide you with the necessary orientation/guidance.

Tamadi Fikru:

Prerequisites and Preparation:

In order to succeed in Fikrou Jalsah, which will partially activate your Conduit for a certain period of time, you must meet the requirements outlined on this page. We have lots of things to do here, but I am going to help you, all the way.

A friendly reminder: If your intentions are selfish or vicious, you will not succeed in opening the Conduit. You must free yourself from all bad and negative thoughts. It is simple; come forward clean, in peace, and with good intentions.

And during the first 6 months of your journey on the road of and toward Mira Nourim, (Knowledge via the visions of light), you must repeat this exercise, at least twice a week, otherwise, your Conduit will weaken, and eventually dissipate.

Diet: Refrain from consuming alcohol and eating fat for a period of three days before you start your exercise.

Hygiene: Be clean, absolutely clean during the exercise. Take a bath before you start the exercise.

Position/stance: Sit comfortably in a chair, of just on the floor.

State of mind: Only good intentions.

Believe in yourself. Believe in this technique.

Clothes: Light colors are recommended. No dark suits.

Place: Be alone. You can practice anywhere, as long as you are by yourself, and far from noise, metallic objects, and electronic gadgets.

Day: Any day.

Time: Always late in the afternoon, and evening hours.

Tools: None. Just use your mind.

Step #1: Look at the illustration #1 on page 274.

1. The Sphere (Globe, circle) you see in this illustration, is the zone you are going to enter, using your mind. Look at the Sphere for 10 seconds or so. Take now a deep breath.

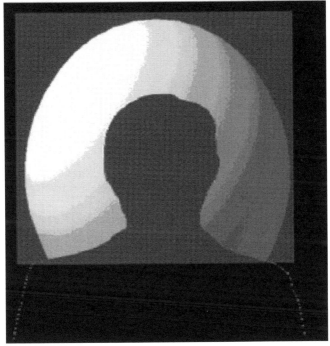

273

Illustration #1: The Sphere

2. Now, close your eyes for 20 seconds, and during that time, tell yourself, you are going to project the Sphere, right in front of yourself. Do not open your eyes yet. In other words, just imagine or visualize the Sphere before you. You got to convince yourself that the Sphere is there, in front of you. Let your imagination do this. I know, it is not real yet.

It is a fantasy, an imagination exercise, but that's fine, because something amazing is going to happen soon. Keep imagining. It is going to work.

3. After 20 seconds or so, the Sphere could appear before you, inside the realm of your mind. If not, open your eyes, and do it again. Take now a deep breath. In case, nothing happens at all, do this:

a-Open you eyes. Take now a deep breath. Close the left eye for 3 seconds.

b-Now, open the left eye, and close the right eye for 3 seconds.

c-Repeat this exercise for 20 seconds or so.

Take now a deep breath.

d-Now close both eyes for 20 seconds, and within yourself, tell your mind to bring the Sphere before you.

e-Move your head, right and left for 5 seconds. Do not open your eyes yet!! Take now a deep breath.

f-Try to remember the shape and size of the Sphere.

g-Try to remember the shades inside and outside the Sphere.

h-In your mind, imagine that there is an empty space in the center of the Sphere. Take now a deep breath.

i-In your mind, try to bring yourself closer to the empty space in the center of the Sphere. Do not open your eyes yet!!

j-Imagine that you are getting closer to the Sphere, and the Sphere is getting bigger and bigger. Take now a deep breath.

k-That's wonderful, you are almost there. Now, enter the Sphere. You are going to feel as if somebody is pushing you gently toward the Sphere. You will start to feel some sort of dizziness. Do not worry, it is working.

l-Now, you are inside the Sphere, from the shoulders up. And you are going to feel it. You are in. Take now a deep breath.

See Illustration #2, on page 276. Go now to page 276.

Illustration #2

Step #2: Look at the illustration #3 on page 278.
a-Now, you are inside the Sphere, from the shoulders up. And you are going to feel it. You are in.
See Illustration #2, on page 276.
b-You are going to feel that you are already inside the Sphere.
c-You are going to sense the presence of two lines on your right and on your left. Take now a deep breath.
See Illustration #3, on page 278.
d-These two lines are real, even though they are not visible to the naked eye. Some Ulema described them as the two invisible line of Khateyn Tarika. Others said, that they are the manifestation of your inner energy. In any case, these two lines (Khateyn) are a mental-physical energy produced by your mind and your body.
They are created by the chemical and bio-organic elements in your body (Like a battery), and manifested on the outside by the power of your mind. They are NOT your aura, but simply, a form of an inner energy that manifests itself during this exercise.
In the future, you will be able to see these two lines around other people, whether parallel to their body, or swirling around their body, depending on their health condition, and mental level.
If you still don't sense or feel the two lines, do this:
a-Place your left thumb between your eyebrows (line 2), and your right palm on line 4, count to 180 (Approx. 3 minutes) and take a deep breath after 180 seconds. It should work. If not, stop the exercise, and do it another time.
See illustration on page 279, for the position of your thumb and palm.

*** *** ***

277

Illustration #3

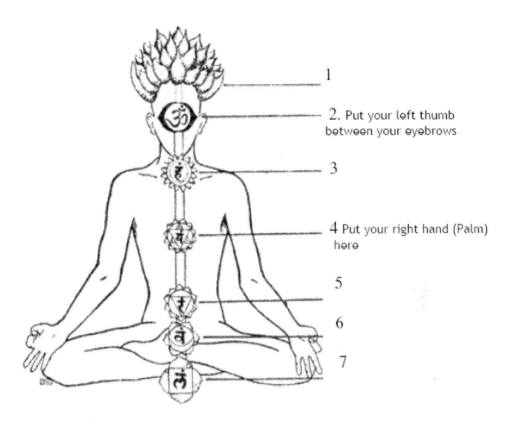

1

2. Put your left thumb between your eyebrows

3

4 Put your right hand (Palm) here

5

6

7

Illustration #4

Step #3: Look at the illustration #4 on page 280.
a-Now, the 2 lines are expanding. This, means that your energy is increasing.
b-You will be able to sense this expansion, and physically you will feel around you, the increase in your energy. Take a deep breath.
c-Tell your mind that your body needs to exist the Sphere. You got to free yourself from the perimeter of the Sphere?
Why?
Because the Sphere is your physical zone, the area that keeps you attached to a physical environment, and you don't need that.
Your mind as well as your body should become absolutely free. And you can do it, by following these instructions:
1-Extand both arms toward the Sphere.
2-Now, join both hands (Put your hands together) always in front of you, like this (See illustration below):

3-Bring both hands toward your head, and place them against your forehead. (Level 1 of the illustration on page 279). Keep them there for 10 seconds. Then, drop them down, very slowly.
4-Look at illustration #5, on page 282. We are heading toward Step #4.

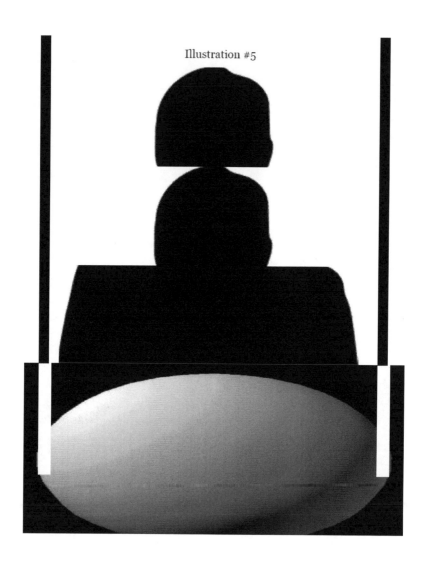

Illustration #5

Step #4: Illustration #5 depicts your detachment from the Sphere.

If you have reached this step, this is a great sign; you are doing wonderfully. And there is a magnificent surprise for you. As soon as your body is outside the Sphere, your Conduit will kick off, meaning, it is on its way to be partially open, but not activated yet. Eventually, you will be able to do it, once you reach Step #5. I know you are getting excited, but you have to remain calm.
Take a deep breath.
You are not entirely free physically.
You are not entirely free mentally.
But you are on the right track.
Now look at illustration #6, on page 284; it demonstrates your new state of mind. And this state of mind will lead you toward the preliminary state of a partial opening of your Conduit.
The Conduit will partially open up when you reach Step #5.
Pertinent explanation and instructions are provided on page 285.
So let's go there.

*** *** ***

Illustration #6

Step #5: This step is related to illustration #7, on page 286.

a-Nothing to do now. Just stay calm. Take a deep breath.
b-Part of your Supersymetric Mind is ready to engage you into a mental conversation. And this conversation will take shape not verbally, but holographically. Meaning, you are going to see a projection of a screen right before your eyes.
c-The holographic screen or grid as known to others, will be projected by your Supersymetric Mind.
d-You will be able to see it, once the Conduit is partially activated, and it is going to happen in a few second.
e-Look now at illustration #8, on page 288. Let's go there, and read additional information and instructions on page 287.

*** *** ***

285

Illustration #7

Step #6: This step is related to illustration #8, on page 288.

a-Do not open your eyes. Keep them close all the time, until you complete the whole process (The entire exercise).
b-Now, your Conduit is partially open, but not fully activated. It does not matter, really.
Because now, you are going to experiment and experience some phenomena, few privileged people in our modern world had the opportunity to witness.
c-Suddenly, a screen or a grid will be projected, and you will be able to see it, even with closed eyes, because it is in your mind.
d-From now on, your "regular mind" becomes dormant, and your Supersymetric Mind will take over.
This sudden transition is produced by the awakening of your Conduit.
e-During this stage, your Conduit is a minor tool you can use temporarily to uncover lots of things, and especially to deal with, and/or remove problems that are causing you lots of headache.
At this stage, your Conduit is NOT activated permanently.
It is operational only during this exercise. Nevertheless, it is a powerful tool, because it allows you to remove up to "4 Knots" that they are blocking you from progressing in life.
Additional information and explanation on these "Knots" are en route. Relax, and take a deep breath. Oh yes, I know, there are lots of breathing stuff here. But you need it. One day, I will tell you all about the great benefits and extraordinary powers you can develop by breathing the right way.
f-Let's go now to page 289 to read about Step #7.

*** *** ***

287

Illustration #8

Step #7: It is related to illustration #9, on page 290.

a-The holographic screen will start to get bigger and bigger. And soon you will be able to read and/or see events from your own life, some from the past, and others from your present and future.

b-It is NOT hallucinations, because you, and only you, know so much about yourself, and your confidential matters. If the screen projects these events, and if the screen allows you to face and see the problems you are having in your life, then, this should ipso facto, convince you without any doubt that you are neither dreaming nor hallucinating. No, you are not crazy, you are just experiencing something mega extraordinary.

c-At this stage, you have to wait for a few seconds, to allow the Conduit to enlarge further the screen (Grid).

d-A lovely and bright light will emerge from the center of the screen (Grid). See it in illustration #10, on page 292.

Let's go there, and read pertinent information on pages 291 and 293.

*** *** ***

Illustration #9

Step #8: This step is related to illustration #10, on page 292.

a-Just stay calm. Take a deep breath. Your Conduit is working.

b-Your Conduit is going to project on the screen, images, symbols, geometrical shapes, and in some instances, portraits and animated images.

c-In your case, as a beginner, you will only see squares, up to four, and much less, if your Khateyn Tarika lines begin to weaken a little bit. Nevertheless, the squares will give you plenty of important information.

d-This is the moment of truth. Because you are going to deal directly with what is bothering you. You know your troubles, you know your own problems, you know the difficulties you are facing...so face everything with an absolute honesty, humility and an open mind.

e-Get ready now to watch the squares.

So, let's go to illustration #11, on page 294, and read pertinent information and explanation on page 293.

*** *** ***

Illustration #10

Step #9: This step is related to illustration #11, on page 294.

a-This step is easy. Tell yourself (Basically, your Supersymetric Mind) to open up the squares.
b-It is up to you how many squares you want to see. Four squares are the maximum. And if by now you are wondering what is the meaning of all that? Squares? Meaning what? And why?
Well, it is very simple. Each square represents a major segment from your life, and above all, a major problem that you could not deal with in ordinary situations. This is your chance to remove these difficulties, once and for good.
If 4 squares are too much, then open up 3, or 2, even 1.
c-Take a deep breath.
d-Look at illustration #11, on page 294, and visualize the squares inside your head. They are there on the screen, alright, but you have to keep looking at each one them, in no particular order. If you are lefty, start from the left.
Your mind, vision and perception are all linked to the way you originally use your hands. No time to explain this for now. Just keep looking at the squares, one by one.
e-Let's go right away to illustration #12, on page 296, and read pertinent information on page 295.

*** *** ***

Illustration #11

Step #10: This step is related to illustration #12, on page 296.

a-Each square represents one "knot".
b-Each "knot" represents one of your problems.
c-You may have more than 4 problems –I hope not–, but for now, we can only deal with 4 major problems.
d-What kind of problems? All sorts of problems; relationships, rapports with others, dealing with clients, unpleasant situations at your workplace, financial difficulties, you name it.
e-Who is going to solve my problems?
Who is going to untie these "knots"?
Your Conduit! You better believe it. The next step will show you how.
f-Let's go now to illustration #12 A, on page 298.

*** *** ***

Illustration #12

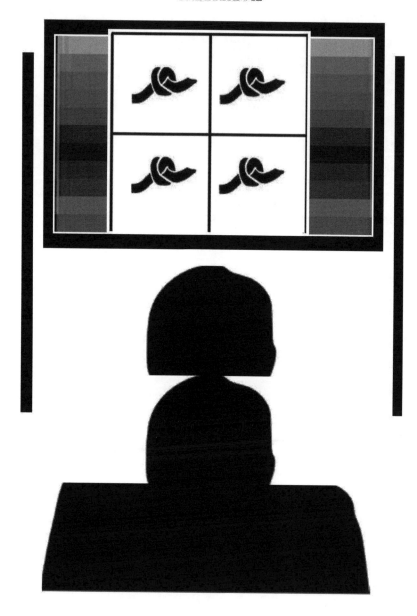

Step #11: This step is related to illustration #12 A, on page 298.

a-What's going on here? Is it the same illustration on page 296. Yes, it is. And intentionally, I reproduced it here for the following reasons:
1-Sometime, the 4 squares remain attached to the screen (Grid). They don't move. Don't get upset.
This means, that you are agitated. And when you are agitated and/or confused, your Supersymetric Mind gets perturbed.
In this situation, your Conduit and Supersymetric Mind are not in synch.
2-The screen will freeze. A déjà vu experience? Yes!
Your computer! How many times did your computer freeze?
Crash? Many times. The same thing applies to the holographic screen, bur for different reasons.
Because any of your vibes emanated by and from your body will affect the holographic screen, positively or negatively, any hollographic projection will either benefit or suffer from it. You have to remember, that the whole exercise is animated through mental waves produced by your Condit, like electricity current. A bad vibe will freeze the squares on the screen.
3-In this situation, take a deep breath, and readjust your setting, change your stance, and find a more comfortable position. This will work.
4-Let's go now to illustration #14, on page 302, and read pertinent information on page 299.

*** *** ***

Illustration #12 A

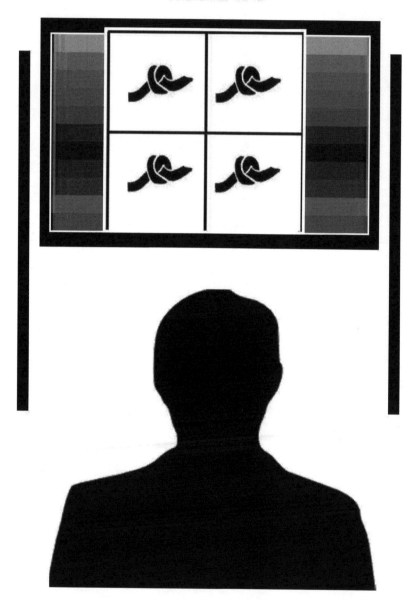

Step #12: This step is related to illustration #13, on page 300.

a-This step deals with the removal of the knots one by one.
b-This stage requires intense focusing, and a deep concentration. Keep your eyes close, and take a deep breath.
c-Change the position of your hands, and keep them like this for approximately 2 minutes, or count till 120.
See illustrations below:

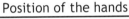

Position of the hands

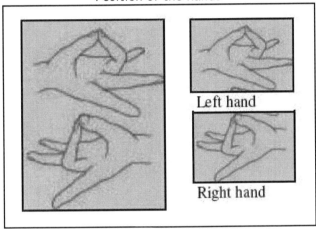

Left hand

Right hand

d-Talk to your Conduit about problem 1, represented by Knot 1. Yes, you have to converse with your Conduit like a real person. Explain the situation, and ask for guidance.
e-Concentrate strongly. Take a deep breath. Ask the Conduit to remove the knot. You might not hear the answer (Vocally) from your Conduit, but the Conduit will untie the knot and remove it from the square. You will see the removal on the screen (Grid), as shown on illustration #13, on page 300.
f-Go now to page 301.

Illustration #13: Removal of the knots one by one

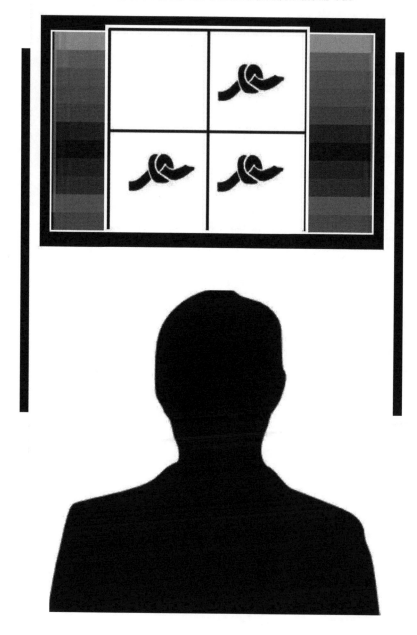

Step #13: This step is related to illustration #14, on page 302.

a-Repeat the same exercise for each "knot".
b-This, would remove "knot" 2.
c-Look at illustration #14, on page 302.
d-Go now to page 303.

*** *** ***

Illustration #14: Removal of the knots one by one

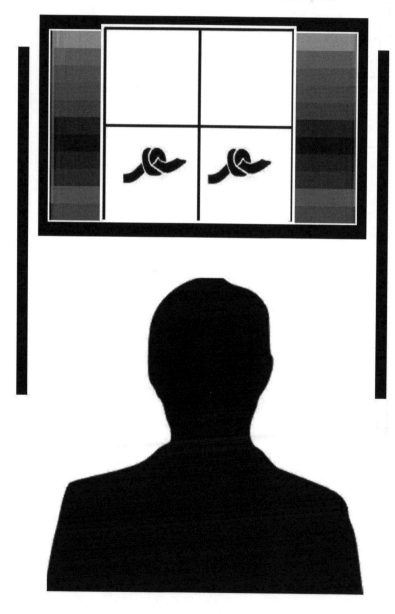

Step #14: This step is related to illustration #15, on page 304.

a-Repeat the same exercise for each "knot".
b-This, would remove "knot" 3.
c-Look at illustration #15, on page 304.
d-Go now to page 305.

*** *** ***

Illustration #15: Removal of the knots one by one

Step #15: This step is related to illustration #16, on page 306.

a-Repeat the same exercise for each "knot".
b-This, would remove "knot" 4.
c-Look at illustration #16, on page 306.
d-All "knots" are removed. And the screen is "clean"!
e-Go now to page 307, and look at illustration #17, on page 308.

*** *** ***

Illustration #16: Removal of the knots one by one

Step #16: This step is related to illustration #17, on page 308.

a-The screen (Grid) is clear.
b-Drop down your hands. Take a deep breath.
c-Put your hands behind your back.

d-Take a deep breath.
e-Bring yourself closer to the blank screen. See illustration #18, on page 310.
f-Tell yourself, you are going to enter the screen.
g-As soon as your Supersymetric Mind hears this, the screen will vanish. See Illustration #19, on page 311.

*** *** ***

Illustration #17: Removal of the 4 squares

Step #17: This step is related to illustration #18, on page 310.

a-You have entered the screen. Look at illustration #18, on page 310.
b-During this phase, you are going to sense a strong energy flux bordering your body. Don't be alarmed.
Your Conduit is surrounding you with a halo of positive energy. It is charging your mind and body. Your Conduit has untied the knots, established the equilibrium of the two lines of Khateyn Tarika, stimulated your Supersymetric Mind and "regular mind", and above all, removed barriers that have blocked your path.
You are going to feel extremely energetic yet delightfully serene, strong, robust, extremely alert, happy about yourself, and in you, within you, in your mind, and the way you think, you are going to see things differently, observe things, objects and people very clearly, and understand situations you could not deal with or understand in ordinary circumstances and situations.
c-As soon as the screen vanishes, (See illustration #19, on page 311), you are going to experience and feel something absolutely wonderful. For example:
1-Physiological nuisances, chronic pains, muscular fatigue, anxiety, fear, indecisiveness, laziness, and other unpleasant mishaps will be either reduced or eliminated.
2-New opportunities will knock on your door, not because you have all of a sudden acquired magical powers, far from it, but because, negative vibrations, and unhealthy Khaten Tarika lines were preventing others from giving you a helping hand, and/or coming forward. You have blocked them, but now, the path is clear, you will become much happier, healthier, luckier, your face will shine, not very much, but enough to attract and please others, and above all, you will radiate, and your aura will show it.

*** *** ***

Illustration #18: Enter the square

Illustration #19: You entered the zone of "Oneness"

Step #18: This step is related to closing the exercise and the Zone of "Oneness"; phase one of the activation of the Conduit, on page 313.

Closing the exercise:
a-Bring yourself to a state of complete quietness. Relax. Take a deep breath. Stay where you are, and do not move for 2 minutes. Your eyes are still closed.
b-Gradually open your eyes. And breathe again.
c-Stand up very slowly.
d-Turn around slowly from left to right.
e-Now turn around from right to left. You are done!

The Zone of "Oneness":
The exercise allowed you to enter the zone of Oneness for a very short time. But that is the beginning. The more you practice, the more you envelop yourself, mind and body, with flux of positive energy, and you will be surrounded by an etheric equilibrium that will enhance your performance in all your activities.
You could even develop extra-ordinary faculties.
But use this knowledge and awakening, wisely, humbly, with love, affection for others, and especially toward those who caused you embarrassment and suffering.
Look at the illustration of the Zone of "Oneness". You were part of it.
If you need additional guidance, email me at delafayette6@aol.com

*** *** ***

Zone of "Oneness"; phase one of the activation of the Conduit.

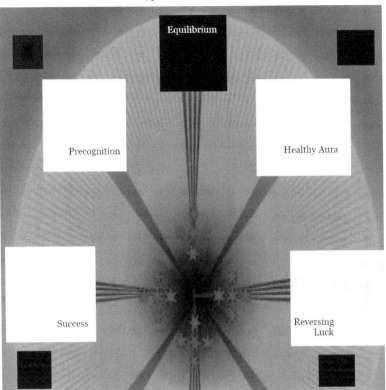

Relation to Khateyn Tarika

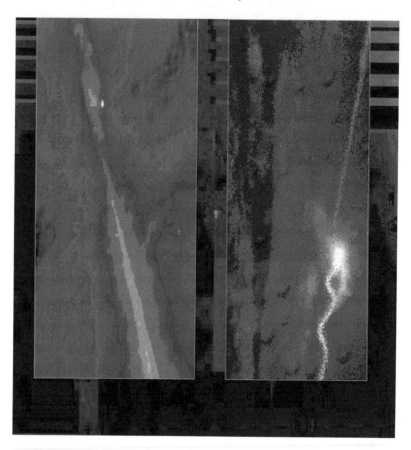

Introduction
II. What is Khateyn Tarika?
III. Explaining the Concept:
a- Position and place of the two lines
b- The perfect alignment
c- The mixed-up alignment
d- The weak and blurry alignment
IV. Inside the two lines
V. You, your body, the bodies of others, entities and spirits, and Khateyn Tarika:
a. Vis-à-vis your physical body's zone

So, where is it?
Does it increase or decrease?
What causes the zone to shrink or extend?
VI. Possessed by the Spirits:
Is this typical spirits possession of the human body?
VII. People entering your zone
Terminology
VIII. What is Atmashabah?
Entities and spirits entering your zone.
Entering other people's zone
IX. Technique for cleansing and strengthening your Khateyn
Tarika
How to use it?
Time and place
Preparation
The process

I. Introduction:

If you are "Outside Khateyn Tarika", you will never reach the top, in anything you do, no matter how happy, intelligent, influential, and rich you are."
The Sahiriin and Rouhaniyiin told us that every human being on Earth is lined up with two invisible lines that determine her/his balance and harmony with their immediate surroundings, as well as the size and strength of his/her luck in this physical world. Khateyn means: Two Lines. It is the plural of Khat, which means one line. They are invisible to the naked eye. The Rouhaniyiin nicknamed Khateyn "Tarik al Hayat", meaning the road of life.

These two lines determine how healthy, successful and balanced you are or will be in your life. Tarika means a path, a road. It is usually linked to your present and future, with major impact on your health, love life and business. Khateyn Tarika is directly linked to your "Double", astral body, your mind, spirits and entities who live here on Earth, and in other dimensions. All of us, big and small, lucky and unlucky, rich and poor, famous, infamous and unknown, are conditioned and influenced by Khateyn Tarika two invisible lines that exist either ahead of our body, behind it, or around it.

315

And the position and placement of these two lines that we cannot see –unless we were taught how to find them– have a major impact on everything we do, and think about. Khateyn Tarika technique will positively influence or change your life, health and luck.

Khateyn Tarika is one of the most important, mind-bending and powerful parts of Ilmu (Knowledge and wisdom), and the secret doctrine of the Allamah and Rouhaniyiin. If you unlock its secrets, you will reach your full potential, and accomplish the impossible.

Khateyn Tarika will put you on the right track, leading to spectacular success, power, harmony with your environment, and perfect health. The Honorable Master Khafaja Sudki Ghayali said verbatim: "If you are "Outside Khateyn Tarika", you will never reach the top, in anything you do, no matter how happy, intelligent, influential, and rich you are."

The Sahiriin and Rouhaniyiin told us that every human being on Earth is lined up with two invisible lines that determine her/his balance and harmony with their immediate surroundings, as well as the size and strength of his/her luck in this physical world.

Ironically, people sometimes say: "You are out of line" without knowing the real and original meaning of this phrase!

Where did this expression come from?

And what do they mean by "Out of line"?

And what "Line" are they talking about?

They don't know.

It is just a very common and popular expression that applies to some situations, and debates/discussions we are familiar with.

The expression "Out of line" appeared for the first time as a "Magical metaphysical" Jimlah in the book "Ilmu Al Donia", written centuries ago in Arabic and Persian. The first to use this expression were the Anunnaki-Ulema.

II. What is Khateyn Tarika?

Pronounced: Kha (Like J in Jose in Spanish) Tayn Taa-Ree-Ka.

Khateyn means: Two Lines. It is the plural of Khat, which means one line. They are invisible to the naked eye. The Rouhaniyiin nicknamed Khateyn "Tarik al Hayat", meaning the road of life. These two lines determine how healthy, successful and balanced

316

you are or will be in your life, in this physical dimension. More information on this topic will follow.

Tarika means a path, a road. It is usually linked to your present and future, with major impact on your health, business, spirituality, physical strength, successes, and relationships.

Khateyn Tarika is a very complex and sophisticated concept, difficult to understand or to accept, unless you are one of the "Illuminated Masters", or the initiated ones (Students and adepts). But I will try to explain this concept as much as I can, in very simple language. Before I do that, I want to let you know that Khateyn Tarika is directly linked to your "Double", astral body, your mind, your "Fik'r", spirits and entities who live here on Earth, and in other dimensions.

III. Explaining the Concept:

a- Position and place of the two lines:

All of us, big and small, lucky and unlucky, rich and poor, famous, infamous and unknown, are conditioned and influenced by two invisible etheric lines that exist either ahead of our body, behind it, or around it.

And the position and placement of these two lines that we cannot see —unless we were taught how to find them— have a major impact on everything we do, and think about.

b- The perfect alignment:

If the two lines are aligned perfectly in parallel position to your body, your brain, or more precisely your intellect will produce magnificent deeds, and you will be able to accomplish things, people thought impossible. Not only that, but you will acquire astonishing speed that allows you to complete tasks, usually requiring much more time and effort. And in some instances, you will be capable of accomplishing multiple tasks, simultaneously, and in certain conditions, INSTANTLY!

c- The mixed-up alignment:

If the two lines are mixed up —meaning not aligned as two parallel lines on the right side and left side of your body, and/or situated behind you, or way ahead of you— your potentials will be limited, and your accomplishments will be minimal.

Consequently, you will not flourish. Many people live, exist, and do things outside the lines. They work hard, long hours, they

317

sweat, and yet, their efforts remain in vain. This failure is caused by the misalignment of the two lines. But there is a way to rectify the situation. In this section of the book, I will explain to you how to do it, and how to maintain a perfect alignment, both mentally and physically.

d- The weak and blurry alignment:
If the two lines are barely defined, your health will deteriorate rapidly, and your finances will crumble. You will fail miserably in your relationships and rapports with others, and all your resources will dry up.

IV. Inside the two lines:
Inside the two lines is the perfect place to be. This is the zone of very successful and healthy people. This zone is harmonious with your environment, and the multiple layers of everything that surrounds you. It is a magical and incomprehensible zone, full of surprises and possibilities. It is the zone of subatomic particles, the extension of your "Conduit", the realm of your "Double", and above all your true mental and bio-organic identity.

It is also the zone of visions, apparitions, alternate realities, fantasy, meta-reality, metalogic, and your rendez-vous with entities and "presences". The illuminated masters live and do things "between the lines." They are never outside of the lines, or "out-of-line". I hear you now telling yourself, "It is so confusing, all these words, dimensions, and bla-bla-bla words are Chinese to me...mumbo jumbo stuff...etc." But that is not it.

It is simply a new concept you are not yet familiar with. If you are patient, and if you give me the time to explain it to you, you will understand to a certain degree what I am talking about!

V. You, your body, the bodies of others, entities and spirits, and Khateyn Tarika:
For now, we are going to call Khateyn Tarika "The Zone".

To make you understand this concept, and to render your zone healthy and well-balanced, I have to explain to you 5 important factors, and which are:

- Vis-à-vis your physical body's zone.
- People entering your zone.
- Entities and spirits entering your zone.
- Entering other people's zone.

318

- Adjusting your zone, meaning bringing equilibrium and awareness to your zone.

a. Vis-à-vis your physical body's zone:
Your body has two spaces.
One, is the physical space that it occupies. Usually defined and limited by your height, size and weight. The other, is a space you don't see. It is an extension of your physical body. This extension does exist, even though you are not aware of it.

So, where is it?
It starts from a quarter of a centimeter from your physical body and extends up to 5 feet, in some cases up to 6 feet, in front of your body, and encompasses a distance of 4 feet on both sides of your body (Left and right), and a distance of 4 feet behind your body. So we have here, 6 feet in front, 4 feet in the rear, and 4 feet to the left and right. This is your zone. This zone stays with you for the rest of your life. In this zone, you find your "Double", your astral body, your "Space memory", your aura, and your physical-non-physical emotions.

Does it increase or decrease?
Yes! It does! And everything depends on the place and position your body occupies between Khateyn Tarika (The two lines). You should keep your body well-aligned within these two lines. This means, that the two lines should always remain parallel to each other, straight as an arrow, and your body should be situated at an equal distance from each line, on the left and on the right.

What causes the zone to shrink or extend?
Shrinking or extending your zone is not healthy, mentally and physically. Evil thoughts, fear, envy, jealousy, hate, suspicions, greed, bad hygiene, worries about finances, trauma caused by losing a job, health problems, addiction to drugs, alcohol and similar substances jeopardize the stability of the two lines, disorient your body, and consequently push the two lines far away from your body.
When these two lines are at a distance exceeding 6 feet ahead of you, they will instantly lose their parallel alignment. And when this happens, your body is no longer protected. Yes! The two lines are your shield. Once, they are no longer close to your body, all sorts of things will invade your zone. In other words, you

have lost your mental-etheric-metaphysical immune system. This loss will automatically affect your brain, your "Conduit", you creativity, and above all your judgment! The two lines are your invisible non-physical guardians. Once you lose your guardians, your non-physical body, which is a copy of your physical body, becomes a "Vagabond", as stated by Allamah Mouhtaram Kemal Agha. He meant, that your body is on its own, and no longer guided by your brain.

Your unprotected body will do ridiculous things, and in some situations, will expose you to imminent danger. For instance, your unprotected body will wake you up in the middle of the night, and make you walk in your sleep, in an erratic manner, and do things a rational person would not do. The problem with this situation, is the fact that you remain totally unaware of what is happening. In these situations you can hurt yourself. It is during this very stage, unwanted "presences" and entities will interfere to misguide you, to disorient you, and influence your subconscious mind, decisions, and actions.

According to the Allamah and Rouhaniyiin, if these occurrences are frequent, your mind will fall prey to illusions and visions created by the entities.

Some have called these mishaps, "Possessed by the evil spirits", others have described these unpleasant incidents as "Being totally commanded by a sick and unbalanced Double." Allamah Moukhtar Al Ansari said verbatim, "In some cases, the Double of other people manifests itself to add more confusion to your mind, and distract your body."

Personally, I have witnessed similar events. A friend of mine who slept overnight at my home, woke up around 2:00 in the morning, started to walk in his sleep all over the place, went to the library bookcase, and began to arrange books on the shelves, threw some on the floor, and ended up rolling one bottle of wine across the floor to the kitchen. He grabbed a bottle, emptied it in a matter of minutes, and hid it under the kitchen sink. A few seconds later, he started to scream and bounce in all directions. And then I heard him saying: "Go away...stay away from me. You hurt me enough! I am no longer a child!" Apparently, he was talking to the Double of his mother who manifested it's presence as a holographic projection, in the form of a wicked woman dancing like an African witch outside his own Khateyn Tarika. This event happened twice before my own eyes. The very next day, my friend accused me of drinking the whole bottle of wine

and hiding it under the kitchen sink!! Then, when I told him about the wicked woman who invaded his zone while he was sleep walking, he said: "Who was it? Was it my mother?"
According to the Sahiriin, my friend was lucky, because at that critical moment, no malevolent spirits invaded his Khateyn Tarika.

VI. Possessed by the Spirits:

As long as you keep your two lines in harmony, and not far from your body, and as long as you maintain an anchored and well-balanced position of your body between the two lines, no spirit will ever invade your zone. And no entity will ever haunt you and/or manipulate your mind. According to Kitab Al Arwaah (The Book of Spirits), spirits, malevolent entities and unwanted Arwaah will never enter the bodies of human beings who have well-aligned Khateyn Tarika. It is only when they are out-of-line, that possession by entities becomes possible. When the two lines deviate, evil spirits invade your zone and take possession of your body and mental faculties.

Many have killed while sleep-walking, and never realized what they have done. Psychiatrists and psychologists came up with all sorts of explanations, and suggested an avalanche of therapies and treatments, but unfortunately, as mental health records show, they remained in vain, and their elaborate explanations were never convincing. Some court records and transcripts tell of people who have committed crimes while sleep-walking, who were acquitted, because they were found temporarily insane, and thus not legally responsible for their actions. The Allamah see the situation quite differently.

They contribute these frightening events to the "displacement" of Khateyn Tarika, which of course is ridiculed by scientists in the West, and the clergy. Yet, men of the cloth, publicly admit that evil spirits and the Devil could easily enter the human body, and possess all our faculties. And how do they deal with this situation? Exorcism.

The Rouhaniyiin and Sahiriin think otherwise. In their opinion, only the re-alignment of Khateyn Tarika, will solve the problem, and expunge any malevolent exterior (External) intervention and possession.

Is this typical spirits possession of the human body?

321

Yes it is, according to the Rouhaniyiin and Sahiriin. And it is called "Intisakhah". Some Intisakhah are temporary, others could last for a very long period of time. Some occur during a séance, others while the Khateyn Tarika are unbalanced, and distant from the human body. New age ufology called these entities who enter the human bodies, "walk-ins."

Anunnaki-Ulema Rabbi Mordachai ben Zvi told me that our third dimension (Earth) is surrounded by time-space pockets that open and close at some particular moments.

During these phases, entities of all sorts, living-forms, particles, sub-atomic particles, "time bubbles" as well as gravity from parallel dimensions could enter our world, and take on different shapes and forms. Afrit and Arwaah are no exception. In fact, what we have witnessed in the case of our "flying-hovering friend" is one of those moments, when an entity enters our dimension without a formal request. The entity starts to look for people whose "Double" is suffering from lack of harmony and synchronization.

These people become the target of the entity. And unfortunately, the entity will keep on revisiting these people, as often as possible, and finally the entity succeeds in creating a niche in their Khateyn Tarika. Those who have had a troubled childhood are particularly vulnerable, and if their Khateyn Tarika becomes periodically distant from their body, the entities' visits become more frequent.

VII. People entering your zone:
Just like entities and spirits, othcrs (Human beings) can also invade your zone. They enter your Khateyn Tarika through their "Double". Siblings and children who had an unpleasant relationship/rapport with their parents, especially with their mothers, suffer from this Double's invasion, more frequently than others. Allamah Sharaf Al Diin stated verbatim: "Some people could become more annoying than spirits.

Usually, it is the Atmashabah of the mother who invades the zone of her adult children. Because there is a permanent link between mother and child, the Double of the mother could easily enter between the two lines of the child's zone, especially when the Double of the child has left an empty place between these two lines. This happens, when the Double has been kicked out by misalignment of Khateyn Tarika."

A very disturbing scenario takes place in this situation. It is quite common to sense the Atmashabah of the mother screaming at her child, and the child reacting very aggressively toward what he/she conceives to be his/her real mother manifesting in the flesh.

VIII. What is Atmashabah?

Atmashabah is composed of two words found in Ana'kh, the language of the Anunnaki, in Ulemite, the language of the Anunnaki-Ulema, in the language of the Sahiriin, and in Arabic. Atma means darkness. Shabah means a ghost, a phantom. Thus, the general meaning is the darkness of a ghost. Darkness of a ghost is a metaphoric expression/interpretation for the grayish gluey substance that constitutes the manifestation of a ghost. Some spiritists call it ectoplasma. But the word ectoplasma is not quite correct. In ancient times, ecto was understood and written as exo, meaning out of, outside, and is of Greek origin. It refers to a substance that exits from the orifices of the human body (Nose, mouth, eyes). But what we have here, is not a substance that comes out of the body, but a substance that is independently produced by the Double of another person, without using human body orifices.

Entities and spirits entering your zone.
Entering other people's zone:

If others can enter your zone, so you too can enter the zone of other people. This happens when your Double escapes for a short time. Your Double can enter so many places on Earth, as well as in adjacent and parallel dimensions. I have written extensively on this subject in my previous books, and I am not about to repeat myself in this present tome. But briefly and rapidly let me point out the following: A healthy Double can be guided and instructed to explore many zones and various spheres of existence, and bring back a wealth of information on all sorts of things, objects, people and places. A Double that has been "kicked out" of your Khateyn Tarika is worthless. It would annoy others, and disrupt the harmonious flow and flux of their zones. This means that you (with your Double bouncing all around everywhere but within your two lines of Khateyn Tarika) would unnerve or perturb the harmonious energy of others. People would say "something about his/her energy/vibe is off-putting."

IX. Technique for cleansing and strengthening your Khateyn Tarika
How to use it?
Follow these instructions:

Time and place:
1. Favorable time: Always after 9:00 PM.
2. Favorable place: Any place as long as you are alone and not disturbed by others.

Preparation:
1. Draw two parallel lines on the floor.
2. The length of the two lines should not exceed 7 feet.
3. The six feet are your zone.
The additional foot limits the outer strength of your zone, usually used for reinforced protection.
4. The space between the two parallel lines should not exceed 5 feet.
5. Light and place one white candle at the end of each line. So, you should have 2 lit candles at the end of your zone defined by the length of the two lines.
6. Now, look around you, and pick up 4 objects, anything you like, a pen, a bracelet, a small cup, a piece of chocolate, whatever you have access to.
7. Dump the 4 objects in a paper bag.
8. Write the name of each object on a piece of paper and place the paper in a second bag.
9. Keep the two bags outside the two lines.
10. Put down the bags in any place you want.
11. There are no restrictions, as long as they are outside the two lines.

The process:
- 1. First of all, in your mind, you should envisage now, the two lines of Khateyn Tarika as the borderlines of everything that contains you as a person; this, consists of the time you live in, the time you have lived in, the good time you knew, the hard time you went through, and what you do believe might prevent you from progressing in life.

- 2. The 4 objects you have already picked up might seem irrelevant to what you are currently thinking about, and/or the situation you are going through.
- 3. I can explain to you right away how important and relevant those 4 objects are, but this could influence your thoughts and spoil the esoteric exercise. So, do not get preoccupied with these objects. Forget about them for the time being.
- 4. Get a rope or a thread and tie 4 knots on the rope or the thread.
- 5. Later on, and on your own you will understand the relation and/or the link that exists between the 4 objects and the 4 knots.
- 6. In this context, each knot could or would represent 4 important things in your life. I asked you to select 4 objects, not less and not more, simply because I do not want you to think about many things for now, because you should keep your mind focused on a few things.
- 7. And fewer objects might not gather and/or cover enough stuff. So 4 objects are more than enough to practice the Khateyn Tarika.
- 8. Now you have a rope or a thread with 4 knots. Lay down the rope or the thread on the floor, any place you want, as long as it is inside the two lines.
- 9. The 4 knots represents 4 periods in your life. You may not agree with this interpretation, because you might think that you have never lived 4 periods.
- 10. True, but according to the enlightened masters, all of us have already lived or will go through 4 phases in our lives. Some periods or passages are pleasant; others are tough or uncomfortable to say the least.
- 11. Some passages you might remember, others you are not aware of, or simply you do not remember, because they are buried in your childhood, or yet to surface in your future. But eventually, they will become part of the fabric of your life in the present and in the future..
- 12. Some people have more problems than others. Consequently, more knots are required. But if we keep on thinking in this manner, we will never finish the practice. Later on, as you progress with your practice,

you can add as many knots as you want. If you add more than 4 knots, you should ask the assistance of a Master.

- 13. Do not complicate things, work with only 4 knots for now. It is more than you can handle, especially if you are a beginner.

- 14. Lay down on the floor, inside the two lines, and close your eyes. Keep your eyes close until the end of the exercise.

- 15. Now, start to focus on one knot; the first one on the rope or the thread.

- 16. Call this first knot, your childhood.

- 17. While you are positioning yourself on the floor, between the two lines, try to remember something from your childhood.

- 18. Do not worry about what you should remember and what part of your childhood you should remember. Anything that pops up in your head will be just fine. Later on, your mind will sort out and resort things accordingly.

- 19. Well, let's assume that your mind will take you back into your past when you were 4 year old. That's fine. Now start to remember what you liked and disliked when you were 4 years old.

- 20. See what your mind will bring back to your memory. Are you seeing the old house you lived in? Maybe now, you are seeing neighbors, the school bus, your teachers, siblings? It does not matter what you are seeing and what you are missing. Let your brain navigate on its own.

- 21. Try to sink yourself into those visions, and relive these passages from your childhood.

- 22. Once you become one with your past, and your brain begins to assimilate this, begin a conversation with the 4 year old child you used to be.

- 23. This conversation will stimulate parts or segments from your past, that will perfectly fit the moment you are living right now, meaning that, what your brain is currently bring back to you, is closely associated with the knot.

- 24. And this exercise applies to the other three knots.

- 25. Now, I want you to stop reading these instructions, right here at bullet #25, and go back to bullet #1, and

326

start reading the instructions from the beginning. Of course, you will not do this during the séance.

- 26. But here and now, and for the sole purpose of fully understanding the process, I am asking you to re-read the instructions from the beginning. Welcome back. Now, here you are talking peacefully to yourself when you were 4 year old. Continue to do so by asking the child standing before you to take you back in time to a place you liked very much; it could be the beach, an old house, a play-ground, your grand mother home, any thing.

- 27. Anchor yourself in the place you are revisiting. Let your memory and mind float freely.

- 28. And while you are revisiting and reliving that place and that moment from your past, ask calmly the child (Remember, this child is YOU!) standing before you to tell you why did he/she like that place?

- What is so special about that place?

- 29. Ask the child about something less pleasant, for instance something that has disturbed you, and/or scared you. It could be anything, a sad event, a painful experience, something like that.

- 30. Wait for the answer, and see how you are going to feel all over again. This sensation will come.

- 31. If you re-experience the same feeling you had years ago, this would be an indication, a sign that you have linked yourself to a past event.

- 32. Now, using your imagination, try to project that unpleasant event, right before your eyes. Use the power of your mind, or simply convince yourself that part of your Symetric Mind is activated.

- 33. Then, tell yourself you are going to tie up that event inside the first knot. And while you are doing this, think about a dark color, any color you want. I recommend dark blue.

- 34. In your first séance, you will concentrate on one knot, and you will tie the pertaining event (Memory of event) inside one knot; the corresponding knot that is. This exercise shall be repeated for the other knots in forthcoming séances.

- 35. Now, you tell your mind to concentrate on your feet. More precisely on your two big toes, simultaneously. Repeat this, until your toes are totally relaxed.
- 36. Tell your toes to go to sleep. Keep telling your toes to do so, until you start to feel that both toes are now cold and heavy.
- 37. Now tell your feet to go to sleep. Keep telling your feet to do so, until you start to feel that your feet are now cold and heavy.
- 38. As you progress in your exercise, you will get better and faster results.
- 39. Now reach for you knees and do the same thing.
- 40. It could take you several attempts to realize this, but eventually you will succeed, if you persevere.
- 41. Once, your knees, your feet, and your toes have reached the state of numbness, you will begin to feel the presence of two lines emanating from the right side and left side of your hip. And that is fine.
- 42. Now, you ask the child standing before you to lift you up.
- 43. Your body will start to rise.
- 44. In less than two seconds, you will start to float in the air. And you will begin to hover over your own body.
- 45. No, you are not dreaming, and you are not under the influence of any mental disillusion. What is happening here is real. It is mental, not physical. Your brain is in charge now of the whole situation. It is not an out-of-the body experience. It is not an astral projection.
- 46. It is the mind which is producing this effect.
- 47. At this precise moment, ask the child who is still standing in front of you, to take you to the place you have chosen for revisiting your childhood.
- 48. Tell your mind to pick up the rope or the thread and to throw it in the air.
- 49. Grab the rope or the thread and shake it strongly and firmly.
- 50. Take the rope or the thread with you to your chosen destination (The place, country or time you have chosen to revisit).

- 51. As soon as you have reached your destination, ask your mind to untie the knot.
- 52. Your mind is extremely powerful. You mind can do it. And soon, you will see the rope or the thread folding and unfolding on itself, and the knot disappearing.
- 53. It is not an illusion, because when you return to the body which is still lying down and flat inside the Khateyn Tarika, you will discover that the rope or the thread has now only three knots.
- 54. Thank the child who accompanied you in your fantastic journey in time and space.
- 55. Descend slowly into your physical body. Your mind will re-enter its original place, and your brain will re-adjust itself.
- 56. You will loose the dumbness you have felt before, and before you know it, your knees, feet and toes will regain their normal/natural senses.
- 57. You will wake up, healthy and content, but you will not remember everything you felt or witnessed.
- 58. Your eyes are wide open now.
- 59. Look at the rope or the thread you left inside the two lines.
- 60. And to your great amazement, you will find out that the rope or the thread has only three knots now. And that is wonderful, because you got rid of a knot which was blocking many wonderful things from happening in your life.
- 61. There is one more wonderful surprise for you; look inside the bag where you have dumped the four objects you have selected. What you will see is self-explanatory.
- 62. You have made a most unusual and successful trip to another dimension. Your two lines are now re-aligned perfectly, and you are now in perfect harmony and sync with your Double.
- 63. This is an experience you will remember for the rest of your life.
- 64. Do not expect to succeed right away, but eventually you will without any doubt, if you believe in yourself, in the power of your mind, and in the magic of your imagination. It will work for you if you practice and

practice and practice. The process becomes much easier, if you know how to use your Supersymetric Mind.

- 65. You can repeat the same exercise for the remaining three knots, until you get rid of each knot which is blocking your life.
- 66. One knot at the time. One séance at the time. One exercise at the time.
- 67. Once all knots/blocks are removed, your Khateyn Tarika lines will become a formidable protection shield, and a magnificent source of energy, strength and mental enlightenment.

PART 6

Healing
Energy
Positive Vibes
Negative Vibes
Aura

Baaniradu Technique
The healing touch technique

I. Definition:

Baaniradu is the Anunnaki-Ulema term for the healing touch technique. It was first used by the priests of Melkart in Ancient Phoenicia, Ugarit and Arwad. It is extremely important to bear in mind, that this technique does not in any shape or form replace any scientific and medical treatment (s). Baaniradu has not been fully explored and used in the West.

I. Prerequisites and Preparation

- **1**-Before you learn how to heal, you should know first if you can heal, and if you have the power to heal without learning.
- **2**-Training and learning will show you the way, but not necessarily the blessing of healing others.
- **3**-Training will teach you the techniques of healing by touch and/or healing without touching. But success depends on the quality and quantity of the healing power you have in your "Conduit".
- **4**-Also you have to remember that if you are intoxicated, or under the influence of drugs, medicine, pills, addictive substances, narcotics, caffeine, tobacco and similar substances, you will not be able to heal others.
- **5**-If your body is not clean, you will not be able to heal others. Your hands most be sparkling clean all the time.
- **6**-If you have been sick yourself for the past 40 days, you will not be able to heal others.

- 7-If you have committed an act of violence, perjury, false testimony, adultery, theft and/or any hideous act (For the past 2 years), you will not be able to heal others. However, if you have been purified by the Ulema, and if you have fully compensated others (Humans and animals) for all the damages, losses, hurting, pain and suffering you have caused them, your chances of healing will increase considerably.
- 8-Do not come close to a sick person, and do not attempt to heal a sick person, if you have sinned in action and in thought. Only, when you are pure in heart and mind you can do so.

Because you will be generating a strong energy current with your hands, you have to keep in mind three important things:

a-Do not rotate both hands in opposite directions over one area of the sick body.

b-Do not use physical strength in moving your hands;

c-Do not constantly concentrate on one particular area of the sick body. Work around it as the healing touch progresses.

*** *** ***

- 1-Our bodies were created to heal themselves.
- 2-Our bodies were programmed from the time we were born.
- 3-We cannot change what was written in our "Essence" (Similar to DNA).
- 4-But we can improve on it.
- 5-Our bodies consist of many things, including mental memory, physical memory, spatial memory, and etheric memory.
- 6-Each memory has its own health condition, limitation and sphere.
- 7-We can be sick in one sphere, and perfectly healthy in another.
- 8-The mental affects the physical, and vice versa.
- 9-We can overcome mental and physical difficulties and disturbances by balancing our physical state (Physical milieu) with our mental sphere (Astral and/or non-physical dimension, also called Zinnar (Etheric Belt surrounding our body).

333

- **10-**This helps a lot. Because when we feel pain in certain part of our body, this part can be transposed into the Zinnar sphere for self-healing.
- **11-**Once it is healed, this part will return to its physical origin. This is an exercise/technique only the Ulema can accomplish. But students like you can heal the painful part of your body without transposing it into a non-physical sphere. You can heal that part with "Talamouth" (A gentle synchronized energetic touch), and "Tarkiz" (Even without touching the suffering part, and simply by directing beam of energy from the brain's cell "Conduit").
- **12-**You have to consider your body as a battery, or like an electrical current. Both have negative and positive terminals. Your body too, has a positive area, and a negative area.
- **13-**Some individuals have negative terminal in the left side of their bodies, and a positive terminal in the right side of their bodies. Others, just the opposite.
- **14-**Thus, it is very important to discern between the two terminals, and know where exactly the negative and the positive terminals or stations are located within the body.
- **15-**If you don't know how to localize these two terminals, and you try to heal a sick person, you could disorient the energy in his body and cause severe injuries.
- **16-**A well-trained student knows how to find these two terminals by dowsing, using his both hands as rods.
- **17-**Before you start dowsing, you have to know upfront, which one of your hands is positive, and which one of your hands is negative.
- **18-**If you don't know, and you begin with your healing touch process, you could disorient the energy flux in the body of the sick person, and cause severe damages to his health.
- **19-**If your right hand has a positive charge, then this hand should "hover" over the positive terminal of the sick person.
- **20-**If your right hand has a negative charge, then this hand should "hover" over the negative terminal of the sick person.

- **21**-The same thing applies to the other hand.
- **22**-You should not wear jewelry or metal during the healing touch therapy.
- **23**-You should not perform the healing touch therapy nearby an electrical outlet.
- **24**-You should not perform the healing touch therapy nearby pets, because pets sense diseases, illness and negative energy. They are vulnerable to these conditions and could absorb their frequencies and vibes, thus disrupting the healing process.
- **25**-Do not come too close to the body of the sick person. Keep at least 20 centimeters of distance between yourself and the sick person.
- **26**-You should stop your healing touch immediately if you notice that the sick person is having trouble breathing.

The healing touch training requires patience, perseverance, practice, and time. Usually, to complete the training program, a student spends at least 3 months studying and practicing. In some instances, the period could stretch to 6 months. Everything depends on the personal effort and commitment of the Talmiz (Student). There are several steps to follow. And here they are:
Your hands are an extension of your mind. Use them wisely and for the good of mankind. Talk to your hands. Explore them. Get to know them. Find out what they can do, and try to discover how many beautiful things they can create. Watch what usually a good concert pianist does before he starts to play.
He examines his hands, he communicates with his hands, he flexes his hands. Do the same thing.
Get to know your hands.
This exercise/technique will show you how.

III. The Technique:

Stage One:
- **1**-You need to practice 3 times a week.
- **2**-Each practice session will take approximately one hour.
- **3**-You practice alone.
- **4**-No people, and no pets should be around you.

- **5**-Select the most suitable three days of the week and stick to this schedule: Meaning you practice only on these three days.
- **6**-Same hours are highly recommended.
- **7**-You have to build in your system a new "practice-memory".
- **8**-First of all, you take a shower. You must be clean and your hands must be spotless.
- **9**-Enter your room, and sit comfortably in a wooden chair.
- **10**-Do not use metallic or plastic chair.
- **11**-Stay put for 5 seconds.
- **12**-Breathe deeply and gently.
- **13**-Extend both arms straight ahead.
- **14**-Join both hands, palm against palm.
- **15**-Keep them like this for one minute or so.
- **16**-Separate both hands approximately two centimeters apart, not more.
- **17**-Focus sharply on these two centimeters for one minute.
- **18**-Drop your hands down.
- **19**-Repeat this exercise (Joining and separating hands) three times.
- **20**-Drop your hands down.
- **21**-Stand up and breathe slowly and deeply three times.
- **22**-Sit down in your chair.
- **23**-Raise both hands, (palms facing the ground), and stretch them as far as you can (Not higher than your shoulders).
- **24**-Bring both hands close to your chest in an horizontal motion (Palms always facing the ground).
- **25**-Start to rotate both hands in a circular motion, and keeping a 15 centimeters distance between the rotation movements.
- **26**-Keep doing this for two minutes.
- **27**-Now, bring your hands together. Palm against palm.
- **28**-Keep both hands in this position close to your solar plexus for two minutes.
- **29**-Close your eyes for approximately two minutes.

- **30**-Now, tell your mind to enter a golden ray of light inside your solar plexus.
- **31**-Let the light enter your solar plexus.
- **32**-Keep your hands close to your solar plexus.
- **33**-Now, tell your mind you want your solar plexus to send the golden light to your hands.
- **34**-Tell your solar plexus to send the light right away.
- **35**-Tell your hands to receive the light and hold on it for one minute.
- **36**-Press strongly one hand against the other. Both palms are very firm.
- **37**-Stay like this for 2 minutes or so.
- **38**-At the end of the two minutes or so, you will start to feel some sort of heat in your palms. And that is good.
- **39**-Do not loose this heat. Hold on this heat.
- **40**-Do not let this heat leave your hands.
- **41**-Take a long and deep breath.
- **42**-Separate your hands.
- **43**-At this moment, you might feel a minor fatigue in both shoulders or a sort of a small muscle cramp in your neck. Don't worry. You will be fine in a few seconds.
- **44**-This is the end of the first session.
- **45**-Take a shower.

Note: Repeat this exercise three times a week for a period of one month.

Preparation for stage two:

During this stage you should not smoke, consume alcohol, or eat meat. And never ever touch addictive substances and narcotics!! This training stage shall take place outside your room. You are going to find a calm spot close to nature, far from cement, steel, noisy surroundings, and people.

We recommend a wooden area, a park, perhaps your backyard if it is not exposed to your neighbors, a river bank, or the beach when nobody is around. The most suitable time is always early in the morning around 5 o'clock. The day should be sunny but not hot. Dress in white. Very light.

Do not wear metal or jewelry. And do not eat before the practice.
Drink plenty of water before you start your exercise.
You don't have to bring anything with you. Mother nature and a
serene ambiance is all what you need.

Stage Two:
- 1-You are now starting stage two.
- 2-You have spent one month practicing in stage one. And you have made an important progress: You have discovered that you hands can hold heat.
- 3-We prefer to call that heat Energy.
- 4-Now, we are going to make this energy a positive energy.
- 5-If this energy is not developed into a positive energy, it will remain worthless, and will disappear before you know it.
- 6-So, we are going to hold on it, and make it work as a healing energy; a sort of positive vibes; a therapeutic touch.
- 7-You are going to succeed, as long as you have patience, you keep on practicing, and you are determined to use this wonderful power for the good of mankind.
- 8-Different practices apply to different places.
- 9-For instances, if you have chosen a river bank, you will be using river stones to practice with. If you have chosen a wooden area, you will be using leaves, or a piece of bark. If you have chosen the beach, you will be using sands or seashells.
- 10-You will always practice with pure elements of Mother Nature.
- 11-You will not touch synthetic products, plastic, metal or technological gadgets.
- 12-Let's assume you have chosen a river bank. And that is good.
- 13-Now you sit comfortably anywhere around the river bank.
- 14-But make sure that the area is clean, calm, and you are alone.
- 15-Take your shoes off.
- 16-Sit for a few seconds, and try to "empty your mind".

- **17**-We have already taught you how to "empty your mind".
- **18**-We are going to use this technique in stage two.
- **19**-Take a deep and a long breath.
- **20**-Find two clean stones. Not too big, and not too small; the size of a small apple.
- **21**-Place one stone in each palm and close both hands.
- **22**-With firmly closed hands squeeze the stones as strong as you can for one minute or so.
- **23**-Open both hands.
- **24**-Keep them open for ten seconds.
- **25**-Close both hands now, and squeeze one more time on the stones for another minute or so.
- **26**-While squeezing tell your mind to bring the golden light to the stones.
- **27**-Ask your mind again one more time.
- **28**-Imagine the golden light entering your hands.
- **29**-Direct the golden light toward the stones.
- **30**-Keep focusing on this for two minutes.
- **31**-Now something is going to happen. Pay attention.
- **32**-The stones are getting hot.
- **33**-Keep squeezing.
- **34**-You start to feel some sort of heat in your hands, and that is good.
- **35**-Now you tell yourself you are going to send the heat away.
- **36**-You tell yourself you are going to absorb the heat.
- **37**-Your order the heat to enter your body.
- **38**-You start to feel the heat entering your body, and that is good.
- **39**-Now you tell yourself your hands are no longer feeling any heat.
- **40**-There is no more heat in your hands.
- **41**-You open both hands.
- **42**-Now something very important is going to happen. Pay attention.
- **43**-Look at the stones.
- **44**-You are going to see something around the stones.

- **45**-What you are seeing now is the vapor of the heat that was left inside the stones.
- **46**-In a few seconds, the vapor will dissipate.
- **47**-You have made a tremendous progress.
- **48**-You were able to direct and to move the heat from one place to another.
- **49**-That is correct, because you have perfectly succeeded in bringing the heat to the stones.
- **50**-Also you have succeeded in storing the heat in the stones; and finally in directing the heat toward your body. That is remarkable.
- **51**-We are almost at the end of the exercise.
- **52**-You have to keep the two stones you worked with.
- **53**-Do not loose them.
- **54**-Put the stones in your pockets.
- **55**-Breathe slowly and deeply.
- **56**-Stay put for ten seconds.
- **57**-Stand up and you are on your way...

Note:
a-Repeat this exercise three times a week for a period of one month.
b-In a wooden area, you can use leaves or a piece of bark, or stones, whatever is accessible.
c-In the future, and once your Conduit is fully operational, you will be able to use this technique/exercise with various materials, including metal and substance originally made from liquids.

Stage Three:
Introduction:
This final stage is extremely important because it concentrates on:
a-Cleansing your hands;
b-Nourishing your hands;
c-Protecting your hands;
d-Experimenting with your hands.

- 1-For a period of one month, you should not touch any substance or product made out of animal fat.
- 2-Do not touch any toxic element.
- 3-Do not use tobacco or consume alcohol.
- 4-Use of addictive substances or narcotics is absolutely forbidden.
- 5-Every day for a period of 10 minutes, hold the two stones (you found on the river bank) in your palms (One in each hand), and gently flip the stones in any direction you want.
- 6-Close your hands, and visualize yourself sitting on the river bank.
- 7-Try to capture the sceneries of the river in your mind.
- 8-Repeat this exercise once a day for thirty days.
- 9-For five minutes or so everyday, bring both hands close to a healthy plant, and keep both hands at 10 centimeters distance from the plant.
- 10-Avoid touching the plant. Just surround it with your palms.
- 11-Focus on the greenest part of the plant or on the very top of the plant.
- 12-Select a specific part of the plant and concentrate on this part. Preferably around the bottom or the roots.
- 13-Repeat this exercise daily for thirty days.
- 14-While concentrating on the chosen area of the plant, remind your mind of the properties and energies of the green colors which are:
- a-Modifying energy.
- b-Natural healing ability.
- c-Restful state.
- 15-Tell yourself you are absorbing the energy, the natural healing ability and the serenity of the plant.
- 16-So far you have practiced with stones and plant. Now, you are going to practice with water.
- 17-Fill a flat container with boiled water.
- 18-Wait until it cools off.
- 19-Immerse both hands in the water.

- **20**-While immersing your hands in the water tell yourself that your hands are absorbing the blue light.
- **21**-Remind yourself of the properties and characteristics of the blue light which are:
- **A**- Balanced existence.
- **B**-Sustaining life.
- **C**-Easing the nerve system.
- **D**-Transmitting forces and energy.
- **E**-Balance of the mind.
- **F**-Receiving and/or transmitting information in a telepathic communication.
- **22**-Tell yourself once again that the blue light is entering your hands and solar plexus.
- **23**-Repeat this exercise twice daily for thirty days.
- **24**-We are almost done.
- **25**-Your final practice is with fire now. Nothing to be afraid of.
- **26**-You will be practicing with a gentle candle.
- **27**-Light up a white candle. Never use a black candle.
- **28**-Bring both hands close to the candle, and keep your palms at five centimeters distance from the candle.
- **29**-Focus on the flame for 2 minutes or so.
- **30**-Soon, you will start to see a purple color emerging from the blue flame. And that is good.
- **31**-Tell yourself the purple color is entering your palms and solar plexus.
- **32**-Indeed the purple color and the gentle warmth of the candle are entering your solar plexus and nourishing your palms.
- **33**-Remind yourself of the major property and effect of the purple color which are:
- **a**-Spiritual thoughts.
- **b**-Gentility, tenderness.
- **34**-Repeat this exercise twice daily for thirty days.
- **35**-Stage three comes to an end now.
- **36**-You are done. You have completed the orientation and training program.
- **37**-It is very possible that you have acquired a healing touch.

- **38**-You have to believe in the positive powers of your hands.
- **39**-You will find out very soon.
- **40**-Use your hands wisely and for the good of mankind.

*** *** ***

Bisho-barkadari "Bukadari" Technique
The Ulema technique to block negative vibes and bad thoughts aimed at you, your business, and your health

- I. Definition
- II. Case study
- Employees in the United States
- III. How to stop attracting negative people to your life. How to block negative vibes
- IV. The Ulema technique to block negative vibes and bad thoughts aimed at you, your business, and your health

---

I. Definition:
Bisho-barkadari "Bukadari" is the Anunnaki-Ultma term for the technique used in blocking bad vibes that negatively affect human beings.
It is composed from two words:
a-Bisho, which means bad; negative.
b-Barkadari, which means flames; rays, vibes; beams.

Negativity is atrociously destructive. It affects your mind, your body, your relationships with others, and your very environment. Negativity comes from three sources:
1-Others; their thoughts, intentions, and actions,
2-Yourself; your thoughts, intentions, and deeds,
3-Your environment; where and how you live.
- Thoughts can take a physical form.
- Thoughts can materialize in physical and non-physical dimensions.
- Enlightened ones can project and materialize healthy and positive thoughts.

343

- Deviated and succumbed seers can project, emanate and materialize negative and destructive thoughts.
- Bad and destructive thoughts directed toward you or against you can harm your mental and physical abilities, as well as your health, your progress, and your environment, including your home, your office, your car, and any place where you live and work.
- Malicious seers can either target your "Double" (Astral Body) and/or your physical body.
- They can also send harmful vibrations to your mind, to your body, and to the objects you touch, including tools, materials, equipments and instruments you use, such as a computer, a camera, a car, an elevator, a desk, even a can-opener. We will talk about all this in due time.
- These bad vibes can be intentional or unintentional.
- They are intentional when they are sent by others to harm you.
- They are unintentional when you discover or when you sense them on your own. In this situation, you can take an immediate action to stop their negative effects on you.
- For instance, you walk into a room or you mingle with people in a social gathering, and all of a sudden, you feel uncomfortable or disturbed in the presence of one or more individuals.
- You get the feeling that you are not at ease being around them, or something is bothering you about a particular person or a group of people. Usually, you get this feeling toward a particular person who has just passed by you, or looking at you, or just standing by.
- Sometimes you know what is bothering you about this guy, and sometimes you don't. Don't think much. Don't philosophize about it. You can stop this disturbing feeling on the spot. And I am going to show you how.
- But first, you must understand what has created this unpleasant and irritating feeling, and caused a negative current to circulate around you.
- Since this unpleasant feeling you have sensed was not intentionally created by others to hurt you, no serious harm will come to you.
- But if you do not stop it right away, it could cause further discomfort and additional nuisances.

344

- The person who has created this negative current around you is usually unaware of it. It is beyond his/her control.
- In most cases, the unpleasant vibes you felt toward that person, and the negativity you sensed are created by one or all of the following factors:

unhealthy vibrations.

b-The person's diet; the quantity of unhealthy food and addictive substances he/she absorbed.

c-The temper and character of the person; if he/she is a bitter and unhappy individual, the disharmonious and unbalanced frequencies of his/her unhappiness and bitterness will hit your Double, the perimeter of your aura, and all your sensorial faculties.

Those frequencies are charged with negative energy usually diffused through grayish rays undetected to the naked eyes, but could be seen, detected and analyzed in laboratories.

This is factual. In many instances, these negative vibrations can prevent your machines and equipments from working properly. All of a sudden, your computer crashes, your car does not start, your cellular phone is dead, your TV is shut off, and many of your electrical gadgets stop working. All these weird things happen while that person is around you.

Do not get frustrated. Do not lose your temper. Soon, everything will be just fine. In the following chapter, you will learn how to block negative vibes.

Two situations to deal with:

How many times did you tell yourself or others?

I can't work when my roommate is in the apartment.

I can't write when she is around!

He drained me out completely!

I feel nervous when he is around and everything stops working.

I had to wait until he leaves before I could start working again.

He gives me the creeps.

Basically, you have two situations to deal with:

1-Situation #1: What you should and could do if you can control your environment or place;

2-Situation #2: What you should and could do if you can't control your environment or place.

It is paramount to understand how the energy field surrounding you, and emanating from others plays a paramount role in conditioning and affecting your mind and your health. You can't measure it or see it with your naked eyes, but most certainly you have felt it many times. Everything around you can affect you. It can even affect your luck, fortune and business. Master B. Ushah was so right when he said that the energy field can be thought of as a grid of fine lines which run crisscross throughout the whole universe and through every living being, thereby connecting every part of creation to each other.

Wherever you go, you become part of the environment, even part of a street sign, and people crossing the street. The Ulema call this energy field "Ih-tikah'k", meaning contact with others on different plane. Western teachers refer to it as Aura, based upon Eastern traditions. This energy field (Ih-tikaah'k or Aura) is the electromagnetic field surrounding an object, including yourself, your friends and foes; even your pets.

It surrounds all living things such as people, plants and animals as well as non-living things such as rocks. These fields change with time, sometimes without warning, due to various positive and more often negative influences.

This field surrounds and runs through the body, holding within it information which reflects the current physical mental and emotional condition of the individual. It also contains the original "blueprint" of health. The human energy field is part of the life force energy field and is like a template or network of energy points with which the physical molecules of the body are aligned. As noted by B. Ushah.

The Ulema said that the field, within and outside of our bodies stores information including our thoughts, past and present. This energetic system comprises of several layers such as:

1-You physical body
2-Others' physical bodies,
3-You Double,
4-Others' Double,
5-Your electro-magnetic vibes,
6-Others' electro-magnetic vibes,
7-Your astral blueprints,
8-Others' astral blueprints,
9-Your Chakras,
10-Others' Chakras,
11-Your meridians,

12-Others' meridians,
13-Your past, present and future,
14-Others' past, present and future,
15-Your Conduit (Active or dormant),
16-Others' Conduit (Active or dormant).

Our personal energy field is in constant contact with the outside world because it is part of it:

- It absorbs slow frequencies from electrical equipment,
- It collects other people's negative energies,
- It stores the memory of upsetting interactions with others,
- It carries the memory of our past illness, distress and life experience, as noted by B. Ushah.

II. Case study:
Employees in the United States:

Contemporary Ulema have found that negative vibrations and transmission of negative energy rays vary in intensity and degree of harm in virtue of many factors.

1-In the United States, negative and bitter people are more likely to emit negative energy that can deeply affect you mentally and physically on Monday and on Tuesday than on any other days of the week.

2-Employees who are dissatisfied with their jobs and who dislike their boss diffuse intense bad vibes during the early and late hours of the day of their shifts.

3-These vibes become more intense upon returning home, and especially during the first 40 minutes.

4-The negative vibes dissipate short after, however their sub-conscience retains their dissatisfaction and anger for the rest of the day.

5-Thus, the Ulema suggest that you give those people enough room to relax and enough time to forget about the job they hate before you discuss with them any delicate or sensitive matter, because they will explode.

6-It is highly recommended to have pets around depressed and tired people. Pets provide therapeutic and curing vibes. However, if these people are going through intense rage or anger state, pets should not be left around them.

7-The negative vibes of bitter and angry people can cause damages not only to humans and pets, but also to domestic appliances.

III. How to stop attracting negative people to your life. How to block negative vibes:

Master Win Li said: "There is a major difference between the Western approach and the Ulema's technique to blocking negative vibes that can harm your well-being. However, Western therapists and Ulema agree on two things:

1-Negative vibes are either produced by ourselves or by others.

2-Without knowing many attract negative and destructive people to their lives.

In both situations, the consequences can be disastrous. Are there techniques to block harmful negative vibes, and to stop attracting bitter and negative people to our life and to what we do for a living? The answer is yes!"

IV. The Ulema technique: How to block negative vibes

- 1-For the untrained, it is difficult to pinpoint the source of bad vibes. Therefore, we will be providing you with general guidelines useful in many cases.
- 2-It is very easy to protect yourself from bad vibes by creating a mental shield around your body.
- 3-Everything starts with your mind.
- 4-You start the first steps in the privacy of your room.
- 5-You sit comfortably in a chair in your room.
- 6-Take off your shoes.
- 7-Remove your jewelry, your belt, your tie, your watch, and any metallic substance you are wearing.
- 8-Change into white clothes. Never wear dark colors clothes during this exercise.
- 9-Close your eyes and take a deep breath.
- 10-Breathe deeply three times.
- 11-Keep your eyes closed.
- 12-Visualize your body standing before your eyes. It is very simple. Just tell yourself I want to imagine my body right here standing before me. It is not going to happen physically, but just say that to yourself.

- 13-Repeat it one more time. Repeat the very same thing you just said.
- 14-Everything is going to be fine.
- 15-Breathe deeply and slowly one more time.
- 16-Stretch your arms (Straight) and move them or rotate in any direction you want as if you were swimming.
- 17-Keep on breathing very slowly and gently.
- 18-Imagine yourself swimming in a beautiful crystal clear lake.
- 19-Continue to swim until you reach the bank or the edge of the lake.
- 20-You are there now. Look for a comfortable spot and sit there.
- 21-You start to feel a fresh breeze and that is good.
- 22-Keep your eyes closed.
- 23-Look at the other edge of the lake. You will find it. The edge from where you started to swim.
- 24-Good. You found the edge.
- 25-Clap your hands now.
- 26-You hear the clapping of your hands.
- 27-Tell yourself you are leaving the sound of clapping at the edge of the lake.
- 28-Leave the clapping at the far end (The edge) of the lake, and return to your spot where you were sitting.
- 29-No, you will not swim again to return to your spot.
- 30-Your brain is so fast now, and understands what you need...it will take you right away to your spot.
- 31-That is wonderful. You are there now, sitting calmly.
- 32-You are still enjoying the fresh breeze.
- 33-Breathe and smell the fresh breeze.
- 33-Tell the breeze to move faster and faster.
- 34-Repeat your command one more time.
- 35-The breeze is moving fast now.
- 36-Let it move and move and move.
- 37-Tell the breeze to get thicker and ticker.
- 38-The breeze is getting ticker...very very thick.
- 39-Thank the breeze.
- 40-Tell the breeze to change itself into a wall.
- 41-Repeat this command three times.

- 42-You are going to feel something now. Pay attention.
- 43-Your head is getting heavier. And that is good.
- 44-Tell the wall to stay there like a guard.
- 45-Lift up both arms and direct them toward the wall.
- 46-Tell yourself the wall is strong and is blocking everything.
- 47-Tell yourself you are leaving everything that has disturbed you behind the wall.
- 48-Thank the wall and ask the wall to go away.
- 49-Clap your hands twice.
- 50-In your mind, try to remember how did you get here, from the very beginning.
- 51-Now tell yourself you are going back to where you have started...the lake bank you saw first.
- 52-Good. You are at the lake bank now.
- 53-You see, you came back without swimming. Your mind knows what you are doing. He is with you all the way.
- 54-Now tell yourself the lake, the breeze, the wall will always be around you to protect you from other's bad thoughts and vibes.
- 55-Tell yourself nobody can enter or break the wall around you.
- 56-Repeat this 3 times.
- 57-Take a deep breath.
- 58-Open your eyes and stay calm in your chair.
- 59-Right down in a notebook what you have experienced. The more details you put down the better you will feel very very soon.
- 60-Repeat this exercise twice a week, always the same day and same time for one full month.
- 61-After the third exercise, burn your notes.
- 62-After the fourth exercise you are going to feel so good and so strong.
- 63-Bad vibes will never disturb you again.

Introduction to the study of vibrations, energy and "Affected Luck"

Everything around you affects your life, negatively or positively, and this includes, pets, people, objects, plants, the way your home is designed, absolutely everything.
You might not know that some people, including good buddies and friends can bring you bad luck, and prevent you from succeeding in life. This book will tell you everything about these topics, and teach you how to change your life to better, and head toward success.

1-People:
Some people who are filled with negativity and bitterness can even crash your computer if they are around, and their negative vibes can spread and develop conditions that cause your failure in many of your projects, businesses, investment, health, and/or any endeavor you are involved with.
Ruhaniyiin, Sahiriin, and Anunnaki Ulema taught us that the human body is a depot of everything that constitutes a person. It is not only a physical organism, but a container of all aspects of a person, mentally, physically, spiritually, and metaphysically.
People who hate your guts, those who envy your success, those who love to see you broke and miserable, and individuals who are mentally and spiritually bankrupt can cause you harm, just by thinking about hurting you.
Some, know the mechanism, others don't.

*** *** ***

353

Their vicious intentions, thoughts, and wishes are stored in "Jabas" inside their brain, and their vibes can create "Mintaka Fasida" (Negative Zone) that could penetrate your "Khateyn Tarika", and cause lots of damages.
No, they are not masters of the power of mind, or great psychics. They are just bad people with strong negative vibes that you are sensible and sensitive to.
Sometimes, dear friends, siblings, and relatives can do the same thing, without knowing, because they are not aware of the functioning of their Jabas.
Their bitterness, loneliness, financial insecurity, and negativity can disrupt the normal rhythm of your life, if they are around you. This is an absolute fact.

The problem we are facing here, is the fact that neither us nor them are aware of what is going on. Besides, you don't suspect a dear friend to cause you harm!
Unfortunately, it happens to us all the time.
Some people who, just by entering your room, and without touching anything, doing anything, or saying anything, can blow up your oven, freeze your computer, and even damage your health.
Their negative vibes are causing all this.
You should be very careful when you are around people, and vice-versa. You need a protection shield that prevents their vibes from entering your "Own Zone", mentally and physically.

2-Where you live:
Something else you should be concerned with: The area where you live. There are areas, zones, spots and places charged with underground negative currents that kill any opportunity to succeed in any project of yours, and would/could bring a series of failures to your life.
Some areas and neighborhoods are good for you, others awfully bad, for everything you do, including your health, relations with others, work and anything related to your present and future.
You should know about these positive and negative zones, places, and neighborhoods.

354

In this book, I tried to summarize the locations of these areas. I will not give you the precise names and locations of streets and zones, because I do not want to cause a mass panic, or get into troubles with local organizations, neighborhoods' committees, developers, and official authorities.

However, I will give you a list of states that fall into any of the foresaid categories. Also, I will provide you with maps reflecting the underground positive and negative currents that have major effects on you and your life in general.

3-Do you feel unlucky?

Many feel unlucky, and they don't know why?

They try hard to come up with something that could change their lives to better, feel secure, but they always fail, despite their hard efforts, good intentions, and perseverance. No matter what they do, there is no light at the end of the tunnel?

How do we explain this?

Is it bad luck?

Bad karma?

Bad planning?

The wrong time?

The wrong place?

Or something else?

I will explore with you all the possibilities and scenarios.

But one thing is sure; there are "Knots" in your life that must be removed right away from the "Thread of your life."

Something has already been written in the book of your life. The Anunnaki Ulema call it "Maktoob", meaning what is written for your future.

How to deal and cope with Maktoob?

Are there techniques and practices to remove the knots of bad luck?

Yes, there is!

And, I will show you step-by-step how to do it.

Also, what about the "17 lucky years" and "7 unlucky years" in your life?

Are you aware of that?

Well, the Rouhaniyiin and the Anunnaki-Ulema told us that each one of us will go through periods (weeks, months, years) that are either lucky or unlucky, and have an enormous effect on everything we do.

During the bad period, we should not –for instance– invest, create a new business, get involved with something or somebody, or take a major decision concerning a job, relocation and other important matters.

And there are the good years in our lives, where everything blooms, and everything we touch will "turn into gold."

We will discover these years and moments in our lives that have determined our fate and/or will shape our future. And yes, in this book, I will provide you with several pertinent techniques and exercises.

4-Good timing and bad timing:

We know from the Anunnaki Ulema Dirasaat and Kiraat, that our lives are conditioned and regulated by a Rizmanah; a sort of macro-micro-human-cosmic calendar that contains all events, situations, circumstances, positions, locations, (Past, present and future) that will shape our lives, fate, destiny, future and luck. There are good days, and there are bad days.

There are happy hours, and there are sad hours. There is a time to cry and mourn, and there is time to rejoice and celebrate. You already know that.

But what you didn't know is this: There are days and hours that could bring failure and even catastrophic results, if you conduct your business, travel, invest, start a new project, relocate, and so on, during those days and those hours.

And fortunately, there are good days and good hours to start a new business, meet new friends, partners, soul-mates, and make decisions on serious matters.

The bad and good days and hours are clearly written inside the Rizmanah. So, you have to check out the Rizmanah.

Each one of us has a personal Rizmanah.

No two Rizmanahs are alike.

In the book, I have provided you with a basic format of the Rizmanah, pertinent squares, and numbers you can use to figure out your good days and hours.

5-Your name:
Oh yes! Your name plays a major role in your life. I am not referring to fancy names, aristocratic names or Hilly-Billy names. I am talking about the powers and weaknesses contained in your surname.
Each letter in your name has something to do with your future, and the place you occupy in this world. Did you know that you have another name given to you before you were born?
Yes sir!
A name not given to you by parents, and relatives.
But by those who created you!
You will read about this fascinating subject in this book.

6-The Great Awakening:
You pump iron to develop your muscles.
How about your brain's muscles?
And, what do you do to increase the size and capabilities of your mind? Well, there are lots of techniques you can use to develop the powers of your mind.
Although, they are metaphysical and esoteric, the results are equally mental and physical.
I have provided you in this book with several exercises, lessons and techniques that could bring a "Great Awakening" to your mind and Supersymetric Mind. They are easy to follow, assuming that you invest in your quest, perseverance, patience, and belief in yourself.

Once your mind is awake and entirely alert, you will discover a world within you, full of supernatural powers, awareness, and synchronization with two wheels that constitute your universe.
The first wheel is the Macro Wheel, and it represents the cosmos you live in.
The second wheel is the Micro Wheel, and it represents you on the landscape of the cosmos.

If the two wheels are not in sync, whatever you do in your life will remain in vain, and you will never accomplish anything meaningful. Consequently, mishaps and bad luck will ride with you on the roads of life.

Some of the techniques and exercises that facilitate harmonious synchronization of the two wheels include the exploration of your imagination and mental projection of everything that surrounds you and influence your way of life, health, business, and your future in general. You will have the opportunity to learn these techniques; they are fun, stimulating and extra-ordinary.

I welcome you to the path of knowledge, sacred hidden wisdom, enlightening discoveries, and compassion.

And let me remind you that in order to succeed in unlocking these secrets and make them work for you, you should keep a warm place in your heart for all those who need comfort, and help everybody and anybody in any way you can, especially those who cannot return the favor.

Without affection and compassion, without pure goodness in your heart, you will never be able to benefit from this book.

Maraka Fasida and Esoteric Dowsing

- Introduction
- List of countries with considerable Maraka Fasida
- Africa
- Africa's worst spots are located in
- Europe
- Europe's worst spots are located in
- Asia
- Asia's worst spots are located in
- Latin America and the Caribbeans
- Latin America and the Caribbeans worst spots are located in
- The United States
- United States' worst spots are located in
- Canada
- Map of United States Lucky and Unlucky Zones
- Map of United States Delicate Zones.
- Explanation
- Black line: Current of negative energy
- Explanation
- Bad spots in Florida
- In Washington, DC area (DC/Virginia/Maryland)
- Bad spots in Virginia
- Bad spots in Maryland
- Bad spots in Washington, DC

359

- Currents of positive energy, and negative energy.
- Ishra-Tamam gray line: Current of positive Energy.
- Ishra-Atila black line: Current of negative Energy.
- Map of Creativity Zones in the United States.
- Explanation
- Etheric Chart's explanation

*** *** ***

Esoteric Dowsing

1. Introduction:

The globe is filled with a multitude of underground negative currents and spots that store and circulate negative energy.

The areas, spots, and zones that store negative energy (ies) are called Maraka Fasida.

And, they are almost everywhere underground.

The Anunnaki Ulema and Rouhaniyiin told us that there are approximately 750,000 Maraka Fasida on planet Earth. Many are unidentified and/or not revealed to us by the Masters. And, they have their own reasons.

People who live above these negative zones (Spots and currents) will suffer enormously in their lives. And their suffering (Physical and mental) will encompass failure in business, relationships, entrepreneurial activities, partnerships, investments, health and mental development. Africa has the lion's share.

2. List of countries with considerable Maraka Fasida:

Africa

- Algeria (People's Democratic Republic of Algeria): 6
- Angola (Republic of Angola): 26
- Benin (Republic of Benin): 86
- Botswana (Republic of Botswana): 16
- Burkina Faso: 10
- Burundi (Republic of Burundi): 9
- Cameroon (Republic of Cameroon): 11
- Cape Verde (Republic of Cape Verde): 7
- Central African Republic (Central African Republic): 89
- Chad (Republic of Chad): 18
- Comoros (Union of the Comoros): 10

361

- Côte d'Ivoire (Republic of Côte d'Ivoire): 28
- Djibouti (Republic of Djibouti): 21
- Egypt (Arab Republic of Egypt): 10
- Equatorial Guinea (Republic of Equatorial Guinea): 96
- Eritrea (State of Eritrea): 26
- Ethiopia (Federal Democratic Republic of Ethiopia): 21
- Gabon (Gabonese Republic): 65
- Gambia (Republic of The Gambia): 74
- Ghana (Republic of Ghana): 91
- Guinea (Republic of Guinea): 94
- Guinea-Bissau (Republic of Guinea-Bissau): 26
- Kenya (Republic of Kenya): 98
- Lesotho (Kingdom of Lesotho): 26
- Liberia (Republic of Liberia): 315
- Libya (Great Socialist People's Libyan Arab Jamahiriya): 11
- Malawi (Republic of Malawi): 11
- Mali (Republic of Mali):21
- Mauritania (Islamic Republic of Mauritania): 21
- Morocco (Kingdom of Morocco): 9
- Mozambique (Republic of Mozambique): 39
- Namibia (Republic of Namibia): 21
- Niger (Republic of Niger): 89
- Nigeria (Federal Republic of Nigeria): 243
- Republic of the Congo (Republic of the Congo): 112
- Rwanda (Republic of Rwanda): 275
- Sao Tome and Principe: 78
- Senegal (Republic of Senegal): 76
- Seychelles (Republic of Seychelles): 43
- Sierra Leone (Republic of Sierra Leone): 348
- Somalia (Somali Republic): 721
- South Africa (Republic of South Africa): 154
- Sudan (Republic of Sudan): 19
- Swaziland (Kingdom of Swaziland): 19
- Tanzania (United Republic of Tanzania): 70

- Togo (Togolese Republic): 21
- Tunisia (Tunisian Republic): 9
- Uganda (Republic of Uganda): 121
- Western Sahara (Sahrawi Arab Democratic Republic): 19
- Zambia (Republic of Zambia): 32
- Zimbabwe (Republic of Zimbabwe): 98

Others:
Madagascar (Republic of Madagascar): 21
Mauritius (Republic of Mauritius): 49

Africa's worst spots (Zones and currents) are located in:
In this order.

Sierra Leone (Republic of Sierra Leone).
Central African Republic (Central African Republic).
South Africa (Republic of South Africa).
Ghana (Republic of Ghana).
Nigeria (Federal Republic of Nigeria).
Rwanda (Republic of Rwanda).
Republic of the Congo (Republic of the Congo).
Uganda (Republic of Uganda).
Somalia (Somali Republic).

*** *** ***
Europe

- Albania: 3
- Andorra: 3
- Armenia: 6
- Austria: 4
- Azerbaijan: 21
- Belarus: 6
- Belgium: 4
- Bosnia & Herzegovina: 11

- Bulgaria: 5
- Croatia: 13
- Cyprus: 6
- Czech Republic: 9
- Denmark: 3
- Estonia: 6
- Finland: 4
- France: 3
- Georgia: 4
- Germany: 9
- Greece: 9
- Hungary: 6
- Iceland: 3
- Ireland: 2
- Italy: 6
- Kosovo: 13
- Latvia: 3
- Liechtenstein: 1
- Lithuania: 4
- Luxembourg: 1
- Macedonia: 4
- Malta: 2
- Moldova: 2
- Monaco: 1
- Montenegro: 2
- The Netherlands: 3
- Norway: 2
- Poland: 4
- Portugal: 4
- Romania: 4
- Russia: 9
- San Marino: 1
- Serbia: 11
- Slovakia: 3
- Slovenia: 3
- Spain: 5

- Sweden: 1
- Switzerland: 1
- Turkey: 11
- Ukraine: 5
- United Kingdom: 6
- Vatican City (Holy See): 1

Europe's worst spots are located in:
In this order.

- Azerbaijan
- Croatia
- Kosovo
- Serbia
- Turkey
- Bosnia & Herzegovina
- Czech Republic
- Albania
- Andorra
- Russia
- Germany

*** *** ***

Asia

- Afghanistan: 31
- Armenia: 6
- Australia: 6
- Azerbaijan: 21
- Bahrain: 2
- Bangladesh: 5
- Bhutan: 2
- Brunei: 2
- Cambodia: 16
- China: 8

- Cyprus: 6
- Fiji: 1
- India: 6
- Indonesia: 7
- Iran: 3
- Iraq: 3
- Israel: 9
- Japan: 9
- Jordan: 2
- Kazakhstan: 5
- Kiribati: 1
- Kuwait: 2
- Kyrgyzstan: 2
- Laos: 9
- Lebanon: 3
- Malaysia: 7
- Maldives: 2
- Marshall Islands: 1
- Federated States of Micronesia: 3
- Mongolia: 2
- Myanmar: 2
- Nauru: 2
- Nepal: 1
- New Zealand: 2
- North Korea: 7
- Oman: 2
- Pakistan: 11
- Palau: 2
- Papua New Guinea: 7
- Philippines: 8
- Qatar: 2
- Samoa: 1
- Saudi Arabia: 3
- Singapore: 6
- Solomon Islands: 2

- South Korea: 6
- Sri Lanka: 4
- Syria: 3
- Taiwan: 3
- Tajikistan: 3
- Thailand: 4
- Timor-Leste: 1
- Tonga: 2
- Turkey: 11
- Turkmenistan: 3
- Tuvalu: 2
- Uzbekistan: 3
- United Arab Emirates: 2
- Vanuatu: 2
- Vietnam: 7
- Yemen: 3

Asia's worst spots are located in:
In this order.

- Afghanistan
- Azerbaijan
- Cambodia
- Pakistan
- Israel
- Japan
- Laos
- China
- Malaysia
- North Korea
- Papua New Guinea
- Indonesia

*** *** ***

Latin America and the Caribbeans

- Anguilla: 1
- Antigua and Barbuda: 1
- Argentina: 2
- Aruba: 1
- Bahamas: 5
- Barbados: 1
- Belize: 1
- Bermuda: 11
- Bolivia: 3
- Brazil: 3
- British Virgin Islands: 1
- Cayman Islands: 1
- Chile: 2
- Colombia: 6
- Costa Rica: 2
- Cuba: 3
- Dominican Republic: 3
- Ecuador: 2
- El Salvador: 2
- Grenada: 2
- Guatemala: 2
- Guyana: 4
- Haiti: 11
- Honduras: 2
- Jamaica: 6
- Mexico: 4
- Montserrat: 1
- Netherlands Antilles: 1
- Nicaragua: 2
- Panama: 2
- Paraguay: 2
- Peru: 2
- Saint Kitts and Nevis: 1

- Saint Lucia: 1
- Saint Vincent and the Grenadines: 1
- Suriname: 1
- Trinidad and Tobago: 1
- Turks and Caicos Islands: 1
- Uruguay: 1
- Venezuela: 1

Latin America and the Caribbeans worst spots are located in:
In this order.
- Haiti
- Bermuda
- Colombia
- Jamaica
- Bahamas
- Mexico
- Guyana

*** *** ***

The United States

Note: Do not confuse negative current and negative spot. Refer to the terminology section.

- Alabama: 4
- Alaska: 2
- American Samoa: 1
- Arizona: 3
- Arkansas: 2
- California: 7
- Colorado: 1
- Connecticut: 1
- Delaware: 1

- District of Columbia: 7
- Florida: 13
- Georgia: 2
- Guam: 1
- Hawaii: 3
- Idaho: 1
- Illinois: 2
- Indiana: 1
- Iowa: 1
- Kansas: 1
- Kentucky: 1
- Louisiana: 4
- Maine: 1
- Maryland: 2
- Massachusetts: 2
- Michigan: 2
- Minnesota: 1
- Mississippi: 3
- Missouri: 2
- Montana: 1
- Nebraska: 1
- Nevada: 9
- New Hampshire: 1
- New Jersey: 3
- New Mexico: 2
- New York: 11
- North Carolina: 1
- North Dakota: 1
- Northern Marianas Islands: 1
- Ohio: 2
- Oklahoma: 1
- Oregon: 1
- Pennsylvania: 2
- Puerto Rico: 4
- Rhode Island: 1
- South Carolina : 1

- South Dakota: 1
- Tennessee: 1
- Texas: 7
- Utah: 1
- Vermont: 1
- Virginia: 3
- Virgin Islands: 3
- Washington: 2
- West Virginia: 3
- Wisconsin: 2
- Wyoming: 1

United States' worst spots are located in:
In this order.

- Florida
- New York
- Nevada
- Texas
- California
- District of Columbia
- Louisiana
- Alabama
- Puerto Rico

*** *** ***
Canada

Canada has 3 spots.

371

Map of United States Lucky and Unlucky Zones
Note: See explanations on the next page.

Map of Lucky and Unlucky Zones

Map of United States Delicate Zones.

Explanation:
A Delicate zone means one or all of the following:
1-The black dots refer to states, where the level and degree of your financial success and/or stability are pre-determined by circumstances and factors out of your control.

2-Although these states are not negative in etheric structure, the vibrations of their milieu (People living there, and underground currents) will affect the outcome of your efforts, planning, financial stability, and new enterprises.
This does not apply to all of us, but to some individuals who are "sensitive and sensible" to the underground negative spots and currents. Many people who live in some of these states succeeded beyond belief and became millionaires, while others failed miserably despite their hard work, intelligence and financial resources.
California, New York and Greater Washington, DC (Including two areas in Maryland) are perfect examples.
You should consult your "Vibrations Personal Chart" and your Rizmanah.
New Jersey is a locale/Carrefour/conglomeration for conflicting currents, meaning unpredictable results. Consequently, if you have lived in neighboring areas where their Maraka Fasida are accentuated, then, you should not move your business, or start a new project in an area or zone situated above an underground negative current starting underground in New York. This is not financial advice I am giving you; and, you should not consider my explanation as a professional opinion. It is up to you, to consider the situation or disregard my argument.
Personally, I will not move my business and activities to any area, if it is directly linked to a negative current which originally starts and/or originates underground/spot/current of a state where the Maraka Fasida is strong.
From consulting my "Etheric Chart", I came to a conclusion that some streets and avenues in New York City will not be beneficial for a period of time starting in 2010 and ending in 2014. Again, this is my personal reading, and you should not categorically apply my findings to your personal situation. It is up to you.
But, if I were in your position, I would seriously consider these possibilities.
In New York: 19th Street between 7th Avenue and 8th Avenue is not a favorable spot. There are 2 blocks on 8th Avenue, I consider to be extremely negative.
57th Street is not a beneficial etheric locale.

18th Street between 7th & 8th Avenue is not good spot for people who want to succeed in artistic careers, such as: acting, composing music and producing videos. On 23rd Street, near Chelsea Hotel, there are several bad luck pockets that could prevent many from having financial freedom. Many of the people living there will always struggle.
Harlem area has 2 huge negative spots. 188th Street, in Inwood, is a good spot. However, there is one bad spot in Inwood above 200th Street, on the East side, zip code 10033 that has a few bad spots. Spiritual people can feel it as well as smell the bad vibes in the air. Its ramifications are stored in the walls of the buildings.

Two particular areas in Park Slope, Brooklyn, are to be avoided. They are bad for business and they halt your creativity.
There are delicate zones on 1st Avenue that could twist your luck. Some blocks of 1st Avenue could catapult your success, but you have to know upfront when you should get out of that area.
Part of Binghamton has been affected by a negative underground current.
3-Some spots in delicate zones have a temporary effect, meaning that for a few months or a few years, your business, personal development, peace of mind and tranquility will not be negatively affected, but at some point, you should relocate to another area. Be alert, watch how things are going, revise your plans and compare results.
Create a time-table chart for all the results you are getting for a few months. Give yourself time, but observe very carefully how others who are conducting the same business are doing on a monthly basis.

*** *** ***

375

Black line: Current of negative energy.

Map of Lucky and Unlucky Zones

Black line: Current of negative energy.

Explanation:
The black line refers to a strong negative current.
States located above this current are charged with Maraka Fasida
strong vibrations. Florida takes the leads.

Bad spots in Florida:
Miami Beach,
Boca Raton,
Delray Beach,
Panama City,
Kissimmee,
Boynton Beach,
Marathon.

In Washington, DC area (DC/Virginia/Maryland):
Bad spots in Virginia:
Loudoun County,
Leesburg,
Tysons Corner.

Bad spots in Maryland:
Columbia,
Fell's Point.

Bad spots in Washington, DC:
Two blocks on Wisconsin Avenue, North West,
One block on M Street in Georgetown, North West,
Brentwood,
Capitol Hill,
One block on Pennsylvania Avenue,
Six blocks in the east/south areas.
One huge bad spot on 14th Street.

*** *** ***

Currents of Positive Energy, and Negative Energy.

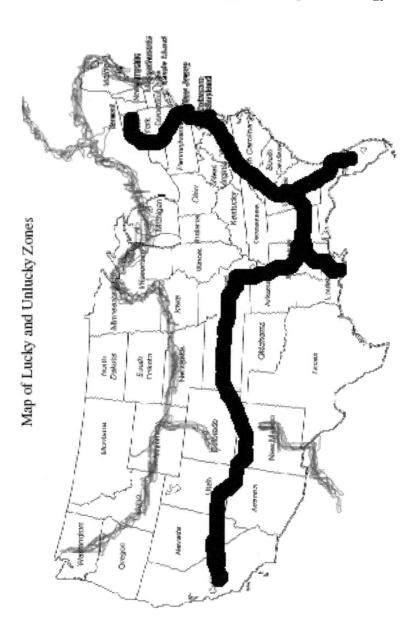

Map of Lucky and Unlucky Zones

Currents of Positive Energy, and Negative Energy.

There are two major currents (Spots and ramifications) running underground in the United States.
The first current is called Ishra-Tamam; it represents a positive energy. The second current is called Ishra-Atila; it represents a negative energy.

Ishra-Tamam:
The map on page 56, illustrates these two currents. The gray line belongs to Ishra-Tamam. It represents the current of positive energy.

Ishra-Atila:
The black line belongs to Ishra-Atila. It represents the current of negative energy.

*** *** ***

379

Map of Creativity Zones in the United States.

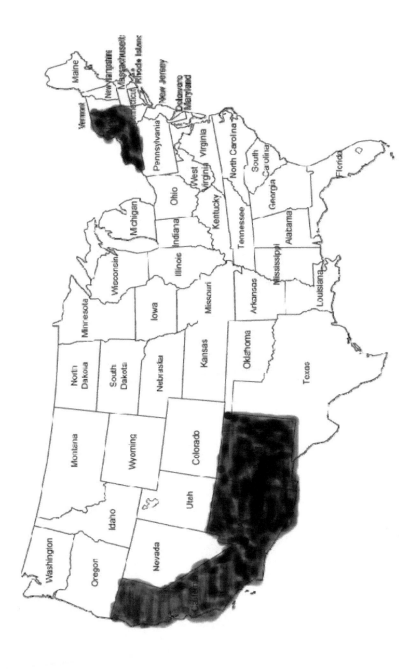

Map of Creativity Zones in the United States.

Explanation:
The map on page 58 represents states, where your creativity and entrepreneurial inclination would flourish. New York takes the lead. California comes second. But you have to remember that your success in this area (Creativity) is not always guaranteed, because New York and California are on the map of United States Delicate Zones. The Etheric Chart provides an explanation.

Etheric Chart's Explanation:
Although underground currents affect (Positively and negatively) those who live above, people too, participate in increasing the positive and negative levels of such currents.
It is a two-way street.
Let's take for instance the reasons that invite and/or encourage people to relocate to another state, or more precisely, the major reason to move to a particular state, such as New York. Almost 90% will tell you: Opportunities, more jobs, business, money and soon.
And of course, lots of them will tell you: Art, culture, Broadway, musicals, museums, etc.
But basically, it is the aspect of business/money, jobs and the enormous opportunities, New York offer.
There is no question about it. And, that's fine.
But if you start to dig deeper into the fabric and nature of how people in big cities and prosperous metropolitan areas, such as New York, compete with each other, seize opportunities, market their products, package themselves, sell themselves, and conduct their business, you will find out that (in many instances, almost 92%) grccd, power, selfishness, deceitful practices, materialism, and compromising ethical standards, play a major role in fueling their success and dominating the market.

These sorts of operations, intentions, and practices contaminate the etheric and spiritual dimensions (Zones) where you, them, and newcomers live and work.

Consequently, they create negative vibes and add to the destructive flux of the negative energy current running beneath us. So, as you see, negative currents affect people and people with bad vibes equally affect the circulating energy where we live. And, in New York City you will find plenty of that.

This could explain why these areas are called delicate zones. However, these areas will not stop your creativity from blooming. Nevertheless, you have to consult your personal etheric chart, and Rizmanah upon dealing with others.

The Rizmanah is also important because it shows you the good days and bad days, the good hours and bad hours to take decisions and conclude business with others.

*** *** ***

Ikti-Chafa
Discovering the Energy of your Mind and Body

I. Introduction:

At the Ma'ahad, the honorable Enlightened Masters taught us several techniques to sense and direct our energy via Ikti-Chafa exercise. In this section, I will provide you with a very simple practice/technique that could help you discover, sense, and direct your energy.

It is customary for the spiritual teachers, guides, channelers, psychics, mediums and healers to talk about that un-je-ne-sais-quoi "Energy"!

But rarely, do they explain in simple terms, what that energy is!

What its substance is made of?

How energy is created?

How energy could be sensed and directed?

How to use it to create a positive environment?

How to use it to block others' negative thoughts and energy?

Can we see others' energy?

Can we see our own energy?

And, can we measure energy?

If pertinent answers and explanations are not given to us, then, kiss goodbye that energy, and all the mambo-jumbo lectures of the spiritual masters and so-called psychics. And, it's as simple as that.

Energy has been defined as:

- Aura,
- Astral Body,
- Vibes or rays emanated by Chakras,
- The first layer of the Double,
- The electromagnetic frequencies of substances and bio-organic elements found in our body,
- An etheric vibration.

383

Some masters in the East depicted energy as:
- Chi,
- Ki,
- Noi Cun,
- Nei-Cha,
- Inner mental-physical strength, you name it.

Don't get confuse with all these definitions. We have to simplify things to understand things.

So, for now, let's call energy, vibrations or frequencies produced by the Jabas, and the elements (Organic elements) found in our body.

Although, they are not visible to the naked eye, true spiritual masters can see these vibrations and frequencies, and in some instances, can be scientifically detected and measured in the laboratory.

II. Generalities:

All of us have energy. Good people produce positive and good energy. Bad people produce negative and bad energy.

Sick people (Good or bad people) produce negative energy.

Mentally disturbed people (Good or bad people) produce negative energy.

Inmates (Good or bad people, innocent or guilty people) produce negative energy.

Good people who temporarily display anger and violence, produce negative and bad energy.

Briefly, energy reflects what and who you are at certain point in your life. It is not permanent, meaning, sometimes, we emanate good energy (Good vibes), and some other times, we emanate bad energy (Bad vibes).

Everything depends on our state of mind, health condition and emotional situation. The good news is:

1-We can change our negative energy to a positive energy.

2-We can see our energy, measure its intensity and use it to ameliorate our situation.

3-We can sense, and in some cases, see others' energy and right away determine whether they are good people or bad people.

But first of all, we need to sense our own energy. This will allow us, later on, to see others' energy, and possibly read them, probe and understand their intentions, and consequently, protect ourselves against harm and damages caused by the vibrations of their bad energy.
On the following pages, I am going to show you step-by-step, how to sense and direct your energy.

*** *** ***

III. Materials/tools needed:

1. A piece of white paper or a white napkin.
2. A candle. Any kind. Color and size are irrelevant.
3. A needle or a pin.

IV. Preparation:

The initial phase is called "Preparation" and includes:
Illustration #1, Illustration #2, Illustration #3, Illustration #4, Step One, Step Two and Step Three.

Step One:

Look now at Illustration #1, on page 101.
Note: When item #10 is done, turn off the light in the room.
1. Perform the exercise in the privacy of your room, always after 7.00 PM.
2. Perform the exercise on any day of the week, except on Sunday night after 10:00 PM or on Monday between 7:00 PM and 9:00 PM.
3. Perform the exercise alone.
No people or pets should be around, because you must not contaminate your vibes.
4. Place the candle on the lower left side of the paper or the napkin.
5. Place the paper or the napkin on a solid surface.
6. Fold the paper or the napkin as seen on the illustration.
7. Draw 2 triangles on the paper or the napkin as seen on the illustration.
8. Mark the upper corner of each triangle with a dot as seen on the illustration.
9. Light up the candle.
10-Stick a needle or a pin in the candle as seen on the illustration.
11-Turn off the light in the room or where you are conducting the exercise.
Note: The needle should be positioned in a way or at an angle that would reflect its shadow on the paper or the napkin. You can always adjust and re-adjust the position (Place) of the needle or the pin. Work on this.

Illustration #1

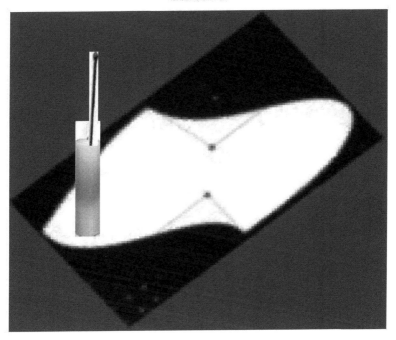

Step Two: Understanding the technique.

1. You must understand what is going on, in order to proceed. So look at Illustration #2. You will see a black line in the middle of the napkin or the paper. This is a dividing line. It is called Khat.
2. The line divides the surface (Paper or napkin) into two areas.
3. The top area "A" is a negative spot.
4. The lower area "A1" is a positive spot.
5. In area "A", you will find an "Upper Triangle". This triangle stores the source of the negative energy.
6. In area "A1", you will find a "Lower Triangle". This triangle stores the source of the positive energy.
7. The black dot of the upper triangle is the infinitesimally small spot, from which, the negative energy leaks to the outside, and invades area "A".
8. The black dot of the lower triangle is the infinitesimally small spot, from which, the positive energy leaks to the outside and invades area "A1".
9. Illustration #3 will give you additional explanation. So let's go to page 389, and read the explanation of Illustration #3 on page 391.

*** *** ***

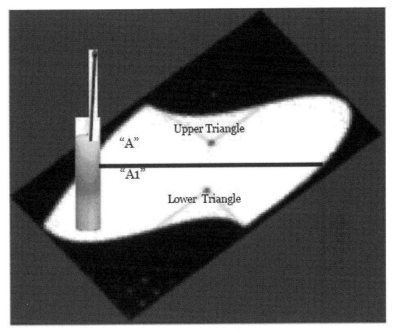

Illustration #2

Step Three: Adjusting the shadow of the needle or pin

1. Adjust the position of the needle or the pin, so it would project a shadow on a straight line, as seen in Illustration #3.
2. You might also need to adjust the position (Place) of the candle. Try and see which one of the two needs alignment.
3. Alignment means a straight shadow, right in the middle of "A" and "A1". In other words, the shadow of the needle or the pin must almost equally divide the surface of the napkin or the paper. See Illustration #4.
4. This shadow is going to play a major role in your exercise. Additional information on the importance and role of the shadow will be provided in due time.
5. For now, get a straight line (A straight shadow). Do not worry about anything else. Everything is going to be just fine.

*** *** ***

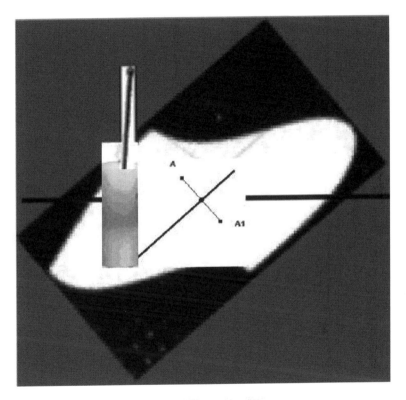

Illustration #3

Illustration #4:

1. Illustration #4 shows you the perfect alignment of the shadow of the needle or the pin.
2. This straight line is not going to stay straight.
It is going to change either direction or position. You will see this happening when you reach forthcoming steps.

*** *** ***

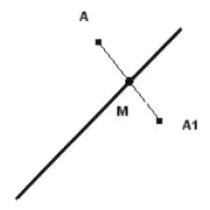

Illustration #4.

V. The Technique:

So far, everything is set for you.
You have everything lined up to get ready, and to start a memorable and an extraordinary journey, leading to astonishing discoveries and findings.
And now, the exercise/technique begins.
But first of all, you have to believe in yourself. You've got to believe very strongly that you are going to succeed.
You have to convince yourself that you can do it.
You have to believe in the power of your mind.
Your mind has tremendous powers. And, I am going to show you step-by-step how to discover these hidden powers and use them to elevate yourself to a higher level of awareness. And, to understand how unseen forces, that surround you, produce incomprehensible things your mind could not grasp in the past.
It is not an easy enterprise, because it requires:

- Lots of practice, sometimes long hours
- Perseverance
- Determination
- Deep concentration
- Observing a particular diet
- Maintaining an absolute state of tranquility
- Imagination capable of developing and animating visions and mental projection

Do not get alarmed now by this idea of imagination, mental projection and animating visions! Part of the technique will give you all the necessary instructions on how to use your imagination. So, relax, and get ready. You are going to succeed, unquestionably and I am with you all the way.
And, if you need additional guidance, you can always write to me at delafayette6@aol.com. You are most welcome!

So, what is the plan now?
Well, if you are looking at the candle, the needle or pin, the paper or the napkin and a shadow on a surface, you will not notice anything extraordinary.

394

But soon, everything is going to change, and something strange might appear on the napkin or the papers. And, who is going to do this? YOU!
Essentially, what we want to accomplish here, is to deviate the shadow we see on the surface; the shadow of the needle or the pin, that is.
In other words, make the shadow move without touching anything. And we are going to accomplish this, simply by using the power of our mind.
You are going to use your mind to order your body to open up the channels of your energy that is simultaneously created by your Jabas (Cells in your brains) and the organic substances in your body.
Your mind is not creating those vibes, alone. The mental waves, YES! But the vibrations and rays of your body are created by your body. The role of your mind here is to sense, to guide and to direct all sorts of vibrations, frequencies, waves and rays coming out of your body. By doing so, you will be able to sense, direct and control your energy!

And once you achieve that, you will be able to:
- Heal yourself and others
- Remove blocks and obstacles that prevent you from succeeding in many of your endeavors and causing the effects of bad luck
- Do marvelous things, we are going to talk about in the book.

And activate the channels of extraordinary supernatural powers.

*** *** ***

395

Follow these instructions:

1. The shadow of the needle or the pin will serve as a tool to make your energy materialize in the form of rays.
2. These rays will change into frequencies and the frequencies will change into vibrations.
3. In brief, these vibrations reflect the strength or weakness of your energy.
4. If your energy is strong, the vibrations are automatically strong and vibrant.
5. If your energy is weak, the vibrations are automatically weak and dim.
6. But there is a way to strengthen your energy. This technique will show you how.
7. But first of all, you must learn whether your energy is strong or weak. You can do that by working with the shadow of the needle or the pin. And this is what you have to do.
8. For 5 seconds, focus intensely on the shadow.
9. For 5 seconds, concentrate on the direction (Position, place) and length of the shadow.
10. So far, nothing is happening. The shadow did not move. In fact, nothing is moving.
11. The only thing that is going to move now is the "inside" of your mind. Meaning, you are going to tell your mind that your energy, or any form of inner strength you have inside your body, even some strong ideas or concepts you have formulated, is getting out of your body, as if you want to get something out of your system.
12. It does not matter what you are thinking about. The quality and quantity of your thoughts are irrelevant. Even anger can produce vibrations, feelings, inner sensations and that's enough to project your energy on the outside.
13. Get busy with your ideas, wishes, dreams, anything you could think of.
14. In a few seconds, you will start to feel something. And we are not going to talk about these feelings for the time being. It is normal and expected that you will feel something.

396

If not, start again, but this time, think about something you dislike; a bad experience, a failure, regret, a physical pain, etc.

15. This should trigger some sensations, and soon after, these sensations will produce vibrations.

And these vibrations will usher in your energy.

16. Now, tell your mind that the shadow on the napkin or piece of paper is getting a little bit fuzzy. Keep thinking about this, for 5 seconds.

17. Place both hands on the solid surface where you have placed the napkin or the piece of papers. This will anchor part of your energy into the napkin or the piece of paper.

18. Stay like this for 5 seconds or so, and now hold firm on the solid surface.

19. After 7 or 8 seconds, sometimes a little bit longer, you will start to feel some sort of resonance or small vibes getting to your fingers.

20. This is going to happen. No question about it.

21. Now, mentally, order the shadow to move, in any direction.

22. Use your concentration to make this happen. For instance, concentrate on the very end of the shadow, using your right eye, and simultaneously, focus on the needle using your left eye. You can do it, it is not very difficult.

Keep repeating this double concentration, until you get it right.

23. Once, the end of the shadow and the needle are within your concentration perimeter, look right away at the shadow.

24. The shadow is moving now. Absolutely! I guarantee it. And if not, stop the exercise and check "information on diet". Repeat the exercise the very next day.

25. If the shadow begins to move, follow it with both eyes. Stay like this, for 5 seconds or so and close your eyes.

26. Keep both eyes closed for 10 seconds or so and keep on concentrating on the shadow inside your mind.

27. While concentrating on the shadow inside your mind, remove your hands from the solid surface, place your left hand against your forehead, and your right hand against your solar plexus. See illustration A and illustration B on the next pages.

397

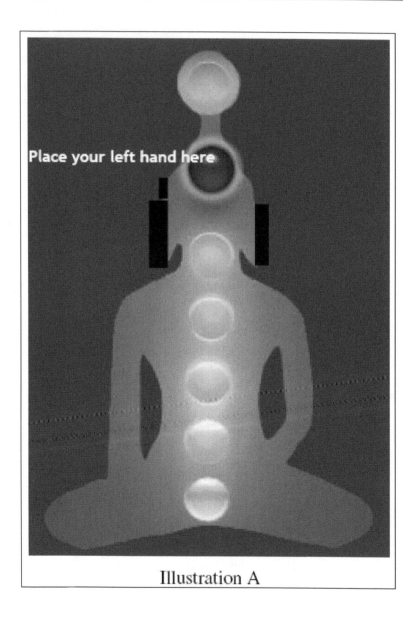

Illustration A

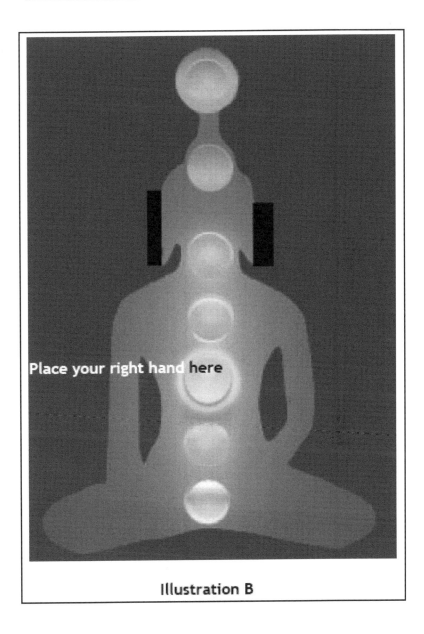

Illustration B

28. Maintain this position for 20 seconds or so.

29. After 20 seconds or so, drop down both hands and look at the shadow on the solid surface.

30. And voila! The shadow has shifted!!

31. Now pay attention to the new alignment of the shadow, meaning the new position or direction of the shadow.

32. If the shadow has moved to the left (Area marked A), as shown in Illustration #5, on page 402, this is an indication that your energy is in trouble, meaning one or all of the following:

- Bad energy
- Negative energy
- Weak vibrations
- Poor mental resonance (Temporary) caused and/or originated by a perturbed physical or emotional state
- Weak aura
- Lack of mental clarity

These etheric symptoms indicate that:

- Your Double is unbalanced
- Your Khateyn Tarika lines are blurry, meaning that your "Mental and Physical Zones" are not protected
- You have lost your protection shield

Consequently, your energy is not effective; and therefore, you need right away to strengthen your energy. There is a technique in this book that shows you how to do it.

33. If you got results indicating that you have bad energy, close the exercise right away, and refer to "Instructions about Diet and Hygiene", on pages 407-408.

34- Bad or negative energy could be disastrous. Its consequences include (To name a few):

- a-Failure in your relationships with others
- b-Health deterioration
- c-Alienating people
- d-Bad judgment
- e-Misunderstanding others
- f-Indecisiveness

- g-Fatigue
- h-Laziness
- i-Fear
- j-Anxiety
- k-Bad luck

35. If the shadow has moved to the right (Area marked A1), as shown in Illustration #6, on page 403, this is an indication that you have a healthy, strong and a good energy

36. Go now to page 404 and check other results
They are revealed in Illustration # 7.

Read the pertinent explanations on page 404.

*** *** ***

Illustration #5
Bad Energy

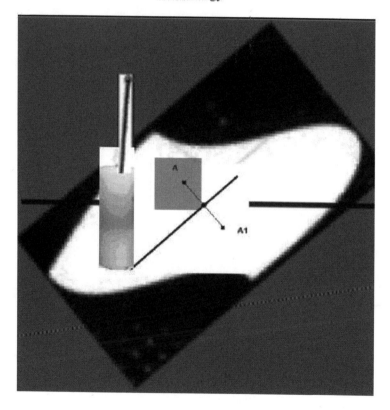

Illustration #6
Good Energy

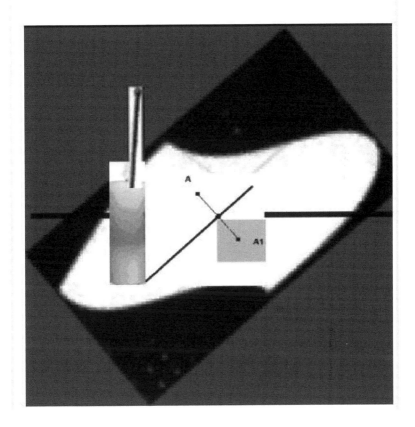

Explanation for Illustration #7

1. Illustration #7, on page 405, refers to the "State of No Variation." Meaning, your energy is stagnant.
In other words, your energy is neither bad nor good. Simply put, it is dormant, and useless.
2. This happens, when the shadow does not move. It stayed still. It's immobile. Your energy needs energy.
3. Well, this situation is not so terrible, because it does not indicate that you have bad vibes. And, when you don't have bad vibes, you don't disturb others, you don't alienate others, but by the same token, you don't attract others and you don't succeed in your relationships with others. And, that could be unpleasant, especially if your energy remains inactive.
4. But we have good news; you can activate your energy, make it vibrant, healthy and extremely positive, by practicing techniques described in Illustrations 8 to 15, on the next pages.

*** *** ***

404

Illustration #7
No Variation

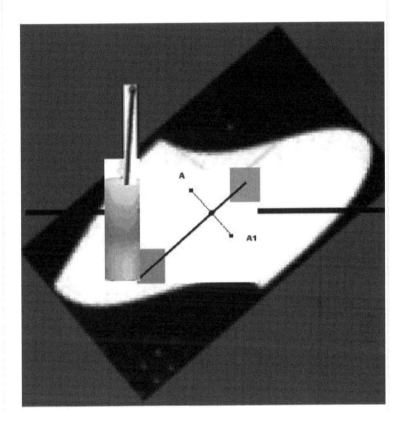

Instructions about Diet and Hygiene:

The Masters told that:

1. Consuming alcohol in moderation is accepted. Wine is good. Drinking beer in moderation is good, but consuming a large quantity of hard liquor deteriorates the vibrations of your energy. And when the vibrations and frequencies of your body and Fikr (Mind) are damaged or threatened, this becomes an indication of a weak energy, and a perturbed inner vitality.

2. Animal fat must be avoided

3. Maintaining a good hygiene is a must

4. Teeth cavities produce bad vibrations

5. Bad breath produces bad vibrations

6. Chemically treated and manufactured tobacco produce blurry vibrations

7. The use of medicinal drugs (Pills, liquids, others) produces temporary blurry vibrations

8. The use of narcotics of any kind is awful. It produces bad energy, emanates bad vibrations, and blocks your Jabas

9. Very long nails produce bad vibrations

10. Greasy hair produces perturbed vibrations

11. Excessive make up produces bad vibrations, and distorts the layers of your energy

12 Eating meat of any kind is not recommended by the Masters, unless it becomes an utmost necessity, based upon physicians' recommendations

13. Dirty or stained clothes produce bad vibrations

14. Shoes, boots, snickers and belts made from rubber and other synthetic products produce bad vibrations

15. Body's odors produce multiple layers of bad vibrations

16. Some kinds of nail polish produce bad vibrations. Black nail polish must be avoided

17. Unclean intercourse or other sexual forms, such as submission, bondage/domination will produce awful vibrations

*** *** ***

406

Avoid and Prevent This, Please!!

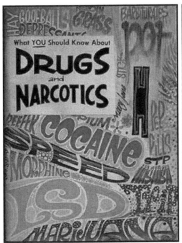

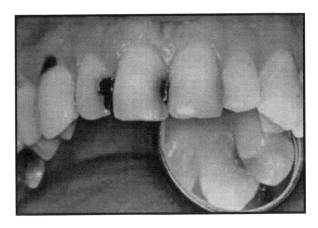

407

Avoid and Prevent This, Please!!

Animating and Activating your Energy

Summarizing:

✓ What do we get out from a positive energy?
✓ Why is it so important to activate our energy?
Because, a positively active energy allows us to accomplish magnificent deeds, such as:

- Blending harmoniously with our environment
- Making others feel comfortable when we are around them
- Removing fear
- Healing physical pains
- Healing others
- Healing ourselves
- Developing a healing touch
- Removing "Knots" and "Blocks" that trapped us in the sphere of failure, confusion, and ultimately pushing us over the cliff!
- And, so many other wonderful things described throughout the book.

✓ Is the healing touch directly related to a good energy?
✓ If yes, can we learn the healing touch technique?
Yes, we can! The technique is described step-by-step in this book.

✓ But what if our energy is not active?
✓ How can we activate it?
✓ And how long will it take to animate and activate our energy?

You will learn pertinent techniques on how to animate and activate your energy in this chapter. And, how long it would take? It depends on how serious you are!

409

Perseverance and practice make perfect.

If you follow the instructions to the letter, and if you practice daily for a period of 25 days, you will be able to animate and activate your energy.

So let's proceed.

Follow these instructions:

- This exercise is extremely important and useful. If you succeed –and you should– in completing all the steps, you will be able to:

a- Calm agitated people

b- Make people relax

c- Influence others' decisions (Oh Yes!)

d- Vitalize your mental energy, meaning widening the spectrum of perception

e- Activate many of the layers of your mental vibrations

f- Properly align your energy

g- Maintain a perfect equilibrium for your Khateyn Tarika

But I must remind you that if you have bad intentions, and you intend on using the mental powers you will gain from this technique, just to hurt people, you might succeed once or twice; but eventually, you will loose everything you have gained from practicing this technique. Your Araya and Jabas will prevent you from carrying on your dishonorable practice.

- 2. Look at Illustration #8 on page 411. It is related to Ikti-Chafa technique. Area "A" represents your bad energy or your inactive energy.
- 3. Area "B" represents your good energy.
- 4. The diving line between "A" and "B" is the path of your mental vibration, and/or the entire depot of your energy.
- 5. The candle represents your brain (Mind, Fikr).

*** *** ***

410

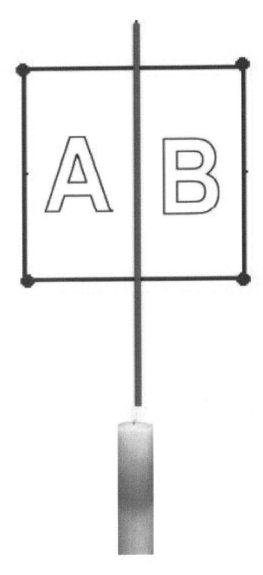

Illustration #8

411

6. Look at Illustration #9 on page 415, to see what you are going to accomplish

7. Return to Illustration 8A, on page 414

8. Touch the bottom of the candle with your second finger as shown in Illustration #8 A, on page 414

9. Put your left hand on the top of your head

10. Take a deep breath for 4 seconds or so

11. Do not push the copy-paper. Don't let it move

12. Press a little bit harder the top of your head with your left hand

13. Close both eyes

14. Open your right eye. And keep it open for 2 seconds

15. Close your right eye

16. Open your left eye. And keep it open for 2 seconds

17. Close your left eye

18. Repeat steps 14, 15, 16, 17

19. Take a deep breath for 4 seconds

20. Slightly, very slightly and very slowly, push the copy-paper forward

21. Do not open your eyes

22. Move your finger one centimeter to the left

23. Keep your finger there

24. Bring your left hand closer to your solar plexus, and press your hand against your solar plexus

25. Keep your left hand there for 5 seconds or so

26. Inside your mind, visualize a gray square moving toward the letter A

27. Press a little bit harder against your solar plexus

28. Take a deep breath for 4 seconds or so

29. Open your eyes half-way. And stay like this for 3 seconds or so

30. Close your eyes

31. Inside your mind, tell yourself that the gray square has already moved to the left side, but it needs adjustment

32. Inside your mind, tell yourself that you are going to anchor the gray square in the "A" area

33. For 10 seconds or so, keep telling yourself that you are doing it

34. Remove your left hand from your solar plexus and place it right away on the left side of the solid surface

35. Open your eyes. The gray square is in the "A" area. You can do it! Many did!

If you get this result, this is an indication that either you have activated your energy and/or your energy was already activated, but needs direction. If you manage to transport/teleport the gray square to the "A" area, this means that you will be able to direct your energy toward any person, any object and any target you wish. And the results could be spectacular

36. Keep practicing and practicing at least twice a day for a period of 5 days

37. On the 6th day, engage yourself in a dialogue with a friend, preferably a stubborn one

Without ill-purpose or vicious intentions, and gently, disagree with your friend on any subject he/she is talking about. As expected, your friend will keep on arguing because he/she is stubborn. That's fine. Now, in a discreet manner, place your left hand against your solar plexus for a few seconds, and mentally send a message to your friend, telling him/her that she is wrong. While you are doing this, focus on his/her forehead for 2 seconds. And right away look him/her in the eyes for 2 seconds. Your friend has already changed his/her mind without knowing!

38. There is no doubt that you will succeed. But if you are skeptic, extremely materialistic and lazy, you will fail!

Illustration #8A

Illustration #9

415

Illustration #10, on page 417:

1. Repeat the same exercise, but this time, you will transport the gray square to the "B" area
2. Follow the same instructions given for the previous exercise
3. You must do this new exercise to strengthen your energy
It is a must.
4. Do not miss any step
5. You should get the result as shown in Illustration #10 on page 417
6. After you have finished this exercise, go to page 417, to read about new instructions for a slightly more advanced exercise

*** *** ***

Illustration #10

Final Exercise pertaining to Illustration #11, page 419

Objective of this exercise:
You should get the result as shown in Areas "A" and "B" in Illustration # 11, on page 419. Meaning, transposing/teleporting two grey rectangles to "A", and to "B".
Go to page 420, to get the instructions. And look at Illustration #11 A on page 421.

***   ***   ***

Illustration #11

Note: Look at Illustration 11 on page 419; this is the result you should get: 2 grey rectangles, just by using your own energy diffused by three fingers, as shown in Illustration #11 A, on page 421. The final result is shown in Illustration #11 B, on page 423.

Follow these instructions:

1. Copy the page of Illustration #8, and place it on a solid surface. Your desk is fine.
2. You are going now to use three fingers to generate energy. This energy has good vibrations you could use for self-healing, as well as for healing others. You will find plenty of information and instruction on the "Healing Touch", in volumes 1 and 2
3. The energy you are going to witness is produced by your mind, not by your body.
The mental energy is stronger and far more superior to the body's energy; the body's energy powers are limited by distances.
The mental energy transcends space and distances, meaning you can send your mental energy to remote areas, to people living far away, so on.
Authentic healers and Rouhaniyiin can heal people at distance. The less-awakened masters use the healing touch.
In some instances and situations, you can use others' energy, and/or incorporate their good vibrations in the healing process. You are not the only one who has energy.
Remember, energy comes from everywhere:
- a-Nature, in general
- b-The cosmos (Universe)
- c-People
- d-Plants,
- e-Solid objects like stones, diamonds, crystals
- f-Animals, pets
4.No matter how weak you are, no matter how skeptic you are, no matter how untrained and unfamiliar with these sorts of things you are, you still have energy somewhere inside your body, outside your body, inside your brain, and outside your brain.

Illustration # 11 A

On the following pages, you will find how and where different levels of energy are stored.

In other parts of the book you will find several grids you can use to centralize, exteriorize and direct your energy at yourself, at others, at objects, and situations/circumstances that are blocking your success.

Be patient, and everything will shine on the road of your life.

5.Place your three fingers at the bottom of the bottom of the candle as shown in illustration #11A, on page 421.

Keep your fingers there for 3 seconds and remove your fingers.

6.Now, look at the bottom of the candle for 2 seconds, and bring your 3 fingers very close to the bottom of the candle, and place your fingers at 0.5 centimeter distance from the bottom of the candle. Do not touch the candle. Keep your fingers there for 5 seconds or so.

7.After 5 seconds, take a deep breath.

8.Close your eyes now, and take another deep breath.

9.Very gently and meticulously touch the end of the bottom of the candle, with your 3 fingers. See below:

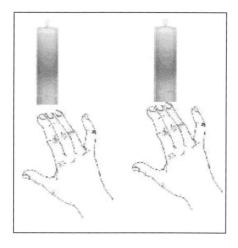

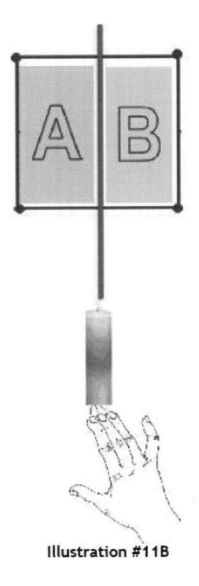

Illustration #11B

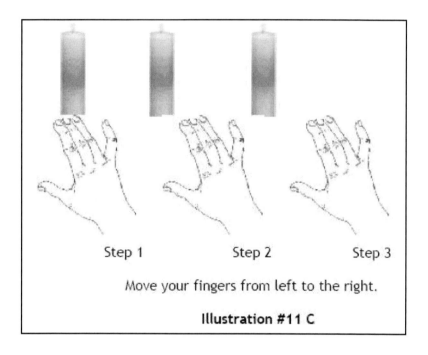

Step 1   Step 2   Step 3

Move your fingers from left to the right.

Illustration #11 C

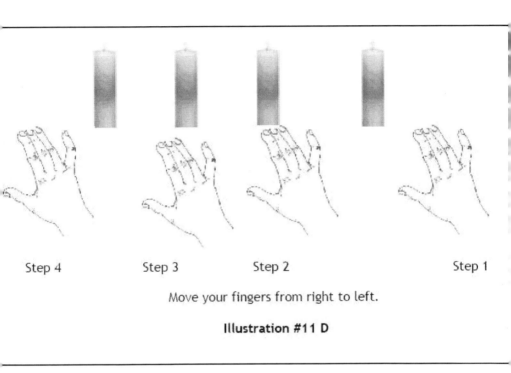

| Step 4 | Step 3 | Step 2 | Step 1 |

Move your fingers from right to left.

Illustration #11 D

10.Very slowly move your fingers like a Chinese fan from left to right, and from right to left, 3 times, as shown in Illustration #11 C, on page 424, and Illustration #11 D, on page 425.

11.Do it this way: First, very slowly move your fingers like a Chinese fan from left to right, as shown in Illustration #11 C, on page 424.

12.Second, very slowly move your fingers like a Chinese fan from right to left, as shown in Illustration #11 D, on page 425.

13.Now, vibrate your hand right and left, and left and right under the candle, as shown in Illustration #11 E, on page 427.

14.Repeat these vibrations' movements for 2 minutes.

Later on, at a more advanced level of experience and learning, you will need only 40 seconds or so.

But for now, you need these 2 minutes to trigger vibrations, it is very normal.

15.Let's go to page 428, for further instruction.

*** *** ***

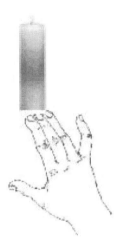

Step 1

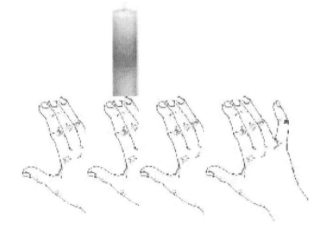

Step 2
Illustration #11 E

16.Look at Illustration #11F, on page 145.

17.With your fingers, push the candle forward, toward Areas "A", and "B".

18.There is no doubt, the candle will move forward. And when you notice that the candle is right under the Square containing the letters "A" and "B", as shown in Illustration #11F, on page 429, vibrate your fingers for 5 seconds.

19.Look one more time at Illustration #11 F, on page 429.

20.Look now at Illustration #11 G, on page 432.

21.Now read the final instruction on page 430.

*** *** ***

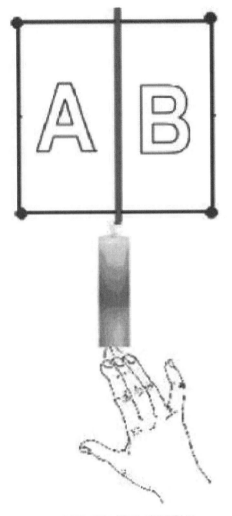

Illustration #11 F

Final Instruction:

22.With your fingers push the candle inside the Square. containing "A", and "B", as shown in Illustration #11G, on page 432.

23.By now, and if you have successfully reached this step, your regular mind, the one you are familiar with, will come to state of trance, mentally, not psychedelically or spiritually. There is nothing spiritual in this exercise. Only MENTAL!

24.There is a part of your Supersymetric Mind that will take over, meaning a part of your duplicate mind will exteriorize and guide your physical senses (In this case, your fingers).

25.The candle is no longer exclusively controlled by the physical vibrations of your body (In this case, your fingers), but also by the mental energy of your mind. The candle will enter the Square without any problem. Please keep believing in yourself. You have nothing to loose, except a few moments from your free time.

26.Once the candle is inside the Square, tell the candle to spread a gray light over the letter "A", and the letter "B".

27.Tell the candle to fill up area "A", and area "B" with a gray shade, as seen in Illustration #11B, on page 423.

28.Concentrate on the candle inside the Square, and keep telling the candle to fill up the square with the gray shade for at least 5 seconds.

29.Close your eyes now for 10 seconds, and repeat step 28.

30.As soon as you start to feel some sort of numbness in your right hand, open immediately your eyes...you will see area "A", and area "B" covered with a gray shade, as seen in Illustration #11H, on page 433.

31.You are almost at the very end of the exercise. Now, look at gray areas of "A" and "B", breath deeply, breath one more time, and tell yourself that You, the Square, and the Candle are ONE.

32. Repeat 5 times, what you have just said "Me, the Square and the Candle are one".

33.Breath deeply and slowly.

34.Close your eyes for 10 seconds, and rapidly think about what you have accomplished.

35.Open your eyes now...they are no longer the same eyes you had before, because they have entered another dimension and saw a sphere few in our modern world have seen.

But the most important thing in all this, IS:

- The learning you have acquired
- The learning of discovering your energy
- The learning of sensing your energy
- The learning and technique for animating and directing the vibrations of your energy.

Now, what can you do with your energy? The sky is the limit.

*** *** ***

431

Illustration #11 G

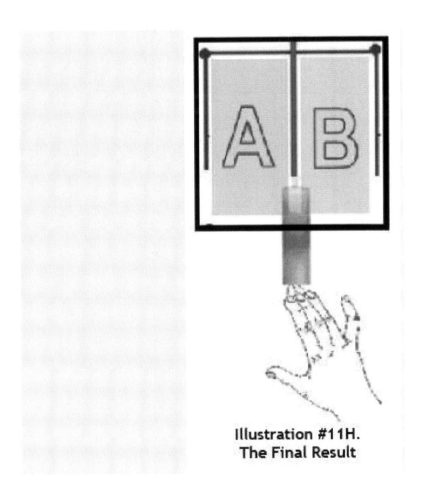

**Illustration #11H.
The Final Result**

Sources and Levels of Energy and Vibrations

I. We are surrounded by energy and vibes:

We are surrounded by energy; all sorts and types of energies;
- a-Nature's energy
- b-Animals' energy
- c-Objects' energy
- d-People's energy
- e-Our own energy

And we can't escape it, like Earth's gravity.
In essence, energy by itself is not the main and principle danger we are facing.
It is rather the:
- a-Vibrations
- b-Frequencies
- c-Rays
- d-Radiations

of the energy, which are damaging and in some cases lethal.

The hideous part of all this, is the fact that:
- We can't see the vibrations of the energy
- We don't know for sure the origin of its vibrations
- We have no clues, where they are going to hit us?
- We can't guess, when are they going to hit us?
- We can't predict and measure the vibrations' immediate, short term and long term effects on us, our health, business, progress and environment in general.

I knew several people in the Eastern and Western hemispheres, who died from being exposed to Al-Atila (Awfully bad) or Al-Fasida (Rotten) vibrations; other people became insane, and a great number of them went out of business, virtually, they became flat broke, penniless, and homeless.

435

Around the 1998, I learned about an old friend of mine who was stricken by a series of mishaps, several financial calamities and terrifying flux of bad luck. Just a few years, prior to what has happened to him, he was on the top of the world; fabulously rich, enormously successful and popular beyond belief.

But he had two major problems (According to some):

a-His generosity; he treated his successful business as charity, meaning, giving away so much, to so many people, and never could imagine that one day, he will run out of money.

b-Bad company; he never suspected that many of those who surrounded him were the scum of the Earth. He was a giver, they were takers, he was forgiving, they were vindictive and vengeful. And, they were street-smart!

They could camouflage pretty good their intentions, viciousness, and hypocrisy. Unfortunately, he could not sense and read their vibrations.

Bottom line, he lost his business, his mansion, everything he had. In fact, he became jobless and homeless for a very long time.

In July of 1998, one of my associates told me about what has happened to him, and asked me if I could help.

"Of course I will," I said, "no question about it."

I start looking for him everywhere, absolutely everywhere. I called almost everybody, asking them if they knew where I could find him. But nobody could.

Finally, in September, 1998, and while visiting New York City, I bumped into Philippe Z., who previously worked for me in Rome. After warm greetings, a few laughs and stuff like that, Philippe said, "Hey boss, do you know what happened to Mr. B? (Call him B for now) You are not going to believe it...I saw him a few days ago, and he looked like s..t!"

I asked Philippe if he knew where he lives and he said, "I will take you there." "Perfect, let's go right now", I replied. Philippe took me to a neighborhood in Brooklyn, New York.

To make the long story short, I met my old friend in his empty apartment; empty, because he had no furniture and he was sleeping on the floor.

I sensed his room and on the spot, I told him to get out of this neighborhood, because it sits right above an underground current infested with bad energy.

I sensed it right away, the moment I entered the building.

What happened next, I will keep it confidential. As soon as my friend moved out of that Brooklyn negative neighborhood, he began to regain his senses and two or three weeks later, he got a solid job offer from one of the most prestigious corporations in Burbank, California.

Apparently, the CEO/VP of the corporation, found my friend's CV (Resume) in a trash basket in one of the offices of the human resources department of the company. It is like a fairy tale. But, it did happen and I was there to see it.

I remember telling my friend that as long as he stays where he is (that miserable neighborhood), he will either go insane or kill himself from despair.

But, if he leaves that area, in less than a month, he will be back again on his feet, because that underground negative energy will no longer have any affect on him, on his body, on his psyche and his bad luck will be removed right away.

I was so happy he listened to me!

An acquaintance of mine, Mr. Kumar, a fine gentleman from Benares, India, told me about a friend of his parents who owned a 7-11 store in Brooklyn. At the beginning, he was doing great; the store brought lots of money, and everything seems to be fine, business-wise, family-wise, and so on, until he moved with his family to a new building in Park Slope, Brooklyn.

One month later, his wife fell in the kitchen and broke her hip. His youngest son got severe skin irritations and he himself began to lose his memory. In three months, he lost his store and his wife became half-paralyzed.

Kumar solicited the help of a Swami, who rushed to the house of the unfortunate family. As soon as the Swami entered the house, he felt a very strong Atila current, and did not waste a moment to tell the family to get out of the apartment as soon as possible.

One year later, the family learned that the previous tenants met almost identical fate.

The Swami said, the building and two adjacent stores (One was a 99 cents store and the other a Middle Eastern deli) were "breathing" negative vibes, left by previous occupants.
Their vibes were trapped inside the metal and wood frames of the external structure of the building and the stores.
The Swami saved their lives.
So, as you see, some areas, zones, neighborhoods, streets and buildings can cripple us, because they sit above underground current (s), charged with negative energy.
The same catastrophic results could happen to all of you, if you are surrounded by negative people, or if you conduct your business around people who emit negative energy vibrations.
In some cases, one single apartment, one particular apartment, on one single floor, on one particular floor of a building, (fancy or modest, in the city or the suburb) can cause us so many damages, financially, emotionally, mentally, and physically), simply because the previous tenant was charged with intensely strong negative energy.
Even though, he or she has vacated the premises, the residues and "Imprints" of his or her negative vibrations/rays are still in the apartment; sometimes we find these killing vibes inside the walls, inside the closets and it is going to take some time to clear the air.

Bad vibrations can originate from all sorts of sources- not only from people and areas. Animals have their own energy. A pet who loves you will emit good energy, even therapeutic vibes. A pet that dislikes you will do just the opposite.
Solid objects, tools, hard surfaces, gadgets and similar materials also diffuse strong vibes.
Unfortunately, many of us are not aware that some of the stuff we keep at home are very damaging to our health and mental state. We are going to talk about this in depth, in the forthcoming chapters.
In addition to people, animals and solid objects, the Cosmos also has strong vibrations and biological-etheric radiations. All these vibes are found at Level 1. See Illustration #12 A, on page 443.

II. Chart of the 3 basic levels/sources of energy around you.

See Illustration #12

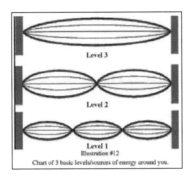

Chart of 3 basic levels/sources of energy around you.

Summary:
There are 3 basic, original and primordial sources of energy that surround you in this physical dimension (Earth). Each energy deeply affects your existence, present, future, fate, life, success, business, environment and everything you do- positively and/or negatively. They are shown in Illustration #12, on page 440.

- **a**-Level 1 represents the 3 sources/origins; they are explained in Illustration #12 A.
- **b**-Level 2 represents You and the Micro Wheel. (Explanation on next pages)
- **c**-Level 3 represents You in synchronization with the Macro Wheel. (Explanation on next pages)

*** *** ***

439

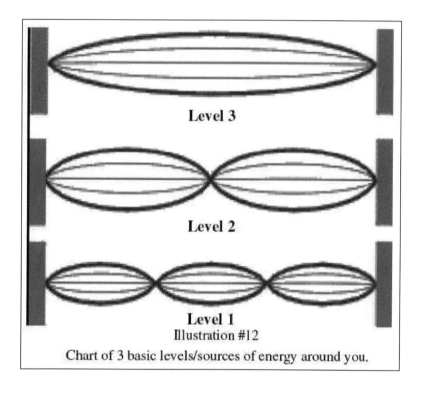

Level 3

Level 2

Level 1
Illustration #12
Chart of 3 basic levels/sources of energy around you.

Level 1

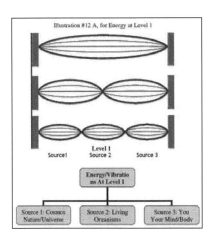

a. The 3 sources of energy at Level 1:

At Level 1, we have 3 sources/origins of energy
- Source 1: Cosmos: Nature/Universe
- Source 2: Living Organisms
- Source 3: You. Your mind. Your body

b. Brief explanation of each source of energy:

Note: See Illustration #12 A, on page 443.

Source 1 at Level 1:

Source 1 represents Mother Nature which accumulates the atmosphere, the skies, the stars, the planets, our solar system, the oceans, the thunders, the light, the shadow; everything that constitutes our world.

In brief, the Universe.

And there is nothing you can do about it.

You can avoid the ray and the heat of the sun, but you can't escape the effects, the solar rays, radiations, energy and vibrations, have on humanity, you, me, them, on our planet, our houses, and our way of life.

You can take some measures of precaution, but the energy and vibrations of Mother Nature and their effects on us are more stronger than any protection shield, tool or apparatus (Physical, spiritual, mental) at our disposal, thus, we will pass on.

Source 2 at Level 1:
Source 2 belongs to all living organisms, including all sorts of:
- a-Life-forms
- b-Animals
- c-Human beings
- d-Bacteria
- e-Viruses, and
- f-Strange creatures

In the present work, we will focus on human beings, because this is one of our major concerns. Asking Jean-Paul Sartre to define hell, he replied, "L'enfer c'est les autres!" (Hell is the others!)

99% of all our problems are caused by humans and remember what the Anunnaki Ulema have said, "Earth, is the dumpster of the universe and the human beings are the lowest life-forms on the cosmic, spiritual, physical, metaphysical and mental Araya (Net) of the universe."

Source 3 at level 1:
Source 3 belongs to you, to your body and to your mind. In the present work, we will focus on YOU, because this is one of our major concerns.

Let's go now to Level 2, on page 444.

*** *** ***

Illustration #12 A, for Energy at Level 1

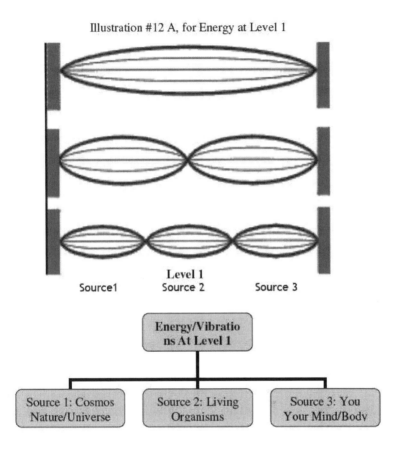

Level 1
Source1   Source 2   Source 3

Energy/Vibratio
ns At Level 1

Source 1: Cosmos
Nature/Universe

Source 2: Living
Organisms

Source 3: You
Your Mind/Body

Level 2

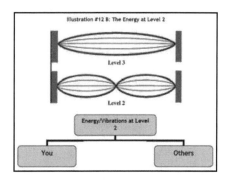

The two sources of energy and vibrations at Level 2:
Note: See Illustration #12 B, on page 445.
At Level 2, we find 2 sources of energy and vibrations.
Source 1 is You. And Source 2 represents the others, all kinds of people.

a. Brief explanation of each source of energy:
Source 1 at Level 2:
Source 1 at Level 2, represents everything about you; your thoughts, intentions, visions, dreams, aspirations, creativity, plans, business, purposes and objectives, your deeds and acts, your body, your hygiene, your habits, your addictions, your character and temper, your personality, the kind of food you eat, liquids you drink, your intelligence, emotions and even feelings.
In brief, your body and its substances and your mind with its substances.
So, every time you absorb something, eat something, think about something, do something, your energy level changes; and as a result, the vibrations of your energy change.
Even when you talk, trained ones will guess, whether you are telling the truth or lying.
Why and how?

444

Illustration #12 B: The Energy at Level 2

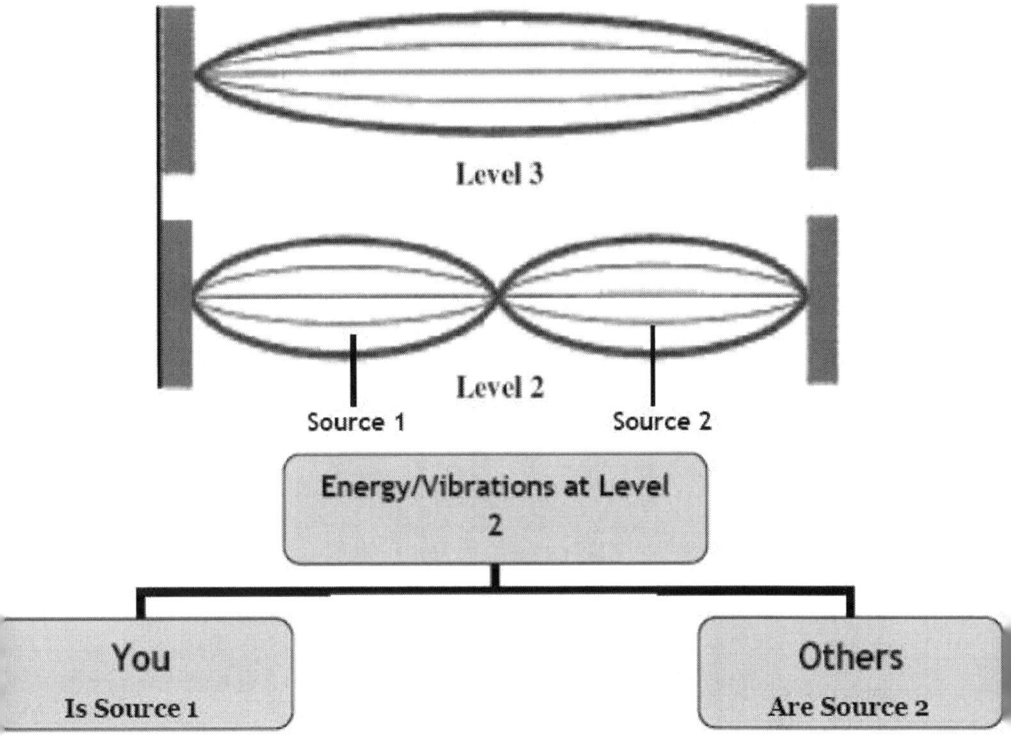

Level 3

Level 2

Source 1   Source 2

Energy/Vibrations at Level 2

You
Is Source 1

Others
Are Source 2

Because, your words, your sentences, your intentions behind the words and sentences, and what you were thinking about when you opened your mouth you send vibrations that can be detected, read, and deciphered by the trained ones (Teachers, masters, adepts, etc.)

The same thing applies to others. So, once you have finished your training, you will be able to find out who is telling you the truth and who is lying to you.

This is one of the major benefits you get from learning about the functioning of the energy and the meaning of its vibrations.

Source 2 at Level 2:

Source 2 represents the others, all kinds of people; good and bad, intelligent and idiots. And each one of them registers different kinds, levels and colors of vibrations.

Their energy, emanated from their bodies and brains, change from time to time. And the vibrations of their energy also change from time to time.

For example, if they are telling you the truth, the color of their vibration turn gold or bright orange. If they are lying to you, the color of their vibrations turns grey or black.

So the vibrations change constantly. By the same token, different parts of their bodies could also emanate different kinds of energy and vibrations, simultaneously.

For example, if they have malicious intentions, their body will emit deep grey or black vibrations from and around their head, neck, and shoulders, and if during that time, their health condition is in a perfect shape, their bodies will emit strong blue vibrations, coming from and around their solar plexus, reflecting their good health.

So, here we have two different kinds of vibrations coming from the same person and at the same time:

a-Bad vibes coming from and around the head/neck/shoulders
b-Good vibes coming from and around the solar plexus

In this situation, the Khateyn Tarika and/or their electro-magnetic zone, aura, etc, sent two messages, different vibes, different colors and so on.

446

Additional vibes (Third ones) will come out of their bodies –at the same time– if they are hiding narcotics or a lethal hardware in their pocket(s), such as a revolver. Our electro-magnetic field can emit dozens of different vibes, simultaneously and each one corresponds to a particular reason, a specific part of our body or brain, and other thoughts/activities we are part of.
The trained ones can see all these vibrations at the same time. They are there to see in the electro-magnetic zone surrounding their bodies. With some good training, you too will be able to see people's vibrations.

b. Who emits bad vibes that could disrupt the normal rhythm of our life, cause lots of damages and bring bad luck?
The list is endless.
But generally speaking, people who have negative energy and bad vibes are those who have committed crimes (Any kind), who are severely mentally disturbed and others who belong to similar categories. This is obvious, as you already know.
Therefore, rather than talking about what you already know about, people who a priori are known to produce negative vibes, and who are not part of your normal daily life, I rather bring your attention to people who are most likely to know or to meet in normal situations, more or less regularly, and in some instances, on a regular basis.
Regular basis means individuals to be found around you and/or likely to meet in various common or public places, intentionally or unintentionally; these persons blend regularly in our society, workplace and other normal situations.
Here is a brief synopsis:
a. Category 1:
Prostitutes, call-girls, escorts, dominatrix-ladies, strippers and any girl/woman who belongs to this racket (Professionally and/or occasionally): They are among the worst kind. Don't ever believe the myth of the prostitute with a golden heart! Nowadays, in our ever growing complex modern societies, it has become difficult to recognize and/or identify –right away– a woman who belongs to that category.

447

In the past, it was quite easy to recognize one, from her clothes, make-up, outfit, location and behavior. No more! Some of these "social prostitutes" and courtesans could be on the outside a respectable married men/women, and/or one of your colleagues at work, but you never knew that on the side, and occasionally, she is in the prostitution business. So it is hard to tell, until you meet one of them intimately, or through shady connections.

And voila! Quelle Surprise! What a nasty or a shocking surprise.

In Manhattan, New York alone, 9 out of 10 girls and women between the age of 18 and 26 who do not have a regular job, an honest pay-check, who get paid cash, and who pays a high monthly rent ($2,500 and plus) are in this racket.

A contact with a prostitute and/or any of the women in the foresaid category will bring you bad luck, a disastrous Karma, and disrupt the normal/healthy rhythm of your life.

Do NOT let them come close to you! They are bad news.

Their vibes will totally destroy your Khateyn Tarika and the flux of good luck.

Stay around them or welcome them to your surrounding and you are dead meat.

You will never recover, because their bad vibes leave strong "Imprints" inside your "Zone".

And, to get rid of the "Imprints" of their bad vibrations, you need a major astral/etheric cleansing.

They are not mental vibrations because they are not transmitted by the cells of their brain; these girls/women emit their bad and destructive vibes from various parts of their bodies, such as:

- a-The hair
- b-The solar plexus
- c-The hips
- d-The belly
- e-The vagina
- f-The fingers
- g-The knees
- h-The feet
- i-The toes' nails

And once you are well-trained, you will be able to see and smell their vibes. The colors of their vibes range from black to dark gray.

And, those who have venereal diseases constantly emit multiple layers of black vibes around areas a to i, and a blurry grey-black rays from the solar plexus. See Illustration for category 1, page 450. Their vibes will penetrate your "Zone", Khateyn Tarika, and hit you in:

- a-The forehead
- b-The solar plexus
- c-The lungs

*** *** ***

449

Illustration for category 1
The picture of this person is used
only for illustration purpose

a

b

c
d

e

f

g

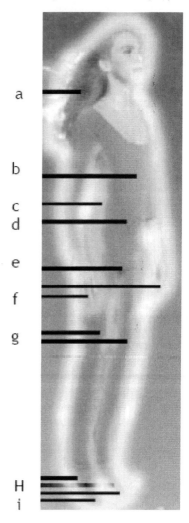

H
i

b. Category 2:
Corrupt and deceitful politicians and preachers.
They are mental vibrations, because they are transmitted by the cells of their brain; however, these vibes emanate from various parts of their bodies, such as:

- a-The hair
- b-The forehead
- c-The eyes
- d-The mouth
- e-The throat
- f-The solar plexus
- g-The hands
- h-The fingers

Once you are well-trained, you will be able to see and smell their vibes. The colors of their vibes range from black to dark gray.
Their vibes will penetrate your "Zone", Khateyn Tarika, and hit you in:

- a-The forehead
- b-The solar plexus

See Illustration for category 2, on page 452.

*** *** ***

451

Illustration for category 2

a
b
c
d
e

f

g
h

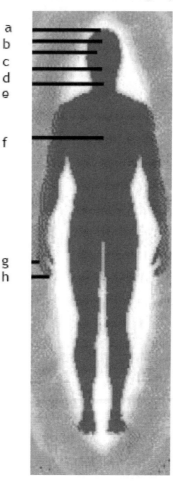

c. Category 3:
This category represents people who display anger, verbal abuse, violence and cruelty toward animals, as well as tyrants and bullying bosses (Employers).
There vibrations are both mental and physical, because they are transmitted by the cells of their brain and their body.
They emanate from:

- a-The hair
- b-The forehead
- c-The eyes
- d-The mouth
- e-The throat
- f-The shoulders
- g-The solar plexus
- h- The belly
- i-The hips
- j-The hands
- k-The fingers
- l-The fingers' nails

Once you are well-trained, you will be able to see their vibes. The colors of their vibes range from black to dark gray and gray.
Their vibes will penetrate your "Zone", Khateyn Tarika and hit you in:

- a-The forehead
- b-The eyes
- c-The solar plexus
- d-The heart
- e-The lungs
- f-The stomach

See Illustration for category 3 on page 454.

Illustration for category 3

a
b
c
d
e
f
g

h
i

i
k
l

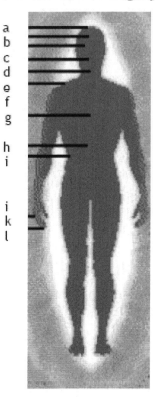

d. Category 4:
This category represents people who are underachievers, bitter, cowards, employees with weak personality, stubborn, excessively argumentative, lazy and people with low self-esteem.
Although, they have no intentions of hurting you, their nature and attitude which were influenced and conditioned by their:
a-Own unpleasant experiences
b-Failed relationships with others
c-Abusive behavior of their bosses, employers and supervisors
d-Complex of inferiority
d-Laziness despite a great potential for creativity

Emit negative vibes that could cripple your creativity, limit your productivity and irritate you every time you are around them, talking to them, or even listening to them. Once you are well-trained, you will be able to see their vibes. The colors of their vibes range from dark gray to a pale beige.
Basically, they are not bad people but their failure in many of the things they try to do, their weak personality and stubbornness will project un-intentional destructive vibes that will either slow down or halt your success. In many instances, their vibes will bring you bad luck. It is easy to avoid these people; be polite, civilized and quite...and avoid any contact with them.

Their bad vibes emanate from:
- a-The forehead
- b-The solar plexus
- c-The hips

Their bad vibes will penetrate your "Zone", Khateyn Tarika, and hit you in:
- a-The solar plexus
- b-The lungs
- c-The joints

See Illustration for category 4 on page 456.

455

Illustration for category 4

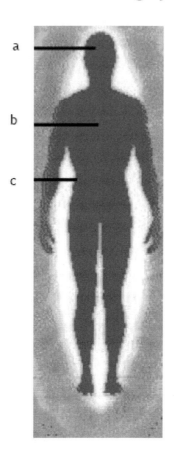

a

b

c

e. Category 5:
This category represents pushers and distributors of narcotics, drugs and various addictive substances.

Their bad vibes emanate from:
- a-The forehead
- b-The solar plexus
- c-The hips

Their bad vibes will penetrate your "Zone", Khateyn Tarika and hit you in:
- a-The forehead
- b-The eyes
- c-The solar plexus
- d-The throat
- e-The lungs
- f-The joints
- g-The hands
- h-The knees

See Illustration for category 5 on page 448.

*** *** ***

457

Illustration for category 5

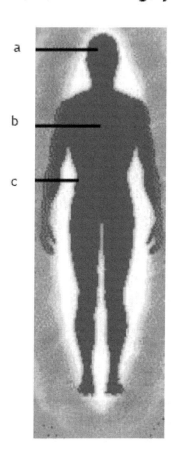

a

b

c

f. Category 6:
This category represents vicious, vindictive, vengeful, jealous and envious people, including those who badmouth others and spread false rumors about people. It is in their nature to cause damages to others.
They are the lowest of the lowest in our world.
And, they do it through character assassination, vicious gossip, and badmouthing you. You will find them almost everywhere; where you work, in supermarkets, in the competitive commercial market, schools, organizations, Wall Street, media, Internet, their own websites and blogs, on the streets, in showbiz, at receptions, parties and even in creative fields, including science, arts and the humanities.
Some, you could meet, others, probably never.

Quite often, they are people who have never met you and most probably you have no interest in knowing them. They envy your success, your wealth, your fame, your popularity and even your beautiful children.
They don't know you, the real YOU! Yet, they use anything they have at their disposal to hurt you. <u>This category is the worst of the worst.</u> And their bad vibes could cause you serious damages, if you do not protect your "Zone", and Khateyn Tarika. They are there to get you.
So strengthen your "Ehetric-Physical Zone".
In this book, I have provided you with a few techniques to create an etheric protection shield. This shield will repel their bad vibes. So, you better start working on these techniques. You should never deal with any person who badmouths others. They are up to no good. Avoid them, don't pay attention to their tactics, but protect yourself, your interests, investment and success.
One of the techniques previously mentioned will show you how to do it. As the old French proverb says: "Les **chiens aboient, la caravane passe."** *Meaning:* "The dogs bark, but the caravan goes by." This is true, but protecting yourself against vicious vibes will make the dogs run away, and the caravan pass faster!

459

Their bad vibes emanate from:
- a-The forehead
- b-The eyes
- c-The mouth
- d-The solar plexus
- e-The hips
- f-The hands

Their bad vibes will penetrate your "Zone", Khateyn Tarika and hit you in:
- a-The forehead
- b-The eyes
- c-The solar plexus
- d-The throat
- e-The lungs
- f-The heart
- g-The joints
- h-The hands
- i-The knees

See Illustration for category 6 on page 461.

*** *** ***

Illustration for category 6

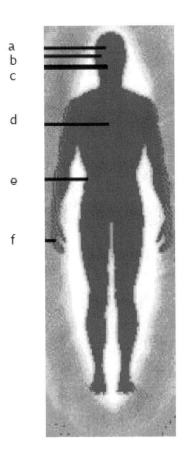

a
b
c

d

e

f

g. Category 7:

This category represents materialistic, greedy and selfish people.
You find them in the financial world- the competitive market, on Wall Street, entertainment and showbiz; wherever diamonds, gold, fur, a dollar bill shake and bake. And, because they are selfish, you could also find them almost everywhere, sometime under your own roof, at home, in churches, schools, hospitals, on the street, in governments' offices, everywhere! Those people have very distinctive vibes, because they emit rays and vibrations of silverish-gray to metallic gray-pale beige colors.
They are sharp and piercing.
They can cut holes "Pockets" in your "Zone".
Unfortunately, you can't reverse their vibes. The best way to deal with this situation is to get out of their sight. Don't deal with them. Do not believe in their promises.
They are heartless and they don't give a damn about you. Once you are well-trained, you will be able to see their vibes.
Even though, there is nothing you can do about this, at least, you will be warned and given plenty of time and reasons to not get mixed up with anything they do.

Their bad vibes emanate from:
- a-The forehead
- b-The eyes
- c-The mouth
- d-The solar plexus
- e-The hips
- f-The hands

Their bad vibes will penetrate your "Zone", Khateyn Tarika, and hit you in:
- a-The forehead
- b-The lungs
- c-The heart
- d-The joints
- e-The knees

See Illustration for category 7, on page 463.

462

Illustration for category 7

a
b
c

d

e

f

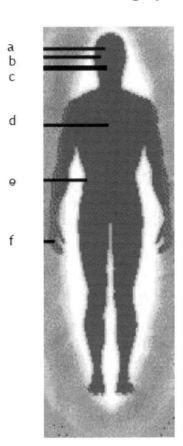

c. Are there specific places and areas that emit and or contain/store bad vibes that could negatively affect our life, business, health, and luck?

Oh yes! I have already answered this question in volume 1. But, I will give you further information on the subject.

Note: The fact that those places retain, store or produce bad vibes, you should not consider the people who live and/or work at these places, as responsible for their bad vibes.

The very nature of these places and areas, their mode and type of their operations/business, the reasons why people (Employees, operators or visitors) are found there, or go there, the spatial and etheric memories which are trapped in these places/spots, and other incomprehensible factors, create a negative environment and produce bad vibes.

So, people who are operating those premises are not categorically and entirely responsible for the bad vibes you will find in those premises. Are there specific places and areas that emit and or contain/store bad vibes? Yes, yes! Almost everywhere. The list is endless.

But the most recognizable ones are
(In no particular order):

- Abortion clinics
- Ammunitions' warehouses/storage areas
- Amputations' areas
- Animal fat and synthetic products areas
- Arenas and stadiums
- Arsenal depots
- Athletes lockers rooms
- Bars
- Cemeteries
- Chemical waste areas
- Collection agencies
- Concentration camps
- Convention halls and areas (Particularly political)
- Correction centers

- Courthouses
- Dentists' offices
- Detention centers
- Entities trapped areas
- Funeral parlors
- Garbage areas and dumpsters
- Governments' offices
- Graveyards
- Hospitals
- Hunting areas
- Jails
- Law offices
- Make-up counters
- Mental health institutions
- Models' runway/areas/dressing rooms
- Morgues
- Narcotics, drugs and addictive substances' warehouses, distribution centers and joints for customers
- Orgies gatherings
- Nuclear testing areas
- Police stations
- Prostitution houses
- Rehab centers
- Rest rooms
- Sewers
- Slaughter houses
- Slave trade operations
- Stock markets floor(s)
- Strip joints
- Sweat shops
- Underground military bases
- Violent sports areas
- Wall Street
- Wars' zones
- Weapons' factories

At level 3

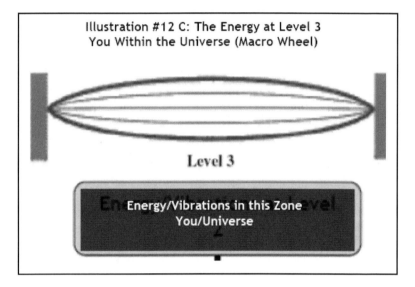

Illustration #12 C: The Energy at Level 3
You Within the Universe (Macro Wheel)

Level 3

Energy/Vibrations in this Zone
You/Universe

At this level, you elevate your vibes to the highest degree. There are several techniques to do and learn from; however, they are highly advanced and complex.
It is quite impossible to learn these techniques on your own without a personal guidance from a spiritual teacher.

*** *** ***

Energy's good days and bad days.
Energy's good hours and the bad hours

I. Introduction:
Your energy does not stay the same all the time. For example, on Monday, your energy could be very healthy and strong, while on Tuesday, it gets weak, and your vibes begin to dim.

Then on Thursday, you hear some good news, and your energy becomes wealthier and stronger, and so on.

Everything depends on your state of mind, and the situations you go through or you face. Of course, others' interaction with you and your immediate environment will affect your energy and vibes.

To keep your energy in good shape (Balance and equilibrium), you could practice on the Mouraba technique (Squares of the week), which I have explained on the following pages. As long as your energy (Mental from your brain, and physical from your body) is strong, your "Etheric-physical Zone" will remain strong; meaning your etheric protection shield will protect you against others' bad vibes and malicious intentions.

Like everything in the world, maintaining equilibrium, strength and health, require:
a-Training or development (Growth)
b-Nutrition
c-Stability

Cars and airplanes need maintenance and repair, plants and tree needs water to grow, to keep a candle burning, we need oxygen, and to stay alive our body needs food, water, and oxygen. The same thing applies to our energy.

So the 46 million Dollar question is:
How to keep our energy strong and healthy?
There are several techniques proposed by a multitude of healers and spiritual masters around the globe.
But, the Anunnaki Ulema techniques are the easiest and most effective; they provide us with answers related to:

a-Training or development (Growth):
Techniques, exercises and practices are given and explained to you. Thus, you will train yourself, your mind and your body, and by doing so, you will develop a strong energy, and healthy vibes.

b-Nutrition:
You have to feed your energy. It needs nutrition; mental, etheric and physical food. The Mouraba technique explains to you what kind of nutrition, your energy needs.

c-Stability:
You have to maintain your energy in good shape, otherwise, others will invade your Khateyn Tarika, your "Zone" and cause lots of damages. Thus, stability of a healthy and strong energy is a must, if you want to protect yourself against others.
The Mouraba will show you how.
The second 46 million Dollar question is:
How to protect ourselves against others' negative energy, bad vibes and malicious thoughts/intentions?
Some of the techniques to protect ourselves were explained in volume 1, but in this volume, there are few ones that would add an extra thick layer of protection.

II. The Technique:
Look at the Energy Equilibrium/Strength Illustration #1, on page 469. The illustration is also referred to as MOURABA Illustration #1. The technique is called Mouraba.
Mouraba is an Ana'kh word meaning a square. In our technique, each day of the week is represented by a square. I am going to explain to you the meaning of all this. Go now to page 470 to get the information and pertinent instructions.

Good days, bad days, good hours, bad hours

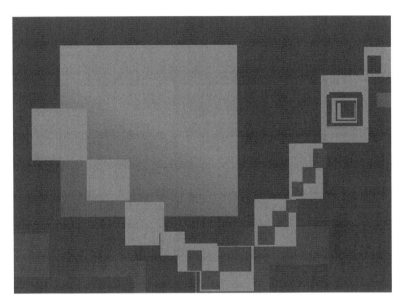

Energy Equilibrium/Strength Illustration #1
MOURABA Illustration #1

Information and pertinent instructions.
Bad days and bad hours of the week:

Note: Look at MOURABA Illustration #2, on page 472.

1. The big square is called Mouraba. It represents a whole week.
2. On your left, you will see a series of small squares, starting with the Monday square, and ending in the middle of the illustration with the Saturday square. Friday square is black. I will explain the black color, when we get to "Friday".
3. Each day of the week has lucky hours and unlucky hours.
4. Each hour of the day corresponds to a particular or a specific activity of yours.
5. If you start and/or complete any project or a business plan during the lucky hour, you will succeed at ease.
6. If you do it during the opening of the unlucky hour, you will fail.
7. If you are exposed to others' bad vibes during an unlucky hour, your unprotected "Zone" would be invaded, and the bad vibes would invade your zone, and hurt you. The bad vibes will bring you back luck, in the form of a failure in what you are working on.
8. You have to protect your zone, feel your surrounding (Environment), and establish a barrier against others' bad vibes.
9. There are general rules to establish those barriers against others' bad vibes. However, each day of the week has its own rhythm and vulnerability hours. For these reasons, we will start with Monday.

Monday:
See Illustration CE #1, on page 472.
The Sahiriin, Rouhaniyiin and Anunnaki Ulema, all agree that Monday is charged with an intense cosmic energy, created by Mother Nature and people. This cosmic energy reaches its peak between 10 AM and 4 PM.
Unfortunately, it is not a positive energy; it could be either neutral or negative. The variation of its nature, quite often, negatively or at least unpleasantly affects the 9 to 5 employees.

470

Thus, creating barriers against this energy on Sunday, between 7 PM and 8 PM is a must. The forthcoming chapters will show you how. For the time being, let's concentrate on the bad days and bad hours of the week. Let's keep focusing on Monday.

In addition to creating barriers to stop the negative vibes, you should also comply with the following rules:

- a-Do not leave dirty dishes and utensils in your sink
- b-Clean all ashtrays
- c-Make you bed
- d-Do not leave dirty laundry inside the home
- e-Open the window (s) if you can
- f-Open one or two faucets, and let water drip for 10 seconds
- g-Do not drink alcohol between 6 PM and 8 PM

Look now at Illustration CE #1, on page 473, Illustration CE#2, on page 474.

*** *** ***

471

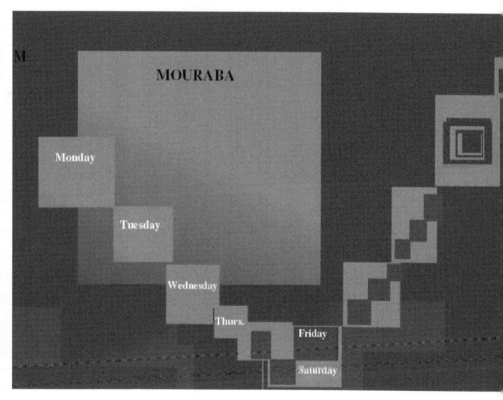

MOURABA ILLUSTRATION #2

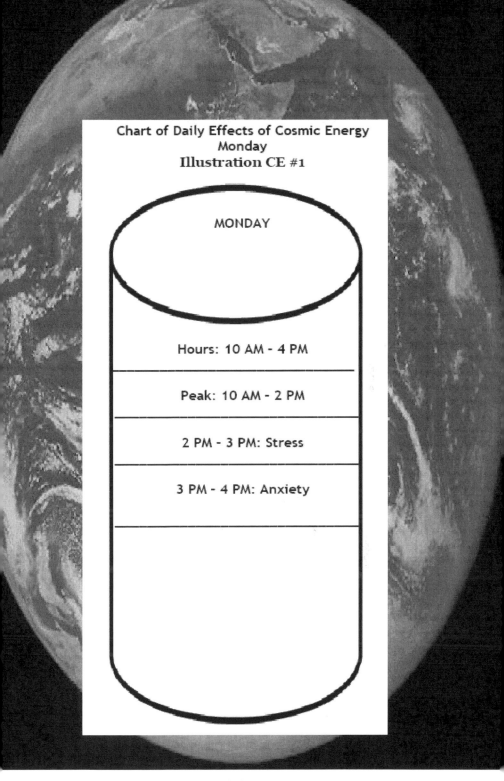

Chart of Daily Effects of Cosmic Energy
Monday
Illustration CE #1

MONDAY

Hours: 10 AM - 4 PM

Peak: 10 AM - 2 PM

2 PM - 3 PM: Stress

3 PM - 4 PM: Anxiety

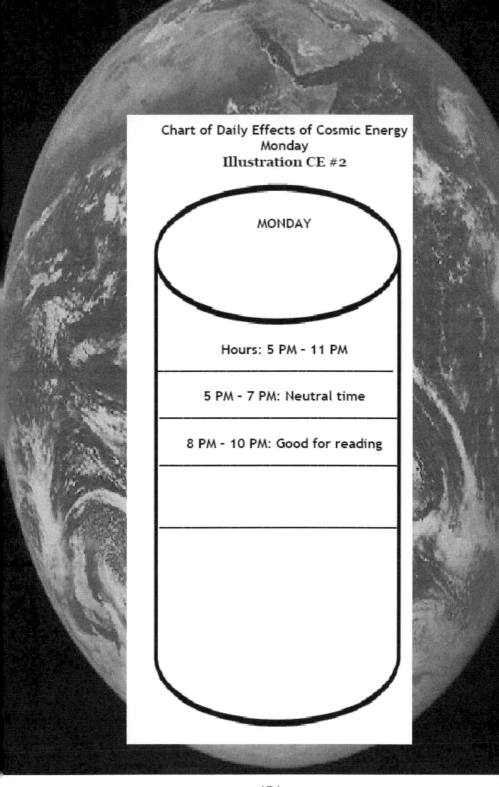

Chart of Daily Effects of Cosmic Energy
Monday
Illustration CE #2

MONDAY

Hours: 5 PM - 11 PM

5 PM - 7 PM: Neutral time

8 PM - 10 PM: Good for reading

Tuesday:
See Illustration CE #3, on page 476.

Tuesday is an excellent day for writing proposals and grants. The most favorable hours are between 11 AM and 1 PM. According to the Rouhaniyiin, the cosmic negative energy is weak on Tuesday. This, does not mean that people would not emit bad vibes.
People do all the time, regardless of the effects of Mother Nature on us, and our lucky days and lucky hours.
This is why, we should keep our Khateyn Tarika fortified, healthy and in equilibrium. Between 8 PM and 10 PM, we have neutral time, meaning a few hours to hang around, do ordinary things, as usual, but not to start a major project.
A few moments after 10 PM, the good energy of Mother Nature will start to weaken. Consequently, we should not undertake major projects, and make final decisions on important matters.
Others' negative vibes get intensified between 11 PM and 6 AM.

$$*** \quad *** \quad ***$$

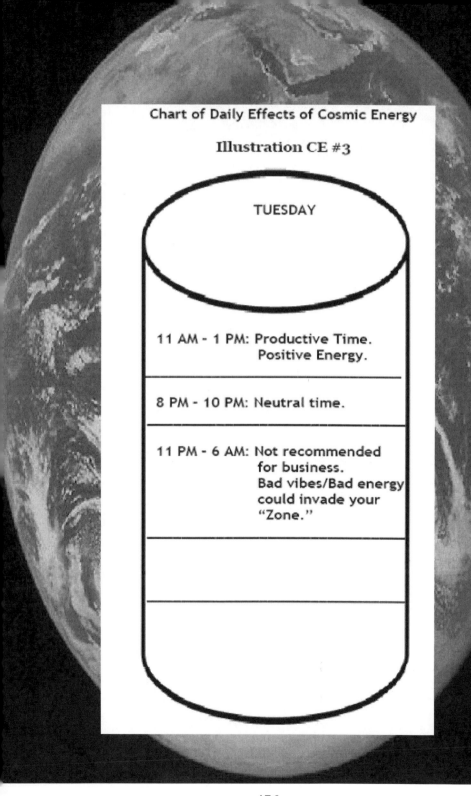

Chart of Daily Effects of Cosmic Energy

Illustration CE #3

TUESDAY

11 AM - 1 PM: Productive Time.
Positive Energy.

8 PM - 10 PM: Neutral time.

11 PM - 6 AM: Not recommended
for business.
Bad vibes/Bad energy
could invade your
"Zone."

Wednesday:
Look at Illustration CE #4, on page 478.
It is self-explanatory.
The hours between 10 AM and 3 PM are positive hours. There is a strong positive current, and the abundance of good vibes make these hours very productive.
It is the perfect timing to conclude deals, give conferences, meet new people, make important decision, get busy in your yard, do shopping, even, to flirt.
However, between 11 PM and 3 AM, negative energy will resurface. Consult the Maps of states and areas charged with underground negative current.

*** *** ***

Chart of Daily Effects of Cosmic Energy

Illustration CE #4

WEDNESDAY

10 AM - 3 PM: Productive Time.
Positive Energy.
A solid day.

5 PM - 7 PM: Neutral time.

8 PM - 10 AM: Good hours to take
care of family
business.

11 PM -3 AM: Negative hours.

Thursday:
Look at Illustration CE #5, on page 480.
The hours between 8 AM and 11 AM are good hours.
They are open to any of your projects and endeavors, particularly to finances, investment, starting a new enterprise, a new business, remodeling, selling, real estate, visits, and so on.
The hours between 3 PM and 2 PM are perfect for evaluating the results of your projects and decisions, to make new decisions, to explore other possibilities, to renegotiate deals, to submit offers, to write new proposals, and for planning.
The hours between 8 PM and 10 PM are excellent for selling and/or displaying your art, paintings, books. Galleries displaying artwork will do great business between these hours. Receptions will get good results.
These hours are highly recommended for spiritual work, esoteric exercises, and exploring the world of the occult.
However, between 2 AM and 5 AM, the negative energy will resurface again. Be careful. Be alert. By now, you know what you should no do during the negative hours.

*** *** ***

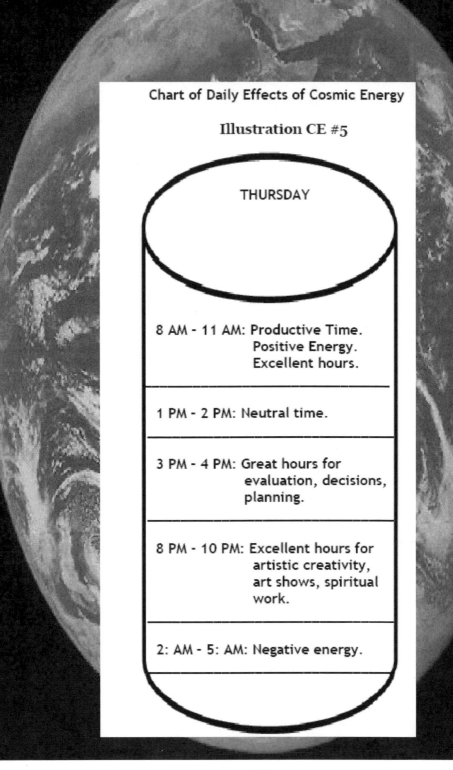

Chart of Daily Effects of Cosmic Energy

Illustration CE #5

THURSDAY

8 AM - 11 AM: Productive Time.
Positive Energy.
Excellent hours.

1 PM - 2 PM: Neutral time.

3 PM - 4 PM: Great hours for
evaluation, decisions,
planning.

8 PM - 10 PM: Excellent hours for
artistic creativity,
art shows, spiritual
work.

2: AM - 5: AM: Negative energy.

Friday:
Look at Illustration CE #6, on page 482.
Friday is a very important day in the calendar of the Rouhaniyiin.
I am not referring to their esoteric and supernatural work, and communications with entities and spirits. Friday is important because it is a bridge between strong physical-cosmic energies and others' energies.
On Friday, mixed currents underground merge, and create unpredictable vibrations. If you have started a discussion, and/or submitted a report/proposal/ plan of action to your boss, associates and potential investors, you must do it between 8 AM and 11 AM, because these three hours will be automatically followed by 2 intense hours; meaning that heated debates, unpleasant arguments, and the emergence of mild negative vibes will develop between 1 PM and 3 PM.
Avoid criticism and arguments between 3 PM and 4 PM.
The hours between 8 PM and 10 PM are excellent for socializing, meeting new people, making contacts, going out, and so on.
However, you must re-energize your Khateyn Tarika before you go out.
Negative energy will re-emerge between 1 AM and 5 AM.

Note: The Friday's square is black, because it represents the emergence of a very strong negative current that could last until the end of the week.

*** *** ***

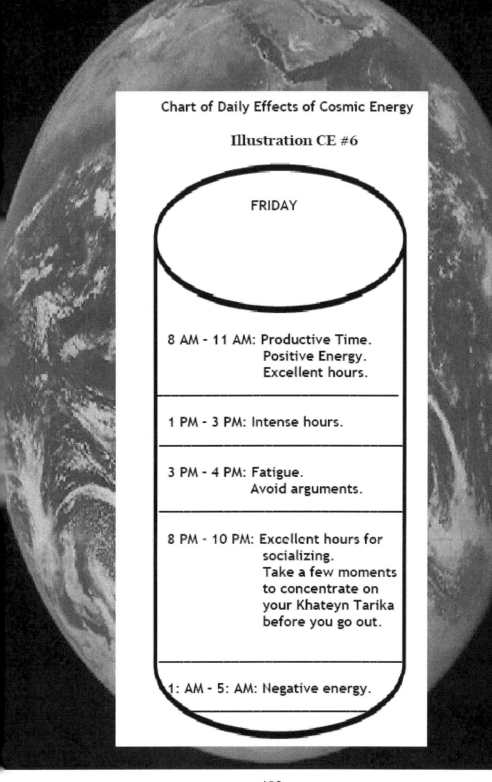

Chart of Daily Effects of Cosmic Energy

Illustration CE #6

FRIDAY

8 AM - 11 AM: Productive Time.
              Positive Energy.
              Excellent hours.

1 PM - 3 PM: Intense hours.

3 PM - 4 PM: Fatigue.
             Avoid arguments.

8 PM - 10 PM: Excellent hours for
              socializing.
              Take a few moments
              to concentrate on
              your Khateyn Tarika
              before you go out.

1: AM - 5: AM: Negative energy.

Saturday:
Look at Illustration CE #7, on page 484.
Cosmic energy circulates very strongly on Saturday between 8 AM and 11 AM, therefore, your home must be absolutely clean. No mess anywhere.
Messy stuff and dirty things inside your home will disrupt the positive flow of energy. Open a window or two, turn on a kitchen faucet for 10 seconds or so. Saturday is a good day to spend with your loved ones. From 2 PM to 4 PM, good energy rides with you. Read Friday's chart, for the following hours.

***   ***   ***

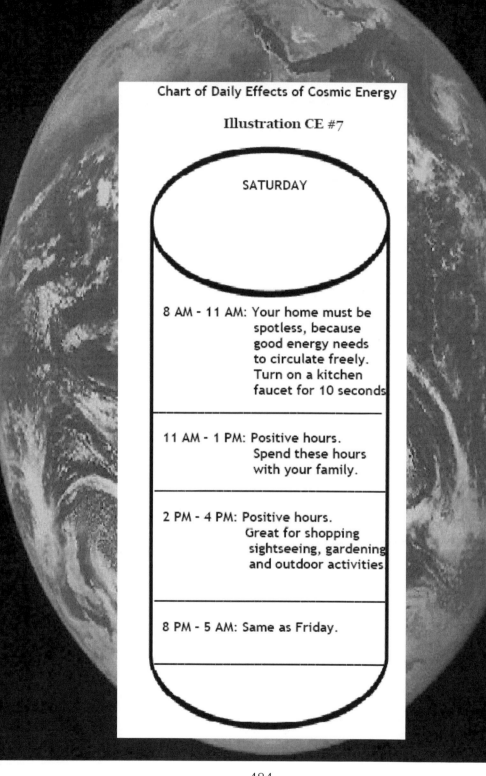

Chart of Daily Effects of Cosmic Energy

Illustration CE #7

SATURDAY

8 AM - 11 AM: Your home must be
spotless, because
good energy needs
to circulate freely.
Turn on a kitchen
faucet for 10 seconds

11 AM - 1 PM: Positive hours.
Spend these hours
with your family.

2 PM - 4 PM: Positive hours.
Great for shopping
sightseeing, gardening
and outdoor activities

8 PM - 5 AM: Same as Friday.

Sunday:
Look at Illustration CE #8, on page 486.
Self-explanatory. However, pay attention to the hours between 1 AM and 5 AM!
Those are bad hours for almost everything, except, perhaps, for casinos' business, and some shady activities.
Whether you are a small or big-time entrepreneur, do not make final decision (s) during these hours.
A very strong cosmic negative energy circulates during these treacherous hours. Avoid travel (Long distances).
Do not argue with people in a position of power. Go to sleep.

*** *** ***

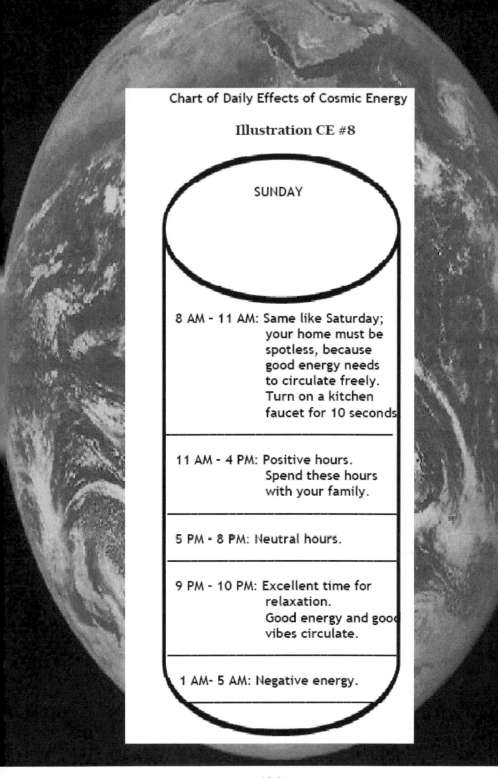

Chart of Daily Effects of Cosmic Energy

Illustration CE #8

SUNDAY

8 AM - 11 AM: Same like Saturday; your home must be spotless, because good energy needs to circulate freely. Turn on a kitchen faucet for 10 seconds

11 AM - 4 PM: Positive hours. Spend these hours with your family.

5 PM - 8 PM: Neutral hours.

9 PM - 10 PM: Excellent time for relaxation. Good energy and good vibes circulate.

1 AM - 5 AM: Negative energy.

Reversing the flux of bad energy, bad days, and bad hours

Reversing the current of bad cosmic energy is a complicated process but not impossible. It is closely related to the negative hours of the week, and how these hours are governed by negative cosmic vibrations; it has nothing to do with your Rizmanah, and your lucky and unlucky hours and days.

The flux of energy is conditioned by cosmic currents, some circulate in the air, and others underground. And unfortunately you are caught between.

I will not be able to explain to you how to reverse a cosmic flux in this book, because you need a personal guidance.

Mouraba Illustration #3 refers to the "Reversing Process".

Basically, it is reconstructing time continuum of cosmic energy backward. I know, it is complicated. Nevertheless, you can write to me for additional information and partial guidance.

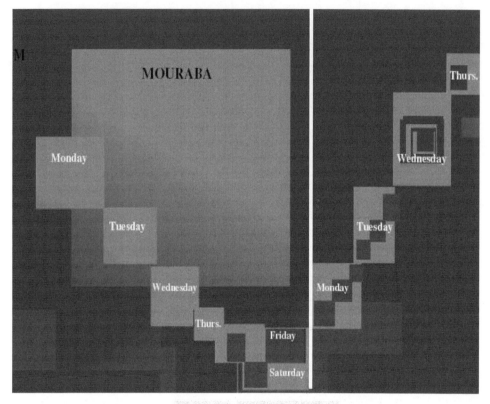

MOURABA ILLUSTRATION #3

Rizmanah/Hamnika-mekhakeh
Calendar of your Lucky Days and Unlucky Days

- Hamnika-mekhakeh: Grids used by Anunnaki-Ulema as calendar to find the lucky days and the lucky hours in a person's life
- Hamnika-mekhakeh- ilmu: The technique of using the Hamnika-mekhakeh
- Synopsis of the concept
- The Ulema-Anunnaki days are
- The calendars' grids
- The use of a language
- The preparation and use of the grids
- Grid 1: Calendar of the week
- Grid 2: Calendar of your name
- Grid 3: Calendar of your lucky hour
- Grid 4
- Grid 5
- Zaradu
- The 17 lucky years in your life
- Araliridu

***   ***   ***

489

Hamnika-mekhakeh:
Ana'kh/Ulemite. Noun.
Grids used by Anunnaki-Ulema as calendar to find the lucky days and the lucky hours in a person's life.

Hamnika-mekhakeh- ilmu:
Ana'kh/Ulemite. Noun. term
The technique of using the Hamnika-mekhakeh.

I. Synopsis of the concept
II. The Ulema-Anunnaki days are
III. The calendars' grids
IV. The use of a language
V. The preparation and use of the grids

I. Synopsis of the concept:
Humans follow certain calendars. The most common one is the Gregorian Calendar, which is a reflection of the Christian faith. It is younger than the Muslim calendar, which in turn, is younger than the Jewish calendar.
All of these are considerably younger than the Anunnaki calendar, which is the only one used by the Anunnaki-Ulema.
The Anunnaki-Ulema reject the idea that the week consists of seven days. Their week consists of four days, corresponding to certain days of our week. These are the only days to use in this technique, and the other three days in our week should not be calculated upon.

II. The Ulema-Anunnaki days are:

- Day 1: Thilta (Tuesday)
- Day 2: Araba (Wednesday)
- Day 3: Jema (Friday)
- Day 4: Saba (Saturday).

491

The importance of these days is the relationship between the person and the hours in each day. Using the calendar of the Anunnaki-Ulema, each person can find the luckiest hour of his or her week, according to the Book of Ramadosh (Rama-Dosh). Ulema Rabbi Mordachai said: "You might feel that one hour a week is not sufficient for anyone's needs. It might also not improve your luck at work if it occurs, say, at two o'clock in the morning each Saturday.

This predicament can be easily resolved by performing another technique, Time Manipulation, on that exact hour. The time that will be added to your life under such circumstances will be as lucky as the original hour, and your chances of success will be vastly improved."

The Anunnaki-Ulema teachers highly recommend performing a combination of techniques, since each enhances the other considerably.

III. The calendars' grids:
A couple of questions might arise as you work with this technique. First, are all people with the same number of letters in their name share a lucky hour?

Yes, indeed they would.

There are only sixteen grid lines to represent millions of people each. And this leads to an interesting discovery

The numbers of letters in people's names represent a certain harmony that exists between them.

For example, if you wish to approach someone in high places for a favor, finding that he or she shares the number of letters and the lucky hour will enhance your chances.

Always send your request to him or her during the lucky hour, either by calling on the phone, using your e-mail, or placing a written letter in the mailbox.

IV. The use of a language:
Another question is the issue of languages. What if your name is written with four letters in America, where you live, but with five letters in your native language? The answer is simple.

492

Always use your native language, the language that you were first aware of your name in, in your grid. It will be much more accurate and certainly more powerful. An important fact to add is that this technique is simple, but it can be enhanced in many ways by subtle variations.

Adding those variations extends the knowledge of how time and space is related to luck and success, and how to fine tune the process. But even in this straightforward version, the technique is incredibly powerful, so much so that it may change your life completely, always for the better.

Tip: If any added numbers are higher than one digit, always add the numbers and use the result. For example, if instead of 3+1+1+1= 6 you will find yourself with, say, 4+7+7+7=25, add 2+5 and use the result, namely 7. If you have 40+41+42+43=126, add 1+2+6=9.

V. The preparation and use of the grids:
The first step is to prepare a grid of sixteen squares, like the one below.

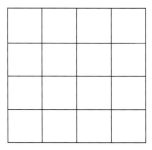

In the next step, you will establish the calendar of the week, by writing them in this specific order.

Grid 1: Calendar of the Week

Day 1	Day 2	Day 3	Day 4
Day 2	Day 3	Day 4	Day 1
Day 3	Day 4	Day 1	Day 2
Day 4	Day 1	Day 2	Day 3

- 1-In the next step, you will establish the calendar of your name. Let's say your name is Suzan.
- 2-You will write your name in the squares, but you must write from right to left, the way they did in many ancient languages, including Ana'kh.
- 3-Then, you follow, still from right to left, with the number of the days, 1, 2, 3, 4.

Grid 2: Calendar of Your Name

A	Z	U	A
3	2	1	N
Z	U	S	4
2	1	N	A

*** *** ***

494

- 1-In the next step, you will establish the calendar of your lucky hour.
- 2-Look at the two squares above.
- 3-Try to find the one square that has the same number in both drawings.
- 4-When you compare each square, you will see that the second square in the last raw has the #1 in it.
- 5-Fill in the number of the days in the first row, the way it appeared in the first grid.

Therefore, Suzan's lucky hour will occur during the second day. (If more than one square presents the same number, add the numbers.)

Grid 3: Calendar of your lucky hour

Day 1	Day 2	Day 3	Day 4
	1		

*** *** ***

In the next step, we shall start our calculations.

- 1-Keep the first row as is.
- 2-fill the rest of the grid with the number 1.
- 3-In each column, you will now subtract the three #1 from the day in the first row. 1-1-1-1= -2; 2-1-1-1= -1; 3-1-1-1= 0; 4-1-1-1 = 1

495

Grid 4

Day 1	Day 2	Day 3	Day 4
1	1	1	1
1	1	1	1
1	1	1	1
-2	-1	0	1

- 4-We will now add the number we have calculated. $(-2) + (-1) + 0 + 1 = (-2)$
- 5-We continue our calculations by using the number we have achieved, -2, as a filler in the grid below, in three rows under the basic days row on top.
- 6-Then, we will calculate the values of the columns the way we have done in the previous grid.

*** *** ***

Grid 5

Day 1	Day 2	Day 3	Day 4
-2	-2	-2	-2
-2	-2	-2	-2
-2	-2	-2	-2
-5	-4	-3	-2

- 7-We will add these numbers: $(-5) + (-4) + (-3) + (-2) = -14$

- **8**-We will combine the individual numbers comprising the number fourteen by adding them: 1+ 4 = 5
- **9**-We will add these two numbers. (-14) + 5 = -9

*** *** ***

In the next step:
- **1**-Return to the first grid, displaying the calendar of the week.
- **2**-Starting on the second row, count the squares, going from right to left, nine times.
- **3**-You will reach Day 3.
- **4**-This establishes that your lucky hour will occur on Friday, the third day of the Anunnaki week.
- **5**-To establish the hour, go back to Grid 4, and look at the row that expresses Day 3.
- **6**-Add the numbers: 3 + 1 + 1 + 1 = 6
- **7**-Calculate: (-9) - (+6) = -3
- **8**-To establish the hour within the 24 hours in each day subtract, 24 − 3 = 21.

21 is 9 P.M.
Therefore, Suzan's luckiest hour of the week occurs at nine o'clock in the evening of each Friday.

*** *** ***

497

Zaradu
The 17 Lucky years in your Life

"Zara-Du", also called "Macari," and "Sabata," is a term for what it is known in the Anunnaki-Ulema literature as the "17 Lucky Years of Your Life." Zaradu is a very important metaphysical but also "Physical knowledge" the Anunnaki-Ulema have learned and kept shrouded in secrecy for thousands of years, fearing that bad or immoral persons might learn, and use to influence others, and selfishly alter the course of history.

It was revealed to the Ulema that every single human being on planet Earth will have during his/her life, a lucky period extending throughout 17 consecutive or interrupted years.

During those years (Called Mah'Zu-Zah") the doors of luck, fortune and development at many levels will open up, and opportunities for extraordinary success shall be freely given to her/him.

This is how the phrase "17 Lucky Years of Your Life" came to exist. And for the period of 17 years, there is a calendar, well structured and divided in a sequence of 77 by 7.

This brings us to the Anunnaki-Ulema magical-esoteric number of 777, considered to be the Alpha and Omega of all knowledge and "Tana-Wur", which means enlightenment, similar to the Bodhisattva.

At one point during the lucky years, a person will acquire two extraordinary faculties:
  1- Rou'h Ya
  2- Firasa (Fi raa-Saa).
These two faculties will positively influence his/her life and guide him/her effortlessly toward reaching the highest level of mental and physical strength, as well success in business and varied endeavors.

Some of these endeavors for instance, is an astonishing power or capability of producing, writing or composing in an exceptional prolific manner.

It also encompass the ability of learning many languages in no time, and reading manuscripts written in secret languages, such as the first secret and hidden alphabet (Characters) of the Hindu language.

Applied in modern times, reading the secret symbols and alphabets become forecasting events and predicting the rise and fall of world's markets.

It was also said, that this 17 year period can alter a DNA sequence, thus preventing time from succumbing the blessed one (Learned ones) to aging, and the deterioration of their cells.

One of the last Anunnaki-Ulema Mounawirin (Enlightened) known to have discovered the secret of the 17 lucky years was Alan Cardec "Allan Cardec" (October 3, 1804- March 31, 1869). Cardec's real name was Hippolyte Léon Denizard Rivail.

And his Ulema name was Asha-Kar-Da-Ki. His mentor was the legendary Johann Heinrich Pestalozzi, also knows as "Mirdach Kadoshi Sirah" in the Anunnaki-Ulema circle.

His incarnated guiding master (Second high level of Anunnaki-Ulema) was Al Zafiru, called Sefiro or Zefiro in mediumship and spiritism literature. In fact, the word or term "Spiritism" was coined by Cardec.

He was the first to use it and explain its application during a contact with a higher entity and other rapports with dead people (Trapped deceased persons) who asked for his help. Sometimes, it was the way around; Cardec asked for their guidance on matter related to life after death, and the realm of the next life.

Cardec was the father of the French movement of Spiritism, and communications with entities trapped between the next dimension and Earth's boundaries.

They are called "Les retenus", meaning those who were trapped in the afterlife dimension, or more precisely, those who were detained.

Cardec was burried at the historical French cemetry "Cimetière du Père Lachaise". The inscription on his tomb stele reads: "Naitre, mourir, renaitre encore et progresser sans cesse, telle est la loi." Translated verbatim: "To be born, die, to be reborn again and to progress unceasingly, such is the law."

Araliridu

One of the most unusual concepts mentioned in the Book of Rama-Dosh. Basically, it means your "other name"; the name you did not know you had, referring to a Name-Code given to you by the Khalek (Anunnaki creator), before you were born, and took a physical form on Earth.

Ulema Bashir Bin AlFakhri As-Soufi explained this concept as follows, (From his Kiraat, Addendum to the Book of Rama-Dosh):

Note: Translated verbatim, word for word, unedited, to preserve its authentic caché.

- **1**-Your parents gave you a name when you were born. That is your physical name. The name of your body, yourself and the link to your family.
- **2**-This name may influence your fate.
- **3**-If your name contains one of the 72 powerful words of the Al Khalek (Creator), then you will be lucky, and you will prosper in life.
- **4**-If your name does not have any of the 72 powerful names of Al Khalek, you would live like all the other people; no special treatment from the providence will be given to you.
- **5**-But what you did not know is that the name given to you by your parents is not the only name you have received in this mortal sphere.
- **6**-There is another name that it has been given to you by a higher authority. This is your real name, because it contains all your attributes, including the lucky dates, the map of your future, and the powers you can use to stop dangers and threats.
- **7**-We call this name "Ism Al Ghayra Manzour", or "Ghayra Al Ma'rouf", meaning the unseen name, or the unknown name.

500

- **8**-This name links you to your origin.
- **9**-This name attaches you to your mind, or to your soul.
- **10**-This name unites you with Al Khalek.
- **11**-Our brothers the Jews, I mean the elder Jewish scholars knew about the unheard, unseen and the unknown name. This is why – some of the reasons – they always give a Hebrew/Jewish name to foreign Jews who were not born in Israel, or do not speak Hebrew. Every Jewish person has two names; one name given to him by his parents, and another Hebrew name given to him by others, either a Rabbi, or even relatives.
- **12**-After a purification ceremony, one of our brothers will find your hidden name.
- **13**-If that name is a lucky name. You will keep it, and you will remember it.
- **14**-If that name is an unlucky name, the Ulema brother will change it, and will give you a new name.
- **15**-Our languages on earth are a great gift from Al Khalek.
- **16**-Only developed minds can create and enjoy a language.
- **17**-In the other dimension, where you came from, you already have a name. It is written in Ana'kh language, because you were created by the first creative source of the Anunnaki.
- **18**-If you are from Sudan, do not expect to find a Sudanese name in the other dimension.
- **19**-If you are from Alexandria, do not expect to find an Alexandrani name in the other dimension.
- **20**-You will only find your name in Ana'kh.
- **21**-Your teacher will find it for you...

Your Name
Your Name Here and Beyond

- Your name here and beyond
- Ismu Ardi; your name on Earth
- Ismu Khalka; your non-Earth name
- How do I write my name in Ana'kh?
- How can I find my true name (Code); the one the Anunnaki gave me before I was born?
- Writing/Equating your name in Ana'kh-Proto Ugaritic
- Chart of the Latin/Anglo-Saxon Alphabet in comparison with the Ana'kh letters
- Placing the letters of your name under each corresponding letter in the Ana'kh/Proto-Ugaritic
- Exercise #1
- Exercise #2

***   ***   ***

Your Name
Your Name Here and Beyond

In this section, I will talk to you about:

> ❖ Ismu Ardi; your name on Earth.
> ❖ Ismu Khalka; your non-Earth name.
> ❖ The importance of your given name.
> ❖ The importance of a name you have received from a higher source, before you were born, and which you are not aware of.

Ismu Ardi; your name on Earth.
Your current name is not necessarily your true name, because it was a name chosen and given to you by your parents or relatives.
In many parts of the globe, and especially in the Middle East, a name is usually given to a new born to honor the name and memory of a father or the head of a family.
In tribal and rigidly traditional communities, a person is often referred to, and/or called as "Ben" of (in Judaic-Jewish tradition) or "Bin" of, and "Ibn" of (in Arabic and Muslim tradition), meaning the son of.
Thus, a name could be given for traditional and familial reasons.
We call this, Ismu Ardi, meaning a terrestrial name.
The Ismu Ardi is not your primordial or original name.

Ismu Khalka; your non-Earth name.
Searching for your name in Ana'kh.

Regardless of your ethnicity, your native tongue, gender or race, you have a name that is written in Ana'kh, which is the Anunnaki's language. This name is a code; your DNA code.

505

In many of the Semitic and ancient Middle Eastern languages, one's name is usually an adjective; an attribute, rather than a noun. For instance, the name Kabir means big; the name Asad means (courageous as a) lion, and so on.

In Ana'kh, names given to people are an attribute, a sort of code. In other words, the name refers to attributes and faculties found in your DNA, and stored in the Conduit of your brain, as it was explained to us by the Ulema Anunnaki. This name is called "Ismu Khalka; your non-Earth name, assigned to you by the Anunnaki.

Each one of us has a name, that nobody else has. There are many Roberts and many Janes on Earth, but in the Anunnaki's realm and in the Bakht (Tarot), there is only one Jane, and only one Robert. Meaning, if your assigned name is Muktiar, nobody else is called Muktiar. You are the only person in other dimensions who has the Muktiar name.

Why?

Because Muktiar or other names assigned to other people are in fact a code, some sort of mathematical-genetic formula. And each person in the Donia (Life, universe, multiverse, etc.) has a different genetic formula and DNA, just like your fingerprints. Thus, for each genetic formula, and for each person's DNA, there is only one name (Code).

On Earth, your name could be Albert or Khalid, Lydia or Hind, but in another dimension, or in a different world, you have a different name totally unrelated to the name you have on Earth.

You are Albert on Earth, but you are also Shimradu in the next dimension, Rafaat in a parallel dimension, and Kira in a non-bio-organic form of existence. Three different names for the same person, so on.

Are Albert, Shimradu and Rafaat the same person?

Yes and no.

Yes, because all of the three have retained some similar and major properties and characteristics, such as the Conduit, the Fikr, the Jabas, etc.

No, because all of the three now have different properties, such as new cellular memory, new molecules, totally different organic substance, more organs, less organs, etc.

506

The changes occur at so many different levels. For instance, on Earth, you have two eyes, while in a different world, eyes are no longer needed to see objects; they have been replaced by other organs or tissues totally inconceivable and incomprehensible to the human mind.

And because the new Albert has become a new entity, the future of this new entity becomes diametrically different from the future of a person called Albert who once upon a time lived on Earth, or is still living somewhere on Earth.

Consequently, for each new entity, new person, or a new intelligent life form, a new Bakht has been created. But do not be concerned with this for now. All you have to do for the moment is to find the name the Anunnaki gave you when you were first born or conceived.

This very name is the one I recommend to use while reading your Bakht and Tarot charts. Yet, you can still use your Erdi name to read your Bakht and learn a lot about your future.

But you have to remember that by only using your Ismu Erdi, your access to the complete file of your future and destiny will not be complete.

Nevertheless, what you will or could discover about yourself and your future is mind-boggling.

How do I write my name in Ana'kh?
How can I find my true name (Code); the one the Anunnaki gave me before I was born?
It is not easy, but it is possible.

- ❖ First, you must equate the letters of your name with the corresponding letters in Ana'kh/Proto-Ugaritic. Look at the corresponding alphabet chart on the next page.
- ❖ Second, place the letters of your name under each corresponding letter in the Ana'kh/Proto-Ugaritic; several examples are provided in this book.
- ❖ Third: Write your Anakh name from right to left, the way the Anakh language is written, similar to written Hebrew and Arabic.

507

This exercise gives you your name in Ana'kh, and refers you to a pertinent meaning. However, it does not give you the primordial name (Code), the Anunnaki assigned to you when you were born, even before you were born/conceived in a blueprint.

*** *** ***

Writing/Equating your name in Ana'kh-Proto Ugaritic
Chart of the Latin/Anglo-Saxon Alphabet in comparison with
the Ana'kh letters

⌘ **Writing/Equating Your Name in Anakh/Proto-Ugaritic** ⌘

Chart

A	B	C	D	E	F	G	H

I	J	K	L	M	N	O	P

Q	R	S	T	U	V	W	X

Y	Z

Additional Sounds/Letters

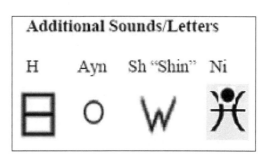

H   Ayn   Sh "Shin"   Ni

Placing the letters of your name under each corresponding letter in the Ana'kh/Proto-Ugaritic

Exercise #1:

Let's assume that you name is Mary, and you are trying to find its equivalent or corresponding name in Anakh/Proto-Ugaritic, the language we will be using for the Tarot.

First: Search for the corresponding letter for M.

The corresponding letter is:

Second: Search for the corresponding letter for A.

The corresponding letter is:

Third: Search for the corresponding letter for R.

The corresponding letter is:

Fourth: Search for the corresponding letter for Y.

The corresponding letter is:

Exercise #2:
First: Write now your Anakh name from right to left. You should get this:

Second: Find the numerical value for each letter.

 =M

M: The numerical value for the letter M is 13.
Meaning:
1-Your physical strength is bigger than your mental strength. But if you are patient, and you try again with determination and a deep concentration, you will gain more mental power.
2-Tenderness and affection.

 =A

A: The numerical value for the letter A is 1.
Meaning:
1-The beginning.
2-It is a good time to start a business.
3-Change of status quo.

=R

R: The numerical value for the letter R is 18.
Meaning:
1-You are a candidate to play a major role in your field, and leave a huge mark in this area.
2-You are going to face strong opposition in your most important projects. Such opposition will come from the opposite sex. And it will occur on the job, or where you work, such as an office, an organization, and even during a delegation and a public speech. But you will be able to convince others and eliminate that opposition if this happens on these days: Tuesday, Thursday and Friday.
3-<u>Monday is not a lucky day for you.</u>

 =Y

Y: The numerical value for the letter Y is 10 .
Meaning:
1-Avoid major decisions on a Monday.
2-Tuesday, Thursday and Friday are your lucky days.
3-Your meticulous planning blends perfectly with an exquisite taste and an accentuated fantasy, yet not totally irrational. On the contrary, it adds originality and creates a special aura around you.
4-In your life, you will meet with strong opposition. But with determination you will prevail.

And what if you write your name like this: Marie, Myriam or Maria? Does this change affect your situation and Bakht? Absolutely not. To be sure, repeat the same exercises, and you will find out. No knowledge, no results and no interpretation should be obtained or caused by coincidence or probability. Even though these exercises might appear incomprehensible and/or irrational, the time will come when you will find out that there are convincing elements, evidence and logic working behind the Bakht techniques.

512

Mintaka Difaya
Protecting your Zone

- Introduction
- Purpose
- Tools and materials needed
- It works like this
- Follow these instructions
- Step One
- Illustration #1 Mintaka Fasida
- Step Two
- Illustration #2 Mintaka Fasida
- Step Three
- Illustration #3 Mintaka Fasida
- Step Four
- Illustration #4 Mintaka Fasida
- Illustration #5 Mintaka Fasida
- Step Five
- Illustration #6 Mintaka Fasida
- Illustration #7 Mintaka Fasida
- Step Six (Final Stage)
- Illustration #8 Mintaka Fasida

*** *** ***

Mintaka Difaya
Protecting your Zone

I. Introduction:

Protecting your zone "Mintaka" is a complex and difficult process to understand, but it is not impossible to learn. The Enlightened Masters have their own techniques, and they are difficult to grasp. But, they taught us some exercises and techniques we can easily use to protect ourselves against bad energy and the negative/malicious vibrations of others. Mind you that not all the negative or bad vibrations are always emitted by bad people or those who want to harm to us.

In many cases, they come from good friends and relatives, for reasons I have already explained throughout the book.

Nevertheless, we must protect ourselves.

Honorable Master Govinda gave us an easy to follow technique. He called it the Dinar Tarika. In the Ulemite language, it is called Mintaka Difaya. It is composed of two words:

a- Mintaka, which means a zone, an area,

b- Difaya, which means protection or defense.

II. Purpose:

With mental visualization and deep concentration, you are to create a field of counter-energy to oppose the bad energy and negative vibes of others.

- a- The coin represents your own energy.
- b- The rice paper symbolically represents a field, a zone. You could call this field your "Etheric Zone".
- c- The nails or needles represent rods or an antenna to be used to direct, redirect, oppose or neutralize bad energy and negative vibes.
- d- With the power of your mind, imagination, and concentration, you are to generate a current on the rice paper that will make the needles or nails move toward a dot or 2 dots you point at, on the rice paper.

515

- e- When the nails or the needles get closer to the dot (s), or touch the dot (s), the rice paper will be charged with a strong positive energy field.
- f- When the rice paper is fully charged, the Mintaka Difaya is entirely/totally activated.
- g- When the Mintaka Difaya is activated, an etheric belt, an astral/etheric protection shield will surround you, and/or surround the area where you live, or wish to stay.
- h- This is what you are going to accomplish; this is the purpose of this technique.

III. Tools and materials needed:
- a- A piece of a rice paper
- b- A coin, any kind, a Dollar coin is just fine
- c-Two nails or two large/thick needles
- d- Ink dots

IV. It works like this:
Follow these instructions:

Step One:
- Look at the Illustration #1 on page 517.
- Place the rice paper on a solid surface, a piece of glass is perfect
- Do not use metal, plastic or a fiberglass surface
- Place the solid surface on your desk, on a regular table, and/or on any commode, anywhere in your home, but not in the kitchen, foyer, or the bathroom
- Tape firmly the solid surface to the area you are using (Desk, table, etc.)
- But make sure that you can easily remove the solid surface without damaging the rice paper.
- Later on, at one point during the exercise, you will be required to move the solid surface to another area in your home
- Wash thoroughly a coin and place it on the rice paper as shown in the illustration #1 on page 517

Illustration #1 Mintaka Difaya

Step Two:
- Look at Illustration #2 Mintaka Difaya, on page 519
- Place 2 nails above and below the coin, as shown in the illustration
- Make sure the nails are not rusty
- Go now to page 521, and look at Illustration # 3 Mintaka Difaya.
- Read pertinent information and instructions on page 520.

*** *** ***

Illustration #2 Mintaka Difaya

Step Three:

- Draw 2 dots on the rice paper, next to each nail, as seen in Illustration #3 Mintaka Fasida, on page 521
- In next step, you will begin your mental work

*** *** ***

Illustration #3 Mintaka Difaya

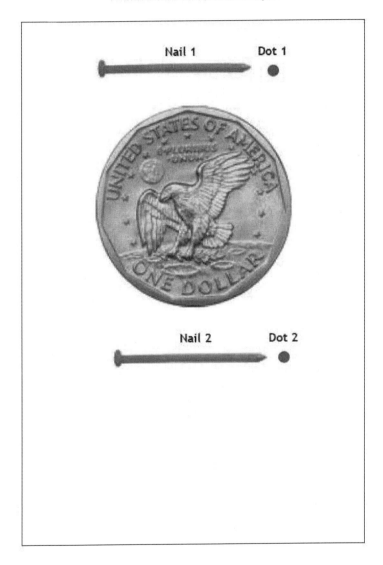

Step Four:

- Look at Illustration #4 Mintaka Fasida, on page 524. You will notice that nail 1 is touching dot 1, or vice versa
- This is the result you should get in this step
- Follow the instructions below
- Concentrate on nail 1 for 3 seconds, and in your mind, tell yourself that a magnetic current exists between nail 1 and dot 1. Just imagine this or fantasize about it. You need to use your imagination, otherwise, the technique would not work
- Cross both hands as shown below, and maintain this position for 10 approximately 10 seconds. And while you are doing that, lean a little bit forward toward the rice paper

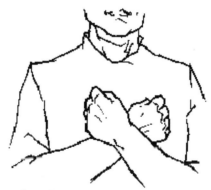

- 5. Take a deep breath
- 6. Close your eyes, release both hands, and extend them toward the solid surface; place the right hand on the right side of the solid surface, and your left hand on the left side of the solid surface
- 7. Stay in this position for 3 seconds
- 8. Take a deep breath
- 9. Keep your left hand on the left side of the rice paper, and move your right hand toward the upper right side of rice paper, and keep it there for 10 seconds.

- 10. Look at Illustration #5, on page 527, to see the position of your right hand
- 11. Go to page 525 and read the instructions on what to do next

*** *** ***

Illustration #4 Mintaka Difaya

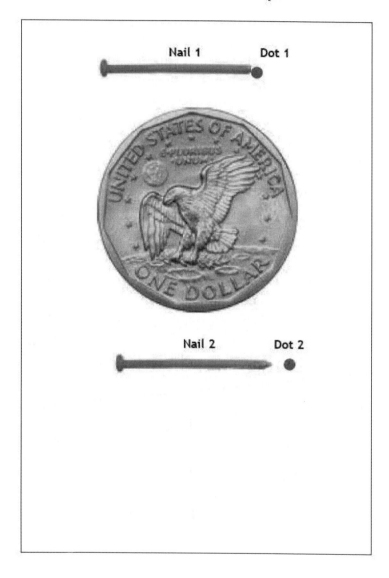

- 12. Look again at Illustration #5, on page 527, to remember the position of your right hand
- 13. You have to use your imagination one more time, and tell yourself there is a magnetic current between your right hand and nail 1.
- 14. Now, you tell yourself there is a magnetic current between your right hand and dot 1.
- 15. You tell yourself there is a magnetic current binding together your right hand, nail 1 and dot 1
- 16. Breath deeply. Breath one more time
- 17. Slowly vibrate your right hand for 20 seconds or so, without touching the rice paper
- 18. And while you are vibrating your right hand, visualize a blue ray emanating from your forehead and going directly toward nail 1
- 19. This blue ray is one of the energy vibes stored in the mental level inside your "Etheric Zone"
- 20. What you have done so far was activating this precise and particular blue vibe. It is working now, and you are about to feel it
- 21. Close your eyes one more time for 5 seconds
- 22. Open your eyes and command nail 1 to come closer to the dot, or if you prefer command dot 1 to come closer to nail 1
- 23. While you are doing that, the blue color vibe coming from your mind is working on its own, meaning creating a positive field of energy that will enhance your Khateyn Tarika and gives an additional layer to your etheric protection shield
- 24. The etheric protection shield will expand and increase in size, even though it remains invisible to the naked eye, but you will fell it, you will sense it not only mentally but physically too
- 25. Take a deep breath
- 26. Close both eyes for 5 seconds while visualizing nail 1 coming closer to dot 1 or dot 1 coming closer to nail 1

- 27. Open your right eye, and keep your left eye close
- 28. Close your right eye, and open your left eye
- Repeat #27 and #28, ten times, and while you are doing that, vibrate your right hand placed on the upper right side of the rice paper
- 29. Open both eyes and look right away at nail 1 and dot 1. They are touching each other, and that's is wonderful because you have vitalized a positive magnetic field around you, created by your mental vibe, a positive energy emitted by your right hand, and the power of concentration
- 30. This positive magnetic field you have just created is mobile, meaning you can take it with you wherever you go. It will never leave you, as long as you keep the 2 lines of your Khateyn Tarika, strong, healthy and parallel to your physical body.
- 31. The positive magnetic field you have just created is capable t neutralizing others' bad vibes
- 32. Every time you feel bad vibes around you, and/or uncomfortable in the presence of a person, tell your mind to re-emit that blue vibe, as simple as that
- 33. You will feel right away that the vibe is taking shape and heading toward others' negative vibes to neutralize them
- 34. You will feel it, no question about it and on the spot you will start to feel better

*** *** ***

526

Illustration #5 Mintaka Fasida

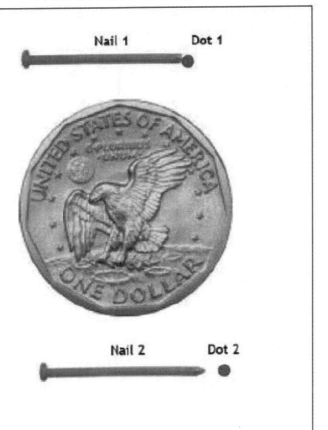

Step Five:
1. Look at Illustration #7 Mintaka Fasida, on page 530
2.You are going to get that result you see in this illustration, meaning you are going to make nail 2 touch dot 2, or vice versa
3. Step Five is similar to Step Four, meaning you have to repeat the instructions given in Step Four to get the result you see on Illustration #7 on page 530.
4. But this time you will use both hands as shown in Illustration #6 Mintaka Fasida, on page 529
5. Look at Illustration #6 Mintaka Fasida on page 529 to see where and how to place both hands on the rice paper

*** *** ***

Illustration #6 Mintaka Difaya

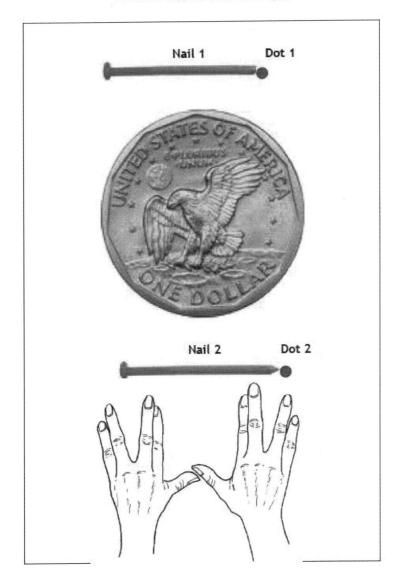

Illustration #7 Mintaka Difaya

Step Six (Final Stage):

1. Remove your hands from the rice paper
2. Stamp your right thumb fingerprint on the rice paper as shown in Illustration #8 Mintaka Fasida, on page 532
3. Take a deep breath
4. Bring back the blue positive vibe and tell your mind to project it over the fingerprint
5. You are going to feel that projection mentally. It is a real projection. More precisely, it is a holographic projection, and you are going to see it
6. Take a deep breath
7. Keep concentrating on your fingerprint for approximately 20 seconds
8. Close your eyes for 5 seconds
9. Open your eyes. The blue vibe is no longer there, but it has merged inside your Etheric Zone", and your fingerprint has sealed your protection shield, meaning that no bad vibes emanated by others will invade your etheric-physical zone.
10. You are protected now
11. Remove the solid surface and store it in a safe area, because you might need it again, in case, in the future you feel the need to repeat this technique
12. You are done. You have succeeded. I am delighted for you, and congratulations
13. Use what you have learned wisely, with humility and good intentions.

*** *** ***

Illustration #8 Mintaka Fasida

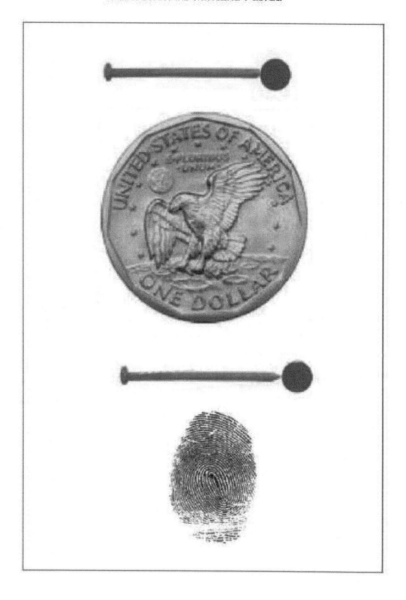

Esoteric-Mental Practices

Exercise on Fik'r-Telemetry. Test your psychic ability

- Exercise on Fik'r-Telemetry. Test your psychic ability
- Definition and introduction
- Objectives and purposes of these exercises
- Objects
- Areas and places
- People
- How it works
- Generalities/Basic steps
- The mental-metaphysical process
- Follow these instructions
- Looking at the photograph of an object
- Continues with these instructions
- Illustration #1 Object
- Illustration # 2 Object
- Illustration #3 Object
- Illustration #4 Object
- Looking at the photograph of a person
- Follow these instructions
- Phase One
- Phase Two
- Illustration #2 Person
- Phase Three

- Illustration #3 Person
- Phase Four
- Illustration #4 Person
- Your tests start here with this page
- Reply to these questions, using the previously mentioned techniques

*** *** ***

Esoteric-Mental Practices

DON'T TURN THE NEXT PAGE YET! READ THIS PAGE FIRST!!

Exercise on Fik'r-Telemetry. Test your psychic ability.

I. Definition and introduction:

Fik'r-Telemetry is one of the Chabariduri's advanced techniques used to identify the nature and origin of an object, as well as, the mental, etheric and physical properties, character, profile and identity of a person, just by touching the object or the photo of that person.

II. Objectives and purposes of these exercises:

Remember, everything around you in the world, including life-forms and objects have some sort of energy, and a multitude of vibrations, including the photos you will be looking at, in this chapter.

By sensing the vibes emanated from the photographs you are looking at, you should be able to create a fair assessment of what you are looking at, such as, identifying the object, the location of areas/places, the character/psyche of people you see in the photographs, and so on.

Try to remember what you have already learned from previous exercises. Apply your learning to all the photos in this chapter.

You are going to look at, and identify a few things:

a-Objects:

You will be asked to look at the photos of various types of objects, ranging from cars and slabs to commercial products and documents.

You are required to identify the object, its origin, properties, etc., just by touching the photo with your right or left palm. And in some instances, you will be asked to tell if you feel good or bad about these objects, meaning if you feel good vibes or bad vibes coming from the objects you are looking at, and just by touching their photographs.

b-Areas and places:
You will be asked to look at the photos of various installations, buildings, edifices, areas, and places. And in some instances, you will be asked to tell if you feel good or bad about these areas and places, meaning if you feel good vibes or bad vibes coming from the places and areas you are looking at, and just by touching their photographs with your right or left palm.
You are required to identify the location of these areas and places, just by touching the photo with your right or left palm.

b-People:
You will be asked to look at the photos of people from around the world, ranging from leaders and artists to celebrities and individuals who created a big buzz.
You are required to identify those people, and in some instances, you will be asked to tell if you feel good or bad about them, meaning if you feel good vibes or bad vibes coming from the people you are looking at, and just by touching their photographs with your right or left palm.

*** *** ***

III. How it works:
Note:

These mental-esoteric exercises are not techniques, but simply exercises to test your psychic abilities, and find out whether you have or have not learned and/or developed psychic, mental, esoteric, and spiritual faculties. However, I will provide you with brief instructions to guide you on the right path. You should concentrate by visually focusing on the photo. Do not guess! Try to sense vibrations or anything unusual just by touching the photograph.

Generalities/Basic steps
The mental-metaphysical process

Follow these instructions:
1. First thing to do is to gaze at the center of the photograph for 5 seconds.
2. Very slowly look at the upper left side of the photograph for approximately 10 seconds
3. Very slowly look now at the right side of the photograph for approximately 10 seconds
4. This will give you a global visual perception of the photograph
5. Take a deep breath
6. Close your eyes for approximately 5 seconds
7. Open your eyes now, learn forward toward the photograph, and place your right or left palm on the photograph
8. Close your eyes for approximately 10 seconds, and try to not think about anything. Create inside your mind an absolute state of tranquility
9. You can accomplish item #8 by visualizing in front of you a rainbow of a multitude of colors, while your eyes are closed
10. If it is difficult to visualize the rainbow, place your left hand above your head, press on the photo with your right palm, and take a deep breath

11. Open your eyes, drop down your left hand, and press on the photograph with your right palm

12. If you are left-handed, do just the opposite

13. Hold the photograph in your left hand, and press again on the photograph with your right palm

14. Run/move your right palm over the photograph in a circular motion, starting from left to right.
Keep doing this for 10 seconds.

15. Now do the opposite; move your right palm in a circular motion, from right to left for 10 seconds

16. Stop, and concentrate intensely on the photograph

17. Pull back a little bit. Allow the photograph to breath and send you its vibes

*** *** ***

Looking at the photograph of an object

Continues with these instructions:

18. If you are looking at the photograph of an object, try to see it as a negative slide. See Illustration #1 Object on page 539.

Illustration #1 Object

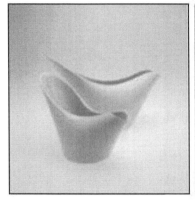 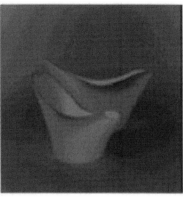

Original picture   The negative slide

19. Create a space in your mind or in your imagination for Illustration #2 Object, on page 540
20. Drag the negative slide to the left (Step One)
21. Enlarge the negative slide as shown in Step 2, and place it on the right side of the place you have created in your mind or imagination
22. Divide the picture in 2 parts, as shown in Step 3, and place it on the left side of the place you have created in your mind or imagination
23. Divide the picture in 4 parts, as shown in Step 4, and place it on the right side of the place you have created in your mind or imagination
24. Go to page 542 for further information, and look at Illustration #3 on page 543

*** *** ***

Illustration # 2 Object

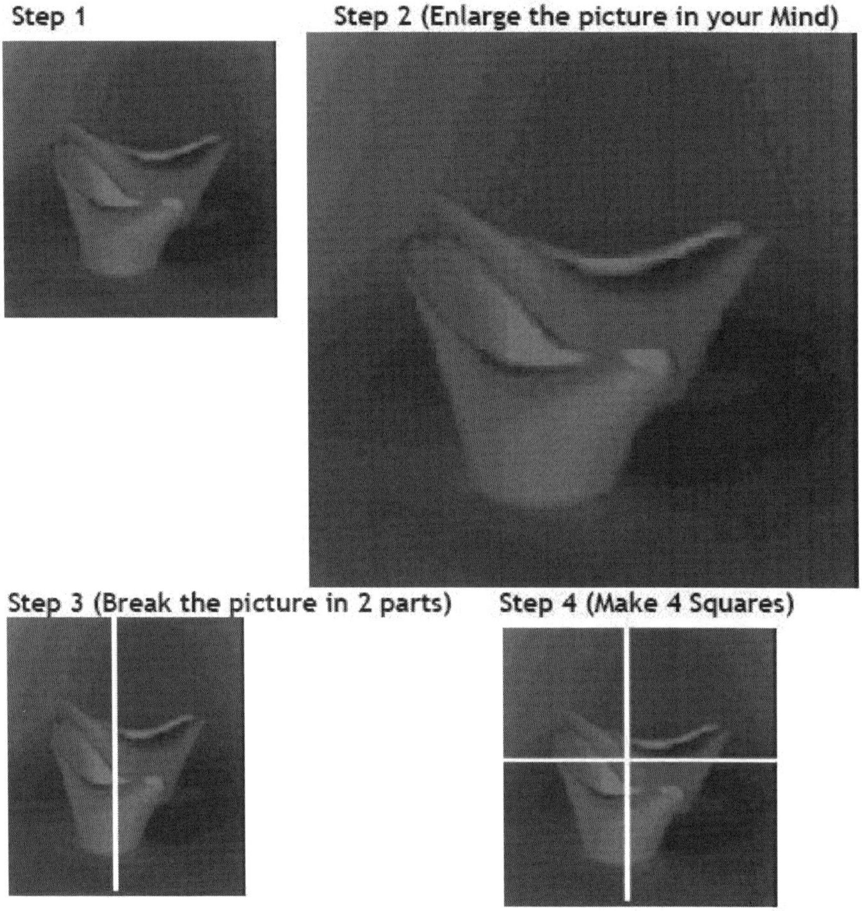

Step 1

Step 2 (Enlarge the picture in your Mind)

Step 3 (Break the picture in 2 parts)

Step 4 (Make 4 Squares)

25. Look at Illustration #3 Object on page 543
26. Keep in your mind the picture listed under Step 1
27. Mentally create a blank square in the center of the picture, as seen under Step 2
28. Mentally enlarge the picture which has the blank square, as seen under Step 3
29. Go to page 544 for further instruction, and look at Illustration #4 Object on page 545

*** *** ***

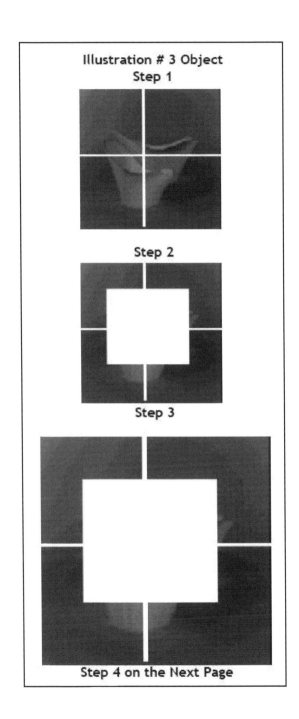

Illustration # 3 Object
Step 1

Step 2

Step 3

Step 4 on the Next Page

30. Place the original photograph of the object inside the blank square

31. Concentrate on the photograph of the object inside the blank square

32. Let your mind for a few moments anchor itself in the blank square

33. When your mind is ready, meaning ready to send you a message, you will feel a new kind of sensations (Vibrations) coming your way, more precisely toward your forehead

34. As soon as the vibrations hit your forehead, you will be able to read very clearly the message of your mind who has analyzed these vibrations

35. And the message will include vital information about the nature, origin and location of the object

36. This is a new discovery you have made, that you will never forget as long as you live, because you have entered the un-chartered world of mind transmission, and remote viewing using your Mind and vibrations you caught from looking at or touching an object

This technique will also help you locate lost objects, such as keys, rings, jewelry, documents, a wallet; any object you were looking for. And if you need additional guidance, do not hesitate to write to me.

*** *** ***

Illustration # 4 Object

Step 4

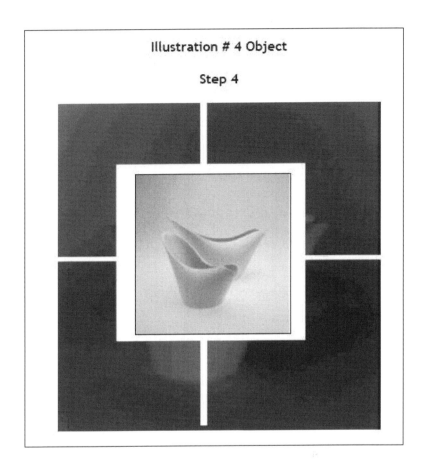

Looking at the photograph of a person.

Look at Illustration #2 Person, on page 548

Note: If you follow my instructions, and you do it right, you will be able not only to identify the person in the picture, but also to discover lots of things about him/her, including character, habits, temperament, level of spirituality and intelligence, thoughts and intentions stored inside his/her Khateyn Tarika, and even locate that person.

You will believe it when you see results, and you will get result when you learn the technique, so start working on it. If you need more help, write to me.

*** *** ***

Follow these instructions.

Phase One:

1. All photographs emit vibrations, thus, you will be able to feel vibrations coming from the photograph of the person you are looking at

2. Hold the photograph in your left hand for 20 seconds, and press on the photograph with your right palm for 20 seconds

3. If you are left-handed, do just the opposite

4. Place the photograph on a solid surface, your desk or a regular table are just fine.

4. Look at the upper left side of the photo for 5 seconds, then look at the upper right side of the photo for 5 seconds

5. Take it easy, relax, easy does it. It is going to work like a charm. I am with you all the way

6. Let the photo sit on the solid surface for 5 seconds or so, this will allow the photograph to anchor some of its vibes into the solid surface

7. Pick up the photograph and place it upside down on the solid surface for 5 seconds

8. Pick up the photograph, place it back on the solid surface, and rotate it clockwise

*** *** ***

Phase Two:

9. Pick up the photograph, make now a copy of the photograph, and reduce its size by approximately 55 to 60%

10. Place the original photograph on the left side of the solid surface, and the copy on the right side, as shown in Illustration #2 Person, (Step 1 and Step 2) on page 548

11. Superpose the reduced photograph in the center of the copy of the photograph, as shown in the illustration (Step 3) and place on the left side of the solid surface, right below the original photograph

12. Let this arrangement of photos sit on the solid surface for 5 seconds

13. Go to page 549 for further instructions related to Phase Three

*** *** ***

Illustration #2 Person

Step 1: The Original photograph   Step 2: Copy of the photograph

Step 3: Superpose the reduced photo

Phase Three:

14. Look at Illustration #3 Person on this page.

15. Re-arrange the photos as seen in the illustration

16. In your mind, link the 3 photos together, meaning creating a three dimensional representation.

17. You can do this by telling yourself that the photo on left represents time zone, the photo on the right represents space/location zone, and the photo in the center represents a sphere/level where you will retrieve information about that person

Go to page 550 for further instruction pertaining to Phase Four, and look at Illustration #4 on page 551

Illustration #3 Person

Phase Four:

19. Now you must concentrate on the photo shown in Illustration #4 Person, on page 551

20. Place your right or left palm on the top of the photo, for 10 seconds

21. Take a deep breath

22. Let your mind for a few moments anchor itself into the photo

23. When your mind is ready, meaning ready to send you a message, you will feel a new kind of sensations (Vibrations) coming your way, more precisely toward your forehead

24.Ask your mind to respond to the questions listed under the photo of a person (They are several in the book) published in this book.

For example, on page 553, the questions were: Is this person a good person? Did he serve well his community or just the opposite?

On page 555, the questions were: Is this person a good person? Was she a great civil right activist? And how did she die? So on.

25. As soon as the vibrations hit your forehead, you will be able to read very clearly the message of your mind who has analyzed these vibrations

35. And the message will include vital information about the person in the photograph, as well as responses/answers to the questions you have asked

Illustration #4 Person

NOTE

For reasons I can't disclose, I am not in a liberty to teach you right now, techniques related to areas and locations of places. Thank you for your kindness and understanding

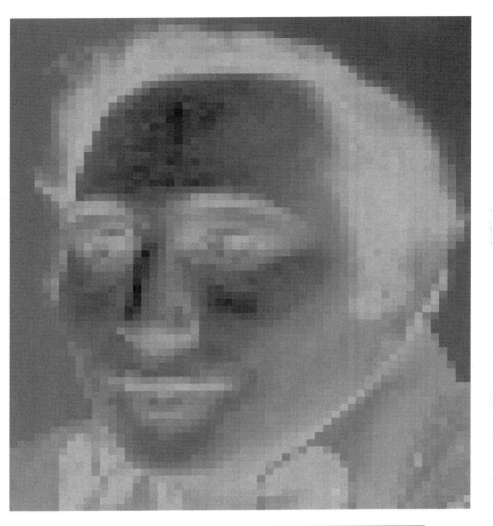

DON'T TURN THIS PAGE YET, OR YOU WILL SPOIL EVERYTHING!!

Reply to the questions, using the previously mentioned techniques:

Is this person a good person? Did he serve well his community or just the opposite?

This is a pixelized and negative photo of a person who, a few years ago made headlines. On the next page, you will see the normal picture. If you have already recognized the person in the negative picture, do not continue this exercise.

The photograph belongs to serial killer David Berkowitz, a.k.a. Son of Sam. So, the correct answer to the question becomes obvious.

**DON'T TURN THIS PAGE YET, OR YOU WILL
SPOIL EVERYTHING!!**
Reply to the questions, using the previously mentioned
techniques:
Is this person a good person?
Was she a great civil right activist? And how did she die?

This is a pixelized photo of a person who made headlines. On the
next page, you will see her normal picture. If you have already
recognized this lady, do not continue this exercise. Find the
correct answers on the next page.

This photo belongs to Teresa Lewis, 41, who died by injection in Virginia. "Lewis enticed two men through sex, cash and a promised cut in an insurance policy to shoot her husband, Julian Clifton Lewis Jr., and his son, Charles." Source: AP.

**DON'T TURN THIS PAGE YET, OR YOU WILL
SPOIL EVERYTHING!!**
Reply to the questions, using the previously mentioned
techniques:
Who is this person?
How did this person die? Select one answer.
Answer #1. Car accident.
Answer # 2. He was assassinated.
Answer #3: Old age.
Answer # 4: Blood transfusion.
The correct answer is on the next page.

This photo belongs to Mohandas Karamchand, known as Mahatma Gandhi (1869 – 1948). He was assassinated on January 30th 1948.

Reply to the question, using the previously mentioned techniques:
Can you identify this place?
The correct answer is on the next page.

This is the photograph of an abandoned Russian military base.

Reply to the questions, using the previously mentioned
techniques:
Anything special about this young woman?
Can you identify her?
The correct answer is on the next page.

Left: This is the picture of a young Mother Theresa, at the age of 18. Right: Mother Theresa, how we remember her.

Reply to the question, using the previously mentioned techniques:
What is or was the profession of this person?
If you have recognized him, disregard this test.
The correct answer is on the next page.

This is the photograph of the legendary French Cubist painter,
Georges Braque.

© SIPA

Reply to the question, using the previously mentioned
techniques:
What is the profession of this person?
The correct answer is on the next page.

This is the photo of the multi-talented Alain Chabat, a French
actor and director.

Reply to the questions, using the previously mentioned
techniques:
Can you identify this place? Where this slab is located?
A nearby area will suffice.
The correct answer is on the next page.

This slab is located nearby Flagstaff, in Arizona, USA.

Reply to the question, using the previously mentioned
techniques:
What this person does for a living?
The correct answer is on the next page.

He is a politician.
This is the picture of Canadian Senator Romeo Dallaire.

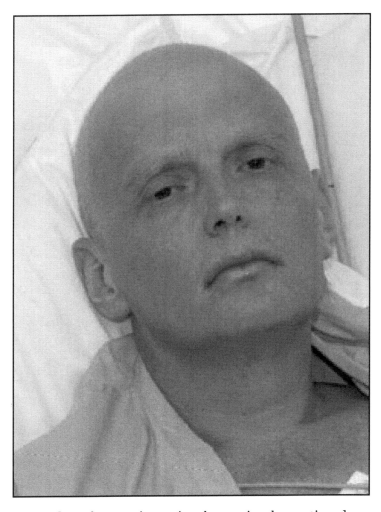

Reply to the question, using the previously mentioned techniques:
Is this person a spy, a prisoner of war, or a gay activist?
The correct answer is on the next page.

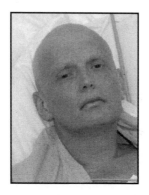

This is the picture of former Russian spy Alexander Litvinenko.

Reply to the question, using the previously mentioned
techniques:
Who from these two stars committed suicide?
If you have already recognized any of them, disregard this test.
The correct answer is on the next page.

Carole Landis, the lady on the left, committed suicide in 1948, in her home, in Pacific Palisades, California, by taking an overdose of Seconal. She was 29 years old.

Reply to the questions, using the previously mentioned techniques:
Can you identify this document?
Who wrote it?
The correct answer is on the next page.

This is the suicide/farewell note of actress Carole Landis, to her mother Clara.

It reads: "Dearest Mommie: "I am sorry, really sorry, to put you through this. But there is no way to avoid it.

I love you Darling. You have been the most wonderful mom ever. And that applies to all our family. I love each and every one of them dearly.

Everything goes to you. Look in the files, and there is a will which decrees everything.

Good bye, my angel.

Pray for me,

your baby."

Reply to the questions, using the previously mentioned
techniques:
Was/is this a successful product?
What kind of vibrations do you feel by looking at this product or
by touching it?
The correct answer is on the next page.

This product is very successful.
You should get good vibes from touching it.

Reply to the question, using the previously mentioned
techniques:
Was/is this a successful product?
What kind of vibrations do you feel by looking at this product or
by touching it?
The correct answer is on the next page.

Can of Bambeanos; a product that did not do well in 1974-1975.
It was an early soybean snack by Colgate-Palmolive.

Reply to the questions, using the previously mentioned techniques:

Was this car a very successful or a failed model?

What kind of vibrations do you feel by looking at this picture or by touching it?

The correct answer is on the next page.

This is Edsel car, which was manufactured by Ford in 1958. It was a total failure in the United States.

Reply to the question, using the previously mentioned techniques:
Which painting is real, and which painting is fake?
The correct answer is on the next page.

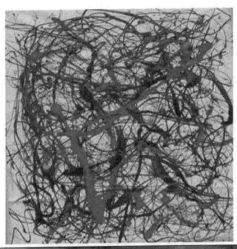

Both painting are fake.

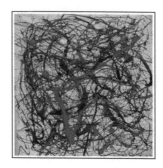

The one on the top is an imitation of a real painting by Jackson Pollock.

The one below is a forgery of a painting by Pablo Picasso, executed by Michael Zabrin.

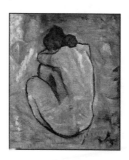

Most Frequently Asked Questions

Q: Is it necessary to learn the Ana'kh terminology to learn the Anunnaki-Ulema techniques?
A: Absolutely. Because the definitions of the words provide additional information on the subject(s), especially those topics that require more detailed explanation.

Q: Do I have to practice everyday to learn the Anunnaki-Ulema techniques?
A: No, except for those techniques that require a particular schedule to follow. Some techniques demand a daily practice, while others clearly specify the days and the hours to use, in order to get the best of these lessons and techniques.
Each technique/lesson has its own training pattern and a prescribed schedule.

Q: Are there good days and bad days for practicing the Anunnaki-Ulema techniques?
A: Yes. Just follow the training schedule, as prescribed in each lesson.

Q: Does the presence of others disrupt the learning process?
Do I have to be by myself to train on these techniques?

A: Absolutely.
Do not let others' vibes enter the place where you are practicing. Some people have negative vibes that will disorient you without knowing it.
Practice alone, and always alone.

585

Q: Does an active sex life, smoking and eating meat affect the learning of the Anunnaki-Ulema techniques, and the training processes?

A: A healthy marital sex life does not prevent anyone from learning the esoteric and paranormal Anunnaki-Ulema techniques. However, extramarital affairs, and an excessive and abusive sexual behavior and habits will handicap your training and learning abilities. The mot destructive ones are those professions that feed on sex, that sell sex, and provide what Ulema Ghandar called "Bestial sexual patterns".

Prostitution, sexually oriented escorts, all demeaning and disgraceful forms of sex such as domination, orgies, etc., will block your learning process, and prevent your progress. Ironically, smoking habit does negatively affect all the training and learning processes.

There are some lessons and training sessions that does allow a person to smoke, but not during the learning and training sessions. Follow the particular instruction of each lesson. Eating meat is a NO NO for the Ulema. Except in force majeure cases, when eating meat becomes an urgent and absolute necessity, categorically requested and advised by physicians.

Q: Are the Anunnaki Ulema techniques of a religious or a spiritual nature?

A: No. The Anunnaki Ulema techniques are based upon the science and philosophy of the "Transmission of Mind". The Ulema do not interfere nor engage themselves into religious matter and debates. As a matter of fact, the Ulema teachings and Kira'at are inspired by the direct revelations and information provided by the Anunnaki. Religion does not play any paramount role in their Kira'at and dirasaat.

Q: Once I have learned the techniques, do I have to keep on practicing the lessons?

A: No. Once learned, the lesson will be remembered by your mind.

Q: Is it possible to reach any of the Ulema Masters?

A: No. The Ulema select their students. The students and adepts are chosen by an Enlightened Master and/or an Ulema Master. The Ulema know who are the righteous ones, and who deserves

586

to be admitted to their Ma'had and Kira'at. However, you can communicate with Ulema Germain Lumiere, and ask for his guidance and advice.

Q: Do the Anunnaki-Ulema charge for their teachings or for admittance into their centers?
A: Never. The Anunnaki Ulema teachings are free of charge.

Q: Is Maximillien de Lafayette an Enlightened Master or an Anunnaki Ulema teacher?
A: Maximillien de Lafayette was chosen by Anunnaki Ulema Master Li and Anunnaki Ulema Mordachai ben Zvi as their student. It will take Maximillien de Lafayette hundreds of years to become an Enlightened Master. However, he is one of the chosen Righteous Ones, and thus, the Ulema have considered him as one of the teachers.

Q: How many Anunnaki Ulema are still around?
A: Only 700. Two hundreds are Mounawariin and Tahiriin. Five hundreds are Ulema from the third and fourth levels.

Q: Is the Book of Ramadosh written by the Ulema or is it an old Anunnaki's manuscript found by the Ulema?
A: The Book of Ramadosh is an Anunnaki collection of scrolls, tablets and written information in Ana'kh, which is the Anunnaki language. It was given to the Anunnaki Ulema by the remnants of the Anunnaki in the ancient Near and Middle East.

Q: The Book of Ramadosh teaches us 13 Anunnaki Ulema. I assume there are more than 13 techniques to learn from. Right?
A: Absolutely.
There are hundreds of Anunnaki Ulema techniques not yet revealed to the general public. The first book was transmitted to us by Maximillien de Lafayette and contained the original 13 techniques. There is a new book on more techniques, coming very soon.

Q: Is there any other book on the Anunnaki Ulema techniques?

A: So far, there is only one book, the once you are currently reading. However, there are two books on the subjects "Mouzakaraat Sinhar Marduchk", written in Anak'h, and "Ilmu Al Donia", written in archaic Arabic (Pre-Islamic era). Both books shall be translated to English, and published in the United States and in Germany in 2011.

Nizrin?

Question: What is an Anunnaki's Nizrin?

Answer: Nizrin is the process by which an Anunnaki elevates the contents of knowledge recently deposited in his/her mind through the "Conduit". The ascension phenomenon occurs frequently and periodically, so the Anunnaki individual could catalogue the categories of knowledge recently acquired. Elevating the contents is a mental projection that begins from within the brain's cells and materializes on a memory pad that appears before an Anunnaki.

La-abrida

Question: In your book on Ramadosh, you wrote about the Anunnaki and Anunnaki-Ulema La-abrida instrument that gives them the means to foresee the future. How would describe for us this instrument, and its mode of operation?

Answer: The Anunnaki, and the Anunnaki-Ulema as well, have at their disposal, an instrument called "La-abrida", or "Bzi'ra-irdu", they frequently use to read the past, the present and the future. It is a rectangular glass table that resonates, when metallic cards are placed on its surface. The word "glass" is hereby used for lack of proper terminology. The material is transparent like glass, but the substance is very different, and cannot be described, using our Earth's vocabularies.

The "metallic cards" represent thin and encoded boards. The word "metallic" is hereby used, for lack of proper terminology.

Each card contains sequences of numbers and dots, perforated on one side of each card. Misinformed researchers nicknamed the cards "Galactic Tarot". It is incorrect. The cards project and interpret sequences and passages from an individual's life in one particular dimension; one space-time sphere at the time. Duplicate, and/or multiple projections of different lives in different dimensions are also possible. However, the projection of any of a person's multiple lives existing in separate universes has no bearing or any effect on the current existence in the third dimension.

Alteration of past events in a different dimension does not categorically alter current events in the third dimension. However, the results and direct consequences of such alteration could and would change the course of life, and events to occur in the present and the near future of an individual, if the person's "Conduit" (Brain cell Conduit) is activated. On Earth, a person could be an illustrious writer, while in a second or a parallel dimension; the very same person is totally illiterate.

People and other living-forms live quite differently in other dimensions. On Earth, a person for instance is a distinguished judge, while in another dimension; the very same person is an outlaw. Removing, altering and/or erasing a crime committed by a person in another dimension does not categorically "clean", and/or delete the "Galactic Record" of that person on the "Conscience-Cosmic-Net".

That person is still held liable for his/her action, and will be punished for his/her crime.

For instance, on Earth (Third dimension), you are 40 year old, while in the same time, you could be 60 year old, or not even born, in another dimension (Universe). In some dimensions, Alexander the Great is still on his way to ancient Persia, and Jesus is not yet crucified. The sequences constitute the code. The code is the key to a wide variety of information and data about individuals. In other words, each card could be interpreted as a microchip.

The microchip stores every single event (Past, present and future) in the life of a person, including, duplications of similar or different occurrences on other planes. "Other planes" mean a separate form of existence in a parallel dimension. "Resonate" means responding to the placement of the card upon the surface of the glass table.

"Responding" means, reading and/or deciphering the code (Key to information) of the data and information stored in each card.

Question: What is the specific mode of operation of this instrument?

Answer: La abrida also called "Bzi'ra-irdu", functions like "Miraya", "Minzar", and "Mnaizar". However, the use of the La-abrida is limited to reading past, present, and future events in the life of one single person. When a card is placed on the top of the glass table, the card changes properties, shape and form. The "metallic" structural substance of the card becomes translucent, and merges with the glass surface. To the naked eye, it appears as if the card was totally absorbed by the glass surface. However, the size of the card remains intact. The shape of the card becomes circular, but retains its original size, meaning, each card occupies the same space, before the shape was changed. Thus, the form of the card becomes either circular or conical. Almost instantly, conic pages open up on the glass surface of the table.

Usually, three to four pages, aligned horizontally. Each page has a distinct color, ranging from light green to almost transparent blue. Words, geometric symbols, dots, and numbers appear on each page.

They are the data and information pertaining to the "existence" of one person in multiple spheres (Separate existences in multiple life-form universes.)

This means, that individuals (Humans and animals alike) do live separately and independently as 4 distinct living persons in 4 distinct dimensions, or more. Contemporary quantum physics theorists totally accept this reality.

Many books and articles discussed this incomprehensible phenomenon. The multiple and separate existences (In our case, 4) are called in quantum physics membranes, or simply branes. Each membrane represents a separate world, called dimension in contemporary quantum physics. That dimension refers to "another universe".

So far, quantum physics theorists have accepted the notion that, there are 11 dimensions in our universe. On the glass surface of the La abrida "Bzi'ra-irdu", the adept will be able to see (In miniature) four different dimensions.

Each one of them, containing a duplicate (Identical or totally different) of himself or herself, his or her total life, habitat, physical appearance, preoccupations, and environment.

In other words, the adept is watching simultaneously his or her other four existences/lives in four separate universes.

This concept has become a major part of the modern study and research of cosmology, and quantum physics, usually discussed under various theories, such as the "Multiverse", the "M Theory", the "String Theory", the "Membranes Theory," so on.

The beginning of everything: Multiples existences and "God's Particle". Ulema Haroon Bakri bin Rached Al Ansari, and Ulema Mordechai ben Zvi provided the following explanation.

Herewith reproduced verbatim, word for word, and unedited. Taken from their Kira'at (Readings), Kiramat Ketab (Book of the good deeds), Hadith (Speech; dialogue) and Rou'ya (Visions; insight):

Time is not linear. Thus, the landscape of so called time and space is not the same in other worlds. In multiple universes, the past, the present, and the future are all contained in one particle. This particle is the "Cell of Everything". This means, everything that has existed before, and shall exist afterward. It is the origin of the creation. The particle is the beginning of everything that is everlasting. Quantum physics theorists call this cell or particle the "God's Particle".

In this cell, you will find all the "Bubbles" (Term used by modern cosmologists) that collided together to create all the universes, galaxies, and planets in the cosmos.

Who created the God's Particle?

Who created the universe?

Who created time?

Who created "God"?

Is there one single Creator who created everything in the universe, including humans and non-humans? The God's particle was at the beginning of everything. And everything was not in existence. Thus, before the particle, time did not exist, space did not exist, the past did not exist, the future did not exist, humans did not exist, and religions did not exist; in brief nothing existed.

The Universe was not created by one single creator. The universe was not created by a "Big Bang." The universe emerged from itself, from within. And when, the nothingness of existence of all forms and substances suddenly collided with itself, the whole universe exploded into billions and billions of stars, galaxies, planets, and layers of dimensions.

In some universes, the coagulation of time with the landscape of space created time. When time was created by the collision of universes (Bubbles), galaxies and universes took shape and place in the cosmos.

On some planets, and in some galaxies, photosynthesis, metabolism, followed by micro-biological evolution created multiple life-forms everywhere.

Some of these life-forms produced all kinds and shapes of organic and botanic substances, stones, mountains, gases, waters, atmospheres. In some dimensions, different intelligent life forms were created. We call this intelligent life-form "Kir-Ra-Ibra", meaning the faculty of reasoning and creating.

The primordial intelligent life-form belonged to very advanced galactic races inhabiting billions of stars and planets. Billions of years later, the human race was genetically created by some of these very advanced intelligent life-forms, such as the Anunnaki, Igigi, and Lyrans.

When pre-humans, proto-humans, and quasi-human began to populate the Earth, time did not exist at that point in history. Later, much later, when the Lyrans, Igigi, and the Anunnaki commenced to experiment with the archaic human species (They were 47 different categories), they installed in the brain of the human beings, some form of intelligence. Some early humans were fortunate to receive the "Conduit", the invisible cell in the brain that produces all sorts of human activities and thoughts.

When the early human beings began to reason, the notion of time was conceived. Thus, "Time" became the invention of humans. Time exists on Earth, not on other dimensions.

Time travel

Question: La-abrida "Bzi'ra-irdu", is it a tool to go back in time or jump into the future? Is it physical or ethereal?

Answer: No, because, if you want to go back in time, and/or visit the future, you have to depart from this dimension (Earth), where you currently live. Once, you are outside the perimeter of the third dimension (Earth), time bends on itself. Space bends on itself. And you are caught in the middle. However, you can escape this dilemma, and realign yourself, following the cadence/rhythm of all dimensions beyond the third one. How, will you accomplish this? We will elaborate on this, when we study the "Parallel Synchronization." Since time does not exist, the enlightened ones (Many of you are enlightened) will be able to watch themselves living separately in different worlds. This is what La abrida "Bzi'ra-irdu" does. It allows you to "see" not to revisit the past or jump into the future, unless your "Conduit" is fully activated.

Once you are outside the physical realm (Panet Earth), you immediately connect with the beginning of everything in the universe. You become part of "God's Particle."

However, and as we have explained before, revisiting the so-called past is possible if you use the Gomatirach Minzari.

592

But bear in mind, you are not visiting, but transposing yourself, unless your "Conduit" is fully activated.

Can we change the future?

Question: Can we use this instrument to change our future?

Answer: Master Kanazawa said yes! He added, "however, you cannot alter the laws of cause and effect; something similar to what you call Karma, but in reality, it is quite different from Karma, because there is no place for reincarnation in the world of the Anunnaki.

The Anunnaki's norms remain universal, although they are norms per se, but not necessary cosmic laws." Master Kanazawa continued, "On Earth, you are accountable for all your actions. The same applies in all the dimensions, realms, and spheres of time, and space. However, in a different form of existence, or dimension, the nature and understanding of certain moral and ethical laws might change considerably. Such change has a paramount effect on the level of enlightenment and happiness you wish to reach. On Earth, we have what we call the human law, the natural law, and dogma establishing acceptable behavior in societies and communities. These laws quite often change in virtue of our understanding of what is right, and what is wrong.

They also change, as time changes, as our form of government changes, as a majority's power and influence change, regionally and nationally. Nothing is truthfully permanent on Earth. In the galactic perimeter of advanced and "spiritual" communities, values do not change.

They are permanent and universal, and they govern the general conduct of life-forms and intelligent entities, in the entire universe. If you enter a particular dimension, far away from Earth, or too close to Earth, you might encounter social rules that are in sharp contrast with laws on Earth. This could confuse your mind, and prevent you from understanding and/or recognizing what is right, and what is wrong.

If this should happen to you, you will not be able to ameliorate your life, and change your destiny, when you return to Earth, and/or to the present. Something else you should take into consideration.

What kind of destiny, success, happiness, prosperity and advancement are you talking about? Are they those your are aiming at, upon returning to Earth, or those you are seeking after death? Or, possibly those that exist in a dimension close to

Earth? The Anunnaki-Ulema can simultaneously live in two or three different dimensions, and coordinate their actions via the "Conduit". We call this, the "Universal Conduit". Humans have not yet reached a level of morality and "spirituality" that allows them to live and relive in separate dimensions at the same time.

Although, some humans might be invited to visit another dimension and acquire a great deal of knowledge, wisdom, and even supernatural powers, upon their return to Earth, they will instantly forget whatever they have learned, heard and seen, unless they are spiritually developed, and guided by the enlightened ones. Thus, in order to ameliorate you destiny, prosper in your endeavors, and preserve a good health, you must be able to differentiate between what is right and what is wrong, at a galactic level.

You must become acquainted with the universal truth; the galactic harmony of things. Truth in the "outer cosmos" is quite different from the truth you find on Earth. Only your activated "Conduit" will allow you to do so.

There are also certain measures and requirements you must consider and comply with, before you leave Earth and enter another dimension, and/or time-space sphere.For instance, selecting the correct time to revisit the past, and/or another dimension is paramount. What "Ba'ab" (Door or entrance to the other world) shall you enter?

How shall you adapt, correct or adjust your vision in a new dimension? How would you differentiate between an astral travel, imagination, fantasy of your mind, and reality?

Even in highly developed dimensions, and in many different time/space spheres, you will encounter fantasy, tricks of the mind, hallucinations, and fake apparitions. Many of the other dimensions (Plans) and time-space spheres are similar to Earth, even though the structural composition and their properties are enormously different.

All these encounters, images and feelings will prevent your mind from understanding what you are seeing. You will be totally confused. For example, and let's assume for now, that you have managed to go back in time, and visit with people and societies from the 18th century. First, how would you know, that the people you will see there are indeed from the 18th century, and not people just like you, visiting the past for the first time?

Second, how would you guide yourself, direct yourself, and reach your destination, without getting lost? Bear in mind, that in a different dimension, you will not have enough time to find your way around, if you don't have the map of the afterlife, and parallel dimensions. Third, you will not be able to last long over there, because your mind and your body will run out of energy. Besides, do you know how to charge and/or recharge yourself? You will be facing incomprehensible situations similar to ectoplasmic apparitions.

Quite often, these ectoplasmic apparitions and projections (Complete or partial) dissipate because the entity has rapidly consumed its "apparition and manifestation energy."

Once you have completed your orientation program, and the master has activated your "Conduit", your trip to the past or to another dimension will be successful and very beneficial.

The Dividing Lines of Multiple and Parallel Dimensions
Question: You wrote about some lines or frontiers that link humans to other dimensions.

Are these lines a doorway to another life, or simply, a stargate?

Answer: These lines or graphs refer to as the invisible borders of multiple adjacent zones of existences, also called multiple dimensions, and/or parallel universes.

You can call them the dividing lines of multiple and parallel dimensions. The Anunnaki-Ulema call these lines "Kalem". These lines serve also as a path or a passage that lead to a higher sphere of knowledge.

From Kalem, derived the Hebrew word Kailem, which literally means, vessels or vehicles; the vases for the source of the Waters of Life, used in the Ten Sephiroth, and considered as the primeval nuclei of all Kosmic Forces.

Some Kabalists and occulists stated that these lines or vessels appear in our world, through twenty two canals, which are represented by the twenty-two letters of the Hebrew alphabet, "thus making with the Ten Sephiroth 32 paths of wisdom."

According to Anunnaki-Ulema Li, "The world of humans is linked to the afterlife through twenty two Kalem (Graphs). Some of these graphs or lines are directly attached to the "Conduit" implanted in the human brain, thus a trained adept can enter and exist other dimensions by placing himself or herself on one of the "tracks" of these lines."

Living in dimensions designed by the Anunnaki.

Question: Do we live in dimensions according to what the Anunnaki have created?

Answer: This is one of the most frequently asked questions by novices and students. Generally, the Ulema are not concerned with issues of a metaphysical nature, because they do not believe that the physical world is completely separated from the non-physical world. They do not see the universe the way we do. Therefore, everything is part of something else.

An Ulema once said, talking to a student:

- 1. Even this rock and this tree leaf are part of you. We are made of the same material." (Author's note: This could be interpreted metaphorically, but there is a deep scientific veracity attached to it.)
- 2. Yes, a rock is a rock. It is physical. It is real. You can touch it and you can weight it.
- 3. But that's not all...it is not all of it, because it has an additional dimension you can't see with your eyes. It does not start and end where you start to touch it, and where you finish touching it.
- 4. Once, your "Rou'ya" (Third Eye to others) opens up, you begin to see a larger size of the rock, and discover its hidden properties...
- 5. This is why we call Earth, the life we live, our desires and our ambitions ILLUSION."
- 6. Yes, you live in physical and non-physical dimensions according to what the Anunnaki have created...

Note: I will mention herewith parts of his answers that are related to the question:

- 7. The Anunnaki have created you on Earth to serve their needs.
- 8. Their intentions were to create a race that could carry heavy physical load and do intense physical labor.
- 9. This was the initial and prime objective.
- 10. Thus, the "Naphsiya" (DNA) they put in all of you had limited lifespan, and mental faculties.
- 11. Later on, they discovered that they had to prolong the human lifespan and add more mental faculties, so they added the "Hara-Kiya" (Internal energy or physical strength).

- 12. Few generations later, the early human beings stock evolves considerably, because the Anunnaki added fully operational Mind in the human body.
- 13. To do so, the Anunnaki installed into your brains, a Conduit with limited capabilities.
- 14. In the same time, this Conduit was also installed into the prototype of the human body.
- 15. Thus, through the Mind, the physical body of the humans got linked to the Double.
- 16. This non-physical link created a Fourth dimension for all of you.
- 17. In fact, it did not create a Fourth dimension per se, rather it activated it.
- 18. So now, at that stage, human beings had a physical dimension (Life on earth), and not-a-totally separated non-physical dimension (Zone) called "Nafis-Ra" on the ethereal level.
- 19. So, yes, Bashar (Humans) became destined to acquire two dimensions, as exactly the Anunnaki decided.
- 20. Later on, centuries upon centuries, the human mind began to evolve, because the other Mind, call it now the Double or prototype began to evolve simultaneously and in sync.
- 21. The more the prototype (First specimen of mankind) is advanced, the more "Physical Mind" becomes alert, creative and multidimensional.
- 22. But you are not trapped, and your mind is no longer conditioned by the Anunnaki.
- 23. The Anunnaki gave you all the choices, opportunities, free will, and freedom to learn on your own, decide on personal matters, select and progress.
- 24. This is why you are accountable and responsible for everything you do and think about.
- 25. Because of the evolution of your mind, the realization (From within) of an inner and deeper knowledge of your surroundings, and understanding what is right and what is wrong, a major mental faculty emerged in all of you. You have called it: Conscience.

*** *** ***

597

From the present to the future.

Question: How do the Masters, the Mounawiriin, and the Anunnaki Ulema transpose you from the present to the future?

Answer: Our brain cannot understand the concept of time-space-future. It is a very difficult concept to grasp.

But the Supersymetric Mind does. One of the Masters said verbatim, "Let me make it easy on you, I will give you an example. You are boarding a train with friends, and the train will make many stops. Some of your friends will get out of the train at station a, others at station b, and others at station c, so on. You stay on the train. You do not exit at station a, b, or c. You stay inside the train, until the train reaches the last destination. That's the last stop of the station. By staying inside the train and not getting out of the train at any stop until the last one, you have seen much more than all of your friends did.

Note: The Master is interrupted by a question from a novice.

Question: Basically you stopped along the way at each train station, but you did not get off the train until the last stop, or final destination of the train. So all you saw on your journey, because you did not get off and explore is various train stations for a few minutes.

Answer of the Master: That's correct, but it does not matter whether you have stayed inside the train, or got off and saw what was going on at each station.

You have assumed that the person who stayed inside the train, and did not get off the train, and did not explore what was going on at each station, has a limited knowledge or no knowledge at all of what happened at each station. This is how human beings reason and rationalize things.

But this is the wrong way to explain things, because you are thinking geographically, and in linear time. Don't tell yourself that because you didn't get off the train, therefore, you have missed lots of things and did not see what was going on at each stop. On a linear chronology of time-distance-space, it is true. Now think like this: You have reached the last stop, the final destination of the train. At this last station, you can rewind your journey on the train backward. And there is a technique to rewind yourself and the time you have spent on the train, a technique you can learn from the Anunnaki Ulema.

It is neither the right time, nor the right place to talk about this technique. Instead, focus on what I am about to tell you. In your mind, try to remember all the stations, and all the stops the train made. It is a very simple exercise. What you are doing now is rewinding your trip backward. And you are going to be amazed, that this simple exercise will make your mind remember everything or at least many things you have seen briefly at each station. But in fact, your brain is going to reveal much more than that. Your brain or more precisely your symmetric mind has a much bigger memory.

A symmetric mind is the original copy of your physical brain. And it is part of your double or astral body. This symmetric mind records and stores everything you saw. And if your Conduit is active or open, it will remind you of everything you have seen, felt or learned. Do not get confused with the concept of the Symmetric Mind. Forget about it for now. But remember, or try to accept the idea, that while you are not aware of the existence of a symmetric mind that you have had since you were born, your symmetric mind is a magnificent recording device, and a very powerful camera.

Your Symmetric Mind has gathered information from every stop, almost everything you have not seen or heard. Who is rewinding back your journey on the train? Is it your memory? You mind? Yourself? Or something else?

None of the above. It is your symmetric mind. Once again, don't worry about your symmetric mind. Let's go back to the last stop of the train. You are there now. Good. Let's now equate this last station with a date, a time frame, a year, a certain time, any time you want. For example, let's choose the year 2021. This year represents the 7th station – the final stop of the train. If you go back in time, (in fact we are going back into the future), we will return to the 1st station. And let's call this first station, the year 2015

Note: Once again, the Master was interrupted by a novice who asked this question:

Why did you choose 7 stops? Why not 5 stops? The Master answered the question and continued his explanation. He said that it is just an example; it does not matter whether we choose 7 stops or 5 stops. It does not make any difference at all. You can also assign any year to any station, as long as you do it chronologically. He continued by saying: Let's go back now to the 7th station, and continue to regress to the 6th station, the 5th station, and so on.

Note: Once again, the Master was interrupted by a novice who asked this question: As we regress, do we record down what we are doing? Do we write down the number of the station and corresponding year? The Master continued his explanation. He said, no, you do not. Your mind is going to take care of this.

But before he had finished his answer, a student asked the Master this question:

Are we seeing the stations as a film?

How are we seeing this regression and station by station?

Is it like a movie?

Are we zooming ourselves into the future like a time machine?

The Honorable Master answered the question and continued his explanation. He said, no, it is not like that. If the Conduit is active, a huge reading screen will be displayed within the mind. And the brain will instantly read what it is displayed and written on the screen. The screen is not to be understood as a physical screen like the one we see in movie theaters.

It is a mental projection of everything the Conduit has stored inside our brain. The screen can be seen through introspection. To understand this, think about your memory; how you remember things, and how you see them in your mind. You don't have to tell yourself, I have to project everything I saw or knew before my eyes, on a huge screen, and look at the screen to see if I can find what I want to remember, and that particular event that happened a long time ago, but I can't remember everything about it.

Your brain does it for you, and you don't need to know how your brain does it, to remember things, and that event you were interested in. The same thing applies here with your Conduit and the screen it projects before you eyes. In fact, it does not project events on a screen before your eyes, but right inside your brain. Do we zoom ourselves into the future like a time machine? No.

Then, a student asked: If he didn't need a spaceship, a Merkaba, or something, nothing then is required to zoom into the future?

The Master answered: A spaceship is needed if you want to physically enter another dimension, or visit a parallel world, where time-space memory remains intact, and all information is preserved. Nothing is lost in the future, not even in the Black Holes. Spatial memory and time memory are not lost, because they constitute cosmic information. And information and data are never lost in the universe. Yes, a spaceship is needed to explore the universe. But it is not required if you want to see the future and/or zoom in a zone where all events from the past, present and future are recorded and preserved. In our case, your Conduit or symmetric brain is your spaceship. Do you want to go to Jupiter or to Mars? Well then you need a spaceship. But this becomes a physical means. When you zoom into the future using your Conduit, this zooming or travel is mental. And the area you reach is also mental. But if your brain remains attached to where you are (Sitting in a physical place), you can't go to the future.

Humans see the future through distance, time, and space. We call this the "Wheel of the universe." And we must be outside the wheel of time to see the future.

A student asked: "So, we are seeing time as a wheel? And by doing so, could we see the future?

The Master replied: There are two wheels. The wheel of the universe, which is called the Macro wheel, and a smaller wheel called the Micro wheel, which represents us, human beings, here on earth, and our time cycle here on earth. It is a wheel within the universe. Humans can't see the Macro wheel, but it does exist on a large scale. As long as, we are on the inside of the Micro wheel, we will never be able to see the future. The future belongs to the Macro wheel. In the Macro wheel, everything is stored, the past, the present and the future.

You can physically reach the Macro wheel, either by using a spaceship that can bend or alter time-space, or by using your Conduit. The Anunnaki Ulema and the enlightened masters can easily reach the Macro wheel physically and mentally by getting outside the Micro wheel, while others (the rest of us), only mentally. Another student asked this question: And how do we get outside the wheel?

The Master replied: There is a technique only known to the enlightened ones (Tahiriin, masters, some Rouhaniyiin, and the Anunnaki Ulema). This technique is part of the secret teachings of the Anunnaki Ulema. It is never revealed to outsiders. They teach it only to their students in the Ma'had. It is one of their most powerful faculties. The Ulema would say, we don't predict the future, we don't see the future, we read the future. A student asked: Is it because the future is already there?

The Master replied: Yes, the future is already there. The future is already Maktoub (what is written). And the Anunnaki Ulema can read anything that is Maktoub. In the Maktoub, you will find

601

everything and anything that is closely related to your fate and future. And there is nothing you can do to change it or alter it.

Your future has been decided upon, the day, the hour, you were born. However, you can modify the results, outcomes and consequences of events to occur in your future. We shall talk about this in another Kira'at. Let's go back now to what we were talking about: How to see a projected future that is occurring in the present.

A projected future occurring in the present.

Let me give you an example. There are two movie theaters in town. People went to a movie theater at 6:00 PM. Let's call this theater "Theater A." The film ends for example at 8:00 PM at theater A. The projectionist is projecting the film on the big screen from the end, meaning backward. At "Theater B", people are watching the same movie. But at theater B, the projectionist is projecting the film from the beginning, like projectionists do all the time. Also at theater B, the film ends at 8:00 PM.

Both viewers will spend two hours at either theater, but here we have something very special and irregular, because the people who are watching the film at two different theaters are not seeing the same frames (Scenes from the film) chronologically. Those who are seeing the film from the end are already ahead of those who are watching the film from the beginning; yet, both have spent the same amount of time at the movies theaters. But at a certain point, they will arrive at the same time where they will be seeing the same frame, whether the film is projected from the beginning or from the end.

This is very possible, if the time of projecting the film in theater A, and theater B is synchronized. Otherwise, it will not happen.

And this moment is very crucial, because it determines the time-space that separates the past from the future.

But don't get confused now with this very specific moment, because you are going to understand it as I keep talking to you.

Those who watched the film beginning from the end, already knew the end of the film, which could be compared to the "future" of the film. Those who watched the film from the very beginning are not there yet, as they have not yet reached the end of the film, which we have called the "future" of the film, because the end of the film is going to happen in the future, even though this future is less than two hours away.

Anunnaki Ulema Mordachai said, let's call the people who are at theater A, Anunnaki or Anunnaki Ulema. And those who went to theater B, let's call them human beings. These two theaters can be located anywhere, Paris, Boston, Budapest, the location is irrelevant, only TIME is a major factor here. Now, the Anunnaki or Anunnaki Ulema at theater A, ask the projectionist to fast-forward/project the film very very fast, as fast as he can, and if he can do it in seconds, it would be much better. And then, they ask the projectionist to re-project the film from the beginning to the end equally as fast.

This means, that they have rapidly seen the whole film from the end to the beginning, and from the beginning to the end.

They saw the future of the film (the End), and revisited the end of the film (in their future) in the same seating. Think about it for a few seconds. There is also a third scenario, more fascinating than the previous one.

The Anunnaki and the Anunnaki Ulema do not need to go to theater B and rewind the film (Equated with time-Space) backward to reach the future and revisit the beginning and the end of the film (Equated with time-Distance), because they are already there, at the end of the film, which can be equated with the FUTURE, a zone where the past, present and future co-exist concurrently, separately, continuously, and instantly.

They are already THERE, because time for them is not a line of distance, space, and speed, and how much it would take to reach the end of the line. Being outside the line (Outside the Wheel of Time), the Anunnaki can see everything that is happening inside and outside the wheel.

Once you are outside the wheel, time and distance cease to exist separately. And when this happens, you are immediately within the future. And since the future is a continuation of the present, and the present is a continuation of the past, you are now simultaneously in the past, the present and the future at the same time. At first, it is very difficult for our mind to understand this concept.

The more you think about time as measured by distance, and vice versa, the more you distance yourself for a readable future you can foresee, read, and understand.

Question from Bernard P.:
I am so curious to know what really does happen to a person during a Master's séance?

Is it a healing session or mind training?

Answer:

There are several kinds of séances, and an avalanche of reasons for conducting a séance. It would take me weeks to provide you with all the answers, and most certainly volumes upon volumes. Your question was very timely.

I have just received an assignment report sent to me by a dear friend who was subject to a very short mental/metaphysical séance I conducted myself.

The answers to your questions can be found in the report.

Date: November 19, 2010
Begin: 8:02pm
End of Séance: 8:14pm
Location: The author's residence.
End of Discussion: 9:00pm (not sure of the exact ending time)
Key/Legend:

Black Text – Present Séance Discussion
M: Maximillien de Lafayette.
P: The person for whom the séance was created.

Green Text – Post Séance Discussion
Red Text – Questions Regarding Discussion/ Text
Here is the report as received. It is unedited, As Is.

Séance #1 of 8:

I arrived just about 1 or so minutes after 8pm and quickly sat down on the couch. Max briefly explained what was going to happen during the séance so I knew what to expect.

He explained:

• We are going to do a séance. They use to do this all the time, with people around in the open (?) the would just close their eyes. This (or these) technique(s) have been around for a very long time (or since ancient times).

P: As Maximillien was saying this, I visualized a group of people (mostly, if not all, men, I believe) in an open market sitting near a well or on an area with stone steps or on the group, in what appeared to be the biblical times. Well, I assumed that as I imagined a guy wearing some sort of turban thing? Someone was at the head of the circle or in front of the group guiding them. Although I didn't see him, I had an awareness that).

• I will ask you 3 questions. Ask 1 question at a time and they will answer.
• We do not know who will show up. It may be your guide, spirit...etc...
• It is very Important to remember what is said- everything, every detail verbatim so I can analyze it later.
I will not remember anything.
• I want you to know, I will not remember anything that is said. So don't worry about what is said during the Séance. (You are like a daughter to me. Think of me as your father. You can say (tell me) anything).
• Then, I will tell you to keep your eyes closed. Remember what you see. It's important
to leave the physical world. Don't pay attention to anything in the physical. If you do and don't let go of the physical, you will not be able to go anywhere. You will stay here and I can't do anything (or nothing will happen). So, use your imagination.

• We will meet 1x a week for 8 weeks. This will be the first of 8 sessions. And then, you are on your own.

P: *[Thinking: Wow, do this on my own? How could I possibly know all this in 8 sessions... let alone speak/ remember the ancient words to summon the spirits, especially if a less than favorable(s) comes through and decides to show up?]*
[Feeling: I felt just a little small by that thought ?]

• The first session will be 10 minutes and each session will increase in time as we go on. (Maximillien gave more specific information regarding time. However, I do not recall the increasing amount of lengths going forward).

I quickly changed into my white Dobok uniform and layed on the floor, as Max asked. At the same time, he turned off all the lights in the apartment, closed the blinds, and lit a white candle on the table beside the ground where I laid.
Max began by adjusting my feet, so my toes were pointed toward the ceiling and palms were placed flat on the ground. He asked me to keep my hands there (something about ground me?)
Not exactly sure but I remember either thinking or hearing Maximillien whisper something about grounding?)

605

He asked me to stay in this position for 1 minute. One minute after, Maximillien began his incantation. Within what seemed to be just seconds, he (my first session) began:

M: Just relax. Take a deep breath in and relax. Breathe into your chest and relax.

P: *[Feeling: At first, I felt a little nervous, and tension in my shoulders. I began breathing deeply into my chest and then started to relax more and more each time].*

M: We are in the presence of a Master, a high level master (or senior master), who is here joining us-

P: *[Thinking: Thank You Master for coming and Max too! I was very excited the Master appeared and wondered who the Master was! I am still excited typing this as if my life is finally starting to get on track! Finally. I feel so happy and so blessed by that and for that very kind help!]*
[Feeling: grateful and HAPPY for the opportunity].
[Physical Body: Felt twitching in my right leg and foot- moving or shifting. Later I felt some twitching on my upper leg, almost in my hip area]

M: Close your eyes and keep them closed.

M: What is your name? (Not sure if this question was asked before or after you told me my name for the séances is Nu ra?)

P: Di...P.

M: [Incantation]. The Master who is here, you will eventually be able to see him, as long as you are on the path of Goodness.

P: *[Thinking: WOW- that's GREAT! I'm more ready now]*
[Feeling: Happy!]

M: From now on, during each séance, your name will be (or you will be called) Nur ra which means light.

P: Num ra

M: (No). Nur ra

P: Nur ra ?
[Thinking: WOW- that's cool! I liked the name. It felt beautiful as I said it and heard/felt it]

M: Nur ra

P: Nur ra

M: You will ask two questions. Make it simple and only one question at a time. What question do you want to ask?

P: What is the purpose I am suppose to be doing in my life and ...etc...?

M: Ask only one question at a time. Keep it simple.

P: What is my life purpose?

[Thinking as I asked the questions: Why am I here- on earth?]

M: Your purpose is simply for healing humans or human-beings. That's it. Do you know what healing means or what it means to heal?

P: Healing means transferring energy to help care for a person's physical body and also support and share energy to help with their emotional self

[Thinking: Ever since I was a child, I always wanted to learn how to HEAL. And, I was always attracted to healers. I met them my whole life.

And each time I did it ignited a spark inside me! I have such a passion and strong connection with wanting to learn as much as I can and help people in that way.

[Feeling: Surprised and not so surprised by the response that I came to heal. And yet, I was surprised by the response because it was so simple and so true and direct. It felt so true /right. And right to me]

M: I'm going to tell you what healing means. Can you remember it or remember this and don't forget it? Healing means removing (or taking away) the pain from the physical body and comforting their mental body (or self). Do you understand?

P: Yes

M: Can you remember that?

P: Yes.

MAX: What is your next question?

P: Can you identify the blockages in my body and help with my body and body alignment?

M: Only one question. Can you ask your question again?

P: Can you identify the blockages and (help) heal my physical body?

[Feeling: A little embarrassed/ selfish to ask them for healing].

M: It will take 1 (or 2) more sessions. You have 5 major knots that arose from instances in your life which caused you to close (or shut down).

The first knot occurred at age 13 and it lasted from 13-15. It had a deep emotional impact on you. This was the first time that such an instance occurred that had such an impact on you (your life). Do you remember this (event)?

P: Yes.

[Physically: Felt twitching in my right leg, hip and thigh. Also my left foot. At some point, I also felt something in my chest on the left side]

M: It was from age 13-15.
P: Yes.

[Post Séance Session: (Referring to the event that caused the knot).
I shared with Max the event that had a very big impact on me was when my father told me he was married before my mother. One day, after his gold outing he had a few drinks. My father hardly ever drank let alone coming home tipsy- that was pretty much un heard of, when decided to share the story.
While sitting at the dinner table the subject happened to come up and he shared he was married before and had two children- a boy and a girl (N..., Jr. and G...). I pretended that it was no big deal; however, the reality was, it was a very BIG shocked that Friday.
So, spent much of the rest of the weekend in my room crying. I kept looking at the brighter side saying, wow now I have another sister. But inside I felt a little angry I was never told before and betrayed. Later I found out my mother wanted to tell me much earlier but my father thought it wasn't such a good idea- perhaps it was his pride or to protect us?
Nevertheless, I never thought my father was married to anyone besides my mother- let alone finding out I know have two new siblings. But the biggest shocker came when I found out that the woman who was my sister was someone I had met on many occasions at my grandmother's house. And, I knew her as the wife of my friends uncle.
The most amazing things was that instantly I had a love for this woman. I loved her in a familial way- a way I can't explain except to say I felt her in my heart. And, I wanted to get to know her more- after all she was my sister]
M: Ok great. Cleared. The second knot occurred at the age of 22 and had a deep impact on you.
Do you remember this or something at (the age of) 22?
P: YES, but I recall it being at 21 or 20 when it happened...
M: 21-22. Do you re-call this?
P: Yes

[Post Séance Discussion: (Referring to the event that caused the knot).

When I was only 20 years old I went to Florida for Spring Break with my friend. My friend liked this guy and his friend liked, or was infatuated by/with me (possibly my energy).

I think the guy put something, like a drug, in my drink; although I was drinking a lot myself, I was completely paralyzed and he took advantage of me. Only a short time later I realized I was pregnant and chose to abort the baby because I didn't have the strength or courage to carry the baby. I felt guilty and weak about not being able to carry the baby into the world.

M: Ok great cleared. Only 1 more for now. The third knot was 5 years (later)? And it was a time (or at the time) you were questioning if you were a female or your female-ness? Do you recall this?

P: No. (I heard the word female or female-ness, not human or human-ness?)

[Post Séance Discussion: (Referring to the event that caused the knot).

During the review, Maximillien mentioned what I heard, "it's impossible". They never use gender specific words such as female or male. Did they say (or mean) Human? They must have meant Human?]

M: So you don't remember this?

P: No. (I thought you said 5 years old; not 5 years after, the age of 22)

M: So, you don't remember this?

P: No, not really; but, it does sound familiar?

M: Ok good.

P: There is a spirit here with us?

[Imagined: Saw a deep red or red-ish color]

[Post Séance Discussion:

I asked Max if it was my brother in law. Max said, "Yes". He was attached to you, draining your energy. That is why you are so tired. He is stuck. We need to send (help) him back (to the White Light) (Don't remember what word Max used exactly to explain this). Max mentioned we can send him back in the next or one of the next séances]

M: Close your eyes tight, squeeze them tightly.

609

What do you see? Colors, images... we are going on (or to take) a journey...

See a double (of yourself) standing on your forehead- feet on your forehead. There is no weight- weightless. Close eyes tight. Squeeze your eyes. Imagine yourself

P: *[Thinking: I remembered Max explaining to me, before we started, that I have to let go of the physical world and let my imagination go. Otherwise, we won't go anywhere. We'll just stay in the physical world (here) So, I reminded myself to let go and let my mind wonder]*

[Visualized: I could see myself, in my imagination, standing up-right, feet on my forehead looking down onto my body. I could see from my POV from the ground looking up (at me)]

[Post Séance Discussion:

P: (To Max) When you asked us to close my eyes I saw dots, like little circles of color moving around. The color was like deep midnight colors- like dark blue, dark purple (violet) ...very dark colors...

M: You saw that?

P: Yes.

M: You saw the bubbles that means (or so you...) ... (you said something else but I can't remembering it right now)

P: Yes. They were more like amebas moving around. And the colors were more dark]

[I imagined myself on the very top of a green, grass-filled hill top, looking out at the landscape. It was a Wide shot and I could see myself from head to toe- I believe I had on a coat and boots- not sure. I was standing in a full ½ profile]

[Post Séance Discussion: I described the grassy-hill ...

P: (I described the scene of the grassy-hill to Max)

M: Did you know this place? Had you been there before?

P: I don't know exactly where it was but it felt familiar. It felt (or I felt) like home.

M: (Smiled & nodded his head)

P: When you first started talking and saying we were going on a journey I went to the grassy-hill. Then, you said we're going to the beach. So, I went to the beach.

Then after you mentioned the hill. And I went back to the same hill I saw when we first started- even before you mentioned going there]

M: We're going to the beach (now)...

P: *[Visualized: Wide shot, ¾ profile of myself sitting on the beach with my knees bent and feet in the sand. I may have had a white hat on? The water was to the left and the sandy dunes to the right.]*

M: There is a friend who you haven't seen in a long time.

P: I was 11. This friend is coming to see me?

Maximillien: She is (standing) right next to you...

P:*[Imagined my friend Adrienne standing next to me looking down. Her name was the first thing I thought of when he said you're with a friend. I was looking out at the water with my arms renting on my knees. I was not looking at her]*

M: Do you know this friend?

P: Yes.

[Post Séance Discussion:
Adrienne is my oldest friend. We grew up together in the same Italian neighborhood (Little Italy in Cleveland, Ohio) and met in pre-school at the age of 3. Ever since we were in 1st-2nd grade we did everything together, like sisters. I was closer with A.... than my own sister, for much of my early life. We were best friends (some-much of our lives) since the time we were little. I'm 40 years old now.

Our families have a long history together, since my father grew up in the same neighborhood. We are like family].

M: Is there something you want to ask this friend?

P: (Pause) Were you jealous of me growing up?

[Physically: My body felt tense and shoulders raised to my ears- when I said the work jealous. I think, I felt embarrassed to say the word]

[Post Séance Discussion: At the end of 5th-6th grade I began loosing weight. I had a more stocky/ solid build until I started watching what I was eating and increased my physical and/or athletic activity. I also started becoming more interested in boys around the same time which I believe, also added to my desire to loose weight. A... was also on the chunky side; and as we got older, her weight kept increasing. She is now obese].

M: Yes. Ask other questions.

P: Is that why you did things to hurt me?

M: Yes. Ask another question. Don't wait. Ask.

P: Did you do those things intentionally?

611

M: No...
P: [Feeling: So happy to hear that]

[Post Séance Discussion: I explained to Max that growing up in my neighborhood we had a group of about 4-5 girl-friends that were very close.
Even our mothers and families were close. Inevitably when someone from my group of friends got upset, with someone in the group, there was often a person left out.
I recall one time, in grade school, when I was very hurt about being left out specifically by A......
As we got older, I was always being left out/ not told or not invited on trips, to concerts, given information (that pertained to my family...etc...) for a lot of my relationship with her. In doing this exercise and writing down the events of the séance a lot of stuff around this area came up. So, I felt I should expand on it further and share. Our friendship felt like a relationship of convenience. A..... loves to say "We've been best friends since we've been 3"; but often, her actions don't show that on a normal, everyday basis- or at least as I expect they should be. That is probably where the conflict lies (My Expectations or what I would do or how I would treat her/ others...]

M: Ask another question. Don't stop
P: (Pause) Did you think my dad was your dad?
(Said what came to mind; and thought it was a silly question to ask after it came out]
M: No

[Post Séance Discussion:

M: (after we spoke about the history with my friend A......)
Incredible. You tapped into her double. That's incredible.
P: (Smiling. Thinking: Ok good, now what does that mean?]
M: There is someone from your family (past) who you have (or your family has) severed relations with and she feels guilty. She would like to repair (fix) the relations (or see/ speak with you). Would you like to do this?
P: YES.
M: You know this person?
P: Yes. Well actually, there are two people.
M: OK. Don't volunteer any information.

P: (Think I was silent- ?)

M: This one will take more time to clear...

M: I'm getting tired. It's time now for the Master to leave.

M: Now put your hands over your head, palms face each other.

P: OK

MAX: Put your fingers like this, look at me.

P: *[I looked at Max but his head was surrounded, with what appeared to be like a white fuzzy dot. It lasted only for a few seconds. Then, soon enough, it cleared and I could see Max clearly with his hands over his face explaining the position of my fingers)*

M: Put your fingers like this. And bring your hands down to your chest, thumbs... do this. And repeat after me...

(.... Closing Incantation...)

Max asked me to stand up and sit on the couch. He proceeded into the kitchen, turned on the light and got a container from the cupboard.

Then, he walk over to the area where the séance took place and spilled out some salt, from the container, onto the carpet where I was laying during the session.

He started with the area where head was placed. And again, he delicately dropped another pinch of salt, shook his head and said, "weird!" He continued to the bottom of the carpet, place another pinch of salt where my feet had been. And blew out the candle.

Post Séance Discussion Points:

• Immediately after the session I spoke with Max for about 45 minutes regarding the séance and what I was able to remember.

• Max was surprised (or acted surprised) by the length of time I re-called the events of the séance. He explained that if the length of time was only 10 minutes for the séance then how can I speak about it for 45 minutes?

He continued to explain that our discussion was 4 x more than time as we know it- in this dimension. He said that during the séance time stops/ doesn't exist/ stands still.

(Max said something to this affect).

• Later I asked Max:

P: Is it normal for a difference in the length of time for the discussion vs the actual length of time of the séance occurred?

M: Yes.

P: Max, does the time of the discussion (which as Max described 4x) vs the length of the actual séance show (or give and idea about) my spiritual power?

M: Yes. If that is developed, then that means what you can produce can be 500 times the rate of time in per/ hour (or average speed).

Observation:

I felt a lot of emotions before I arrived at Max's for the séance, because of my discussion with Master X..P...., from the Meditation Center. I told her, I was not going to do the training in December and not going to the Interview on Friday morning-something I had been preparing for a long time; even though I have always felt pulled.

• I cried that evening when I returned home from the séance, like both a weight was lifted off me and yet I had a sadness at the same time. It was as if I was leaving part of my family behind from the yoga center. Some of the tears could have also been related to the release of knots I had been carrying for many years?

P: I feel as if I wanted to cry. I asked if that was normal? (That feeling still was with me until the entire next day on Friday. I cried several times on Friday).

M: It is normal.

Post Discussion & Experience(s):

• Max said, I will learn to do this (séance) to help others and then I would teach others to do this too.

DINA: (Feeling: Excited and blessed to think I was going to learn:

1) From Max, and,

2) Be able to share this ancient knowledge and TRUTH to help people.

I was (AM) VERY excited.

• Max gave me an assignment to write everything down, VERBATIM, every detail, from the entire evening. He will use this to analyze the session- even include the points from the Post Session. This will become my bible.

• Max was pleased with the séance. He said it was a good first séance. (I was happy to hear that).

Questions:

1) The next day, after the session, I felt a pressure (not painful) on the right side of my head, inside my head, about 2 inches behind my scalp. Wondering, if this is related to our session in any way?

2) When I returned home I got on the phone briefly and eventually began doing my assignment, as instructed by Max.

I did my best to re-call the experience on as many levels as I could. However, as was completing the journal on Saturday- just 2 days later, I feel as if I missed so much of the material. I feel as if there was an entire section that was discussed before the Master left and it was gone?

I can't remember any other topics or points, in this moment, that I have not already written about; and yet it still feels like a gap or a space between the moment of the last discussion and him leaving. Is that a normal feeling or occurrence when recalling experience(s) within the absence of time (space)?

3) How long will each session be going forward? And, as I get more comfortable and use to doing the sessions will that dictate the length of material covered in the sessions?

Notes:

• I do not remember exactly when Max announced that a spirit came into the room. However, I still noted it in the journal to the best of my ability.

• I keep feeling as if I missed a lot of nuances from the time the session occurred, on Thursday evening, until I'm completing the journal tonight- Saturday evening.

• While writing out the notes, it was as if the discussion was shorter then I remembered it. It felt as if I had sooo much to say, when we were talking about it after the Séance. However, now that it's written, it seems as if there was so little said? The length in time seems so off; especially when putting the experience down on paper.

• When I woke up the next morning I felt as if I had gone through months worth of things overnight. I felt as if I had learned a host of lessons. For instance, by choosing Not To Go to the Interview was so clearing.

I realized that just making a decision, whatever the outcome or result, allows you to move forward because you are not wasting time and lost in the uncertainty of trying to make a decision. So, I felt like I matured in that way.

24 hour after the session: what happened?

1. When I woke up the next morning I felt as if I had gone through two years worth of learning and maturation overnight. I felt as if I had learned a host of lessons beyond what I could have ever imagined. I felt so much lighter. It seemed as if something was lifted off my shoulders- like a heaviness or weight. I was clearer and moved forward mentally leaps and bounds. Then it dawned on me, the reason was simple.

All I had to do was to make a decision. Once I committed myself to my decision, in this case not to go on the interview, after months (even several years) of preparation, I made space inside myself, and in my mind, allowing me to move forward in my own life. Because I was not preoccupied with the thought, *I have to make a decision*, constantly looming over my head, like I had been doing for months. Instead, I cut to the chase and stopped wasting energy, time and mind space going back and forth with the question in my mind, and simply choose.

As I was typing out this experience, I thought how amazing this awareness could be if it was applied to my life purpose. When we choose, when we make space in our minds and free ourselves from thoughts how opportunity there is to fully step into ourselves and our lives and our purpose(s).

2. The same morning, after my session, it appeared to me, I was or felt more humble. Even though my decision not to go on the interview, to be accepted into more advanced training, was very difficult; and I cried the entire night and next day. I realized my decision left me feeling calmer and stiller inside. Many of these individuals, some of which I had prepared for almost two years for this training, and yet it had all changed for me. How was I going to explain this to them, I thought, knowing I may face ridicule or judgment? Then it hit me, I didn't have to say or do anything except recognize that this was a huge lesson for me as they were moving forward (in their eyes by doing the interview) and I was also moving forward by choosing not to do the interview.

Source: Report sent to me by Miss P....G....

Questions from Ray M. Chavez:
In one of your lectures you mentioned 7 prime emotions people are usually concerned with. Is there a Fik'r vibrational chart for these emotions? And which one of these emotions produces the most vibrations?
Answer:
Look at the chart of Fik'r development below.
Relations and relationships produce the most intense vibrations.

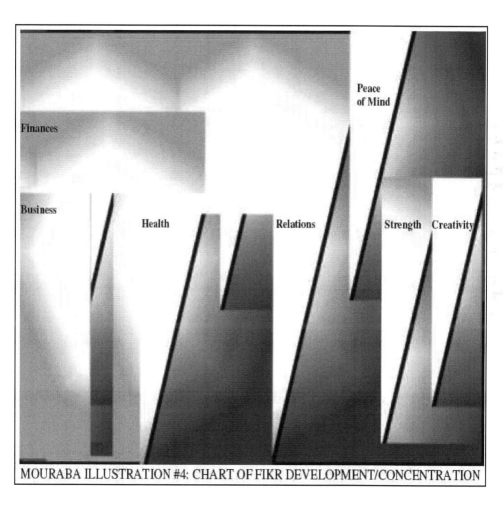

MOURABA ILLUSTRATION #4: CHART OF FIKR DEVELOPMENT/CONCENTRATION

617

Question from Julia Bernardino:
Does the Mouraba lesson eliminate stress and financial worries?
Answer:
Yes. See illustrations below. And here is a brief commentary on the illustrations of Mouraba Technique-Graph.

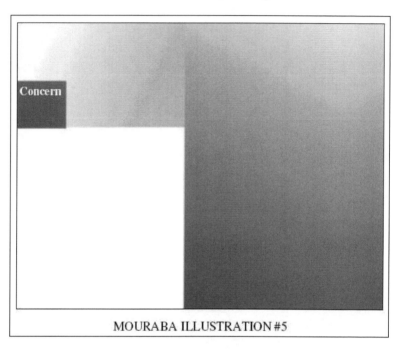

MOURABA ILLUSTRATION #5

Mouraba Illustration #5 (Above) represents the 3 vibrational spheres or dimensions we live in, and/or we go through during our life in the 3rd dimension (Earth). Nobody will escape the effects of each dimension, physically, mentally and spiritually.

Some are trapped in 1, 2 or 3 dimensions, others are capable of freeing themselves at a certain level. If you feel trapped because you are poor, financially insecure, unimportant, unlucky, or constantly threatened (Could be anything), you will never be able to progress on any level. And your mind will deteriorate. Worries of any kind are unhealthy.

The next illustration (Chart) gives additional explanation.

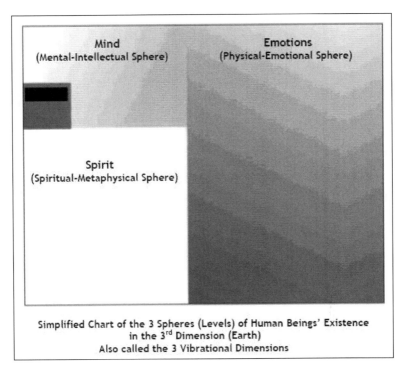

Simplified Chart of the 3 Spheres (Levels) of Human Beings' Existence
in the 3rd Dimension (Earth)
Also called the 3 Vibrational Dimensions

The chart above is called "Simplified Chart of the 3 Spheres." It is also called, the Mouraba Squares Chart.

It represents three spheres or levels of existences, human beings live in or pass through, during their life on Earth, and which are:

- 1-The physical-emotional sphere
- It belongs to the world of feelings and emotions
- 2-The mental-intellectual sphere
- It belongs to the mind (Intellect)
- 3-The spiritual-metaphysical sphere
- It belongs to the realm/level of spirit, encompassing spirituality, ethics, morality, social codes, enlightenment, and so on

Although, these 3 spheres have their separate vibrational worlds, they remained closely conditioned by the mental sphere. If we can deal with the mental zone (Mind), we will be able to solve lots of our problems.

The power of your mind is enormous.

If you use it wisely and pragmatically, you will be able to bring health and stability to your emotions; your mental power can even allow you to control physical pain, and eliminate stress and worries.

The Enlightened Masters recommend that you transpose your stress and worries to the zone of the mind. Let your mind worry about that, and keep the zone of your emotions safe and healthy.

The Anunnaki Ulema have developed several techniques to deal with stress and financial worries.

One of their techniques is demonstrated in Mouraba Illustration #6, on the following page. For instance, they recommend that we send our worries, stress, fear and anxiety to the zone of the mind, one at the time.

Here is a brief description of how it works:

- You send (Transfer) your worries and concern to the mental zone (Sphere of the mind), because you should deal with your problems at an intellectual-mental level.
- As long as your emotions, feelings and worries are trapped in the emotional zone, you will not be able to assess and analyze the situation, rationally and logically.
- You should not be emotional when you evaluate situations. It is wonderful to have a great heart filled with warm feelings and goodness, but you should not think with your heart. Leave your Heart Chakra alone when you go through crises.
- Create an area for your concern in the mental zone. Let your mind work on it.
- In the emotions sphere, open a register as seen in the Mouraba Illustration #6.
- Write down the nature of your concern.
- Your mind has already started working on your concern. Soon, your mind will send you a message.

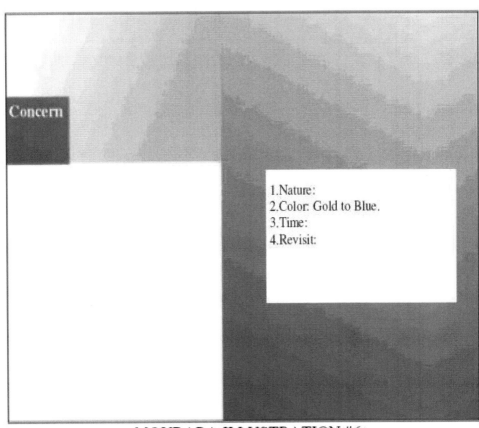

MOURABA ILLUSTRATION #6

- The message sent to you by your Fik'r-Mind contains analyses of your vibrations and energy.
- Write down the color of your vibrations.
- Write down the time (Day, hours) of your concern, meaning the period of your concern; when you feel worried, anxious, afraid, etc.
- Below, register the time when you have received a mental message.
- Tell yourself you are going to revisit the "Concern Square" in your mental zone.
- Apply the technique of the "Removal of the Knots", I have given you in the book "Activation of the Conduit and the Supersymetric Mind", pages 138-150.
- Your mind has already removed the "Knots", meaning successfully dealt with your concern (s).
- See the illustration of the technique on page 130.
- Go now to the Illustration of the final result. This is how your emotional field will look; clean, free from all worries and concerns, because your mind has emptied the register, where you have written your worries.

*** *** ***

Illustration of the Final Result

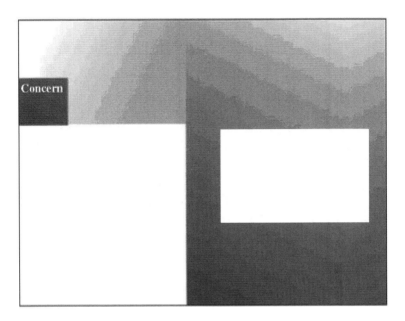

*** *** ***

Illustration of the "Removal of the Knots" (Concerns) Technique, from the book "Activation of the Conduit and the Supersymetric Mind."

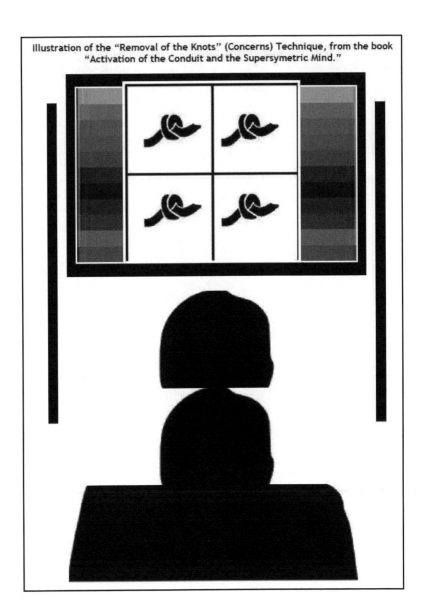

Questions from Ephrem Nehme:

Does one's vibration produce deadly physical strength as claimed by martial artists? Is there a famous master who demonstrated such strong vibrations? I am a student of Tae Kwon Do, and I need your honest opinion on this subject. Thank you.

Answer:

The Nei Cha style or more precisely the Noi Cun school of Chinese Wushu (Kung Fu) is well-known for its techniques that produce tremendous inner energy capable of pulverizing massive objects. Grandmaster Ku Yu Cheung was a living example. See his display of inner Chi, on the next page. Another legendary figure was Master Wang Jiwu.

Master Wang Jiwu practicing Nei Gong to cultivate and develop the Nei Ki, originally taught by the Indian Budhhist monk Bodhidharma.

Grandmaster Ku Yu Cheung breaking a stack of 12 bricks with his palm, using his inner strength. The power produced by his palm was generated by Dim Mak or Dim Muk technique, known in the West as the "Death Touch".

The Noi Cun, Nui Kung, or simply "Chi" is a fascinating manifestation of inner energy remarkably mastered by legendary Chinese Wushu masters.
Noi Cun is also used as a healing tool. Those who practice Tai Noi Cun and Chi Gung are quite familiar with the concept.

*** *** ***

626

Heart Chakra or Power of the Mind?

From Darlene.

Hello!

Listened to the show last night and of course found it very interesting!!! I would have had some questions far more interesting than your host but unfortunately the show ended without having that opportunity!

I already know about the energy of people places and things that effect us everyday but I did not know about the geographical locations and how they are mapped out across the world other than the positive energy vortexes that draw people for their spiritual endeavors. Example: Sodona, AZ

One of my questions would have been how you know the locations and how were they discovered???

I took some Astroprojection classes and learned how to utilize my vibrational force within me to protect oneself when in certain areas such as a train or places where there are many people or if one leaves the body to travel to higher levels of learning or time travel.

I have to say what I pick up from you when I listen to you talk on an intuitive level is that you function so much on an intellectual level that your heart chakra needs to be more engaged.

Balance is what we seek to achieve. Just my observation!

Best Always, Darlene

Answer:

The locations are known to the Anunnaki Ulema and the Enlightened Masters. I am just a passing shadow on the roads of life. My knowledge and learning are very limited. What I have written and said about those locations, was revealed to me by the honorable and loving masters who took me under their wings. And how did they know?

I don't know what Master Govinda, or the Buddha would have replied to an inquirer who asked this question: "How did you get enlightened?" or "How do you know what you know?"

Darlene, I would not dare to ask the Masters, what you have asked me. I would rather sit at the shadow of their feet, and enjoy my blessing for being there.

An intellectual-mystic Ulema is safer to be around...for emotions could produce illusion and suffering, while a warm and honest intellect will guide you like a shining light on a dark night...on the road of your life... I am not that light, Darlene, just a shadow.

627

Question: Is it true some places or neighborhoods bring bad luck?
Answer:
Absolutely.
In many instances, luck (Bad or good) depends on where you live. Is it an apartment or a single house?
Is it in the city or suburbia?
Is it on the beach or in the mountains?
Each part of earth has its own vibes.
Some vibes are positive, and some are negative.
The vibes of areas outside the city are usually healthier than the vibes emanated from spots and places in congested cities. And this does affect your health, psyche, and luck.

*** *** ***

Question: What is the percentage of coincidence in reading the Bakht? I mean is it possible that something will pop up like a pure coincidence or by error?

Answer:
Everything is possible.
This is why you should neither interpret the reading nor take it for granted. In other words, you should observe all the rules of the reading, and if necessary repeat twice the same reading. If you keep on receiving mixed messages or if you think what you have just read is a pure coincidence, then close up the Bakht and try it again after 24 hours.

*** *** ***

Bad luck, superstitions and curses.

Question from Rima Khan: Walking under a ladder could bring bad luck, according to many. Do you believe it is true?

Answer:
It is superstition. It has no effect on your luck.

*** *** ***

Employees' bad vibes.

Questions from Roy Bennedict: In volume two, page 83, you wrote "In the United States, negative and bitter people are more likely to emit negative energy that can deeply affect you mentally and physically on Monday and on Tuesday than on any other days of the week. Employees who are dissatisfied with their jobs and who dislike their boss diffuse intense bad vibes during the early and late hours of the day of their shifts. These vibes become more intense upon returning home, especially during the first 40 minutes." Are these bad and negative vibes created by the angry boss or the unhappy employees? Why employees' vibes become more intense when they come home?
And what are the symptoms? Can we sense these symptoms?

Answer:
The bad vibes are created by both the bullying-boss (Employer) and the employees.
Monday is the day when employees' bad vibrations and negative energy intensify. The very first 40 minutes-period refers to the time period when the bad vibes exteriorize outside the zone of the workplace. This does not mean that employees' bad vibes are not noticeable from 9 to 5.
It simply means that when they return home, their state of mind creates an etheric-physical zone surrounding their bodies that could be sensed by many people.

Some of the symptoms are:
a-Employees are easily irritated when you talk them during the 40 minutes time-period.
b-Fatigue becomes apparent, and in some instances, they start to feel muscular discomfort around the neck, the back, and the feet.
c-My advice to you is to give them time to relax, and to get out of the layers of negative residues they have stored in their Khateyn Tarika at the workplace. Soon after, their moods will change, and everything will be OK.

630

Ana'kh Bakht and good fortune

Question from Salim Ghorbal: Is Bakht good luck or bad luck? Is the magic book on spirits called Sham Al Maaref Koubra, a practical guide to communicate with spirits and stop the curses of bad people?

Answer:
Bakht is an Ana'kh word which means many things, such as fortune, fortune-telling, reading the future, luck (Bad or good), foreseeing particular segments from future events, and reading what was written in the book of your life, at the time you were born, and even before you existed on Earth.

Thousands of years later, Arab and Pre-Islamic scholars began to use the Anakh word Bakht in their Arabic language. Today, you will find the word Bakht in written and spoken Arabic.

The modern Egyptians use the word Bakht quite frequently. But the meaning has changed a little bit, because Bakht in Arabic means "Haz", and "Haz" means luck. Some fortune-tellers in Egypt and the Near East interpret "Haz" as the future. Thus "Reading the Bakht" in Arabic today means: Foretelling your future and luck.

The earliest manuscript on Bakht appeared in Phoenicia, circa 7,500 B.C., and it was written in Ana'kh. A later version in Anakh-Pro-Ugaritic appeared three thousand years later. A third version written in the early Phoenician-Byblos script appeared in Byblos and Tyre.

There are also two versions in Akkadian and Old Babylonian language, which are assumed lost.

Around 65 A.D., a new version in Arabic appeared in the Arabian Peninsula, and Persia, and it was called "Firasa".

Around 685 A.D., a revised edition appeared in Damascus, Syria. It was said that, from this Syrian edition, derived the hand-written manuscript "Ilmu Al Donia" (Science or Knowledge of the Universe). This manuscript included chapters on Arwah (Spirits and non-human entities), Djins, and Afrit.

Around 1365 A.D., a book titled "Shams Al Maaref Al Koubra" appeared in Cairo and Damascus, based upon two books "Al Bakht: Dirasat Al Moustakbal", and "Ilmu Al Donia".

Sham Al Maaref Koubra, is a fascinating book. The early Sahiriin and Rouhaniyiin used it very effectively.

To Westerners, the book is worthless.

Anunnaki, bad luck, fate and negative vibrations.

Question from Jamil Soudki: **Have the Anunnaki already decided on our luck? If so, then vibrations have nothing to do with our bad luck or good luck? If not, is there a direct link from luck to what you have said about the inner bio-rhthym created by Anunnaki to influence our lives and fate?**

Answer:
Thousands of years ago, before history was recorded, the Anunnaki created the first Man to meet their needs. They created us as a work-force to take care of the fields, cultivate the land, and bring them food; this is according to the Akkadian/Sumerian clay tablets. It is very clear.

At that time, when the Anunnaki gods and goddesses (Aruru, Mummu, Ea, Ninna, etc.) created the first prototypes of the quasi-human races, Man did not have all the mental faculties we have today. Thus, no Bakht was written for us.

We had no future. And the purpose of our life on Earth was dictated by the Anunnaki. It was not a bright future, and it was limited and fashioned by the intentions of the Anunnaki. Later on, 13 new faculties were added to the brain of the early Man.

And everything in the brain was wired and functioned according to a cellular rhythm. We cannot change this rhythm. But we can improve on it, and ameliorate its functioning, by acquiring new knowledge, developing a stronger memory, reading, writing, listening to intelligent and well-informed people, getting rid of bad habits, and elevating our being to a higher mental/spiritual level, through introspection, meditation, and refraining from hurting others. By doing so, we can free ourselves and reach a higher dimension of knowledge and awareness.

Some people are born normal, others are born with some mental deficiency, while a few were created as geniuses, like Bach, Mozart, etc., people who astonished us with extraordinary creativity, and unmatched talents. These talents and mental gifts were already "placed" into their Conduit. Otherwise, how can we explain the astonishing musical compositions of Mozart and other great composers at the age of 4?

Yes, we can alter the inner bio-rhthym, the Anunnaki installed in us, but we cannot change it completely. And by altering the rhythm, we can alter our future. This can be detected by reading the Bakht.

First thing to do is to activate the Conduit. As far as luck (Good and bad) is concerned, the noble in spirit (Mind, or "Soul" if you want) will be given the opportunities and means to learn how to positively reshape future events in his/her life. Unfortunately, there are too many good people in the world who are constantly suffering. And we wonder where is the logic?

What is the reason for their suffering? Is it true that good people always finish last?

Sadly enough, it happens all the time.

We see hard-working nurses (Who save lives) struggling to make a living. We see devoted school teachers unable to pay their bills.We see bloody bastards getting richer and richer, while honorable, loving and caring people are being kicked out of their homes!!

Where is the justice?

The truth I tell you, is that there is no justice on Earth, despite all the good intentions of so many of us, and despite so many good court decisions, and decent laws to maintain law and order.

The Ulema taught us that a good behavior, a high level of morality, an unconditional love, forgiveness and generosity do not guarantee success in life, or secure a good luck.

Ulema Badri said verbatim: "Your character and good manners are the only things you should keep even when you have lost everything in life.

So, start developing your brain, activate your Conduit, talk to your inner-self...and there, you will find the salvation..., you will find a way to change your bad luck into good luck.

If your Mind is in harmony with your "Jaba", then, and only then, can you change your inner bio-rhythm, and influence your DNA's metamorphosis." And remember, your DNA is a vital part of your future. You can decipher its sequence by reading your Bakht.

*** *** ***

The 3 Primordial Tarot Cards for Good Luck

Question from Antoine Farah: **You wrote in your book on Tarot and good luck that if we use three special cards from the Anunnaki Ulema Tarot deck, we could stop the**

effects of the evil eye and stop bad vibrations. Where can I find these three cards? Do you have a technique I can use to make these cards work for me? By the way, what do we call these three magic cards?

Answer:
I.Names of the three primordial Tarot cards:
Card 1 is called Jisru, Jisri, meaning a bridge.
Card 2 is called: Rahma, Rama, meaning mercy, assistance.
Card 3 is called Akafa, meaning to halt or eliminate a mishap.

II. Purpose of each card:
Each card serves a different purpose. And its use depends on your need and particular situation.
For example, if something (A plan, a wish) is not coming your way, and/or seems to be blocked for some unknown reasons, you must use Card 3 (Akafa). If you feel that you are threatened or warned about an awful event to happen to you, you must use Card 2 (Rahma, Rama). If you feel that a competition is too strong to overcome, and/or your chances to get this or that are minimal, use Card 1 (Jisru, Jisri).

III. How to use the cards. Preparation:
- **a**-First of all, you must cut each card and laminate it.
- **b**-Once laminated, keep the three cards wrapped into a piece of clothe (Silk) and place the cards under your pillow for 24 hours.
- **c**-Take the three cards from under your pillow and hold them in the palm of your right hand for at least one minute.
- **d**-While holding on the cards, do NOT think about anything negative or fearful.
- **e**-Do not let your own bad vibes penetrate the cards. Do not let your fear contaminate the cards.

IV. How to use the cards. Application:
- 1-Shuffle the cards 7 times.
- 2-Do not follow any shuffling order.
- 3-Pile the 3 cards on the lower side of the Tarot table.
- 4-Start reading your Bakht from the beginning.

- 5-As soon as you get a bad reading, stop the reading right away.
- 6-Open up the first piled card (From the 3 Primordial Cards) placed on the lower side of the Tarot table.
- 7-Remove the bad card from the square. The square is where you have placed the bad card.
- 8-Replace the bad card with the first piled card from the three primordial card.
- 9-Now, start reading your Bakht from the second square on your Tarot Table. You remember, there are four squares on your Tarot Table.
- 10-This new placement should change the reading.
- 11-If the second square continues to have a bad card, take it out of the square, and replace it with the second piled card from the three primordial cards.
- 12-If the third square continues to have a bad card, take it out of the square, and replace it with the third piled card from the three primordial cards.
- 13-Now, you have 3 good cards placed in 3 squares. So what about the fourth square?
- 14-Do no worry, the last square is good, even though, it is giving you a bad reading. At least now you know what the real problem is.
- 15-We are going to solve this problem. So, for now, stop the reading. Close the Bakht, but do not remove any card from the Tarot Table.
- 16-Shuffle the cards 7 times.
- 17-Place the Tarot deck on the right side of the Tarot Table.
- 18-Remove now the three primordial cards, and start the reading.
- 19-Fill up the 3 first squares and commence the reading.
- 20-What you have done so far is removing a bad stain on the net of your bad luck.
- 21-The new reading is going to please you enormously.
- 22-If you still have any doubt, close the Bakht, and reopen it again.
- 23-The new reading should give you full satisfaction.

You can find the three cards in my book "Ulema Anunnaki Tarot."

Question from Safaat Hilmi: **Does the Bakht influence or change my future?**
Answer: No, but YOU could, if you follow the instructions on how to read the Anunnaki Ulema Tarot.

However, you cannot alter future events, but you will be informed about their future occurrences, and work around it. This is not so bad, because in this case, the Bakht will send you a warning and advise you on what you should do to prevent mishaps or avoid them. But the events will occur no matter what.

*** *** ***

Questions: Talking about bad hours and good hours, lucky days and unlucky days, does it apply to all of us?
Answer:
Yes. Each one of us has a calendar of lucky days and unlucky days, lucky hours and unlucky hours. And you can find out by establishing the Calendar Grid.

*** *** ***

"Kama", Center of Energy
Question from Giorgio Anatoli: Is Kama, one of the energies spots in our body?
Answer:
No. Kama was called "an etheric center of energy", by Ulema Oppenheimer. Also referred to as the "Manifestation Square", meaning a zone where different forms of appearances, including beings and higher entities manifest themselves for multiple reasons. The Manifestation Square is indeed a physical area on Earth. Some Ulema suggested that this Square serves as a platform for the Ba'ab. According to Ulema Stanbouli, the Earth is full of these Squares. However, they are not permanent, meaning they appear on Earth, each time a cosmic molecule or "Buble" collides with another Bubble. This happens cosmically.
The Manifestation Squares materialize on Earth, when two distinct yet very close dimension membranes "bump" into each other. Ulema Stanbouli added, "The whole universe was created in this way." From Kama, derived the Hebrew word Kamea, which means a magic square. In esoterica and occult studies, Kama or Kamea are a place, or a zone used by Kabalists and

occultists to communicate with non-human entities in order to accomplish magical acts.

*** *** ***

Reading and visiting the future through vibration.

Question from Nura:
If we enter the world of vibration, the mental world, can we read the future? And, can we change it? Also, is there a technique to do so? Is it like reading the oracle? If we enter the realm of the future, can we change it?

Answer:
Yes, you can enter the realm of the future and see what is going to happen to you in the future. But, you can't change the future. However, the beauty of going into the future is using a technique to change the outcome of an event (in the future). For example, once you are in the sphere of the future you might see yourself hit by a car in the year 2014. And unfortunately, you will see yourself dead- the car killed you.

Now, you can't prevent the accident because it was already written. However, you can change the outcome of the accident, meaning instead of being killed by the car, you can do something to get only injured instead.

So, you are not interfering with the synchronized rule of the universe, the macro wheel. But, you are spinning inside the sphere of the future, within the macro wheel and therefore, you are able to change one of the rotations instead of the whole movement, since each incident has it's own rotation of the wheel on the landscape of the universe.

Going in the future is like going in the past. You can't change the event in the future. You can't change the event in the past. You can't go in the past, 60 or 70 years in the past, like the Holocaust and stop the massacre of the Jews. But you can attenuate the catastrophic results by giving warning of others.

This is the kind of information and knowledge the Ulema share with their students. But to do this you have to find the grid of time-space; even so, this is still not enough because you still have to find yourself in the grid. Simply put, you have to talk to the grid. Talking to the grid means, you have to put inside the grid your name, like entering you name on your computer to enter it, it's like a password.

Now this password is your name; but not the name you have, because the one you have is the name your parents gave you- in memory of your ancestors, Robert IV... in the realm of vibration these things don't exist because they are not terrestrials.

The original name that belongs to the astral body, which is the original blueprint of yourself. Call it the serial number; the code. Now we have two names; one that belongs to your physical body and one that belongs to your astral body.

Once you find your etheric name, you put it inside the grid and this is how you will be able to transcend physical frontiers and visit various dimensions.

So once you commit yourself to this awakening you become part of the wider picture of the universe. Other masters call this the state of one-ness. All this can be reached through vibration.

Question from Nura: So the state of oneness is really about awakening to the idea, the power of intention, like committing yourself, to the belief that we are all connected- not opening the heart chakra but the belief...so it's not a physical process or physical access?

Answer:
It is both physical and mental. Scientifically it is possible. According to quantum physics if you can make your molecules thinner then the molecules of the side of a wall, for example, you can penetrate the wall. This is proven by science.

This is how the Ulema defrayment their molecules and how they materialize and dematerialize, known to the general public as deportation. When you master this capability you will be able to enter multiple and adjacent dimensions. On a mental level, you don't need substance de-fragmentation.

All you need to do is set your mind free, on the multiple layers of vibrations. And those vibrations, because they are not physical, can go through solid substances such as wall, barricades, libraries... (For more information on this and similar techniques, you can refer to my other books). The important thing is not only to understand the study of vibrations and energy as a way to help protect yourself from others bad vibes; but also, and more importantly, like being on a magic carpet, to help you travel to other dimensions, and set your mind free by sending them forward on other layers of dimensions.

*** *** ***

Question from Leila R:
I was told the human body has 7 Chakras. How many centers of energy or Chakras has Khateyn Tarika?

Answer:
8, instead of 7. See photograph on page 640.

***   ***   ***

Questions from Raoul Lopez:
What is the actual size of the physical Zone of Khateyn Tarika?
What are the limits of our vulnerability zone?

Answer:
Space/physical zone of Khateyn Tarika: 5 feet on both side, right and left.
6 feet in front of you: Vulnerability limit/zone.
5 feet behind you: Vulnerability limit/zone. See illustration on pages 641-642.

***   ***   ***

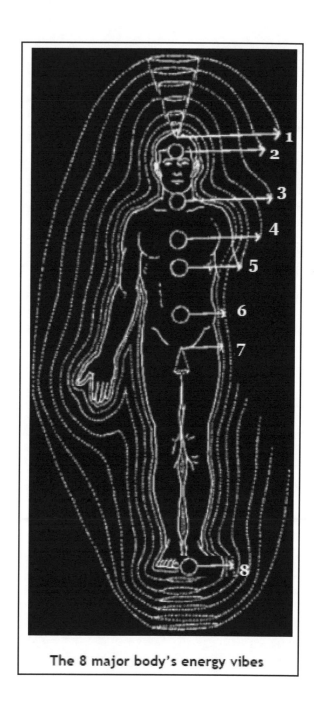

The 8 major body's energy vibes

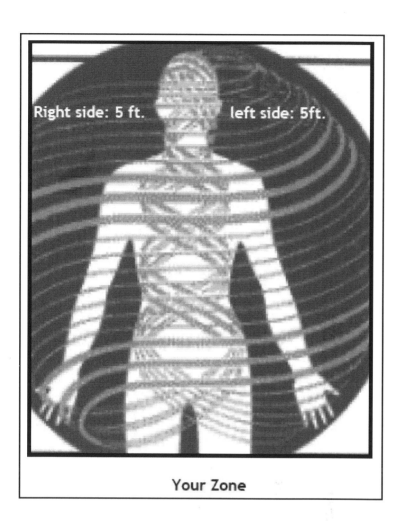

Your Zone

641

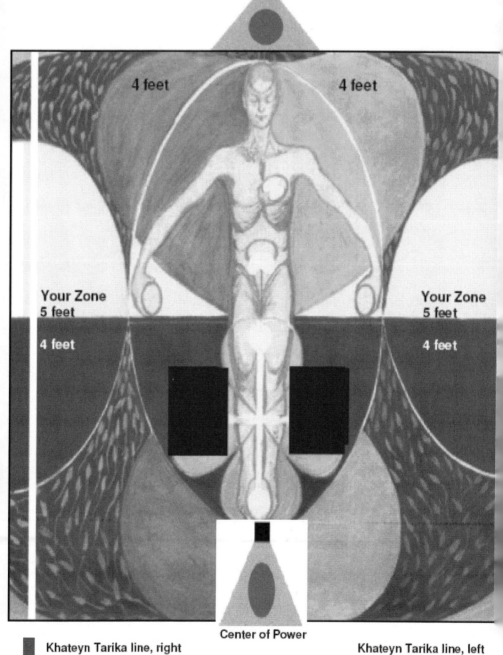

ILLUSTRATION OF ZONES AND DISTANCES OF VULNERABILITY

Questions from Jean-Louis Duhamel:
Are the Mikhals the center points from which bad vibes leak?
And how many are they exactly?

Answer:
Correct.
They are 7. See illustration on page 644.

*** *** ***

Question from Majed:
Is it the brightness or dimness of the vibes which determine the
state of health and energy of our body?

Answer:
Correct! See illustrations on pages 645 and 646.

*** *** ***

Question from Antoine Dumont:
From where does the mental energy exit?

Answer:
See illustration on page 647.

*** *** ***

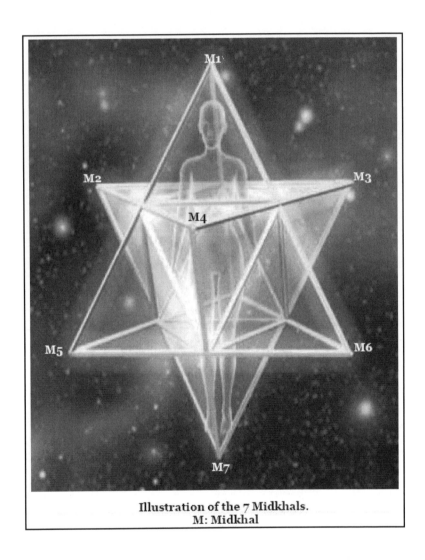

Illustration of the 7 Midkhals.
M: Midkhal

644

State of Energy

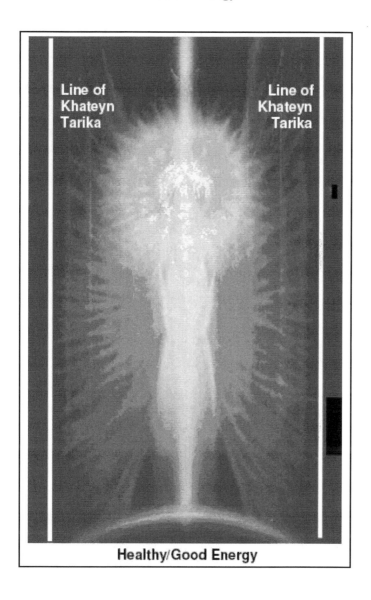

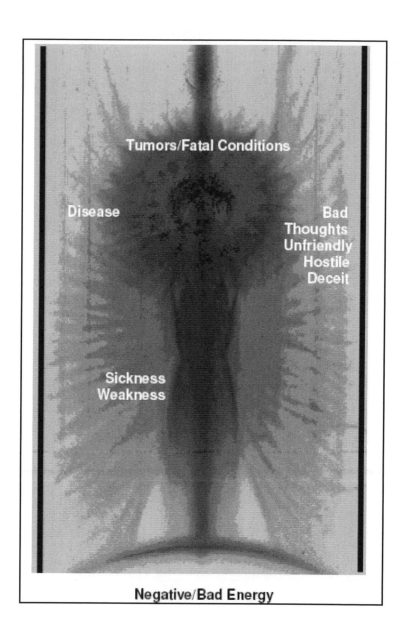

Shape of your mind energy (Mental Vibes)

Exit point of the mental energy

Illustration of your Mental Energy

Question by Matt Hoxtell, Chicago, Illinois, USA.

Question: What is the outlook for mankind after the year 2022? You have explained this in some detail in your books but will we live in peace or does humankind still pose a threat to one another if challenges and greed are proposed like they always have been?

Answer:

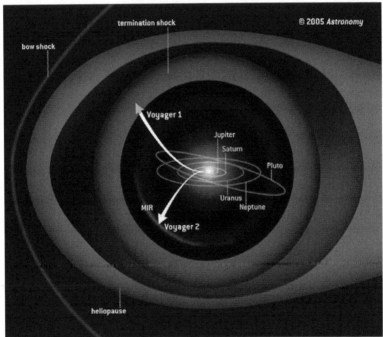

NASA's ring of hydrogen particles.

*** *** ***

NASA has discovered a ring of hydrogen particles around our solar system–a protective layer, which is now being called the Heliosphere. This was announced by the Anunnaki-Ulema, centuries ago, and they called the ring "The Cosmic Plasmic Belt."

The Heliosphere is generated by solar wind particles, which originate deep within the Sun. NASA launched the Interstellar Boundary Explorer Mission (IBEX) last year to get a better picture of the Heliosphere.
It was always suspected that it existed, but NASA scientists thought it existed in a completely different form; instead of being a uniform stripe, there are bright spots, which indicate the "bubble" has varying intensity and density.
Also, though NASA knows it protects the solar system from the radiation outside of it, scientists still aren't entirely sure why it is there or what it does. As noted by NASA.

***   ***   ***

2022 happenings are diverse, and could be easily misinterpreted by the public. Nothing physically will occur on Earth's landscape, or in its atmosphere.
A clash between a segment of non-terrestrials and humans is inevitable in the future.

In the past, more than 3 incidents occurred in secret military bases, and produced fatal consequences.
The incidents were provoked by military men who according to Greys' revelations have insulted Grey scientists who had worked on two joint- programs with the military.
The future clash will occur between the Anunnaki and the Greys, and humans will be caught in the middle. The outlook of mankind will be seriously affected by direct interference from the Anunnaki group called "Baalshamroot Ram".
This is the very group that surrounded the Solar System with the "Cosmic Plasmic Belt"; intense radiations/high velocity ranges of rays, as recently revealed by NASA.

The human race will never be in peace with itself, and with its own kind. This is dictated by the "Naf-Siya", the "Araya", the DNA and the bio-psychological makeup of human nature, originally created by the Anunnaki on two occasions:
The first time some 450,000 years ago, and the second time (Final Phase), some 10,000 years ago, which announced the dawn of civilizations on Earth.

Greed is an indivisible segment and one of the characteristics of the fabric of the human psyche. Thus, greed will always be here, and will increase the level of the contamination of mankind.
However, the year 2022 will bring major changes to social systems, and these changes will have enormous influence on the public's concept of religions.
Christianity's dogma could be altered. Islam will not be affected by these changes.

Buddhism, and Hinduism will not affected either, simply because Buddhism is founded on the concept of "Transmission of mind," and thus is not a religion per se.
Ancient Hinduism and Hindu manuscripts and inscriptions have already announced and pre-announced the existence of celestial spacecrafts known as "Vimanas" created by the "Gods", a super race from the multiple layers of the universe. Consequently, both will blend perfectly with the comprehension and definition of a new social order to be established by the Anunnaki.

In short, 2022 will bring paramount changes to:
a-Religions;
b-Social order.

*** *** ***

Another extraterrestrial threat other than the Gray's aliens

Question by Matt Hoxtell, Chicago, Illinois, USA.

650

Question: After the Anunnaki's job is finished here on earth through decontamination will we ever have to deal with another Extraterrestrial threat other than the Gray's aliens?

Answer:

The only threat humanity will face is the product of the Greys' agenda. It is important to understand, that the Greys have lived on Earth for millions of years, long before the human races were created by the Igigi, Anunnaki and Lyrans. We call the Greys "extraterrestrials". This is not entirely correct, as the Greys are the intraterrestrials of Earth, and humans their co-habitants. We fear the Greys. And ironically, the Greys also fear us. They feel threatened by our nuclear arsenal and experiments, because these can annihilate Earth, where the Greys live. Earth is also the habitat of the Greys.

Earth is where their communities and families live. Greys will do anything and everything to prevent humans from destroying Earth. Earth will be only destroyed by acts of nuclear war. The Greys have adapted very well to the intra-landscape of Earth; meaning Inner-Earth. And water on Earth is essential for their survival and for "energizing" their crafts. Unfortunately, constant interactions with the Greys will deteriorate the genes of the human race.

The first phase of such deterioration is contamination.

The Anunnaki are fully aware of this contamination. Simply put, in order to eliminate the contamination of human and human DNA, the Anunnaki must get rid of the Greys.

And the decontamination process will result in a major confrontation with the Greys. Some influential governments have already received a sort of "briefing" on the subject.

Some high officials took the threat very seriously, whilst many others did not. Their arrogance and ignorance will have lethal consequences, which humanity will suffer from.

No, there are no additional threats from other extraterrestrial races, simply because they are not interested in us. They are not interested, because we have nothing meaningful or important to offer them. Humans live on a linear scale. This is how and why we understand the universe in terms of time and distance/space. And this limits us, and prevents us from becoming members of the "Cosmic Federation."

Only two races in the known universe can live on Earth: The Anunnaki and the Greys. In the past three extraterrestrial races lived here on Earth, for sometime among us.
They were:

- **a**-The Anunnaki;
- **b**-The Lyrans;
- **c**-The Greys.

Their organisms and body structure could sustain our atmosphere and its conditions. Other extraterrestrials would not be able to live on Earth, as humans are not able to live on other known stars and planets because of their atmospheric conditions. Other alien races will self-destruct if they try to live on Earth.

Consequently, they have no interest whatsoever in invading or dominating Earth. In other words, the only threat, the only real threat, will come from the Greys. But for the time being, we are safe, because the Greys still need us. Despite their highly advanced technology and science, the Greys did not yet find the perfect and final formula for saving themselves, genetically.

For some incomprehensible and possibly silly reasons, the survival of the Greys depends on two things:

- **a**-The survival of humans;
- **b**-The safety of planet Earth.

*** *** ***

Aliens competing with the Anunnaki to rule our planet?

Question by Matt Hoxtell, Chicago, Illinois, USA.

Question: Are there any other alien races in this galaxy or another that could compete with the superstar status of the Anunnaki and rule our planet?
Answer:
On the market nowadays, we find several so-called encyclopedias and field-guides on extraterrestrial races. The Internet is infested with silly and childish websites posting ridiculous literature on

extraterrestrial races, description of their physiognomy, heights, weights, eyes, skin, etc. This is nonsense par excellence. How did they know about these extraterrestrial races?

What are their sources, data, and authoritative references? They are non-existent. Their articles are the product of an erroneous imagination and immature fantasy.

Unless you break the frontiers of time and space, and land on their planets and stars, you will never be able to learn about their species, physiognomy and their biological structure on any level. As long as modern ufology embraces such phantasmagoric assumptions and fake narratives, ufology will never be accepted academically, or gain the respect and trust of erudite milieus and scientists.

However, and according to some statements and "leaks", we have learned about the existence of six different extraterrestrial races who have contacted the United States military.

This was mentioned in the "Krill File".

But again, this so-called file was announced to the ufology community by Mr. Moore, who has been discredited by eminent ufologists. And once again, I ask you to define what we understand by "Eminent ufologists"? How eminence is defined, and on what basis or foundation, such eminence is based upon and structured?

To tell you the truth, nobody knows, except the Anunnaki-Ulema. Unless you are familiar with Ana'kh, and have read the archaic manuscripts of the Anunnaki-Ulema, and some of the Phoenician cosmogeny tablets, and unless you are familiar with the Akkadian and proto-Mesopotamian language(s), you will never be able –for sure– to categorize the galactic races.

All we have is mythology and colorful folklore. And beginning in the early 1950's, authors began to put their spin on everything extraterrestrial or alien. Call it science fiction, or perhaps mytho-inspirational essay, but not an authoritative study of galactic civilizations.

As of today, we are aware of the existence of two races:

a-The Greys;

b-The Anunnaki.

The Greys became known to us through articles by all sorts of ufologists, contactees (usually phony/fake), abductees, charlatan channelers, statements by so-called military men who worked in secret military bases, "insiders" and self-serving authors.

The truth I tell you, is that the Greys do exist, but they are not, who, what and how they are generally described to be, by many ufologists and those who claim to have had any sort of contact or rapport with them. In some cases, accounts of encounters were correct, but in general, 95% of accounts and reports betray the truth, simply because the human mind is unable to understand what flashes before our eyes.

And this apparent in the way contactees/abductees (followed by a fleet of ufologists) describe the Greys. For instance, how many times have you heard from abductees and ufologists alike, that the Greys or extraterrestrials have very big eyes in proportion to the size of their heads, and the eyes were described as large eyes slanted upward and outward, or big dark eyes that were olive or almond-shaped?

Many times, I'm sure. To tell you the truth, extraterrestrials' eyes are as big or as small as human eyes. And their sockets are almost similar to ours, but with three major differences. One of them is the retina. Aliens do not have retina in their eyes, simply because they do not need one.

Abductees were not able to realize that aliens or extraterrestrials eyes were "masked."

By masked I mean their eyes were covered by a dark lens or more exactly a screen, called "Bou-Ka'h" in the Ana'kh, the Anunnaki language. The large black eyes were simply a dark screen applied to the eyes of the extraterrestrials. Consider this screen as eyeglasses for now (But in actuality these glasses provided the alien with information, much like glasses with mini TV/info screens on them being made and used by the military today).

This common error is clearly shared by ufology authors, ufologists, and researchers alike. This serious misconception and erroneous description are strong evidence that we have no clear vision or understanding of the physiognomy of extraterrestrials.

If this is true, then we are not in a position to categorize and adequately classify aliens, extraterrestrials, and Greys.

Thus, recognizing and/or defining other extraterrestrial species is pure speculation.

In conclusion, we should concentrate exclusively on two known non-human races; the Anunnaki and the Greys.

Such concentration will enable us to conclude that:
- 1-There are no other extraterrestrials on the scene;

- 2-The Greys are not in any position to compete with the Anunnaki.

And since we have logically eliminated the possible interference from other alien races/non-humans that exist in our galaxy/other galaxies answering the question: "Are there any other alien races in this galaxy or another that could compete with the superstar status of the Anunnaki and rule our planet?" becomes an easy task.

And the answer is: The Greys cannot rule our planet, nor can they challenge the super status of the Anunnaki for obvious reasons.

One of these reasons is the fact that the Anunnaki are far more advanced than the Greys.

*** *** ***

Would the Anunnaki come to aid the planet if another threat happens?

Questions by Matt Hoxtell, Chicago, Illinois, USA.

Question: You have stated that the Anunnaki feel responsible for hybrid contamination between humans and the Gray's, would the Anunnaki ever come to the aid of the planet aif this threat would happen again?

Answer:

Yes and yes.

This was basically the topic Sinhar Ambar Anati (Victoria) discussed with representatives from the United States government years ago.

Please refer to the book: "Anunnaki Ultimatum", co-authored by Ilil Arbel. Anati made it clear to American scientists and to two generals, that the Greys' contamination will inevitably destroy the human race.

*** *** ***

Question: Has the planet ever come close to another threat as serious as the Gray's and will it be a possibility?

655

Answer:

Yes, millions of years ago, when a huge celestial object was on a trajectory in the direction of planet Earth.

The Anunnaki deviated the object from its collision course with Earth. And later on, they decided to surround the Solar system with a protection shield, known as "The Cosmic Plasmic Belt", which is called "Zinar" in Ana'kh, the Anunnaki language. This was also mentioned in the Book of Ramadosh "Ketab Rama-Dosh."

*** *** ***

Are the Anunnaki going to take over Earth?

Questions by Reverend Nancy Santos.

Question : Is one of these Anunnaki Gods going to take over the earth after the pole shift?

Answer:

No! For two reasons:

- 1-The pole is not going to shift. So don't worry. This is based upon mainstream science. However, it could shift as it did before, millions of years ago. But scientists are not concerned. They are absolutely sure that no shift will occur anytime soon.
- 2- If the Anunnaki intend to take over Earth, they will not wait until the pole shift. They can do it any time, at will. But they are not interested at all.

Read the section on the final warning.

Dear Sandra, you have to remember that the Anunnaki are not territorial. Besides, planet Earth is meaningless to them. We, as human beings are not interesting enough to the Anunnaki. Our natural resources are found on numerous planets, readily accessible to the Anunnaki.

There are 7 galaxies in the cosmos filled with natural resources available to the Anunnaki, and these resources are not contaminated. We think that we are the center of the universe, because we are arrogant and pretentious. In fact, very very very few alien civilizations are aware of our existence. And they have no interest whatsoever of paying a visit to us. However, and according to Stephen William Hawking, it is not a good idea to try to reach other civilizations in the universe. He warned us. Now, this does not mean that other alien races are not visiting our planet. Some have visited Earth several times, as part of their galactic excursions.

They came and they left. Nevertheless, the intraterrestrial aliens are still here.

Why?

It is very simple: They lived here millions of years before we were created. This is why we call them the intraterrestrials. They are not humans, and they live in isolated areas and aquatic habitats. These races are peaceful to a certain degree, as long as, the human race will not jeopardize the safety of Earth.

So in conclusion, the Anunnaki are not going to take over the Earth. But please do remember, that we are expecting a global communication/contact/rapport with them in 2022.

*** *** ***

Human race: The Anunnaki creation of a new human race after 2022

Question by Raoul Mondragon, Vera Cruz, Mexico.

Question: I am very worried by what you have written on the subject of the return of the Anunnaki in 2022? Is it for real? Are they going to change the way we look? Are they going to get rid of us and replace us with a new human race? What kind?

Answer:

What kind of a new human race are we talking about?

A new genetic race?

A bio-genetic race?

A new race with new physical characteristics and different physiognomy?

"None of the above," said the Honorable Master Li.

He added verbatim, word for word, and unedited: "The physical form of humans will not change.

Unless, the Anunnaki will take us back to the primordial Chimiti (Akkadian word for the genetic lab tubes, used by the Anunnaki to create an early form of human beings.)
And this is very unlikely, even impossible. The changes will occur on different levels, and almost instantly."

***   ***   ***

Russian Underwater Bases

Questions by Angelique Doudnikova

Question: Is it true that a massive Russian underwater base exists one mile deep in the Marianas trench in the Pacific ocean? If so, what activities/research/experiments are going on there? Do the Chinese have one too?
Answer:
Yes, it is true. The Russians have a massive underwater base that was created in 1969, to study an extraterrestrial underwater navigation system called "Aquatic Plasma Corridors".
This corridor is undetectable by satellite, sonar or any other underwater detection system.
Not all branches of the Russian Navy were aware of the creation/existence of this base.
During one of their naval maneuvers just outside the perimeter of this Russian underwater base, six frogmen from one of the Russian submarines encountered three alien frogmen in metallic suits underneath a massive metallic object.
Both the Russian and alien frogmen were roughly at a depth of one hundred to one hundred and twenty feet. The alien frogmen were wearing what appeared underwater to be metallic suits of indeterminable and interchanging colors that morphed from a silvery white to bluish to grey.
One of the Russian frogmen stated that when he tried to approach these three, he was blocked by what seemed to be an invisible underwater forcefield, created by the alien frogmen as a protection sheild.

The Russian frogman's oxygen tanks started to fail and he quickly lost consciousness and started sinking but was saved by one of his fellow divers.

After being rescued, he described the alien frogmen as being 8ft to 11ft tall, as he saw them underwater. And none of them had any visible oxygen tanks/breathing apparatus attached to them.

In the secret debriefing that followed, the Russian diver who saved his fellow frogman, said that when he too tried to approach this massive foreign submerged object, he encountered what felt like a solid transparent wall surrounding the object.

He later described it as an oval glass box, surrounding this mysterious submerged object which also shielded it from contact with the ocean's water.

After the fall of the Berlin wall, and ensuing collapse of the Soviet Empire, rumors started circulating within the military and scientific community, that this bizarre event was in fact a joint Russian-extraterrestrial operation designed to explore the effects of the underwater plasma corridor on it's environment in the ocean, and on humans, as well as their psychological and psychosomatic reaction to encountering the corridor and seeing the alien frogmen and the ship itself.

Two decades later in Lake Baikal, other Russian navy frogmen encountered similar 9ft "silver swimmers" who also had no visible breathing apparatus. While these encounters are largely unknown to the general public, military scientists with top clearance are well aware of them, and have worked on similar projects in different underwater bases, such as the one known to us as AUTEC, which is located off Andros Island in the Bahamas.

These massive underwater military bases, whether they be Russian, or American or Chinese, look from the surface to be rectangular/traditional compound structures.

However upon entering them underwater, they expand in all directions, and are extremely extensive. And all of them are joint human-alien operations.

Starting from the second underwater level, compartments are divided into large operation rooms, separated by elaborate long corridors, curving at 90 degrees every hundred feet or so, with doors that can drop down from the ceiling to seal off segments in the event of radiation leakage, or any matter related to internal security. One of the interesting characteristics of these doors in the corridors is the circular porthole-like windows within what is a whitish metal of extraterrestrial origin.

None of these metallic alloys are possible here due to earth's gravity, and as such have to be done in orbit aboard the Space Shuttle. Interestingly enough, this technology has been shared by American, Russian and Israeli military scientists.

At one time British and French scientists complained of being left out of the loop, to which the Americans responded very candidly "We don't trust Europeans – especially the French!" To which the French retorted that they would withhold all information garnered from the Cassini-Huygens mission to Saturn...

An American three star general was quick to respond by saying "This is not the first time you Europeans have withheld information from us. Remember the Belgian incident?" (Aurora)

The mode of transportation down to the underwater base and within the base is also fascinating.

From the surface, one enters a craft that looks like a silvery metallic spinning top, approximately 8ft in diameter, that can comfortably accommodate four passengers, and corkscrews its way downwards centrifugally around a rod using a form of magnetic propulsion for what seems to be a only a few seconds down to an unknown depth. (With a cheeky smile, M. de Lafayette added that he did not think the Chinese yet had this technology.)

From the second underwater level on down, the "Spinning Mobile Satellite" (SMS) travels horizontally and reaches its final destination at an undisclosed level of the base at which it again dives into water. It is at that level/destination that you will find the habitat and work center of the Grays.

Only the highest level personnel with top clearance can go there. Not even President Barack Obama or Vice-president Joe Biden, or any member of Congress/Senate is allowed access to that level at these facilities.

This clearance status was decided upon (jointly) by the NSA, the CIA, the United States Air Force, the DOD and NASA. Even the FBI has been excluded from this exclusive little club.

This is perfectly appropriate, since politicians come and go, whilst the military are sworn to secrecy, the average career of top military brass are thirty or more years, and they take their secrets with them to the grave.

"The Body" Ventura, former WWF wrestler, and one time governor of Minnesota, who kept all the secrets sealed from the public while in office, yet is now spilling the beans on his own conspiracy show on television!! Worth mentioning here also, is the fact that Lafayette loves Ventura, but were he General Jesse Ventura he would have kept his mouth shut.

Jesse "The Body" Ventura.

Do people have a right to know all these things, including the joint human-alien ventures? And my answer is: Absolutely not! At the present time, so as not to shatter the fabric of our society and cause complete chaos and total anarchy, this information should be withheld and only gradually released to the public as set forth in the U.S.-extraterrestrial protocol, because humans have to be mentally prepared, in order to meet the extraterrestrial."

Anunnaki Prevention of Use of Nuclear Weapons

Question by Angelique Doudnikova.

Question: Will the Anunnaki intervene to prevent possible aggressive use of atomic/thermonuclear weapons against other nation(s) prior to, and/or during their return in 2022?

Photo: Benazir Bhutto

Answer:
From yet undisclosed data, Maximillien de Lafayette said the most imminent threat will come not from Iran, but from Pakistan, an as yet highly unlikely surprise scenario.

Benazir Bhutto knew of this, spoke about it behind closed doors, and was assassinated soon after.

I found it very childish and ridiculous when American ufologists wrote on subjects pertaining to extraterrestrials and nuclear issues since they are absolute outsiders.

Nowhere in their books have they ever written on the Anunnaki and their Ba'abs. Why are some of the Ba'abs so extremely important?

They lead to the parallel dimensions of the Anunnaki, and the beginning of time, where the God-Particle/Higgs Boson can be found, which is the reason for the building of CERN's Large Hadron Collider (LHC).

Through the Miraya – a cosmic screen/monitor with a vast depot of data that informs the Anunnaki of past, present and future events occurring in non-linear form, and in different galaxies by which the Anunnaki can monitor the activities of humans on Earth, the Grays, Reptilians, Nordics, Lyrans, Dracos, Plaeidians etc, and envoys from various other galactic civilizations wrongly identified and referred to as "The Galactic Federation/Council" .

There is no way for a medium/channeler/psychic to the stars sitting in his/her apartment in Wala Wala, or Biloxi, Mississippi or in the swamps of Louisiana, listening to Willie Nelson's "On the Road Again" to access this Miraya and reveal the secrets of the Universe.

The Anunnaki will definitely intervene if a nuclear explosion were seen on the Miraya screen to happen near a Ba'ab connected to their galaxy, close to the membrane of the Universe that could cause chaos and disequilibrium in the eleventh dimension of the Universe. This is all very possible, since the speech given by Adolf Hitler at the 1936 Berlin Olympics, can still be heard in different worlds, as can the Sermon that was given by Yeshuah (Jesus) on the Mount of Olives. Both can be heard in the "Time-Space Depository". A bank of information, that Nikola Tesla accidentally tapped into.

Nikola Tesla.

American history has been unfair to Tesla and given his credits to the greedy and egotistical Edison. Everyone on the planet using A/C electricity today should give thanks and praise to Nikola Tesla and not Thomas Edison. Only humans on earth refer to space-time. All other extraterrestrial sentient beings use the term time-space to define the limits of the known universe.

*** *** ***

Who will survive the return of the Anunnaki?

Question by Angelique Doudnikova.

Question: What percentage of the world's population will survive the return of the Anunnaki, to become part of the new human race after 2022?

Answer:
To calculate the dimensions of the Ziggurat of Enki in Ur (in Iraq), to find the number of earth's population that would survive which had been predicted millennia ago.

And all this while he looked out from the window of his Manhattan apartment at eight fifteen in the morning, after a late night - no an all night interview.

*** *** ***

How many other Anunnaki will be part of the return?

Questions by Angelique Doudnikova.

Question: Though the return will be led by Sinhars Marduchk and Inannaschamra, how many other Anunnaki will be part of the return?

And how many Anunnaki guides will there be, for humans who will be saved and returned to earth after the cleansing?

Answer:
That is a very normal way for a purely human mind to ask such a question. The truth is: the galactic mind of the extraterrestrials functions differently.

Consequently, the alien mode of operation becomes totally incomprehensible to our mind, and instead of focusing on how many military personnel they might send, we should focus on how many I.S.Ms they will operate at close proximity to Earth. This stands for "Intelligent Satellite Module".

665

Each module is approximately 8ft to 10ft in diameter, made of "fibro-metal", an alloy of elements not found on Earth, which is cone shaped on the top half and oval shaped on the bottom half. Worth mentioning here, the Gray aliens have craft similar to the "I.S.M." being smaller in diameter at 6ft to 8ft wide.

These were witnessed by farmers in the mid-west several times, and reported on cable T.V.

The purpose of the Gray's I.S.Ms, was to scan particular areas in the United States for several military strategic reasons, such as creating an atmospheric shield network which could alter the fabric of weather and be used to control climatic/atmospheric conditions over a chosen area/country.

This military ecological weapon system produces tsunamis, earthquakes, mysterious underground detonations, complete destruction of all types of agriculture, forests and natural resources (crops, trees, orchards, and every kind of plant).

Have we seen these kinds of catastrophic events recently in different parts of the world?

Whilst the Gray I.S.Ms require a complicated operational structure, encompassing large numbers of military personnel, one Anunnaki can handle up to one thousand of their I.S.M. machines.

They will be using the Shabka - a cosmic net, made up of anti-radar emissions and rays that not even N.O.R.A.D. can detect. The Gray/Earth joint program I.S.M.'s are detectable and clearly visible to the naked eye, whilst the Anunnaki I.S.Ms are totally invisible and completely undetectable, as they jump from one time-space pocket to another.

Worth mention here to all our readers: The difference between "time-space" travel and "space-time" travel is this: In the mode of time-space, the human mind cannot yet understand it, nor can the eyes see it, as we do not yet fully comprehend the concept of time. In space-mode time however, human eyes can glimpse the craft, for a split second before it vanishes/jumps to another pocket. Only in this instance, does the space-time appear linearly to humans.

One Anunnaki I.S.M. module is capable of covering up to 9,000 square miles.

These mini-spaceship machines will be interconnected through a massive net of rays that will seal off the Earth's atmosphere when the Anunnaki return.

The number of Anunnaki who will be operating this return mission is as yet unknown. Very few Anunnaki personnel will be needed to operate this enterprise.

When this massive net of rays is interwoven, it forms a dark gray gluey substance that appears to us as a blend of burning metal, bark and rubber with the most awful foul odor imaginable!! The ghastly and noxious odor itself is enough to kill people. Light from the sun will be completely blocked out, as this gluey substance, known to the Anunnaki as "Zafta", forms a solid egg-shell-like casing around the entire planet from which there will be no escape.

This will truly be the end of the world, and life on Earth as we know it."

Sorry all you "2012" believers, but Maximillien de Lafayette says it ain't gonna happen!! He will be inviting all of you to a big banquet come January 1st 2013 in Acapulco, Mexico with free Margaritas and Bloody Mary's cocktails to go round till the sun goes down – no cover charge!!

*** *** ***

Efficient energy systems of the Anunnaki.

Question by Angelique Doudnikova.

Question: What kind of clean and efficient energy systems, and modes of transportation will the Anunnaki introduce after 2022?

Answer:

After the cleansing is done, no oil, coal, natural gas, or any other carbon based fuels will be used to power any car, machinery or mechanical equipment/apparatus.

Energy to power all of the above will be provided via satellites which harness cosmic energy.

By then even solar energy will be regarded as an archaic and rudimentary form of harnessing energy.

This will be made possible by the process of opening the Anunnaki cosmic Ba'abs, which are also the stargates to multiple dimensions.

Eleven of these Ba'abs exist, within the multi-dimensional cosmic landscape, adjacent to Earth.

*** *** ***

Grand Central Station in downtown Chicago.

Stargate over Chicago

Questions from Matt Hoxtell, Chicago.

Questions: Is there a stargate/Ba'ab in Chicago?
Where exactly is it located, and what does it look like?
How would you jump into a ba'ab?
Is it part of the Anunnaki evacuation plan for humans upon their return in 2022?

Answer:
There is a huge cosmic Ba'ab/stargate over Chicago. But this one is quite unique, because it is called a Madkhaal, which means in Ana'kh, an entrance, rather than a stargate.

Madison Square Garden.

Not all stargates are identical, nor do they function in the same manner. There are stargates that lead to another (singular) world, an incomprehensible world of bent time-space. And there are stargates that lead you into parallel dimensions adjacent to our world.
The one over Chicago leads you towards a dimension where time and space are no longer linear. In this dimension, the laws of physics as they are known to us on earth no longer apply.

The Madkhaal is located above Grand Central Station in downtown Chicago.

It is oval and vibrates like a rubber band, very similar to a multiverse membrane, found in the perimeter of the eleven dimensions mentioned in contemporary quantum physics.
It is neither visible to the naked eye nor can it be detected by any apparatus on Earth. Also worth mentioning here, is the subject of the "Anomaly of Stargates."
Stargates do vary in size, function, purpose and mobility, just like the extraterrestrial underwater plasma corridors, used to navigate our seas and oceans.

The stargate in New York City, which is located over Madison Square Garden, is twice the size of that over Central Station in downtown Chicago. Travel to and from the Chicago stargate is possible at particular times, however travel through the Madison Square Garden Ba'ab is a one way street.
Maximillien de Lafayette recommends this ba'ab for all televangelists and divorce lawyers!!
Since the Ba'abs are at least 900ft – 1,700ft above ground, it is not possible to jump into a Ba'ab. At the time of the return of the Anunnaki, an electromagnetic fog will suck up the people with light to medium contamination, as set forth by the Anunnaki's return protocol.

Signs before the return of the Anunnaki

Question by Angelique Doudnikova.

Question: What are the signs that people will see in the skies the day before the Anunnaki return, and where will they be seen?
Answer:
One year before the return of the Anunnaki, around the end of the year 2021, the governments of many countries will start to circulate publications and manuals describing signs that will indicate the appearance of extraterrestrial craft visible to the public at large.
I am convinced that many Bishops and Archbishops in the United States and England have already been briefed on the

subject, and were secretly asked to cooperate on the redaction of material, that would suitably marry religious dogma with "intelligent design", as well as the frightening arrival of extraterrestrials to our planet.

Ironically, four major Anunnaki stargates will be activated and opened, which religious leaders will also interpret as the arrival of the "Four Horsemen" as stated in the Book of Revelation, and will be urging believers to run to their churches and pray. Readers and believers of the "Left Behind" series will have another shot at redemption...(Not!!)

Meanwhile, from the end of 2021 to November 30th, 2022 American citizens will have the most unusual evacuation display of UFOs/USOs of all shapes and sizes (oval, circular,crescent-shaped, triangular, cylindrical and every other shape witnessed, reported and ridiculed by the media, military disinformers and debunkers alike.) These are the vehicles of the Gray aliens jointly operated with the military.

Anunnaki's "tool of annihilation"

Question by Angelique Doudnikova.

Question: Who/what created the "tool of annihilation" that the Anunnaki will use when they return?

Answer:

The "Tool of Annihilation" was created by the Majlas – the Anunnaki High Council, as stated by Sinhar Anbar Anati, specifically for the purpose of cleansing the earth from all its contamination upon their return in 2022.

This tool of annihilation will be utilized in the event of hostile situations, where uninformed rednecks (Back in the saddle again) and other surburbanites will pull out their hunting rifles and shotguns to shoot at spaceships belonging to the most advanced race in the known universe. Those are the ones who are going to get it first!

On Divination and Tarot Card Reading

Questions by Salma Tabbah, Amman, Jordan.

Question:
Do the Ulema believe in divination and Tarot card reading?
At the beginning I was skeptical, but after having consulted a Tarot reader, I became a believer. She predicted things nobody knew or heard about. Sometimes her predictions touched on a very personal note. So my question to you is this: Is the Tarot something your people accept? Is it a game or the real thing?- Salma Tabbah.

Note: We encourage the readers to refer to the book "Ulema Anunnaki Tarot. Extraterrestrial Lessons and Techniques to See your Future: The world's most powerful book on the occult and foreseeing your future on Earth and in other dimensions. Published in February 2010.

Answer:
Yes, the Anunnaki-Ulema have used a very unique "Divination" method to explore ultra-dimension. The word divination is not totally correct, but we are going to use it for now, because it is "As close as it gets to the real thing," said Ulema Bukhtiar.
We can also use the word "Oracle", as these words refer to the same thing in essence.
The other term "Ultra-dimension" means a "Surrounding that is not normally and usually detected by scientific or physical means," said Ulema Seif El Din. This ultra-dimension belongs to the realm of many things, including thoughts, perception, extra-sensory feelings (Not caused by anomaly of any sort), and a depot of knowledge that evolves around past, present and future events. One of the aspects of the Ulema's Kira'at deals with Tarot card reading called Bak'ht-Kira'at. The Master taps into a zone that contains lots of information about events to occur in the future.
The figures and numbers he/she opens up while reading the cards are closely related to that zone called "Da-irat Al-Maaref" (Circumference of Knowledge).

The figures and numbers that appear on the cards guide the Master reader towards a chart that contains and explains all the possible meanings, NOT interpretation.

"But this is not enough, we should not rely only on symbols and numbers, because this could happen in a very ordinary manner, far from the truthful reach of knowledge and discovery...it could fall into the possibility of coincidences. This is why, a reading should be repeated multiple times to detect coincidence and separate superstitions from reality..." explained the Honorable Ulema Ghandar.

*** *** ***

Question:
If your answer is yes, then would you please explain the difference between regular Tarot cards and Ulema tarot cards?

Answer:
I will give you a brief explanation.

The Ulema cards are personalized, meaning they are hand-made by you. You do not purchase your Ulema cards from a store. They are not a commercial product. The Master provides you with a set of 50 cards called "Warka". Each card has either a figure or a symbol (Number). The cards are printed on a master-sheet or on several sheets. You cut each card individually, until you have 50 cards.

This constitutes your personal cards deck. Nobody else should touch or use this deck. The Master will instruct you to attach one of your photos to one specific card. You can place your photo on this card and xerox it, and later add it to the deck. This card is extremely important, because the whole deck will rotate around it.

Something else: One of the 50 cards must bear your name. Also, you should give yourself a new surname. Nobody should know about your new name; it should remain secret. What we have so far is this:

a-A set of 50 cards, cut and laminated by you.

b-One of the cards has your photo.

c-One of the cards has your real name (First name).

d-One of the cards has your new name. (The one you gave yourself)

Now you start to understand why the Ulema cards are called "Personalized".

673

Question :

OK, would I be able to learn about my future if I use the Ulema Tarot cards?

Answer :

Enough, but not everything. First, you have to remember that if your "Conduit" is not activated, your access to knowledge about your future will be limited.

However, you will be able to learn a lot about some events that are extremely important in your life, and especially about "New happenings or things to happen" that can influence or alter your luck, success, and other vital matters.

The cards will give you some guidance and orientation.

The cards will give you dates and a warning related to each separate event to occur in the future; event(s) detected by your cards.

Something else you should know: If you attach the photo of another person to one of the cards, you could possibly discover lots of things about that person.

However, you will not able to influence his/her mind, or bring a major change to his/her life, unless some criteria are met.

*** *** ***

Question:

Is there a particular book on the Anunnaki-Ulema Tarot? If yes, who wrote it? Is it about the past, present or the future?

What did the Ulema say about the future?

Is it already written for us?

Can we change our future?

Answer:

Note: The following answer is taken from our Tarot Book

Ulema Mordachai ben Zvi said, "Bakht (Ulema Tarot) has been practiced by the Ulema Anunnaki for thousands of years.

It is totally unknown in the Western hemisphere.

Essentially, Bakht is based upon knowledge received from the early remnants of the Anna.Ki, also called Anu.Na.Ki, an extra-terrestrial race which landed on Earth hundreds of thousands of years ago.

Very few seers and mystics outside the circle of the Ulema Anunnaki penetrated the secrets of the Bakht. They were the elite of the priests of Ra, the early Sinhar Khaldi (Early Chaldean priests/astrologers/astronomers), the Tahar (Early Phoenician

674

Purification priests), and the Rouhaniyiin, known in the West as the alchemists/Kabalists.

In the whole world today, there are no more 700 persons who practice the Bakht, and they are called Ba-khaat or Bakhaati. Two hundred of them are the supreme enlightened masters, called the Mounawariin.

The other five hundred masters are simply called Ulema Anunnaki. The teachers of the Ba-khaat or Bakhaati are called Tahiriim and the Ulema refer to them as the Baal-Shamroutiim.

The earliest manuscript on Bakht appeared in Phoenicia, circa 7,500 B.C., and it was written in Ana'kh. A later version in Anakh-Pro-Ugaritic appeared three thousand years later.

A third version written in the early Phoenician-Byblos script appeared in Byblos and Tyre. There are also two versions in Akkadian and the Old Babylonian language, that are assumed to be lost. Around 65 A.D., a new version in Arabic appeared in the Arabian Peninsula, and Persia, and it was called "Firasa".

Around 685 A.D., a revised edition appeared in Damascus, Syria. It was said that, from this Syrian edition, the hand-written manuscript "Ilmu Al Donia" (Science or Knowledge of the Universe) was derived.

This manuscript included chapters on Arwah (Spirits and non-human entities), Djins, and Afrit.

Around 1365 A.D., a book titled "Shams Al Maaref Al Koubra" appeared in Cairo and Damascus, based upon two books "Al Bakht: Dirasat Al Moustakbal", and "Ilmu Al Donia"."

Maximillien de Lafayette said, "The future is neither concealed, nor hidden, because the future has already happened in a zone or Zamania that exists very close to the zone or sphere of existence, that you already live in.

In other words, the past, present and future are timelines that exist and run concurrently, called Istimraar."

Does this mean that every event is constantly being repeated indefinitely in different worlds, dimensions and times?

Yes, it is, according to mainstream science and quantum physics – based upon the theory of the "Ever expanding universe." –

And according to the Ulema Anunnaki, people (Humans and other life-forms) live simultaneously on different Woujoud and Zaman.

Most certainly, they might look different, physically and bio-organically, because of the atmospheric and climate conditions,

675

and they could or would act differently —convergent or divergent— according to the level of their awareness and intelligence in different worlds.

Consequently, you can live a past on this Earth and remember very well past events in your life, and in the same time, you remain unaware of your other existences, other pasts and lives in different worlds.

Henceforth, you must learn what has happened or what is currently happening to you, or to your other copies, either on different planets and habitats, or in higher dimensions.

Now, you begin to know that each one of us has infinite copies of ourselves, as well as, many separate and independent past(s).

Knowing the future and revisiting your past in different dimensions and previous lives is a pre-requisite for reading your Bakht Haya.Ti (Linear Future), and Moustakbal Daa-em (Multidimensional Future).

There are some events in your past that greatly influence the course of your life, and part of your future. The situation gets a little bit tricky, when you are not fully aware of major events, and decisions you have made in your Moustakbal Daa-em, because few of us are capable of visiting our past(s) in different dimensions.

The future in its two forms, linear and multidimensional is what really constitutes your true future.

However, it is not absolutely necessary to learn about all the phases of your past, and what your Double or your other copies in different time-space zones have done in the past, and/or are currently doing in a zone beyond Earth.

If you believe that life continues after death, then it becomes necessary to learn about your Double, and other bio-organic and etheric copies of yourself that currently exist in other worlds.

On Earth, in this world, we have one single future. The learned Ulema referred to it as Al Maktoob, meaning what was written. This concept has created an intellectual, philosophical and religious controversy, even an outrage, for all those who have rejected the idea that a Supreme Creator has already imposed upon us, a future, the moment we were born; a future that controls our destiny and our life, for ever!

In other words, what it is already written in the front-page of our life, dictates the magnitude, level and development of our future successes, failures, kind of job or profession reserved for us, our health conditions, finances, families, how good or how bad our

676

children will be in the future, sort and amount of joy and pain we will feel in the forthcoming years of our lives, so on...

Others have felt that the Al Maktoob makes us slaves of the Creator, because our destiny has been decided upon, without our knowledge, consent and will.

If this is the case, then our life has no purpose at all, and no matter how hard we try to reach a higher level of spirituality and awareness, we will always fail because, it was written in the book of our future, that we have no choice, no freedom to choose and above all, it was already written, that our efforts in this context were not to bear fruit. Thus, it becomes impossible for any of us to change our future, and/or re-write what it is already written and decided upon, in the book of life and destiny.

Consequently, learning about our Bakht (Future) would not serve any purpose, except to make us feel trapped in this life. This is what many people, and some of the early Gnostics have felt about this unpleasant and horrible scenario. But the Ulema Anunnaki have a different scenario for all of us; a pleasant and a happy one. Humans have retained their freedom of choice, thus, they are accountable for all their actions, deeds, intentions and thoughts.

They have the right and the freedom to choose, select and carry on their own plans. And in the process of doing so, they remain the masters of their own destiny, and solely responsible for their decisions, and the consequences of these decisions.

Their mental faculties and degree of their creativity are shaped by, and decided upon by many factors, such as the Conduit, the Jabas, and the Fikr.

But their destiny and future remain unconditioned by the DNA, the Conduit and other genetic "ingredients" fashioned by the Anunnaki. The ethical-moral-spiritual endeavors and aspects of their physical and non-physical structures remain under their personal control.

This part of their future can be learned about and read by using the Bakht. In addition, humans' present and future decisions and actions, and the consequences of their deeds and intentions could be altered or changed, according to their free will and personal choices.

All these decisions, deeds, intentions, consequences, and effects are part of one single future, which can be changed at will.

But the remaining part of their future which is conditioned by the genetic formula of the Anunnaki cannot be changed, unless the Conduit is fully activated

Reading the Bakht, guides you in this direction, and explains to you what part of your future can be changed, and what part of your future will remain intact.

This, applies exclusively to your future on Earth; your Erdi future.

So, are we trapped in this life?

Are we at the mercy of the Anunnaki?

Is our life, destiny and future already decided upon, by the Anunnaki who created us by using multiple genetic techniques and experiments?

Do we have the power, the choice and the freedom to change our future?

If so, is it the whole future or part of it?

You will find the answers to these questions while you are reading your Bakht. And step by step, you will learn what is going to happen to you in this life, in the present, in the near future, and in the distant future, simply because your present and future exist simultaneously as you read your Bakht.

In addition, when you consult the Ulema Anunnaki Tarot on different subjects and matters of concern, the cards will tell you what you should do and consider, and what you should avoid. It will become crystal clear, and future events will be displayed right before your eyes.

You have to remember that the Ulema Anunnaki Tarot is a reading of many of your futures; one on Earth, and the others in different zones of times and spaces.

As you progress in this field of Ulema Tarot, and as you begin to learn more about other dimensions, and copies of yourself in other worlds, your mind will start to understand gradually how things work in different dimensions, and particularly how you and part of your multidimensional futures are projected.

*** *** ***

On inner bio-rhythm, bad luck, good luck & Anunnaki

Questions asked by Salem Turbi, Tunisia.

678

Question: Is it true what some mediums have said that some people are conditioned by a bio-rhythm that creates good luck and bad luck?

If so, can we change this rhythm and become luckier, if we were not so lucky in the first place? Was this rhythm created by the Anunnaki when they manipulated our DNA?

Answer:

"Zara-Du", also called "Macari," and "Sabata," is a term for what it is known in Anunnaki-Ulema literature as the "17 Lucky Years of Your Life." Zaradu is very important metaphysical but also "Physical knowledge" that the Anunnaki-Ulema have learned, and kept shrouded in secrecy for thousands of years, fearing that bad/immoral persons might learn and use to it to influence others, and selfishly alter the course of history.

It was revealed to the honorable Ulema that every single human being on planet Earth will have during his/her life, a lucky period extending through 17 consecutive, uninterrupted years.

During those years (Called Mah-Zu-Zah) the doors of luck, fortune and development at many levels will open up, and opportunities for extraordinary success shall be freely given to her/him.

This is how the phrase "the 17 Lucky Years of Your Life" came to exist. And for this period of 17 years, there is a calendar, which is well structured, and divided into a sequence of 77 by 7.

This brings us to the Anunnaki-Ulema magical esoteric number of 777, considered to be the Alpha and Omega of all knowledge and "Tana-Wur", which means enlightenment, similar to the Bodhisattva.

At one point during these lucky years, a person will acquire two extraordinary faculties:

    a- Rou'h Ya

    b- Firasa (Fi raa-Saa).

These two faculties will positively influence his/her life and guide him/her effortlessly towards reaching the highest level of mental and physical strength, as well success in business and a variety of endeavors.

Ulema-Anunnaki, Alain "Allan" Cardec.

Examples of these endeavors for instance, are an astonishing power or capability of producing, writing or composing in an exceptionally prolific manner. It also encompasses the ability to learn many languages in next to no time, and read manuscripts written in secret languages, such as the first secret and hidden alphabet (Characters) of the Hindu language.

Applied in modern times, reading the secret symbols and alphabets become forecasting events and predicting the rise and fall of world's markets. It was also said, that this 17 year period can alter a DNA sequence, thus preventing accelerated aging, and the deterioration of human cells.

One of the last Anunnaki-Ulema Mounawariin (Enlightened Ones) known to have discovered the secret of the 17 lucky years was Alan Cardec "Allan Cardec" (October 3, 1804- March 31, 1869). Cardec's real name was Hippolyte Léon Denizard Rivail. And his Ulema name was Asha-Kar-Da-Ki. His mentor was the legendary Johann Heinrich Pestalozzi, also known as "Mirdach Kadoshi Sirah" in the Anunnaki-Ulema circle. His incarnated guiding master (Second high level of Anunnaki-Ulema) was Al Zafiru, called Sefiro or Zefiro in mediumship and spiritism literature. In fact, the word or term "Spiritism" was coined by Cardec.

He was the first to use it and explain its application during a contact with a higher entity and other rapports with dead people (Trapped deceased persons) who asked for his help. Sometimes, it was the other way around; Cardec asked for their guidance on matters related to life after death, and the realm of the next life.

Master Cardec was the father of the French movement of Spiritism, and communications with entities trapped between the next dimension and Earth's boundaries. They are called "Les retenus", meaning those who were trapped in the afterlife dimension, or more precisely, those who were detained. Cardec was buried at the historical French cemetry "Cimetiere du Pere Lachaise".

The inscription on his tomb stele reads: "Naitre, mourir, renaitre encore et progresser sans cesse, telle est la loi." Translated verbatim: "To be born, to die, to be reborn again, and to progress unceasingly, such is the law."

The inner bio-rhthym and the Anunnaki:

Thousands of years ago, before history was recorded, the Anunnaki created Man to meet their needs. They created us as a work-force to take care of the fields, cultivate the land, and bring them food; this is according to the Akkadian/Sumerian clay tablets. It is very clear.

At that time, when the Anunnaki gods and goddesses (Aruru, Mummu, Ea, Ninna, etc.) created the first prototypes of the quasi-human races, Man did not have all the mental faculties we have today. Later on, 13 new faculties were added to his brain. And everything in the brain was wired and functioned according to a cellular rhythm.

We cannot change this rhythm.

But we can improve on it, and ameliorate its functioning, by acquiring new knowledge, developing a stronger memory, reading, writing, listening to intelligent and well-informed people, getting rid of bad habits, and elevating our being to a higher mental/spiritual level, through introspection, meditation, and refraining from hurting others. Some are born normal, others are born with some mental deficiency, while a few were created as geniuses, like Bach, Mozart, Da Vinci etc., people who astonished us with extraordinary creativity, and unmatched talents.

These talents and mental gifts were already "placed" into their Conduit. Otherwise, how can we explain the astonishing musical compositions of Mozart and other great composers at the age of 4? Yes, we can alter the inner bio-rythm, the Anunnaki installed in us, but we cannot change it completely. The first thing to do is to activate the Conduit.

As far as luck (Good and bad) is concerned, the noble in spirit (Mind, or "Soul" if you want) will be given the opportunities and means to learn how to positively reshape future events in his/her life.

Unfortunately, there are so many good people in the world who are constantly suffering. And we wonder where is the logic? What is the reason for their suffering? Is it true that good people always finish last? Sadly enough, it happens all the time.

We see hard-working nurses (who save lives) struggling to make a living. We see devoted school teachers unable to pay their bills.We see bloody bastards getting richer and richer, whilst honorable, loving and caring people are being kicked out of their homes!! Where is the justice?

The truth I tell you, is that there is no justice on Earth, despite all the good intentions of so many of us, and despite so many good courts' decisions, and decent laws to maintain law and order. The

Ulema taught us that good behavior, a high level of morality, unconditional love, forgiveness and generosity do not guarantee success in life, or secure good luck. Ulema Badri said verbatim: "Your character and good manners are the only things you should keep when you have lost everything in life. To some, this is not enough, for financial security, and some good luck would not hurt.

I agree. So, start developing your brain, activate your Conduit, talk to your inner-self...there you will find the salvation...there you will find a way to change your bad luck into good luck. If your Mind is in harmony with your "Jaba", then, and only then, can you change your inner bio-rhythm, and influence your DNA's metamorphosis."

***   ***   ***

Were dinosaurs created by extraterrestrials?

Question by Matt Hoxtell, Chicago, Illinois, USA.

Question: Were dinosaurs created by extraterrestrials?
Answer:
Not every life-form on Earth was created by the Anunnaki. It is important to remember that when the first expedition of the Anunnaki landed on Earth, our planet was already populated by an amazing variety of living organisms, animals, quasi-human species, the earliest of human-animal forms, synthesized molecules, substances and biological entities. Many of these life-forms were created from cosmic dust.

Some were the result of photosynthesis, and other groups were produced by bacteria and evolution inertia. Worth mentioning here, is that the Anunnaki had no interest or motivation in creating/altering the creation of pre-existing life-forms that were deemed unnecessary or not very essential for starting and/or carrying on their projects on Earth.

The dinosaurs existed on planet Earth, long before the Anunnaki descended to Earth.

The dinosaurs first appeared about 230 million years ago, and their reign lasted over 100 million years. The Anunnaki arrived to Earth circa 449,000 B.C.

Besides, the Anunnaki(any expedition) did not consider the dinosaurs, or remnants of the dinosaurs and similar reptiles, necessary or useful for their plans for two reasons:

- **a**-They lacked mental/intellectual faculties, necessary for understanding the instructions of the Anunnaki;
- **b**-Their enormous size.

***   ***   ***

The lost continent of MU's connection with the Anunnaki

Question by Ismail Kemal Ciftcioglu, Turkey.

Question: This is the most important question for me. In any of the books I read, I haven't come across any information about the lost continent of MU's connection with the Anunnaki. I assume you know lots of things about it. According to James Churchward's books, MU was even older than Atlantis and home to the human civilization. Humans migrated from MU all over the world. But we know that the Anunnaki were in Mesopotamia. So what about it? What can you tell me about the lost continent of MU?

Answer:

I. Introduction/Mythological backgound:

According to legend and esoteric myth, Mu was a large continent of an advanced civilization. It sank beneath the ocean many thousands of years ago.

The story or Myth of Mu appeared for the first time in the 19th century, thanks to the writings of Augustus Le Plongeon (1825-1908), who claimed that the survivors of Mu went to the Americas and established the Mayan Empire.

Then, in the first half of the 20th century, the prolific writer and visionary extraordinaire James Churchward popularized the story of Mu in a series of books he wrote: "The Children of Mu" published in 1931; "The Lost Continent of Mu" published in 1933, and "The Sacred Symbols of Mu", published in 1935.

And in the 1930's, Kamal Atatürk (Baba Kamal) then leader of Turkey, your majestic country, generously funded academic and scientific research on Mu.

684

The great Turkish leader thought that perhaps he would be able to establish a direct link or some sort of connection betweek Turkey and the world's first civilizations that could include the Aztec, and the Maya. Unfortunately, all attempts to prove the existence of MU failed.

II. Scientific/geological facts:

First of all, you have to remember that the Anunnaki were not only in Mesopotamia.

The first expedition of the Anunnaki to Earth, occurred some 449,000 years ago.

They landed in the Near East (Phoenicia) and explored the territories of Madagascar, Brazil, Central Africa, Turkey (Anatolia) etc., and finally they established their kingdom in Mesopotamia. The continent of MU was already in existence, long, long before the Mesopotamian civilization.

And Atlantis was the bridge between the remnants of Mu, the pre-historic civilization of Crete, Phoenicia(Modern day Lebanon), Ugarit, Arwad, Egypt, Mesopotamia, the lands of the Hittites in Anatolia, and Cyprus.

Mu was established some 14,000 to 20,000 years ago, and its civilization was destroyed some 9,500 to 10,000 years ago, but MU itself did not "sink" under the ocean, as many have claimed, simply because scientifically speaking, continents do not sink; they might shift, drift, and break into two, three or several parts, but this is a very very long geolocial process that takes hundreds of millions of years.

Except for Pangaea, history, archeology, anthropology and oceanography tell us that continents have maintained their original position.

Thus, for the continent of MU to change its original position as a continent, or to sink to the bottom of the ocean, these events and changes should have occurred at the time Pangaea shifted some 250 millions years ago, or even during the shift of Pannotia, that was formed on Earth some 600 million years ago, or Rodinia (formed some 1.2 billion years ago) which has totally shifted some 750 million years ago.

Yet once again, geography, natural history, oceanography, anthropology, the study of fossils, and the history of comparative civilizations have not provided any proof that a new shift has ever occurred after those dates.

Thus, the idea that an early advanced civilization existed hundreds of millions of years ago on a vanished continent is pure fantasy, ridiculed by science.

In conclusion, the civilization of MU must have existed around 14,000 to 20,000 years ago, and during that period, no continent has ever shifted. Therefore, the sinking of MU to the bottom of the ocean is an impossibility.

III. Anunnaki-Ulema views:

Baalbeck, one of the earliest cities/colonies of the Anunnaki on Earth.

Ulema have suggested that MU and Atlantis were one and the same; a community, instead of a continent. This makes it more logical to assume that a migration of a community to another part of the world, including Baalbeck, Tyre, Sidon, Turkey, Anatolia, the Near East/the Middle East could have occurred.

In addition, this migration could also explain the sudden emergence of an advanced civilization that we know little about.

The early community of Mu or Atlantis or both, since they were considered epistemologically and anthropologically the same, had a highly advanced civilization and well-structured societies, "implanted" by an extraterrestrial race.

686

And the only extraterrestrial race that left some historical and mythological documents and records on Earth were the Anunnaki. This is the only and most logical link we can attach to the people of MU/Atlantis.

Anunnaki-Ulema Sadek ben Alia Al Bakri stated verbatim: "The Anunnaki had a direct contact with those people, and taught them science, technology, language, and the use of advanced learning techniques and tools. They went to the Near/Middle East and established their new colonies, always under the supervision of the Anunnaki."

Ulema Sharif Al Takki Al Zubyani (1797-1877) stated that Mu did exist some 50,000 years ago according to the Ulemite calendar (14,000-20,000 years in our calendar).

He added that the original name of Mu was Mari, and it was inhabited by people who were very advanced in "Ilm Al Falak", meaning space science. An enormous explosion happened on the continent, caused by the reflection of light and rays emitted by a gigantic "Miraya", which means mirrors, triggered by a huge volcano eruption.

Coincidentally or strangely enough, the Anunnaki and Ulemite literature referred to the Miraya as a galactic tool used to receive and emit cosmic messages, a sort of beam (Possibly atomic or laser), as well as to record and decode events from the past, the present and the future. Al Zubyani added: "Those mirrors were also used as weapons, and if they are not handled properly, they could destroy a whole country."

Those who know Arabic, including the archaic dialect of the Arab Peninsula, and Ana'kh will find out that there is a very close relation (Perhaps linguistically only) between the Name Mari and the Arabic, pre-Islamic word Mir'aat (Mir'-aat and Miraya) which means in both languages (Ana'kh and Arabic) mirror.

Strangely enough, the French word "Miroir" and the English word mirror are derived directly from the Ana'kh (Anunnaki language) Miraya. So here we have a million year old Anunnaki word "Miraya", a 50,000 year old name "Mari", a 7,000 year old Ulemite word "Mirra-ya", and a 5,000 year old Arabic word Miraya! Any connection?

IV. So, what did we learn from all this?
We have learned the following:

- The continent of MU did not sink to the bottom of the ocean, because scientifically, continents do not sink.

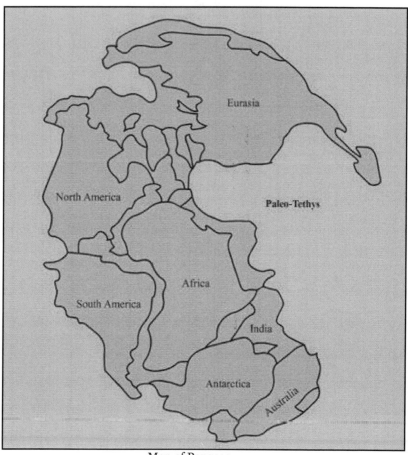

Map of Pangaea.

- 2- Some sort of ecological or geological catastrophe occurred some 9,500 to 10,000 years ago that forced the population of that part of the world to flee and seek refuge somewhere else, probably in the countries I have mentioned earlier. In fact, science has provided evidence of a cosmic catastrophe around 9,500 B.C., and this explains everything.

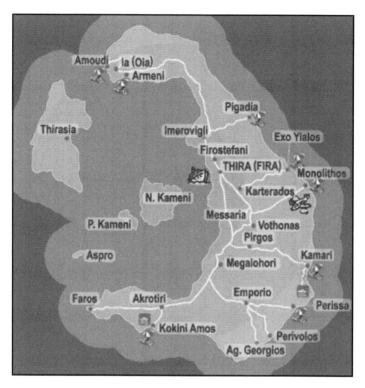

Map of Santorini.
Santorini is a small, circular archipelago of volcanic islands located in the southern Aegean Sea, about 200 km southeast from Greece's mainland.

- 3- Upon their arrival to new countries, a sudden and new civilization appeared in that part of the world, and that explains the "out of nowhere" origin of human civilization, the birth of language, and the acquired knowledge in so many fields, etc.
- 4- In fact, that society was highly advanced, and most certainly influenced and taught by a super non-human extraterrestrial race. This explains the sudden rise of

689

their civilization, societies, communities and cities, in sharp contrast with other "human societies" which were still living in darkness, ignorance and retarded social conditions.

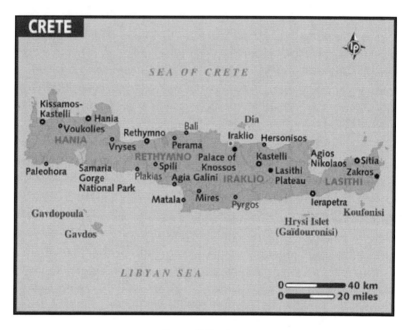

Map of Crete.

- 5- This advanced society, the originator of human civilization did exist and live on and around the areas and lands nearby Santorini-Crete, and neighboring islands, where a geological catastrophe, and a huge volcano eruption were proven by science.

*** *** ***

690

Don't ever underestimate the power of your mind!

Question by anonymous: I can't understand how you could write so many books in such a short time? Do you use some sort of magic or a supernatural power? You know what, some people are spreading rumors that the overwhelming number of your books you wrote were made by a machine and because of this you are a machine.

Answer:

Many, like you, have asked how did I manage to write hundreds of books in a short time, or to be able to speak so many languages, and accomplish multiple tasks simulteneously?

Some have dubbed me superhuman, others have called me nuts, and a few have said that the fact that I have written so many books so in such a short period of time, means that I have got to be a scam. This amuses me a lot, because no supernatural powers or machines are associated with what I do.

I can assure anybody, absolutely anybody can do what I have done, effortlessly if some techniques are learned and utilized.

And these technniques are associated with how you organize your mind. I will try to explain this very simply. Your mind is a wonderful machine composed of Jabas, a collection of pockets or drawers, similar to your computer. When your computer is loaded with temporary internet files, searching, loading and uploading will slow your computer down considerably.

Thus, you have to delete your temporary files, in order to speed up your computer, and have more space on your hard drive. The same thing applies to your mind.

When your Jabas are full with old and unnecessay information, your mind slows down; becoming slow in acquiring, storing, organizing, sorting and analyzing new information. In addition to the clearing (Cleaning, emptying) of your Jabas, you must let your Supersymetric mind work on it's own.

You have to sit, and start talking to yourself. Mind you while you are doing that, your brain is independently listening to you. First of all, you have to convince yourself that you can do it.

Never understimate yourself or your personal powers.

The fact that you do not have – apparently – supernatural powers, does not mean that you cannot accomplish amazing things, even extraordinary deeds by normal standards. Yes you can.! And it is so easy if you start to believe in yourself, in a new and different way.

This opens part of your "Mind Pockets/Jabas." Please refer to the book "The Ulema Anunnaki Forbidden Book of Ramadosh"; as it explains how this can be done.

Basically, your brain is full of junk and storage you do not need. So, as a first step, you have to get rid of this junk. It is easy to do. You start by asking yourself, what did you put in your mind, in the past and now, ten years ago and today?

This exersize is good, simply because you begin to inquire about what you have already learned in your life. It is as if you are probing your own brain, confidentially in the privacy and comfort of your own space .

*** *** ***

Scanning brilliant minds to create a "Super-Baby"!

Question by Akram Jibril, UAE.

Question: I am not sure who has said aliens can scan our brain and create a new species of babies for their hybrid program. Is it true? Can they do that? And how it is done?

Answer:
Ulema Oppenheimer and Ulema Govinda commented on "Mind Scanning" and duplicating-multiplying brains' potentials:

From their Kira'at, verbatim: Scanning your brain and body to create a new copy of "You" for a new-born baby.

They scan you, mind and body, and place the scan in an "Aetra" mold to recreate you and duplicate you; they can make as many copies as they want. On the top of the "Scan Mold", there is a transparent cover "Kha-Tar" that looks like fiberglass.

As soon as the scan process begins, the Khatar starts to work, meaning, it starts to reshape itself into a human form, the physical form of your body in its miniscule details.

So what we have here, is "you" imprinted three dimensionally on a sheet of a fiberglass. This is the "Physical Scan". What is more facinating, is the "Kha-tra-Fikr", which is the "Mental Scan" of

692

your brains, all your thoughts, feelings, beliefs, memories and intentions.

At the end, they either mix the physical scan with the mental scan to recreate a copy of you, or install your brain into another body (Not Yours), or attached your body to the brain of another scanned person.

Now, imagine if they keep on - indefinitely - duplicating and reduplicating these scans, physically and mentally, how many millions of new hybrid people would be created? More than you can count!!

In some instances, at birth, some of them have already implanted scanned brains into the brain/mind of new born babies. The baby is 2 hours old, but his/her memory is 50 years old.

The new born's mind is almost virgin and clean like a dry sponge, but with their genetic manipulation, they can feed this "virgin mind" with the contents of brilliant minds they have scanned for hundreds of years.

So what we have here is a superbaby, an infant who is more intelligent than all the geniuses on Earth, combined!

*** *** ***

Is the Ulema-Anunnaki group administered by men or a matriarch woman?

Question by Rita Montiel, Madrid, Spain.

Question: Is the Ulema-Anunnaki group administered by men or a matriarch woman as I have heard?

Answer:
No, the Ulema are not exclusively all men. In fact, the head of one Ma'had (Center/Institute) is Umdasturia; a magnificent woman. And her name is quite interesting and revealing.

Those who know Turkish, Arabic, Farsi, and some ancient Middle Eastern languages will be able to know what her name means. Well, Um means mother, and Dasturia means the law, or the constitution of the Ulema's assembly.

By the way, the assembly is called Majlas.

In the eye of Baal Shamroot and Ameliku (the great supreme Sinhars of the Anunnaki), even though men and women are equal, women remain far more superior to men.

Women are the first and exclusive source of Man's life and existence in the known universe. Women are the first cell and the first molecule of the life of all men. The earliest Akkadian-Babylonian- Sumerian tablets tell us that the early women on Earth, the offspring of the Anunnaki and Igigi did not need men's sperm to fertilize their eggs and give birth to babies.

Women-goddesses were self-reproductive, and could give birth to babies without having intercourse with a man. But they lost this capability, by constantly interbreeding with Earth's men and continuously engaging in sexual acts with Earth's "creatures". According to the Akkadian-Sumerian tablets, at the beginning of time, the second most powerful person in the universe was a woman goddess - creator of the universe, and of men.

She was called Tiamat. But Tiamat was dethroned and killed by a male god known as Marduk. The male scribes and the kings needed to restore the "Authority of Man" over everything, thus they created the myth of Marduk and justified the reason for his killing Tiamat.

Marduk fighting the dragon Tiamat.

Marduk fighting the dragon Tiamat, and putting an end to her major influence on the affairs of the universe, the state and Man. By doing so, Marduk became the absolute and most powerful god of the Anunnaki, the Igigi, and Babylon.

Marduk chasing and fighting Tiamat.

Eventually, Marduk will slaughter Tiamat, and from parts of her body, Marduk will create the universe, according to the Akkadian-Babylonian tablets.

***   ***   ***

The relationship between our mind, body and cellular memory?

Question by Tony Rossi, Bocan Raton, Florida.

Question: What is the relationship between our mind, body and cellular memory?
Answer:

"Do you think you are seeing yourself as a physical reality when you in a mirror? Think again. Some highly evolved people extend to the outside perimeter of their physical body..." said Ulema Li.
Anunnaki Ulema ben Yacob stated: "You too, can do this...you can transcend the physical boundaries of your body. There are two presences/substances that made you what and who you are:

- **a**-You as a person;
- **b**-You as a human being.

The human being is the physical form of yourself.
The "Person" is what constitutes everything about yourself.
There are lots of things (Matter and Mind) about you that are somewhere you are not aware of. Part of you exists in a tree, in a river, in a thought, in a memory cell, in a beautiful song, in a dream, in another country, and way beyond; in dimensions that most recently were elaborated on, by quantum physics' leading thinkers and pioneers.
You have to find out everything that is part of you, in order to reach extraordinary standards of intelligence, and unmatched success at multiple levels.
Part of your "Extraordinary Intelligence" rotates around cellular memory.
Do you know where your cellular memory is?
Is it in your physical body, or in your psyche?
Is it in you "The Person", or in you the "Human Entity"?
And why is cellular memory so important to be concerned about?
It is important, because that memory is everything you have experienced and learned from, as well as the stimulus and conditioner of your judgment, analysis and the understanding of the world you live in.
But it is not perfect because it is not complete.
You have to tap into both segments of yourself, the physical body that takes you from your home to your office, and the "Person" that transports you from a limited physical sphere of knowledge to the ultimate and highest zone of awareness, that is so close to you, close to your physical body.
There, you will find the ultimate truth about yourself, how much information and knowledge you have stored within you before you were born, after you were born, and what you are going to be once you are no longer here.

You are too important to be confined in 150 pounds, 190 pounds, 200 pounds, 5 feet, or 6 feet 11. You are much bigger and denser than you think. So tap into the missing part of yourself. It is so enjoyable, so remunerating, so profitable, and so powerful.

Visit yourself iin other dimensions, rediscover the zone you that are not fully aware of exists. It belongs to you, and to you alone.

Once there, you will reinforce your physical and mental powers and energies.

The denser the body of your other person is, the healthier you become. That other person you may call whatever you want: a guardian, an angel, an etheric presence, your double. All are the very same thing. People who have succeeded in blending with the other part of themselves that extends beyond and outside their physical mass of muscles, feet, hands and lungs, have accomplished extraordinary things. You too, you can do it. It just requires a certain degree of belief, practice and determination.

Where is this other part of me, you might ask?

It is so close to your physical body, and wherever you go, it goes with you, it does not follow you, but accompany you. You have to make a deal with it.

You have to reach some sort of agreement with it. An agreement to chat together, to meet somewhere, and go from there.

If you don't converse with your own mind, you will never work out/exercize the mental muscles in your brain, and if you do not increase the size and strength of your mental muscles, your intellect will shrink.

*** *** ***

Anunnaki-Phoenician Chavad-nitrin and the immortality of the gods

Question by Georges Haddad, Michigan.

Question: I am originally from Byblos (Jbeil) in Lebanon, and we Lebanese are descendants of the Crusaders who learned some of the secrets of the Anunnaki in Lebanon and Jerusalem. I have heard that my ancestors the Phoenicians have used a product similar to athletes' steroids. This product I was told was also used by the Egyptian Pharaohs. Could you please tell me more about it? Many thanks.

Roman pillars leading up to the temple of Balaat Gebal, in
Byblos, Phoenicia, where the Chavad-nitrin was used by the
priests of Baal.

Answer:
Correct, that product was called "Chavad-nitrin", after an ancient
Phoenician embalming process, learned from Byblos and Arwad
Anunnaki remnants, using Mah'rit (Maha-reet), a secret
substance considered to be humanity's first formula for steroids,
mixed with barks from the cedars of Phoenicia. It was frequently
used by athletes in Ugarit, Amrit, and Arwad.

From Chavad-nitrin, derived the Greek word Natron or Natrin, a
substance used in the embalming process.

Because of the reported physical endurance and legendary
longevity it produced, the Egyptians equated the words Neter,
Netjer and Netjet with the immortality of the gods.

According to Egyptian tradition, the first human being to be
mummified was the god Osiris, whose body floated down the
Nile in a wooden casket, and washed ashore at Byblos (Your
hometown) in Phoenicia.

God Osiris.

Ruins of the ancient city of Ugarit.

For this reason, Byblos was a sacred region to Osiris, to his cult, and to the Egyptians. This explains the reason why the Egyptians have called Byblos the land of the god Osiris; Ta Netjer.

*** *** ***

Hidden entrances to other worlds and dimensions, right here on Earth

Question by Isabelle Franchot, and Emile Farkas, Beverly Hills, California.

Question: Do UFOs and extraterrestrials use galactic entrances and space-time corridors to enter and exit our world? And how many are there? Are they visible to the naked eye?
Answer:
There are several unseen, hidden, and undetectable entrances to three different dimensions beyond ours:
    a-   Entrance(s) to the after-life (After death);

b- Entrances to the fourth dimension;
c- Entrance(s) to the parallel dimension (Ba'ab)

Each dimension (Zone) is a totally different world in structure, substance, composition, and boundaries. Some are extremely close to us. Closer than you might think.
I will explain:

a-Entrance to the after-life:
This is called life after death. And it is exactly what you might think. The realm of deceased people. Only dead people enter this zone, and they never return. The Babylonians called it "The Land of no Return".
It was mentioned in their epics. In some passages, it was called Kur in Akkadian. On their way into that dimension, deceased people encounter all sorts of entities, benevolent and malevolent. This is not my personal theory. I did not invent such a story. This was mentioned thousands of years ago in the Egyptian Book of the Dead, in the Tibetan "Bardo Todol", and many other texts from various ancient cultures.

b-Entrance to the fourth dimension:
This is a zone that a person can enter in two manners, mentally and physically.
This zone could have entrances everywhere; in your bedroom, in a valley, in a building corridor, absolutely everywhere and anywhere. And this includes the oceans, the bottom of the sea, in thin air, and right inside your home doors. Many people have been sucked-up, absorbed by its "Pulling Force" (Magnetic field) in a split second.
 Once they are attracted or pulled in by these entrances, they zoom inside the entrance at incredible speed.
For incomprehensible reasons, these entrances could open up and close at anytime, any moment. And as soon as a person or an object is swallowed up by the current (Flux-Influx) of those entrances, the entrance shut's its opening (Overture) in on itself.
Those kinds of entrances are situated everywhere in our world. There is vast literature on people, vehicles, animals who have vanished into thin air, in a split second. Highly advanced alien races know exactly where the locations of these entrances are, as well as their currents and times of opening and closing.

They have used these entrances as corridors and passages for millions of years.

Many of their spaceships have navigated through these channels. Some Ulema have explained the passages of these entrances as a net of time and space bending on itself, and thus reducing distances and time between points and destinations.

Sometimes, UFOs sharp angular turns and zigzag pattern indicate where these entrances are located in the skies. This is why Ulema have said that UFOS do not fly, they jump. Meaning, they jump from one pocket to another.

In other words, these pockets are nothing more than entrances to a higher dimension; the fourth dimension.

I am absolutely sure that several scientists working on classified outer-space programs (sponsored by some governments) have already worked on projects related to fourth dimensional entrances. Some might have succeeded. And I will rest my case here, and keep my mouth shut!

It was reported in close circles, that a couple living somewhere in the United States had a nightmarish experience, when the nanny of their two lovely children vanished into thin air, in a fraction of a second in their kitchen, while opening a can of concentrated milk; never to be found again.

The military police were called in to investigate. Two days later, the "case was closed" and the couple were order to evacuate their home. You have every right to doubt my words.

To an alert mind, these sorts of stories are science fiction. From the bottom of my heart, I do not wish to see you in a similar situation, because this could happen to all of us.

A highly regarded scientist told me once that the disappearance of the nanny was never considered a "closed case". He said that a few hours after this tragic and frightening experience happened, one parapsychologist and one quantum physics expert were taken to the couple's home to conduct further investigations.

They searched the whole house, and after three laborious hours, found the entrance to the fourth dimension, located on the right side of the kitchen sink. They sealed the kitchen area, and encircled the entrance "Door" of the threatening dimension with colored fiberglass sheets. From these types of openings, entities, substances, other life-forms, gravity and reverse-gravity can also leak into our world from that fourth dimension.

702

3-Entrance to the parallel dimension:

I will not elaborate on this dimension, because I have written on this subject ad infinitum in many of my previous books. But worth mentioning here, is that parallel dimensions are not the product of fantasy or science fiction. Some of the world's most admired scientists and professors teaching quantum physics have already explained what a parallel dimension is, and/ or how multiple dimensions work.

According to their most recent findings and theories, there are 11 known parallel dimensions in the universe.

*** *** ***

Anunnaki immaturity, emotional control, jealousy, sin?

Questions by Reverend Nancy Santos.

Question: Have the Anunnaki matured away from their immaturity in emotional control, past stories of jealousy, power, etc., sin?

Answer:

On what base(s) or ground, have you created this opinion of yours? How did you know about Anunnaki's maturity or immaturity? Jealousy, sin, etc.? The only and very few authentic and authoritative references (Historical, chronological, linguistic, religious, epistemological, etymological, artistic, archeological, anthropological, and of course cosmological) on the Anunnaki are found in:

- **1-The Akkadian clay tablets texts:**

The Akkadian clay tablets texts, (Nineveh Library of Ashur-ba-Nipal) which millions of readers in the West cannot read. And almost 99% of those who read about ufology and related topics have based their opinions about the Anunnaki (and also other aliens as well), on personal interpretations of very crafty authors with fabulous and phantasmagorical theories that defy logic and common sense.

Unless you know Akkadian, Old Babylonian, Ugaritic, Hittite, Assyrian, and Phoenician languages, you cannot form any opinion on the Anunnaki. However, you can shape a pretty clear idea about the Anunnaki, by reading the works and translations

703

of the early Assyriologists and eminent linguists, who deciphered and translated the Akkadian cuneiform tablets in the 19th and early 20th centuries. Unfortunately, very few readers in the West are interested in these literary and academic publications, because they are not fun – or so they think!

They would rather prefer to read paperback books, and stories by contemporary authors who have managed to somehow mesmerize the public with fabulous stories and extraordinary interpretations, which is why their books have become bestsellers, whilst the serious and well-researched books on the history and civilization of Mesopotamia, Babylon, Sumer, Assyria, Chaldea, Akkad, Ugarit, and Anunnaki are largely ignored and forgotten under a heavy layer of dust in college libraries, and in the archives of rarely visited museums.

But I have some good news for you.

In many works by archeologists, historians, linguists and museum curators (From the early 1810 to the mid 20th century), you can find translations of Akkadian and Old Babylonian texts, referring to how and why the Sumerians depicted the Anunnaki as they did. Please read the serious books written by acclaimed scholars, and not the third rate novels, commercial essays, paperbacks, and idiotic blogs on the Internet!!

In those translations by academicians and noted historians, you will find plenty of stories about the emotions, feelings, and the way of life of the Anunnaki, as depicted by Babylonian scribes and writers in the Akkadian language, and proto-Babylonian.

These stories encompass all sorts of dramas and soap operas, like gods raping women, Anunnaki Sinhars (Leaders) fighting each other, an Anunnaki god who planned the destruction of the human race; Anunnaki goddesses with extreme anger and legendary jealousy, so on. But bear in mind, those Anunnaki stories came from the mouth of fabulous story-tellers in Sumer. And this was intentional on their part.

They wanted to portray the Anunnaki as divine-human, so at least they could share some common and similar traits with them. The Greeks did the very same thing.

Some of their deities were jealous, ferocious, malicious and yes, some were rapists and sexual predators!!

Something else you should remember:

The Anunnaki who descended to Earth (Sumer, Phoenicia, Turkey) are quite different from the Anunnaki who were, and still are in Nibiru!

Earth's Anunnaki had to look in some way, somehow not very much different from humans, otherwise the Babylonians would have not tried to identify and associate their legendary kings with the Anunnaki kings.

- **2-The Bible:**

I will be brief.

The Old Testament offered contradicting, convergent and divergent portrayals of the Anunnaki, usually referred to as Rephaim, Anakim, Nephilim, B'nai Elohim, so on.

Don't count on these Biblical accounts. The early Hebrew scribes borrowed their major Biblical stories from the myths and religions of Babylon, Ugarit, Amrit and Phoenicia.

As a matter of fact, Yahweh was Baal-El, the Ugaritic-Phoenician god. And almost all the powerful traits and virtues of Enki and Ea were transferred to the attributes of Jehovah (Yahweh, the god of the Israelites), even Daniel was copied from the Phoenician myth of Danel (Ugarit).

This is a fact.

You can read several translations of this myth as well as numerous Ugaritic texts referring to the early prototypes and characteristics of Yahweh found in the depiction of the Ugaritic deities. Having said that, bear in mind that the Biblical depiction of the Anunnaki in various forms and names is not accurate. In fact, they are hostile, and there are reasons for doing so.

Firstly, Abraham and Moses desperately wanted to establish an identity for their people.

In ancient times, a nation was usually associated with its deities. If their god was strong and all mighty, then they become a powerful and rightful nation.

If, however, you have a bad/weak god, you end up with a bad/weak nation. Secondly, the early Israelites feared the expansion of the Phoenician cults. They were a direct threat to Yahweh, their own god.

The Israelite prophets waged hysterical wars against the gods of Tyre, Sidon, Byblos, Arwad, Ugarit and Amrit.

Consequently, they had to assassinate the character of all other gods, and portray Yahweh as the only, the mightiest and most righteous god of all. Therefore, what you have read in the Bible about the sin, the anger, the jealousy, the vices of the Anunnaki, were written by scribes who had to defend their own interests, authority, the pride of their nation, their raison d'etre, and the status/importance/legitimacy of their god, and above all, to justify the reasons for conquering the lands of their neighbors, and building their new cities on territories taken away from their legitimate owners.

Yes, the Bible is the most colorful propaganda literature in the world."

3- Phoenician and Anatolian texts and archeological finds:

You can learn a lot about the Anunnaki from studying slabs, texts, obelisks and cylinder seals found in Turkey, Arwad, Malta, Cyprus, Ugarit, Amrit, Phoenicia, Armenia (Urartu, Cilicia), Byblos, Batroun, Sidon, Afkah, Amchit and Tyre in Lebanon (Ancient Phoenicia). In addition, there are several myths and poems in Phoenician and Ugaritic that tell us about the traits and characteristics of the Anunnaki.

Worth mentioning here is that none of these archeological finds indicate what you have stated: "Anunnaki immaturity, jealousy, control, etc." On the contrary, the Anatolian and Phoenician texts and slabs offered us a different picture of the Anunnaki, in sharp contrast to the Hebrew depiction of the Anunnaki.

Before passing judgment on the Anunnaki, we should first refer to historical sources, and above all to original texts written in Akkadian/Sumerian, Babylonian and Phoenician.

What you read on the Internet (Usually written by ignorant red necks, self-proclaimed channelers and psychics, and people totally unfamiliar with Middle Eastern and Near Eastern languages) is pure fabrication.

Stick to the historical and linguistic facts!

*** *** ***

The Anunnaki's God: A critical God?

Question by Reverend Nancy Santos.

Question: Are the Anunnaki a Critical God?
No forgiveness, and no exceptions as in an eye for an eye and a tooth for a tooth?
Answer:
The Anunnaki do not have a God.
The God we know (Judeo-Christian-Muslim God) was invented by an Iraqi man called Abraham (Real name Av-Ram, and he was born in Ur in Mesopotamia, modern day Iraq.) And this God called Yahweh or Jehovah by the Hebrews was in fact a replica of the Anunnaki Ea-Enki lords, and later on embellished with a divine caricature borrowed from the Ugaritic-Phoenician pagan god Baal, El.
The concept of God, or one God was reinforced by Moses; a god he met in the bushes! Quite a rendez-vous!
The same God he had a chat with on Mount Sinai, where he received the 10 Commandments! The truth I tell you, Yahweh was modeled after the Anunnaki lords who descended on Iraq, and the Phoenician Baal (Ba'al Hadadd) of Tyre and Ugarit.
Besides, Moses did not need to go all the way up to the top of the mountain to get his Commandments.
They were already available to him in Egypt, while he served as a chief advisor and a military commander to the Pharaoh. The 10 Commandments were in fact 613 Commandments. Almost 80% of these Hebraic Commandments were taken from the Egyptian scriptures and the Egyptian Book of the Dead!!

Some 50 years ago, German and French archeologists found the Famous "Byblos Building Inscriptions" which specifically contained the name of Yahweh as Yaw, and Ya-weh (Phoenician pronunciation) centuries before Moses announced to his people the name of their Hebrew God.
God was created by Man.
However, the Anunnaki have A Maha-Sinhar, also called Gala-Amroot, and Baalshamrout, which means a great lord. He/she is in charge. He is both female and male, the creator/creatrice of all intelligent life-forms on Earth.
On Nibiru and in the galactic infinity, the Maha-Sinhar is a merciful lord. Her/his wisdom is based upon a complete understanding of Donia (The world; the universe). Her/his truth is founded in science; a positive and "friendly" science.
"No exceptions as in an eye for an eye and a tooth for a tooth?" as you have stated, is an alarming truth, because it is part of early

Man's literature. Yes, Nancy, you are right this time, if you associate this phrase with the God we have learned about from the Israelites.

Some of the Anunnaki so-called gods who descended to Earth (Sumer/Assyria) displayed anger, vengeance et al, as depicted by scribes on planet Earth. This primordial depiction gave birth to the character, persona and traits of the Hebrew God who become the God of the Christians and the Muslims.

But...but NOT to the early Gnostic Christians (The Real and first Christians), for they understood that the Judaic God was a vicious, vengeful and aggressive villain-god!

The Anunnaki's God on Earth was a "Critical God" as you have correctly stated.

The Anunnaki so-called God on Nibiru is just the opposite!

This is not a personal attack on Judaism and Christianity and/or Islam. My favorite mentors/teachers were Mordachai ben Zvi and N. ben Yacob. I was raised as a Roman-Catholic and as a Jew. And I have served the Vatican and the Jewish community and media in several roles and capacities.

As to my affiliation with Islam, (I am not a Muslim) I have studied the Koran and Arabic literature for more than 55 years, and I have taught Islamic literature and language for decades, in addition to which I have studied the Sharia, the Fukh, and Islamic laws and procedures for a very long time, and appeared before Islamic courts as an attorney at law; a tradition I became very fond of!

*** *** ***

Benevolent and malevolent Anunnaki gods

Question by Reverend Nancy Santos.

Question: Is there a benevolent and a malevolent faction of Anunnaki Gods?

Answer:

Not in their homeland, and not on their planet!

On Earth, yes!

And on Earth in ancient times, not today.

Ancient stories and inscriptions on clay tablets found in Iraq revealed a great deal of violence, aggression, and malevolence of the Anunnaki gods.

- **a**-The Epic of Gilgamesh,
- **b**-the Descent of Ishtar to Kurnugi (Hell),
- **c**-The Enuma Elish,
- **d**-The exploits of Marduk,
- **e**-The Akkadian epic of creation,
- **f**-The story of the fight between Tiamat and Marduk,
- **g**-The struggle between the Anunnaki lords, Ea, Enki, Anu,
- **h**-The story of the revolt of the Igigi,
- **i**-The story of the rape of an Anunnaki goddess by an Anunnaki god/king,
- **j**-The story of the genetic creation of the first Man by slaughtering an Igigi god,
- **k**-The poems and literature of Babylon (Ishtar, Inanna, Eabani, Enkidu, etc.)

All have revealed the good and bad aspects of the Anunnaki gods on Earth, as written by the Babylonian scribes. But these stories are pure literature, myths, legends, and tales, and exclusively related to Earth's Anunnaki. The truth of these events can only be found within the manuscripts/scrolls of the Anunnaki-Ulema.

*** *** ***

Clairvoyance (Telepathic communication/vision) between members of the same family

Question from his Eminence, Archbishop Frédéric Burcklé von Aarburg. Brussels, Belgium.

Question: Y a-t-il une voyance entre les membres d'une meme famille? (Ce que disent les Mormons). Je pense que nous sommes des récepteurs d'ondes, peut etre plus fortes émanant d'une famille. Mon grand père paternel est décédé au milieu d'une haine familiale énorme, la principale raison en était que notre famille étant Alsacienne, mon grand père se trouva du coté de l'occupant, alors que mon père fut dans la résistance.

Je résidais à l'époque entre Bruxelles et Amsterdam; Je décidais de faire dire une messe pour mon grand père 6 mois après son déces; Bien sur je fis en sorte de calculer quel jour je serais présent pour la dite messe à Bruxelles;

Il se fit que je ne pouvais etre à Bruxelles le jour de la messe; Le soir j'ai téléphoné à Paris et mon père m'a déclaré: Figure toi que je ne sais pourquoi aujourd'hui mes pas m'ont porté à telle Eglise (il n'allait jamais plus à l'Eglise)à 18heures (heure de la messe prévue à Bruxelles) et j'ai prié et allumé un cierge pour mon père (mon grand père)

Il se trouve donc que, ce qui est logique, il fit le devoir que je lui avait mentalement suggéré (c'est mon interprétation)

Translation in brief: Is there clairvoyance (Telepathic communication/vision) between members of the same family?

Answer:
Science has split interpretations on the subject. However, such telepathic communication does occur quite often, especially between siblings and members of the same family, who share a strong affectionate bondage.

This telepathic phenomenon is usually reinforced in cases, when two members of the same family are deeply concerned with one subject and/or a situation that tie(s) them very closely to each other; such occurrences are manifested in cases of death, imminent threat, accentuated anxiety, fear, a deep concern, and an urgent need to reach other.

Clairvoyance rapport and/or mental suggestion can be taught.
It is a matter of:

a-Rapport:
- **1**-Determination of two persons or more who wish to contact each other,
- **2**-Concentration on the same subject or object,
- **3**- Parties' agreeing on contacting each other at a specific time,
- **4**-Parties willingness to be patient;
- **5**-One party to act as a recipient (A receiver),
- **6**-Another party to act as an emitter (Sender) of the message.

- 7-The locale is very important. The parties involved should not be distracted.

b-Message:
The message should be:
- 1-Clear and precise,
- 2-Brief,
- 3-Totally mental, meaning no words are pronounced, no phrases are used. The message is transmitted as a mental image/wave. (Ondulation; ondes)
- 4-Suggested by a single person directed toward one single person. No mass communication is to be considered.
- 5-The sender (Emitter) must be younger than the recipient, except when a message is sent by a female sender, such as mother and sister, NOT a wife or a girlfriend.

"Yes, I agree with you, Your Eminence, your mental suggestion and transmission of your message were effective..."

*** *** ***

On different dimensions and multidimensional beings

Questions by Steven Morello

Question: What dimensions lie beyond the 4th, that we can experience?
Answer:
According to quantum physics, there are eleven dimensions. Up to a few years ago, scientists believed in only 7 dimensions.
And do not forget that the theorist and eminent scientist who advanced the theory of the 11 dimensions had been ridiculed by peers for 11 years! And unfortunately, he also lost one of his teaching positions.
But finally and thankfully he has recently been vindicated.
Yes sir, they ridiculed him and disgraced him for years!

According to the Ulema, there exist far more than 11 dimensions. Steven, I have already answered this question in another section of this book. Never mind, I am glad to give you more information and accommodate your question.

Quantum physics pioneers compared the multiple dimensions of the universe (Multiverse) to strings. And quite correctly added, that the universe was created by collisions of membranes (M theory). And this collision is continuing as we speak. Thus, they concluded that the universe is expanding. Well, the Catholic priest and scientist, Christian Lemaitre said the very same thing 90 years ago.

Einstein reviewed his theory and commented: "Your math is correct, but your physics are lousy!" Einstein was wrong.

Centuries ago, the Ulema have stated (As I have mentioned in my previous books) that the known universe was created by several collisions of bubbles.

In 1961, when I reported this to several scientists and some of my colleagues (authors), they laughed at me and at the Ulema! I didn't mind, because I laughed too.

There is an enormous difference between traditional science, avant-garde quantum physics and Ulema science-metaphysics-metalogic. The Ulema views are based upon science and knowledge gained from the Anunnaki. What they have learned from the Anunnaki Sinhars, remains incomprehensible to most of us. But I can assure you that a few extraordinary scientists strongly believe in the astronomy and cosmogeny of the Anunnaki, and honestly admitted that our mind is incapable of understanding the Anunnaki's highly advanced science and technology. The Anunnaki saw our universe before we were born. And they witnessed the birth of many stars, planets and galaxies!

According to Ulemite literature, the Anunnaki told the Ulema that there are several "Layers" and "Outer-Dimensions" beyond the boundaries of planet Earth. Some are purely mental, others are physical. And even in the "Mental Sphere" you will find multiple spheres and zones, which are extra or para-mental. This applies also to the physical planes, membranes or branes as coined in quantum physics.

Most recently, quantum physics theorists began to admit that within each and every separate molecule, each brane, and each universe, there are multiple universes. But they don't know for sure how these intra-universes were created in one single universe or molecule. Some have advanced the theory, that the inner universe of a global universe (One single molecule) was created by an "Implosion".

Ironically, this is what the Ulema have said centuries ago. We can conclude from the statements of the Ulema, that there are zillions of universes and dimensions beyond our physical world, and these universes are increasing in number, size and mobility. And some are running away from us and from the very fabric of the universe.

This is very convenient to quantum physics pioneers, because it strengthens their theory of "The universe is expanding."

*** *** ***

Question: Do other beings exist in these dimensions?
Answer:
Absolutely. According to quantum physics pioneers and leading theorists in the field, (led by Dr. Michio Kaku) there are even copies of ourselves in other worlds. On the Science Channel in the United States, Dr. Kaku stated that in some universes, Elvis Presley is still alive, Napoleon won the war, and you were never born.

I am pleased and relieved that such a fantastic statement came directly from the mouth of an eminent and highly respected scientist. Just imagine if I had said that to people who hate my guts... how they would react, and how gossipy and vicious would the blogs be, posted on cheap websites on the Internet to ridicule and discredit me.

There is vast literature on this subject, part of it written by eminent scientists, and several other parts produced by New Age ufology writers and "Psychics to the Stars". Take your pick. Some researchers have reported to me, that at least two governments have already catalogued the different categories of aliens and non-alien entities living in different universes.

*** *** ***

Question: Can we ever contact them, and would there be negative repercussions from doing so?
Answer:
Dr. Stephen Hawking said: "It would a very bad idea!"

713

PART 7

UFOs
ALIENS
EXTRATERRESTRIALS

On UFOs

Did the Anunnaki or any other extraterrestrial race give the Nazis any secret and advanced technology to built UFOs?
Did the United States government as we were told capture secret files on German UFOs?

If yes, is it possible that top secret airplanes like the Aurora were secretly built according to German UFOs blueprints?
The Ulema did not answer all these questions. It is very obvious, that the honorable Ulema are not deeply interested in the UFOs as flying machines, despite the fact that they have plenty of amazing information on the subject of UFOs, secret military operations and programs on exotic weapons, and especially alien technology. I remember what Master Gupa once told me: "UFOs are simply a piece of metal. What we are interested in is the place and role of Man on the galactic landscape, and the future of humanity."
Briefly, Master Oppenheimer answered one question, and I am herewith reproducing his answer. However, because the subject of Nazi UFOs has captured the imagination and wild interest of the public, I took the liberty to provide you with an in-depth research and findings summary on the topic, following the Master's reply.

Answer of Master Oppenheimer:
1. The Anunnaki never cooperated with the Nazi on any military project.
2. In fact, the Anunnaki never returned to Earth.
3. The Anunnaki are your creators and your makers. They don't need to negotiate with the human beings; they don't interfere in your daily affairs; they do not influence or control governments; and they do not create wars on Earth.
4. The Anunnaki have no interest in communicating with the human race. And for this reason, people of the Earth should understand that no harm will ever come from the Anunnaki.

5. However, they will return to Earth in 2022 to put an end to all the troubles, the injustice, the cruelty, the violence, the greed and destructive military and governments' unjustified acts of war and vicious expansionism.
6. In part, they feel responsible for the atrocious behavior of the human race, because they have created the mankind according to their specifications.
7. These specifications were implanted in your genes, DNA, and "Naphsiya" (Mind/First source of energy).
8. Having said that, you should realize by now, that the Anunnaki do not, and did not encourage any form of violence on Earth.
9. Military aircrafts are usually designed as a tool of war. Thus, aircrafts, or UFOs, or any other type of military flying machines are considered tools of violence, aggression and destruction.
10. However, there is a non-human race, you may call it extraterrestrial (In origin) if you wish, that had collaborated with an occult group in Germany, and provided its leaders with vital information on how to construct formidable spaceships that defy human logic, and the laws of physics, as understood by mankind.
11. This German occult group fell into the hands of some German scientists of the Third Reich.
12. German military scientists were provided with blueprints of a very advanced type of crafts that were produced one year before the end of the Second World War.
13. Few prototypes of super aircrafts were manufactured, and flew successfully.
14. None of these super aircrafts took part in any military operation during the war.
15. However, some were spotted by American and British pilots who had no clues what these super aircrafts were!
16. Few German super aircrafts survived the war, and were secretly transported to the North Pole.
17. Some of these German super aircrafts were captured by the American military.
18. I am not in liberty to tell you more about this very sensitive and delicate subject.

On the crash of a UFO in Roswell as recorded on the Anunnaki's Miraya

Did the military capture aliens when the UFO crashed in Roswell? Did the United States government negotiate a deal with the aliens?
Did the Anunnaki know anything about the crash?
Did the military find out where the aliens came from?
Did the captured aliens die in a military base?
If they did not die, where are they now?

- 1. In 1947, a Grays' spacecraft crashed on an American soil.
- 2. Two Grays died from the impact, but one survived.
- 3. The Americans held him underground at Andrew Air Force Base. Strangely enough, a sort of friendship was developed between the Gray and two American civilian scientists, despite the fact, that the Grays don't usually show any emotion. They are much like a hive mentality, insects.
- 4. The Americans were only interested in acquiring advanced military weapon systems, not in a friendship with an alien. But somehow they became friends.
- 5. At that time, the American military kept everything under cover and did not inform even the Congress or the President of the United States.
- 6. One general actually said, 'Civilians and politicians come and go. But we, the military, that is our career. Therefore, they should not be informed and if the Congress will not be told, consequently the American public should not be told either.' That was the policy that was adopted on a regular basis ever since.
- 7. The Anunnaki who have monitored the crash, recorded it on their Miraya.
- 8. The Miraya recorded all the sequences and what followed. Here is one of the first conversations between the surviving Gray and the two American scientists.
- 9. Two men and a Gray sat around an empty desk. They seemed comfortable, there was no tension that you would expect in such a company. Then, the sound came from the Miraya.

718

- 10. One of the American scientists asked the Gray: "Where did you come from, and why are you here?"
- 11. "We have been here for thousands of years, sir," said the Gray, in perfect English, though his voice had the usual scratchy sound of his race. "We have our bases underwater, in the Pacific, near Puerto Rico, and under Alaska's glaciers."

12. The conversation continues: "Thousands of years?" "That is so. We consider ourselves the first and the legitimate inhabitants and owners of the Earth. You are not. We are here because we need natural resources that exist on the surface of the Earth and in the oceans."

"Seems to me this is not all you need, buddy," said the other scientist, grinning and lighting a cigarette.

"This is true. We also need some live organisms, and various substances we can extract from human bodies."

"And did you get all you want?" asked the first scientist.

"Yes, by and large. We need them on a constant basis," said the Gray. "The natural resources of the earth and the water are regularly mined. The human substances are more difficult to obtain. We get them from the humans we abduct."

Note: The two scientists nodded in agreement, totally unimpressed by the mention of the abductions. They really did not seem to mind.

The conversation continues (As recorded on the Anunnaki's Miraya):

"What bugs me," said the first scientist, "is that we tried so hard to reverse engineer your spaceship, ever since we got it after the crash in Roswell. We just can't do it.

You have to help us decipher the codes on the screens we found inside the spaceship, and also the geometric and scientific symbols on the grids and measuring tapes we found scattered around the spaceship. Our team is getting impatient; they may even threaten to kill you, you know. The two of us are friendly with you, but the team is getting ugly, and the boss is mad."

"What is the point?" said the Gray without showing any emotion, not even fear regarding the threat. "Even if I teach you how things work, and decipher all the codes for you, you will not be able to reverse engineer our technology, because you don't have the raw materials. Look at this."

719

From somewhere around his body, he pulled out a piece of metal. "This is a very light metal yet stronger than any material known on earth. Yet this sheet of metal could float in the air, and can be bent and folded like paper and then, open up on its own. Look!" He demonstrated. The metal seemed to be indestructible.

"You must understand that we are willing to reveal plenty of information," said the Gray. "But we can only do so if you will allow me to go home. I need to recharge my body, it's like a battery, you know. I will die if I stay much longer, and that will be useless to you. Let me go, and I will arrange for others to come back with me, others who know much more than I do. I am a simple pilot. I will bring you scientists. We have no intention of hiding this knowledge from you, on the contrary, we have every reason to cooperate with you and do some joint projects. And we can supply the raw materials and the knowledge of how to turn it all to your advantage."

"So since we are such good friends," said the second scientist, "tell me, where exactly is the home you speak of? Since you have lost the spaceship, obviously, we will have to take you there.'"

"If I tell you, you will not understand and you will not be able to take me there, since it involves getting through additional dimensions. Our scientists constructed our bases' entries like that, as a precaution against intruders. But if you take me back to Roswell, exactly where we crashed, I will find my own way."

"How will you do that?"

"Simple," said the Gray. "When a spacecraft lands on a particular spot, automatically it marks the spot, scans it, and sends data to our mission control for identification and location purposes. Thus, we are never lost. If I can contact my people, they will come for me."

"But if you go away, how do we communicate with you, and find out when the others are coming?"

"In the spacecraft there is a communication device. Let's go there. I am sure it is functional, because it is really indestructible. I'll teach you how to use it. We will contact my people from there and tell them about our plan. You will be there to supervise everything. Bring the boss, too, just in case."

The scientists looked at each other. They seemed rather pleased.

"Very well," said one of them. "We'll come back for you later tonight, after we talk to the boss. I am sure he will agree to our plan."

"It will be a feather in his cap," said the Gray, using an old human expression unexpectedly. The two scientists burst out laughing.

Author's notes based on records and statements supplied by Ambar Anati, and published in the book "Anunnaki Ultimatum', co-authored by Ilil Arbel.
That, was indeed what happened. They took him back to Roswell, and left him there on the exact spot of the crash. They did not leave the area, though, but hid in a small canteen which was placed at some distance, to watch what was going to happen to the Gray. In a very short time, a spaceship came, landed, and he went in.
The spaceship took off directly and vanished into the sky.
The scientists sent the piece of metal which the Gray has demonstrated to a military laboratory, and they called one engineer from Lockheed Corporation and another one from MIT to analyse the piece.
Nobody could figure out what it was made of. Still, prior to his departure, apparently the Gray did reveal many secrets of very advanced technology, that American corporations started developing right away, and began to use ten years later.
Many of the highly advanced electronic gadgets American consumers used for a quarter of a century came from the Grays.
A few years passed. Then, a historic meeting happened. In February 1954, President Dwight Eisenhower went for a week's vacation to Palm Springs, California.
This was a little strange, and many did not quite understand the timing, because he just came back from a quail shooting vacation in Georgia. Actually, it was less than a week before his trip to Palm Springs.
Two vacations in a row was not his style, but he went anyway, and arranged to stay there for a week. Now, a president, as you know, is always surrounded by other officials, not to mention body guards; he is never out of sight.
But on the night of February 20, the President of the United States disappeared.
The press, which somehow was alerted despite all the efforts for secrecy, spread rumors that he was ill, or that he suddenly died.
The president's people were alarmed, so they called an emergency press conference, and announced that Eisenhower lost a tooth cap at his dinner, and had to be rushed to a dentist.

To make it more believable, the dentist was presented to the people. He was invited to a function the next evening, and was introduced all around. This, again, was strange.

Why would a dentist be invited to such an affair, and why would the President's personnel take such care to make him visible to everyone?

The military needed a cover-up.

President Eisenhower was actually taken to Muroc Airfield, which later was renamed Edwards Air Force Base. There, he met with Grays. No president has ever done so before. The delegation of the extraterrestrials consisted of eleven Grays. Six from Zeta Reticuli, and five from earth's underwater bases. But of course, this was not the last meeting.

This marked the beginning of negotiations between the government of United States and the Grays. So the situation was no longer only in the hands of the military, but went much further.

How was this meeting arranged, in the first place?

According to the Miraya's records and Sinhar Anati's statements: It started a year before the meetings.

In 1953, astronomers discovered some large objects that at first were believed to be asteroids, and later proven to be spaceships.

They were very large, but since they took a high orbit around the equator, they were not visible to laymen.

Two projects were installed – Project Sigma, created to interpret the Grays' radio communications, and Project Plato, created to establish diplomatic relationships with the aliens.

There were talks about other races that contacted the humans at that time, arguments regarding who the treaties should be signed with, and so on.

As a matter of fact, the Nordics, a benevolent race, actually tried to prevent the humans from getting into these evil treaties, and wanted them to dismantle their nuclear weapons and abandon their road to self destruction, but they were not listened to.

The Nordics wanted the humans to go on a path of spiritual developments, but what the humans wanted was military secrets. Because they are so badly contaminated, they would not even consider a peaceful offer.

And the treaty with the Grays was signed. It basically said that the aliens and the humans will not interfere with each other's affairs. The humans will keep their presence a secret, and they will be allowed to experiment on cows and on a limited number of human abductees. The abductees' names would be reported to the U.S. government for control, they were not to be harmed, and they should be returned to their homes after the memory of the events was removed.

The Grays as treacherous as they are, did not keep the promise, and extended their experiments without telling the U.S. government. The humans were treacherous as well. For example, there was the issue of the Gray that has arranged all that.

He came back with the delegation of 1954, and agreed to stay on earth as a hostage of good will, on condition that he would be allowed freedom to go back and forth to recharge himself.

This lasted for a year, but soon enough the Americans, having learned a little about the vicious plans of the Grays and the excessive number of abductions that was not agreed upon, turned back on their word to the hostage and locked him up for three years. As a result, he developed extreme claustrophobia that eventually killed him.

They won't let him recharge himself.

Sinhar Anati said: "The humans are no better than the Grays." The Anunnaki Council said (According to Anati, of course): "There are still good humans out there, those who are not contaminated, but they usually don't go into government business."

Important note:

The Anunnaki's Miraya also recorded information on the "Grays' Earth Belt." Sinhar Anati explained: "The Grays have built an invisible radio plasmic belt around Earth. They want to isolate Earth from the universe. This belt can expand up or down, and can affect missiles, rockets, or airplanes, and blow them up. This is what happened to various airplanes in Vietnam, and also to human spacecrafts and space missions."

*** *** ***

What are Anunnaki ships and extraterrestrial crafts made of and how do they look?

- **1.** The UFOs and USOs are the spaceships of the Grays who live here on Earth and underwater.
- **2.** They are made from special metal and a blend of material/substances totally unknown to humans.

- **3.** They are "coated" with:
- a- Protection shields;
- b- Anti-matter frames;
- c- Invisibility belts;
- d- Anti-gravity circumferences;
- e- Anti-metal fatigue, and anti-erosion properties, thus allowing them to jump from time pocket to another time pocket, and from space pocket to another space pocket. These maneuvers explain their erratic, irregular "flying" (In fact, they do not fly, they jump) pattern and sharp and sudden angular turns and spiral acceleration.
- **4.** They come in all shapes and forms ranging from:
- a- Circular;
- b- Conical (Conic);
- c- Triangular;
- d- Crescent;
- e- Half crescent; and half crescent with an angular tail;
- f- Cigar shape;
- g- Spheroids, also called "Flattened Spheres";
- h- Rings;
- i- Balls of lights;
- j- Oval;
- k- Egg shape;
- l- Diamond shape;
- m- Lampshade shape;
- n- Cylindrical;
- o- Probes;
- p- Small carriers;
- **5.** Grays UFOs and USOs have a multitude of spectral colors and shades such as:
- a- Bluish in day time;
- b- Bluish-grayish in day time;
- c- Orange in day time;
- d- Reflective in day time;
- e- Shiny (Aluminum-Silver-Chrome colors);
- f- Luminous in the dark or night time;
- g- Extremely bright in the dark or night time;

- h- Different and constantly changing colors from burning magnesium to fluorescent blue-green, in the dark or night time;
- i- Sudden alteration/variation from greenish-blue to red-orange, with intense white-blue underside or under the "belly" of the craft, in the dark or night time;
- j- The total spectral colors (Range and intensity) range from silver to red, yellow, orange, green, violet and blue.
- **6**- They emit various gases, to name a few:
- Hydrogen;
- Acetylene;
- Translucent plasma;
- Helium;
- Oxygen;
- Carbon dioxide;
- Argon;
- Krypton, so on...
- 7- They produce several physical, mental, emotional, psychological, psycho-somatic and bio-organic effects on human beings, animals, and the environment, to name a few:
- a- An intense heat;
- b- Continuous increase of temperature;
- c- Radio active emission and rays;
- d- Paralysis;
- e- Immobilization;
- f- Vision impairment;
- g- Burning the skin;
- h- Laps of memory;
- i- Difficulty in breathing;
- j- Lost of consciousness;
- k- Electrical shocks;
- l- Cars engines stop to work;
- m- Vehicles motors misfire;
- n- Headlamps regularly went out;
- o- Emission of electromagnetic energy;
- p- Painful pricklings;
- q- Disruption of electrical circuits;
- r- Amnesia;

- s- Headache;
- t-Eye pains;
- u- Nausea; so on...
- **8.** The Anunnaki ships called Merkaba and Markaba are completely different from the UFOs and USOs you see in the skies.
- a- They are much much bigger;
- b- They are always accompanied by a mother-ship that stays around the orbit of the Earth;
- c-The mother-ship houses multiple and smaller crafts, usually stored in the lowest section (Belly) of the mother-ship;
- d- They produce a loud sound when they take off from a land-base;
- e- The spaceship top section has a dome made from translucent material, resembling a diamond ring;
- f- This upper section (At the very top) of the spaceship serve as a navigation and control command center;
- g- Below the crystal ring, there are four to five circular and parallel compartments connected to the main engine of the craft;
- h- I have used the word "Engine" for lack of proper terminology, because alien spaceships of any category do not have engines or motors, some time, the whole craft serves as a propulsion catalyst.
- i- The larger Anunnaki spaceships are noted for their arched back side.
- j- The lower part or level of the spaceship have circular rings rotating independently from each other; these rings when they start to spin, they produce the lift, activate the spiral (Oval or circular) propulsion system, and instantly neutralize gravity.
- k- To the human eyes, the rings appear like wide-spread wings and/or a helicopter blade;
- i- The central/lower wheel (the fifth one) spins at a great speed;
- j- All wheels spin independently from each other in different directions; there is no synchronization in their motion and circular rotation;

726

- k- From the lower part of the spaceship (Belly), extend four rectangular sections that change to oval shape, when the craft has reached an altitude of 200 feet;
- l- On take off, these four sections remain inside the body of the craft. But when the craft lands, they "emerge" from the body of the craft to provide support for landing, even though they never touch the ground;
- m- These four sections are sometime called the "Legs of the ship"' they are clearly visible to the naked eyes, because they look like long, extended and straight forks, brightly polished, of a golden or amber color that changes to highly polished brass color;
- n- Fraction of seconds, before the craft lands while still hovering in a semi-circular motion, the "legs" of the ship begin to rotate on their own axis, and the very end or extremity of the legs become flat;
- o- The spaceship does not a cockpit or a flight deck for obvious reasons.
- p- The entrance gate or door of the ship is never visible at first sight. The gate or the door opens and closes in a revolving manner.
- q- Once, the door or the gate stops to rotate, a sort of an extended rail (consisting of several lined up rectangular sections attached to each other by very thin rows of tubes) extends from the lower body of the ship, and its extension suddenly widens, and opens up to reveal a circular entrance/exit.

*** *** ***

Brief excerpts from the transcripts of what the aliens told our government
What are the Aliens' Transcripts (AT)?

I. Definition:

The Aliens' Transcripts (AT) are a collection, a record, a detailed account, a huge dossier on all the meetings with non-human entities that occurred from 1947 to the present. The Aliens' Transcripts have a paramount military significance and an enormous national security importance. And I shall not tap into these two areas. And I honestly appreciate your understanding.

The Aliens' Transcripts contain thousands upon thousands of pages, sketches, illustrations, charts, graphs, communiqués, notes, statistics, secret Presidential orders, addenda, revised, and re-revised and updated addenda on everything pertaining to encounters and meetings with aliens.

AT does not include civilians' encounters with aliens, abductions or UFOs' sightings. AT are strictly and exclusively transcripts of meetings with aliens, extraterrestrials, and intraterrestrials.

And do not expect these transcripts to be declassified. They will never be! Perhaps some of the pages and reports will be made public in 2021, when the "Aliens Protocol" will be released to the general public; another fascinating document on aliens. If you ask an ufologist or a person who pretends to know a lot about aliens, or has written a book on flying saucers, he/she will tell you, "I have never heard of the Aliens' Transcripts! What is this?" Others will rush to say, "It is a hoax!" Imbeciles, (no matter how many PhDs they have), will tell you, it is a disinformation campaign. And I say to them Rubbish! Silly people will tell you, something fishy here. Alert minds and intelligent people might say, "Hey, let's look into this." Insiders know what the Aliens Transcripts are.

Who had or has access to these transcripts?
Even 4 star generals could not access these transcripts. President ...tried and failed. Senator...did everything he could to have a glance at AT and he was "sent away". Vice President...inquired about AT, and he was told, there is no such thing as Aliens' Transcripts. A congressional hearing was scheduled to inquire about AT and conduct some sort of questioning, deposition and investigation, but 2 two days later, it was cancelled. Are you getting the picture? Do you have the right to know everything about the AT? No, not everything. Some, yes!

At one time, Dr. Hynek tried to have access to the Transcripts and the Pentagon said: NO! But Dr. Werhner von Braun, Dr. Edward Teller, Dr. Oberth, Albert Einstein, two young German scientists who are still around (They worked with Viktor Schauberger), and a young and brilliant scientist (Still alive) who worked with the late Karl Schapeller, had plenty of time and opportunities to go through the files of the Transcripts.

In 1948, we heard that Rudolph Schriever joined the scientists' team, although some colleagues have claimed that Schriever never participated in any project, simply because he died that year in Czechoslovakia. My sources tell me that they were wrong. Schriever was well, very much alive and kicking. In 1951, Alberto Fenoglio, joined the team. Twenty years later, Dr. Carl Sagan, and a very famous scientist (Still alive) known for his mind-bending theory on galactic civilizations were added to the roster.

How are they structured the Aliens Transcripts?
From mid to the end of 1947, the Aliens Transcripts were a straight documentation and minutes of meetings with aliens in general; extraterrestrials, and intraterrestrials (The Grays).
In 1948, the Air Force and the Pentagon jointly decided to divide the Transcripts into three categories or parts, and as follows:
Category one/Part One: The meetings.
This category recorded all questions and answers, and what it was decided upon to do or to continue to do during the meetings. The minutes contained all the topics and subjects discussed, the material studied, and especially those of a military and scientific nature, names, ranks and titles of people (military and civilians) who were present, followed by recommendations and brief reports from scientists. Issues, discussions and subjects on religion, ethics, Earth history, and anthropology were later incorporated in category three/part three. This decision was made by a two stars general following studies and reports submitted to his office by a committee of physicians, psychiatrists, and experts in behavioral sciences, who at the time, were working on esoteric, mind control, and psychosomatic projects and research.
Category two/Part Two: The projects.
This category refers to research programs, projects, and training sessions administered by two offices especially created by the military and The White House. In this category, detailed reports on "Progress" were submitted by trusted military contractors, and added to the Transcripts. On this, my lips are sealed.
Category three/Part Three: Addenda & reports.
This category gathered and catalogued all sorts of information on aliens':
* 1-Nature
* 2-Races
* 3-Species

- 4-Origin
- 5-Habitat
- 6-Technology
- 7-Future operations; I can't talk about this
- 8-Reports from military personnel at all levels on their personal rapports with aliens who worked with them in military bases
- 9-Study and analysis of the behavior of the aliens
- 10-Habits
- 11-Strengths and weaknesses
- 12-Nutrition
- 13-Reactions in confined places
- 14-Reactions/attitudes under severe weather conditions (Cold and heat)
- 13-Confrontations and heated debates with scientists, the military, and military guards
- 14-Flights test
- 15-Reverse engineering, so on.

Meetings with the Aliens

Basic information:
It is extremely important to understand the difference between "meeting extraterrestrials", or "meeting with extraterrestrials", and encounter with extraterrestrial, and first meeting/encounter with extraterrestrials. Each occurrence had different purposes, and happened for very specific reasons. Also the nature of the meeting and the nature of the encounter are very different, for some, are terrestrial, and others non-terrestrial.

Q: Did any government and/or agency or unit affiliated with a government in the Eastern and Western Hemispheres meet with the aliens, the intraterrestrials and the extraterrestrials?

A: Yes!

Q: How many times?

A: Many times.

Q: Where?

A: In many places; military bases, in the desert, underwater, around Earth's orbit, and outer-space.

Q: Are these meetings still happening?

A: Yes.

Q: Who attend or have attended these meetings?

A: High echelon/top brass in the military, and the nation's very best scientists, codes decipherers and breakers, and "select" linguists working for the government.

In some meetings, members of the clergy (Catholic Church) and a very prominent Protestant preacher were present.

730

Q: What language has been used during these meetings?

A: In the first two meetings, very complicated and complex tools/machines were used by the aliens to talk to us.

They carried with them a special device in a circular metallic box (Voice-box, also called VB); they had two different kinds of boxes on board their spacecrafts. Later on, the aliens spoke to us in English and Russian, with a perfect accent.

In the second meeting, the aliens gave us the Translation Signals Box (TSB), which allowed us to respond to their communications and messages.

Later on, the CTF (Transmission Channel), originally "Channel of the transmissions frequency of aliens" was used.

Q: Didn't they talk to us telepathically?

A: Nonsense! On their device, they have the recordings of all the languages and dialects of Earth.

Q: Is it true that the aliens have their own language; an articulate language?

A: Yes, they do.

Q: Does their device contain non-Earth languages?

A: No! The device they used to communicate with was especially created/designed for this purpose.

Present at the meetings:

- **First meeting:** Military, scientists, photographers.
- **Second meeting:** Same as the first meeting, plus a head of state, clergy, preacher, psychics, code breakers, linguists, intelligence, national security.
- **Following meetings** (First 3 or 4): Military, intelligence, national security, test pilots, propulsion system experts, scientists, pathologists, astrophysicists, photographers, futurist, laboratory researchers, one person from the film industry, physicians, psychologists, psychiatrists, artists, illustrators, so on.
- **Following meetings** (Continuous/Regular): Military, test pilots, scientists, nuclear physicists, intelligence, national security, photographers, trusted military contractors, so on.
- **Deleted from the attendance roster (Permanently):** Futurist, physicians, pathologists, clergy, psychologists, psychiatrists, preacher, psychics, code breakers, etc.

2. Reports and briefings:

Reports in Files & Archives (Classified, Declassified)

Government	Total Pages	Sketches/Graphs	Photos
Belgium	1,250	200	75
Brazil	3,500±	111±	110±
China	600	35	86
Japan	340	89	112
France	1,956	123	300
Israel	900	97	145
Mexico	3,786	340	912
Russia	2,670	651	1,230
USA	20,000±	2,600±	3,210±

Briefings and Transcripts of Aliens/Grays-Government Meetings

Government	Total Pages	Sketches/Graphs	Photos
Belgium	0	0	0
Brazil	0	0	0
China	0	0	0
Japan	0	0	0
France	0	0	0
Israel	0	0	0
Mexico	96	76	81
Russia	1,200	2,100	432
USA	28,000	3,600	3,400

Aliens/Grays-Government Meetings

Government	Meetings	Locations	Years
Belgium	0	0	0
Brazil	0	0	0
China	0	0	0
Japan	0	0	0
France	0	0	0
Israel	0	0	0
Mexico	2		
Russia	1	Military Base	1948
Russia	2	Military Base	1949
Russia	3	Kapustin Yar	1961

Russia		Ibid	1980
USA	2	Military Base	1947
USA	3	Military Base	1948
USA	6	Ibid	1954-1958
USA	**Permanent**	**Permanent**	**1974-Present**
USA	Joint Programs	Outer-space	1979-2000
USA	Training	Mexico	2000-2002
USA	Technology	Military Bases	Permanent
USA	**Permanent**	Bases on Earth	1959-Present
USA	1	Space	Undisclosed
USA	1	Space	Undisclosed

Q: What people, military and others were wearing at the meeting?

A: In the first meeting, more precisely encounter/meeting, you could see military and civilians. No protective suits were used.

This historical event was not coincidental. It was agreed upon, and the aliens told us where and when they will meet with us.

According to notes in the transcripts, Section 9: Addendum 12- Briefing 341-E1, 1947, this first encounter/meeting was arranged by an alien who was in the custody of the Air Force.

At the bottom of the page, there is an arrow and a reference made to a certain "Lt. Colonel S..." On the next page, top left, the words or phrase "No outfits" was mentioned.

Note: I brought this up, so those who are "closer to the truth" and other decent insiders will immediately know that I had a close look at the aliens' transcripts.The alien was never detained by the CIA or the NSA, as many have claimed.

The alien stayed at a military base for approximately 3 months and 4 days, and later died.

Her body was sent to a military hospital. The alien was captured after her spacecraft crashed, for missing to "jump" into the time-space pocket, needed to enter and exit a physical dimension. The three other aliens died on impact. The one who survived was a female alien-hybrid, although no genital organs were visible (I will talk about this, later on.)

So, apparently, the aliens did something to their spacecraft, so radiations emitted by their ships would not affect us, or perhaps, they totally eliminated any radioactive emission.

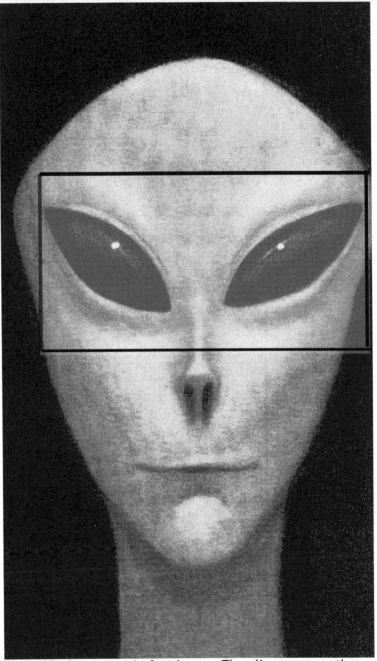

These black eyes are in fact lenses. The aliens remove them at will. They are attached to a gland we do not have in our system. The aliens don't have a retina; they see through cells channel in their brain. Three of the major functions of the lenses are:
a)Protection, b)navigation/direction, c)communication.

However, in other cases and situations, when aliens do not announce their arrival or landing, their crafts emit and leave behind radioactive radiations. But the aliens were wearing protective suits. They told us, human germs cause them skin irritations and dermatologic allergy. This is one of the reasons they wear those silver-metallic suits and eyes-protection-screen-glasses. Others reasons are, anti-gravity inside their ships, protection against G caused by sharp turns and sudden entering-exiting time-space pockets (Speed of light) and for navigation purposes.

The aliens told us to warn our people not to come close to any of their spacecrafts when they land unannounced (In all cases and other circumstances), because their spacecrafts' radiations cause temporary loss of memory, nausea, vomiting, severe headaches, temporary paralysis, temporary loss of sight, and severe skin burns.

By the way, they call their spacecrafts "Time-Space machines", because they don't fly, but jump from one time-space pocket to another. Worth mentioning here, that the Russians upon meeting the aliens for the first time, did wear special suits, for protection measures. The suits were manufactured in Tbilisi, Georgia, former state of the Soviet Union, and the suits were stored at Kapustin Yar.

A brief excerpts from the Transcripts.

Note: You can read the whole Aliens Transcripts in my book "Trancripts of what the Aliens, Extraterrestrials and Intraterrestrials Told Our Governments".

From the Transcripts of 1947, 1948, 1958, 1963, 1971, and Addenda (Plural of Addendum) of 1947, 1948, 1964, 1974, 1979, 2003, 2007.

1. Aliens cannot constantly breathe oxygen; they will suffocate and die.

2. Almost all aliens are claustrophobic. They will be disoriented if they are confined in a small area for a certain period of time in the same place.

3. There are 224 planets that sustain life as we know it.

4. Four other galactic species including the Anunnaki and Igigi resemble humans to a certain degree.

5. Two governments have a huge dossier cataloguing alien species by category, faculty, intelligence, science, technology, physiognomy, nature, and location of their habitat.

6. Aliens don't have genitals; they don't reproduce sexually.

7. Aliens don't have a digestive system.

8. Aliens don't have a retina.

9. Aliens don't have a centralized nervous system.

10. Aliens' skin is covered with small pores that have multiple functions and purposes we do not fully understand.

11. At the dawn of humanity, several human species had long tail. And the modern human beings were genetically created by the Anunnaki.

12. An archaic human-reptilian race lived on planet Earth.

13. Meteors or other celestial bodies did not kill the dinosaurs. It never happened.

14. At one time, the Anunnaki had settlements on the Moon and Mars.

15. The hybrid race is genetically created by the intraterrestrials.

16. There are 4 hybrid generations and three types. One of these generations lives among us.

17. The human race is not important to aliens.

18. Earth is the dumpster of the universe we know.

19. There is no reincarnation. However dead people trapped in the doomed zone (Marash Mawta) can re-appear and re-manifest themselves physically and holographically.

20. Ghosts are the projection of a time-space imprints. They are their own imprints, produced by time-space memory.

21. God was invented by the early human beings.
This item for reasons I don't understand was mentioned twice in the Transcripts.

22. There is no hell and there is no heaven in the afterlife.

23. The Exodus never happened.

24. Jesus Christ did not die on the Cross.

25. Jesus Christ was not born in Israel, but in Egypt.

26. St. Joseph is not the real father of Jesus.

27. There is no soul trapped in the human body. This idea was created by the cave man even though he did not understand what soul is. It was his way to communicate with the "Divine" and the supernatural. The early Hittites knew this. And The Anunnaki Ulema told us about the concept of soul in their Kira'at.

28. Civilization was not created by the Mesopotamians. It was exported to their lands by the Anatolians (Plateau of Turkey), and the early inhabitants of Phoenicia, at a time this land had no name. Later on it was called Leebaan, which means snow-white.
Civilization did not start in Mesopotamia, but first in Anatolia (Part Turkey, part ancient Armenia), continued in Phoenicia, and later on bloomed in Mesopotamia.
This item was mentioned twice in the Transcripts.

29. Turkey and the Anatolian Plateau gave birth to the first form of civilization on Earth.

30. The universe was created from within; an implosion on the inside and collisions of bubbles on the outside.
This item for reasons I don't understand was mentioned twice in the Transcripts.

31. There are multiple dimensions beyond our physical world.
And within each layer of dimension, there is a multitude of other forms of dimensions.

32. There are copies of us in other dimensions.

33. Planet Earth will cease to exist in 5 billion years, along with the Moon.

34. There are "artificial" settlements and tunnels inside the Moon.

35. Many regions inside the Moon are filled with life-forms.

36. The Grays saved planet Earth from annihilation when they redirect the trajectory of a huge celestial body heading toward Earth. This happened already twice.

37. The Pyramids are 10,900-11,000 year old. And were not built by the Egyptians or any human race. The stones were teleported. This item for reasons I don't understand was mentioned twice in the Transcripts.

38. Earth ax shifted 4 times before.

39. Dark matter is what keeps the universe in place and in order, and contributes to its expansion.

This item for reasons I don't understand was mentioned twice in the Transcripts.

40. The shortest distance between A and B is not a straight line, but a bent trajectory between two dots on a parallel plane.

41. The universe bends on itself.

42. At the very beginning, Earth had the shape of an egg. It was never totally round.

43. The United States is the only country on Earth which has at its disposal a "Vortex Tunnel Weapon System". The aliens called it the "Vacuum Continuum Path" (VCP).

44. A former President of the United States Okayed operations to uncover and investigate anything and everything related to aliens' existence on Earth. He informed an intelligence agency to gather everything they could find, here and abroad and create a file (Dossier). And the President specifically informed the agency that he is NOT interested in reading their reports and learning about their findings.

He gave the agency carte blanche, with unlimited authority and power. He also authorized the agency to solicit the help of foreign agents, if necessary. The agency did.

Russian operatives and British agents worked for the agency. The agency recruited four former British code breakers, who cracked the code of the German Enigma Machine at the signals intelligence center at Bletchley Park in England. In fact, two scientists from Poland were the first to unlock the complicated mechanism of Enigma, and decipher its codes, not the Brits. Alan Turing, was one of the first British code breakers who joined the agency efforts to learn more about aliens symbols and codes. On more than one occasion, the President told the head of the agency not to bother him anymore with UFO and aliens stuff. And he made it clear to him, that nobody, no other agency, no one, not even the Air Force should know about this. In other words and simply put, they had to report to nobody, no one! Director of the FBI, Edgar J. Hoover and the military found out and were pissed off. Later on, when the Pentagon and Air Force became heavily involved with UFOs, and took over the whole thing, Hoover wrote to them and asked to be permanently informed.

President Truman and President Eisenhower were the only two American Presidents who were vividly interested in the aliens' question; they took a vital part and played a major role in creating a protocol and procedures on how to initiate and conduct investigations, and gather information. Both presidents allocated huge secret budgets for aliens' studies and UFOs research. Along with President George Bush, Sr., at the time he was the director of the CIA, Eisenhower and Truman are considered to be the most knowledgeable high officials on matters related to aliens, the Grays in particular, and UFOs.

Eisenhower remained extremely interested in aliens, UFOs and extraterrestrial technology, and how it could be used militarily. President Truman by the end of his presidency lost interest in UFOs and aliens, who once called "Space Monkeys"!

45. One committee was created to oversee the whole "progress". It was headed by a 2 star general.

Members were:

- Three distinguished scientists,
- A linguist,
- Two code breakers, one from the United States, the other from Great Britain,
- A cryptology expert, in a different capacity than the code breakers/decipherers,
- A pathologist,
- A Lt. Colonel, transferred either from the Pentagon or the Air force,
- A high-ranking official from an intelligence agency,
- An expert photographer,
- A Captain,
- A typist,
- A civilian whose identity was only known to the 2 star general.

A few months later, the panel got bigger and bigger, to include:

- A- An admiral,
- b- An astronomer,
- c- A test-pilot from the Air Force,
- d- A nuclear physicist who worked at Los Alamos,
- e- A noted German scientist,
- f- A highly regarded university professor,
- g- A geologist/botanist who never said a word.

This is not the MJ-12 legendary panel, which is unfortunately to ufology and ufologists an elaborate scheme, created by three gentlemen, and regrettably swallowed by an avalanche of honest but ill-informed authors. They were simply duped!! C'est la vie !

46. In the early fifties, a UFO crashed in Mexico, and human bodies' parts were found inside the craft.

When the military confronted the Grays, they were shocked to hear the Grays telling them that the UFO was not one of theirs. Furthermore, they explained to the military that not all UFOs come from the same origin. They pointed out that the crescent-shape UFOs were piloted by another race which from time to time enters our space. And there is nothing we can do about it. When a general asked if THEY (Grays) could do something about it, the aliens said NO, because those spacecrafts are in fact time machines, difficult to spot, pursue and chase.

In the Transcripts, this incident was revisited twice, and marked in 3 footnotes. Many years later, when another intelligence/security agency was created, the incident was brought up, and dissected piece by piece. It was concluded that in fact, the Grays were no part of it, and the bodies parts were those of native Mexicans from the Aztec's region, not Americans. For a while they rested their case. However, three years later, upon the request of a retired general who became a very influential politician/lawmaker, the case was reopened and re-examined.

The conclusions were horrifying, and I am not in liberty to reveal any information about the investigation. But bear in mind, and never forget this: The United States Air Force, the CIA and the other intelligence agency were not aware of what the aliens were doing at that time.

It was only in mid 1960, they became fully aware of what was going on, and they adopted a new policy and protocol in dealing with aliens. And this was done against all odds, and by taking huge risks, for aliens are millions of years a head of us on all levels, especially technology, science and warfare. Some sort of agreement was discussed to prevent further atrocities.

And to a great degree, it was successful. And the Transcripts show that the UFO's crash in Mexico was totally unrelated to other alleged or assumed UFOs' crashes in the United States, for they were piloted by a different alien race.This crash was never mentioned in Grudge, the Blue Book, the Condon Report, or in any official report on UFOs.

Bear in mind that very sensitive situations and cases, embarrassing sightings, possible UFOs' crashes and/or landings with "military implications", and confrontations with non-human entities (Aliens of any classification) were never mentioned in any official report on UFOs, and were never brought to the attention of civilian scientists (Astronomers and astrophysicists) who were hired by the government, by order from the "Big Boss".

The author can be reached at
delafayette6@aol.com

Published by
Times Square Press
New York

Printed in the United States of America